THE MIND THAT IS
CATHOLIC

THE MIND THAT IS
CATHOLIC

PHILOSOPHICAL &
POLITICAL ESSAYS

JAMES V. SCHALL

THE CATHOLIC UNIVERSITY OF AMERICA PRESS
WASHINGTON, D.C.

LIBRARY OF CONGRESS CATALOGING-IN-PUBLICATION DATA
Schall, James V.
The mind that is Catholic : philosophical and political essays / James V. Schall.
p. cm.
Includes bibliographical references and index.
ISBN 978-0-8132-1541-9 (pbk. : alk. paper)   1. Christianity and politics—
Catholic Church.   2. Political science—Philosophy.   I. Title.
BX1793.S325 2008
282—dc22   2008020523

Socrates: "Shouldn't we offer a prayer to the gods here before we leave?"
Phaedrus: "Of course."
Socrates: "O dear Pan and all the other gods of this place, grant that I may be beautiful inside. Let all my external possessions be in friendly harmony with what is within. May I consider the wise man rich. As for gold, let me have as much as a moderate man could bear and carry with him."

—Plato, *Phaedrus*

We have been promised something we do not yet possess, and because the promise was made by one who keeps his word, we must trust him and are glad; but insofar as possession is delayed, we can only long and yearn for it. It is good for us to persevere in longing until we receive what was promised.

—Augustine, Discourse on Psalm 148 (5th Week, Easter, Saturday)

That is what is peculiar to theology that it turns to something we ourselves have not devised and that is able to be the foundation of our life, in that it goes before us and supports us, that is to say, it is greater than our own thought. The path of theology is indicated by the saying, credo ut intelligam. I accept what is given in advance, in order to find, starting from this and in this, the path to the right way of living, to the right way of understanding myself.

—Joseph Cardinal Ratzinger, "What in Fact Is Theology?"

It is not only possible to say a great deal in praise of play; it is really possible to say the highest things in praise of it. It might reasonably be maintained that the true object of all human life is play. Earth is a task garden; heaven is a playground. To be at last in such secure innocence that one can juggle with the universe and the stars, to be so good that one can treat everything as a joke—that may be, perhaps, the real end and final holiday of human souls.

—G. K. Chesterton, "Oxford from Without"

Le problème est de savoir en d'autre termes si la référence ultime est politique ou s'il y a des référenes ultimes par lesquelles la politique elle-même est jugée. Ce problème est peut-être le problème essentiel d'aujourd'hui. Et si nous tenons tellement à Dieu, c'est à cause de cela. C'est parce que nous pensons qu'un monde où la référence politique serait la référence ultime est un monde où les libertés ne seraient plus possibles.

—Jean Cardinal Daniélou, *La crise actuelle de l'intelligence*

For if some (things) have no grace to charm the sense, yet even these, by disclosing to intellectual perception the artistic spirit that designed them, give immense pleasure to all who can trace links of causation, and are inclined to philosophy.

—Aristotle, *Parts of Animals*

CONTENTS

CONTENTS

PART IV. THE MEDIEVAL EXPERIENCE

PART V. IMPLICATIONS OF CATHOLIC THOUGHT

PART VI. THINGS PRACTICAL AND IMPRACTICAL

PART VII. WHERE DOES IT LEAD?

ACKNOWLEDGMENTS

The origin of each chapter is found at the beginning of the chapter. However, I would like to thank the publishers and editors of the following journals and sources for permission to reproduce material of mine that appeared in their pages. Chapter 1, *Second Spring;* chapter 3, *Logos;* chapter 4, Lexington Books; chapter 5, *Gregorianum;* chapter 6, *American Scholar;* chapters 7, 13, 18, and 21, *Fellowship of Catholic Scholars Quarterly;* chapter 8, *Classical Bulletin;* chapter 9, *The Thomist;* chapter 10, Sheed & Ward; chapters 11 and 14, *Perspectives on Political Science,* Heldref Publishers; chapter 12, Rodopi Publishers; chapter 15, Ignatius Insight online; chapter 16, *Review of Politics;* chapter 17, *Modern Age;* chapter 19, *Policy Review;* chapter 20, *New Pantagruel;* chapter 22, Benbella Books, and for the appendix, the Claremont Institute.

The director of the Catholic University of America Press, David McGonagle, and his staff have been, as always, most helpful and competent.

THE MIND THAT IS
CATHOLIC

INTRODUCTION
"A CERTAIN CRIME UNOBSERVED"

Many a man is mad in certain instances, and goes through life without having it perceived: for example, a madness has seized a person for supposing himself obliged literally to pray continually—had the madness turned the opposite way and this person thought it a crime never to pray, it might not improbably have continued unobserved.

—Samuel Johnson, 1780

In a famous query in the *Gorgias* Socrates talks to Chaerephon, the very man, as he tells us in the *Apology,* who asked the Oracle, "who was the wisest man in Greece?" Socrates tells him to ask Gorgias, the philosophic-orator, precisely "what he is" (477c).[1] When anyone attempts to answer such a question for himself to himself, always a difficult and humbling endeavor, he comes up with an odd series of possible responses. He can, as in my case, answer: "He is a human being." "He is a man." "He is a cleric." "He is an American." "He is an academic." No doubt, one could add many further qualifications, from perhaps, "He is mad" to "He is 'elderly,'" to "He is sometimes coherent." As we see, this effort may prove to be dangerous if extended too far.

In this book, I intend to present, in a more unified form, a selection of specifically "academic" essays written since my first "academic" essay, on justice and friendship, was published in *The Thomist* in 1957. This essay was part of my master's thesis in philosophy at Gonzaga University, written under Father Clifford Kossel, S.J., a man of profound intelligence and insight. Though shortened and rewritten, this essay constitutes chapter 9 of this book. In many ways, it contains themes to which I frequently return,

1. Throughout this book, when Scripture, Plato, Aristotle, or Thomas Aquinas is cited, the standard reference citation—that is, (John 3:12) for Scripture, (234b) for Plato, (11234a) for Aristotle, and (I-II, 76, 2) for Thomas Aquinas—will be inserted in the text at the place where identification is needed.

which is why I include it here even though its "rhythm" is more pedantic. The last citation in this particular essay, from Chesterton's *Dickens,* has long been one of my favorite passages. It comes as close as anything I have seen or read since to capturing both the inspiration of my own intellectual life and, indeed, the essence of Christianity's reflections on itself about our own destiny and individual meaning, themes that constitutes the last three chapters of this book. Ultimately, we begin and end in friendship.

The essays included in this book are "academic," though sometimes lightsome in tone. I use the term "academic essay" in contrast to the shorter essay, for which I have a great fondness, myriads of which I have written over the years in sundry journals and papers. Indeed, the subtitle of my book *Idylls and Rambles* captures the sort of thing that I love to write and in which, often, one can come closer to the truth than in most other ways. Its subtitle was "Lighter Christian Essays." I associate myself with the shorter essay because, as Josef Pieper remarked in his book on Aquinas, the short *articulus,* in which the core of Aquinas's thought appears, is in fact a brief one- to four-page essay. But I also like the short essay because of the wit and humor that we find in the essays of the English Catholic writers like Belloc and Chesterton. These latter writers, both heroes of mine, combine a certain poignancy about our existence with a sudden glimpse of delight into the truth of things in whatever they see. Charlie Brown, the *Peanuts* hero, also appears in these pages for the same philosophic reason.

It is no accident that I have chosen to begin these introductory reflections with a passage abut "madness" from another of my heroes, Samuel Johnson. I should add that, in my younger years, under the bemused influence of my nephews, then young boys, I used to cite *Mad* magazine quite regularly. Too, I love "The Maniac," the title of the first chapter of Chesterton's *Orthodoxy,* exactly a century old in 2008. Christian intelligence is also, at times, called, even by its upholders, "absurd" or "mad." But this particular word has a distinguished place in the heart of Christian philosophy, under the Greek forms of its origin in "mania" and "enthusiasm," something touched on in chapter 17. These very words recall Ronald Knox's *Enthusiasm* and Josef Pieper's *Enthusiasm and the Divine Madness,* both wonderful books. Chesterton says in *Orthodoxy* that the "maniac" is not an irrational man, but rather a man of one idea that he holds to with the greatest insistence. This one idea, however, is outside the balance that comes with seeing where things fit together. In the instance that Johnson cites, the man who "prays always" might well be considered "mad" by most people, but not the man who never prays at all. In fact, by objective standards, the latter may well be more "mad." To the "mad," sanity itself is bound to seem "madness."

We are Christians and Catholics when we realize that it was St. Paul who told us to "pray always." This is the same Paul who is also called "mad." In one of the great passages in Acts, the Roman governor, Festus, says to Paul, after Paul explains why Christ had to suffer, "Paul, you are mad; your learning is turning you mad." To this judgment, Paul simply replies, "I am not mad, most excellent Festus, but I am speaking the sober truth" (Acts 26:24–25). The contrast between "the sober truth" and "great learning" driving us mad is at the heart of the reception of revelation among the learned. Both tragedy and amusement are contained in this record of coming to terms with what I here call "the mind that is Catholic."

While I also use the term "Christian" as perfectly acceptable, the term "Catholic" is generally more exact for what I have in mind in these essays. Insofar as a diversity of theological and philosophical presuppositions exists within Christianity, I do not here intend to deal with these differing interpretations. There are, indeed, "heresies," positions that are not Christian in their understanding of reality. I am concerned rather with that central tradition of intellect that sees itself and defines itself as precisely *Catholic*. Thinking within that tradition is what I have tried to do here. I am not concerned with its deviations but with Catholicism's central understanding of itself. I think it is from within this tradition that we best address ourselves to human and ultimate issues. I do not pretend that I could not be wrong or that my understanding is always the best. What I do think is that the effort to take reason and revelation in themselves and in their relation to each other does result in the best understanding of God, world, politics, man, and indeed, reality as such. This is, perhaps, a "minority report," but it is, I hope, worth making nonetheless.

All of the essays in this book, I think, circle around the same point, that things do fit together, that reason is very powerful in its own order, but that, at its best, especially at its best, it leaves us with a certain longing, a certain unsettlement, an abiding intellectual search. At the same time, it is possible to think with a knowledge of and belief in revelation without thereby harming reason or its legitimate powers. What I suggest in these pages is that, in fact, we think better, more consistently, when both are taken into account. Revelation is addressed to intellect, and on its own terms. And intellect is "addressed" to something beyond its own scope precisely because it always remains open to *what is*. This openness is why the title of this book is precisely *The Mind That Is Catholic*. It is all right to think of political and philosophical things in the light of revelation. But it is also important that those who consider themselves recipients of revelation also think and think well. We only know that revelation is addressed to us, in a more complete sense, if we too have seen the limits or extent of our reason.

It is not always easy to find a forum in which one can write and think comfortably about reason and revelation as if it is necessary for intellectual integrity to do so. Often Catholic scholars must write, to be published or heard, as if their whole mind did not exist. They are expected to talk as if revelation either did not exist or had no effect, just the opposite of what revelation says of itself. Likewise, nonbelievers write as if their view of the world needs no attention to a vast reality closed to them, usually at some stage, because of their own choices. A realism exists in the mind that is Catholic that is aware of dire events in the world. Reality does not always conform to intellectual theories.

Catholic thinking is not utopian in character. In this it differs from much modern thought. Chapters 14 and 19 on Machiavelli and war are intended to suggest that the Catholic mind does not hesitate to confront difficult issues. For these, the mind that is Catholic has concepts and understandings that enable it to remain human in the full sense of seeing ourselves as finite human beings who will also die, but who have themselves a supernatural destiny. I have often been struck in these pages that balancing transcendence, politics, philosophy, and our inner-worldly purpose is both delicate and possible when reason and revelation are seen as open to each other.

At the beginning of each chapter, I have identified the original published source of each essay. I have grouped them in broad subject divisions. The reason for this arrangement is to see that certain themes, especially those of the inner life of God, the Trinity, friendship, and truth recur in differing contexts. Within these essays is a concern for precisely political philosophy as it has presented itself as a unique and controversial search for its own truth within the more complete understanding that comes with philosophy and theology. I remain largely Aristotelian in this sense. Political philosophy cannot be itself without also being aware of the household, which it cannot by its own methods completely grasp, and of the activities of leisure that transcend even politics.

A further theme in these essays is that political philosophy can be especially dangerous when it conceives itself to be a metaphysics, a complete explanation for all things. Benedict XVI touched on this delicate issue when, in receiving a new ambassador from Moldova, he remarked: "For too long Moldova suffered from the imposition of a totalitarian utopia of 'justice without freedom.' The West, by contrast, continues to be exposed to the danger of an alternative utopia of 'freedom without truth,' issuing from a false understanding of 'tolerance.'"[2] It is no accident that both of these problems are conceived in terms of "utopias," itself an abiding consideration in political philosophy, as we see several times in these essays.

What I intend to show in these essays is an awareness, through intellectual history, of the continuing themes that are most often present and considered central in precisely the "Catholic" mind. I do not use that term as if it needs itself be "mysterious," though, as I suggest in chapter 17, mystery and mysticism are not to be neglected in our comprehension of what we are. I have selected themes from the classical writers, especially Plato, though I am much dependent on Aristotle and Aquinas. Some chapters deal with the impact of revelation, others with how things fit together as a whole. Philosophy is said to be, and is, a quest for a knowledge of the whole. I consider that quest to be partly what is at stake here.

I also believe that intellectual questions are not just questions. They are intended to have answers. The mind that is Catholic is one that expects answers because it understands that such expectation constitutes the kind of beings that we are. We are not only seekers after the truth, but finders of it. But we are also, as I suggest in chapter 20, beings that can "choose" to reject it. This willingness to reject truth is something that I often noticed Aristotle "noticing." He understood that we are not likely to think correctly if we do not live correctly, if we have not acquired the natural virtues open to us.

The mind that is Catholic, in short, seeks to be open to all things, including those things revealed to us, insofar as we can grasp them. Our minds are not divine minds. This mind, at its best, does not neglect what we call the "Fall," that is, some sense of our disorder and some Platonic realization of its relation to our knowledge of ourselves. Plato, indeed, is often the mind that enables us most clearly to see the Catholic mind. Maybe

2. Benedict XVI, "To New Ambassador from Moldova" (lecture, May 18, 2006), *L'Osservatore Romano*, English ed., June 14, 2006, 8. Speaking on this same theme from the Gospel account of the third temptation of Christ in the desert, Benedict XVI wrote: "The Christian empire or the secular power of the papacy is no longer a temptation today, but the interpretation of Christianity as a recipe for progress and the proclamation of universal prosperity as the real goal of all religion, including Christianity—this is the modern form of the same temptation. It appears in the guise of a question: 'What did Jesus bring, then, if he didn't usher in a better world? How can this not be the content of messianic hope?'" *Jesus of Nazareth* (New York: Doubleday, 2007), 42–43.

this influence is what Nietzsche suspected in the famous passage in *Beyond Good and Evil,* when he called Christianity the "Platonism of the masses."[3] These considerations of Plato, begun in chapters 5–7, are why I have ended these essays with a discussion of *Narnia,* which has its own Platonic overtones, within the "ultimate meaning of our existence." All of these reflections point to the Trinity, with the understanding that God is not alone and does not intend anyone else ultimately to be lonely, unless that individual so chooses. These are the things that the Catholic mind is "about." But mind itself points to being, to *what is.* We end up, while remaining precisely ourselves, in being not solely in our minds. This indeed is our glory, to seek "face-to-face" a Glory that we did not make, that Glory which ultimately we can only behold and praise and, yes, celebrate.

3. Friedrich Nietzsche, *Beyond Good and Evil: Prelude to a Philosophy of the Future,* translated by R. Hollingdale (Harmondsworth, England: Penguin, 1975), 14.

PART 1

ON CATHOLIC THINKING

1 THE MIND THAT IS CATHOLIC

The miracles seem in fact to be the great embarrassment to the modern man, a kind of scandal. If the miracles could be argued away and Christ reduced to the status of a teacher, domesticated and fallible, then there'd be no problem. Anyway, to discover the Church you have to set out by yourself. . . . Discovering the Church is apt to be a slow procedure but it can only take place if you have a free mind and no vested interest in disbelief.

—Flannery O'Connor, "Letter to Cecil Dawkins, July 16, 1957"

The mind is an infinity, even if it is an infinity of nonsense. The mind of man is divine, even in the unfathomable nature of its darkness. Men can think of anything seriously, however absurd it is. Men can believe anything, even the truth.

—G. K. Chesterton, "Fancies and Facts"

I.

Near the end the sixth of C. S. Lewis's Chronicles of Narnia, entitled *The Magician's Nephew,* the young hero, Digory, has been tempted by the witch to take an apple, contrary to the instructions of Aslan, the Christ-symbolic character in these stories, back to his home.[1] There, in England, Digory's mother lies seriously ill with no hope of recovery. He wants to give the apple to his mother. The magic apple will give her an inner-worldly immortality. Like the witch, she will not die. The witch uses this devotion to his mother as the bait for Digory to break the law. The witch herself has already broken the same law in order to possess a kind of hopeless immortality.

Digory, after much struggle, finally rejects the witch's proposal to give

---

This essay was originally intended as a lecture for the Australian Catholic Students' Association Convention in Brisbane in July 2003. Due to illness at the last moment, I was unable to attend. Professor Tracey Rowland kindly read the lecture in my stead. The lecture was published subsequently in *Second Spring* 7 (2006): 19–25.

1. The last chapter of this book ends with a longer reflection on the Narnia adventures.

his mother disobedient immortality. When we take something good in the wrong way, Aslan explains to Digory and his friend Polly, "The fruit is good, but those who take it loathe it ever after." Polly thinks that because the witch took the fruit in the wrong way, she could not be immortal. But exactly the opposite is the case, though the witch suffers another kind of punishment. This is how Aslan explains the witch's situation: "Things always work out according to their nature. She [the witch] has won her heart's desire; she has unwearying strength and endless days like a goddess. But length of days with an evil heart is only length of misery and already she begins to know it. All get what they want: they do not always like it."[2]

The title of this chapter is "The Mind That Is Catholic." Though C. S. Lewis was not a Catholic, I think his mind was. I am not interested here in the oft-discussed question, among Catholics, about why Lewis was not a Catholic. But I am most interested in the observation that "all get what they want: they do not always like it." To understand the import of that principle, we need certain orthodox doctrines on the nature of reality. We need to know that pride is the ultimate sin, the sin of our willingness to create our own world. Too, we need the Greek doctrine of the immortality of the soul and the subsequent punishment for injustice and reward for good, the theme in the last book of the *Republic*.

Things work out according to our nature. We are free in our wills. The punishment for our sins, for the wrong use of our wills, is not so much external pain inflicted by someone else, God, say, or some alien power. Rather, it is the internal awareness that ultimately we get what we choose. And when what we choose is not according to what we are, not according to the order of things, we eventually find that we do not like what we choose. We do not really want it. What we are is not best explained to us by what we think we are or by what we choose to make ourselves to be, presupposing only ourselves.

This reflection is, if I might put it that way, the Catholic mind at work. *The Magician's Nephew* is, in a way, the retelling of the Book of Genesis, the story of the Creation and Fall. May I suggest initially that all of our lives, when we come to recount them, are themselves a retelling of this same story, the story of what we choose, the story of whether we ultimately choose *what is* or ourselves to be the central event in our existence.

2. C. S. Lewis, *The Magician's Nephew* (New York: Collins, 1955), 174.

II.

During my Roman days in the 1960s, a friend of mine knew the famous Australian novelist Morris West. We'd occasionally be invited, as foreign clerics, to his lovely home, as I recall, out in some distant Roman suburb. In thinking of this Australian visit, I wondered if West was still alive. On the web, I found an interview with him by Ramona Koval on the Australian Broadcasting Company *News* (1998), about a year before his death in 1999. Koval asked West, at the time in a hospital, to look back on his own life, "at those times in which you think things are just falling apart." When he thought his own world seemed most confused after his years in the monastery, West realized that it "takes such a long time to learn. And even those who are nearest and dearest to you, you can't teach. You simply have to prepare them, and you have to be there." West concluded that "life is not about doing good" but "being loving, and . . . respectful of human nature."[3]

Of course, on rereading that passage from Morris West, we know that life is both about doing good and being loving and respectful of human nature, not either one or the other. Though it is a rather popular, catchy notion, the very idea that we can actually love someone without willing his good is simply contradictory. Love means seeking and acknowledging the good in what exists, and doing it for the sake of that good. We can, to be sure, love some good wrongly, but not because it is not good.

We need to understand that we have a nature, an inner configuration, which we did not give to ourselves, that what we are itself points us to what is good and to the love of *what is.* The enterprise of actively becoming aware of this record, this uniqueness belonging to no one else, constitutes the inner history of each of us. Whether we like it or not, we have, as Augustine said, "restless hearts." The only thing we cannot do is to deny this truth of ourselves, but even should we try to do so, we know what we deny. The essential content of our intellectual lives is to confront the question of whether there is an object, a good, in which this experienced restlessness ceases.

III.

No one can begin to talk of Catholicism today without first acknowledging the clerical scandals in various places, especially in the United

---

3. Found at www.abc.net.au/rn/arts/bwriting/west.htm.

States, that have marred its visage. That similar scandals have happened in the long history of the Church is not particularly consoling, though it needs understanding. Who does not fret about the slowness of Church officials to recognize and do something about what came to public notice not from within the Church but largely from publicity in the world press?

But we can become too discouraged by such events. They may actually indicate that the essential core of revelation was right about what to expect from human nature at all times and places. We need to recall what I take to be the central point of Mel Gibson's *The Passion of the Christ*, namely, that Christ suffered and died for sinners, prominently numbered among whom we each must first count ourselves. The fact that we are sinners is no comfort, of course. But it also serves to remind us of the purpose of the Incarnation in the first place, namely, to redeem us, to invite us to repent. To my knowledge, no place in Scripture or in Catholic teaching ever suggests that a time will come in this world when this acknowledgment and repentance for our sins do not arise among us.

If we had no need of redemption, the work and events of the Incarnation and the drama of Christ's life and death, as we understand them, would have been unnecessary. The Catholic mind maintains that, in no area of life, personal, political, or religious, are we immune from the results of the Fall or the hope of the Redemption. A secular mind holds that it has no need to account for anything beyond itself and no necessity to account for itself to any standard higher than any it proposes to itself.

How this latter view is a rather boring and deceptive way to picture the reality and nobility of our *de facto* existence, I will leave you to figure out. The main trouble with an atheistic humanism is not that it is atheist, but that it is not a humanism. The "ground of our being," to use Eric Voegelin's term, is something already established and that not by ourselves.

The Pharisees in the Gospel were, in one famous incident, engaged in learned debate over the penalty of stoning for the woman caught in adultery. Christ challenged them: "Let him who is without sin cast the first stone." With this remark, he taught us a graphic lesson, as did the Pharisees, who one by one quietly slipped away, leaving Christ alone with the accused woman. The "go and sin no more" admonition that Christ finally directed to the woman is not necessarily a guarantee of our or her never sinning again even after our acknowledging such sins. This possible "sinning again" is the old problem about delaying baptism till the point of death, as the likelihood of sinning again was so great. Such was a misunderstanding of the sacraments but not of the worrisome proneness of mankind to sin again. It is often helpful to be reminded that the effect of the Fall will ever be present among us, even in the highest of places, perhaps especially there.

IV.

In his "Dialogue concerning Heresies," Sir Thomas More has a very Augustinian sounding subheading: "Reason, as well as Faith, Is Needed for the Interpretation of Scripture." Here is More's explanation of this heading:

> Now in the study of Scripture, in devising upon the sentence (meaning), in considering what ye read, in pondering the purpose of divers comments, in comparing together divers texts that seem contrary and be not, albeit I deny not but that grace and God's especial help is the great thing therein, yet useth he for an instrument man's reason therein. God helpeth us to eat also but yet not without our mouth.[4]

This is the classic Catholic mind at work. In one sense, Christ multiplied the loaves. But what caused us to be what we are formed us with mouths whereby to eat such loaves. Christ may have healed the lame to walk. We have to free ourselves from determinist ideologies that claim *a priori* that miraculous events are impossible, in order to acknowledge what in fact does happen, even a miracle.

Christ did not teach anyone with no legs to walk, though we moderns have restructured our sidewalks without curbs and put the legless in machines with the help of which they can get about in our cities. Thomas More, in this brief passage, has summarized the whole theological method—that is, we first read the Scripture for what it says; we then carefully seek its exact meaning, its words, and situation in place. We look at differing proposed understandings of what is said. We compare various texts that apparently are contradictory. Meanwhile, we know that Scripture cannot contradict itself. Our intellectual task is thus to show, on evident grounds, that it does not in fact do so.

Scripture was given to us as a record that once upon a time, certain lame men were healed by a certain evidently unusual Man. It was also given to us, however, so that, in reading of such events, we ask ourselves whether, in theory, they could have happened naturally. We are not ex-

4. Sir Thomas More, "Dialogue concerning Heresies," *Essential Thomas More*, edited by James J. Greene and John P. Dolan (New York: Mentor, 1967), 200.

empt from examining whether, in practice, the witnesses were reliable, whether the structure of the world is such that nothing outside its normal cyclic laws can happen. It is, in other words, one thing for us to know that a miracle happened. It is another thing to have a philosophical understanding of the world that permits such things to happen within it. The miracle of the world is not merely that extraordinary things, outside of normal events, such as the lame walking, can happen in it. It is also the intellectual awareness that ordinary things can also happen within it. The latter may, at bottom, be more impressive than the former. Sir Thomas More was right: "God helpeth us to eat also, but not without giving us a mouth." This is the Catholic mind at work.

This same Sir Thomas More, himself no mean philosopher, in a "Letter to Dons at the University of Oxford," dealt with the relation that we Christians have to Greek philosophy, of which he did not claim to be the "sole champion." This is the reason-revelation question as the Catholic mind sees it, something developed by John Paul II in *Fides et Ratio*. Many scholars at Oxford, Sir Thomas admitted, did indeed know the usefulness of the Greeks. "For who is not cognizant of the fact that in the liberal arts, and especially in theology, it was the Greeks who discovered or handed on whatever was of value. In the realm of philosophy, with the possible exceptions of Cicero and Seneca, what is there that was not written in Greek or taken directly from the Greeks?"[5] Both in this comment about the place of the Greeks in theology and philosophy, and in his comment about heresies, More notes the special place of intelligence, of mind, in thinking about what God has revealed to us.

To this emphasis, I might add, More is not ignoring other intellectual systems, past and present, unknown to Hellas. He praised the Greeks not because they were Greeks but because they were mind. I might also add that, as Socrates, perhaps the most Greek of them all, understood, the Greeks themselves also held this position. Greek philosophy, as Aquinas himself would note, could be wrong on this or that point. But if it was wrong, it was on the grounds that it was philosophy, not that it was Greek. Thus it could be corrected by better philosophy without denying the Greeks their culture. A Catholic mind, reflecting on what is revealed, can see what at times needs philosophic correction. Revelation can make what we already are more manifest to us.

<hr>

5. More, "Letter to the University of Oxford" (March 29, 1518), ibid., 108.

Tracey Rowland, in her insightful book *Culture and the Thomist Tradition*, has noted what happens when the cultural images and artifacts, the music, the words, the poetry, of Catholicism lose their proportion to their object. Plato had long ago also noted that our souls can become disordered by the music we hear and by the poetry we read.

The very purpose of revelation was not only properly to define God, but to establish forms of response to the divine reality in terms of beauty and order that were worthy of Him. The Mass exists not as a human invention but as a divine one, itself designed to show mankind what it has so long sought to know, namely how God is to be worshiped. This worship includes the right understanding of what goes on in this same Mass.

Both in the Eastern and Western church, we have surrounded the Sacrifice of the Mass with noble and worthy words, gestures, vestments, all designed to express the awe that we experience in beholding the glory that we are given through the Sacrifice of the Cross. Beauty is itself educative in its delight. When it is undermined, when what goes on is no longer worthy, when the great mystery is trivialized, the cultural results are devastating. As Rowland puts it:

> By depriving people of these riches through the policy of accommodating liturgical practices to the norms of "mass culture" . . . the post-Conciliar Church has unwittingly undermined the ability of many of its own members to experience self-transcendence. . . . As a consequence, plain persons fall into the pit of nihilistic despair and/or search for transcendence in the secular liturgies of the global economy, whereas the more highly educated pursue strategies of stoic withdrawal and individual self-cultivation which are destined to end in despair, and even madness.[6]

The Catholic mind understands with Aristotle that a small error in the beginning leads to a large error in the end. The historical alternatives to the proper and dignified worship of God as established by God ultimately lead to despair and madness. In our inner souls, we are only made for true worship. Nothing less than everything will give us rest.

VI.

At the beginning of the fifteenth and last book of Augustine's treatise on the Trinity, he briefly sums up what he has written in the previous fourteen books. His overall intention in writing this now famous book is not

---

6. Tracey Rowland, *Culture and the Thomist Tradition* (London: Routledge, 2003), 168.

polemic. He wants to account for the Godhead in such a way that it makes some sense to the human mind. In order to do this, Augustine again calls our attention to the fact that we have a mind, the reflection on which enables us to understand how something can be one and yet within it have a relationship of otherness, how God can be the one God of the Old Testament and the triune God of the New Testament without contradiction, without absurdity, something the Catholic adamantly holds to be the case. What the inner life of God is like, after all, is the highest of questions to which all other inquires are related. The pondering of this doctrine is more likely to teach us what we are than any other topic.

"Wanting to train the reader in the things that were made, so that he might know Him by whom they were made," Augustine explains, "we have now at least arrived at His image, which is man. But it is man in that by which man is superior to other animals, namely, in reason and understanding, and whatever else can be said of the rational or intellectual soul that pertains to that thing which is called 'mind' or 'rational soul.'"[7] Catholicism is not afraid of intelligence.

Thinking about the Godhead is, no doubt, a difficult accomplishment. Revelation was primarily directed at our salvation. It was not a treatise or direct explication of what the inner life of God is like. Still Augustine was quite capable of being annoyed at those who refuse to bend their minds on the subject but are content merely to repeat Scripture, which is, indeed, the origin of our understanding of the Trinity in the first place. Augustine could not tolerate intellectual laziness even in ordinary people.

I emphasize this pique of Augustine because, I think, it is another good example of the Catholic mind at work. If someone is not capable of or is not interested in reflecting on his own mind to see what is true there, namely, that mind, will, and being are of one person, yet reveal different powers, why believe Scripture about "the highest Trinity which God is?" No human mind can fully grasp it. Many people believe in Scripture with unshakeable trust. On this basis, with the help of "prayer, study and a good life," surely they can seek "to understand . . . that what is retained by faith may be seen *in* the mind, insofar as it can be seen. Who would forbid this? Nay rather, who would not exhort them to do this?"[8]

In other words, Augustine is rather impatient with those who do not

7. Augustine, *On The Trinity*, edited by Gareth B. Mathews (Cambridge: Cambridge University Press, 2002), 167.
8. Ibid., book 15, chap. 27, 331.

think about what Scripture sets down. It is not enough just to know it. Augustine does not think our relation to God is completed only by believing. It includes the effort further to understand. "This (combination of soul and body) is a work of such wonder and grandeur," Augustine continues,

as to astound the mind that seriously considers it, and to evoke praise to the creator; and this is true not only as that work is observed in man, a rational being and on that account of more excellence and greater worth than all other creatures, but even in the case of the tiniest fly. It is God who has given man his mind. . . . The mind becomes capable of knowledge and learning, ready for the perception of truth, and able to love the good.[9]

The mind can fail in this, Augustine admits, but this failure too is part of its drama, without which we could not be the kind of beings we are.

In conclusion, chapter 46 of the third volume of St. Thomas's *Summa contra Gentiles* is entitled *"Quod anima in hac vita non intelligit seipsam per seipsam."* It is a question related to Augustine's discussion of the relation of the mind to the Trinity. Basically, it states that in this life, our mind or soul does not understand itself through itself. The only mind that understands itself through itself is the divine mind. We have a mind, but not a divine one. But this human mind must first be put into activity by knowing what is not itself. Once it knows what is not itself, the mind can reflect on itself to know that it also is. Aquinas states that "according to Augustine's meaning, our mind knows itself through itself, in so far as it knows concerning itself, that it is. Indeed, from the fact that it perceives that it acts it perceives that it is. Of course, it acts through itself, and so, through itself, it knows concerning itself that it is." In this short epistemological passage, we already have the foundation by which we can reject a persistent modern view. This is the notion that by denying the mind's ability or capacity to know the truth, we can justify ourselves for deliberately not knowing what we can know.

What has this observation to do with the mind that is Catholic? These are my conclusions:

1. "Let he who is without sin cast the first stone."
2. "All get what they want; they do not always like it."
3. "God helpeth us to eat also, but yet not without our mouth."

---

9. Augustine, *Concerning the City of God against the Pagans,* translated by Henry Bettenson (Harmondsworth, England: Penguin, 1984), 1072.

4. Even the case of "the tiniest fly" is of "such wonder and grandeur as to astound the mind."

5. "Discovering the Church is apt to be a slow process, but it can only take place if you have a free mind and no vested interest in disbelief."

6. "Men can think of anything seriously, however absurd it is. Men can believe anything, even the truth."

In the end, this is the Catholic mind, to hold the truth because it knows that it is itself mind open to *what is,* to what is true from whatever source its evidence might arise, even from common sense, even from reason, yes, even from the revelation handed down to us.

2 "INFINITIZED BY THE SPIRIT"

Maritain and the Intellectual Vocation

Discursive and demonstrative arguments, doctrinal erudition, and historical erudition are assuredly necessary, but of little efficacy on human intellects such as God made them, and which first ask to see. In actual fact, a few fundamental intuitions, if they have one fine day sprung up in a mind, mark it for ever.

—Jacques Maritain, *Notebooks*

During that academic year of 1921–1922, I had only one or two occasions to speak to Maritain. . . . I had to give an "exposé" on the question: The role of sensible experience in the development of knowledge; I asked Maritain what had to be touched upon to treat the question from a Thomist point of view. He answered that there were three points to consider: 1) the origin of ideas, 2) no thought without an image, 3) judgment is hindered when the senses are impeded. And he sent me to the Summa Theologica.

—Yves Simon, *My First Memories of Jacques Maritain*

Educators must not expect too much from education. . . . St. Thomas holds that the teacher actually engenders knowledge in the soul of the pupil, and this is equally true of moral habits and of virtue; but, in so doing, he (the teacher) acts as an instrumental and not as an efficient cause.

—Jacques Maritain, "Philosophy and Education"

I.

Though realizing that it is but one, we live, if you will, in two worlds. The first is the world of things already in being and functioning by themselves according to what they are, by their own resources. Such a world is simply there through no activity or cause of our own. We can learn something of how it "works," but it is already there working by itself without us.

This paper was originally presented at the American Maritain Association meeting at the Catholic University of America, October 2005.

In this sense, we are ourselves included in this world of things that come to be without ourselves being the primary cause of what it is for them to come to be or of what they are. The world was simply "there" before we recognized that it was actually there or before we worried about what it was. And unless we are not quite normal, few of us ever maintained that the world was only there because we put it there, or, even worse, maintained that nothing was there but our thoughts about what was there.

The second world, that makes the first world alive and vivid to us, is mostly invisible. It is the world of thought itself as it reflects on these already existing things *that are.* Through thought, we seek to know and delight in *what and why things are.* Thought primarily changes our internal world; it leaves the ongoing world as it is.

Allied to this latter internal world and an essential part of it, however, is the world of practical intellect. This practical world relates to the knowledge of the things that can be "otherwise" through our own activities of making or doing. These latter realities, things made and things done, come to be only because we human beings, in all our oddness, already exist in the first world. The practical things are the products of our personal causality and need not, as such, exist.

We have in existence, then, things put there by our art and craft capacities, boats and trains and "picture shows," as we used quaintly to call them. Such things could not be there at all without these human capacities of making and doing, though that too always presupposes a first world already there. Such practical things have their own intelligibilities, their own mode of being, their own "truth," insofar as they relate to the correspondence of what we intend to put into existence with what we actually put there.

We also have the ethical and political world, the world of "doing" or "acting." Like the art/craft world, ethical and political acts are put there by our free choices about what we ought and shall do as human beings governing ourselves, our families, our voluntary and necessary institutions. This ethical world is obscurely visible to us in our intentions, in our virtues and vices, in our deeds and misdeeds. But it is a world of intense interest and vibrancy to us, about which we cannot not know something or be completely indifferent. Man is, after all, as Aristotle famously said, a "political" animal. He added that he is also one who "laughs."

The scholastic philosophers used to have the phrase that went—*vivere viventibus est esse;* roughly translated, it can be rendered: "For beings who are alive, their *to be* is 'to live.'" In the case of rational beings, to which we happily belong, their living is not simply being conscious of life's pulsations, though there is that too. Their living includes, is subsumed into, their knowing—*et esse et vivere intelligentibus est intelligere*. In other words, if I might put it that way, the life of the mind, the intellectual life, the intellectual vocation, is a vivid reality constantly bursting forth in all minds. By such activity, we know not only ourselves but initially what is not ourselves.

Thus, reflective activity on what is not ourselves enables us also at least indirectly to know ourselves, the great Socratic project. And this interior, or invisible, vibrant life of our minds is, in a way, the most important thing about us, provided we do not lapse into what Maritain often warned about, namely, the "angelism" of a Descartes. According to this view, we think that we would be better off not to have bodies at all. But we are not and are not intended to be, after all, pure minds, pure spirits. This wholeness, body and soul, is no defect in our being. We are persons with minds that illumine all that we are and do, all that we see and observe. It is only because we also have minds that there is light in our otherwise intellectually dark world. We are the beings in the universe, from within it, that combine mind and body in such a manner as to remain still one being, as Aristotle already saw.

Certain inner activities, then, are proper and typical to our kind. In a 1994 *Peanuts* sequence, Lucy is earnestly talking to little Rerun about what she has in her hand. He intently is watching her. "See, Rerun?" she explains to him, holding it out for him to observe, "It's a jump rope." In the next scene, we see Lucy alone vigorously flipping the rope over her head and skipping over it as it falls. She continues in demonstration, "You twirl the rope and you jump up and down, like this." In the third scene, Rerun, clearly puzzled, continues to watch her from a distance while Lucy makes a further clarification: "Then you count how many times you jump." In the last scene, we see Lucy, for once, completely flummoxed. As she looks straight down at him, he asks her, simply, the great question, "Why?"

That utterly amusing scene, I think, touches the essence of the philosophic vocation. "Why on earth, Lucy, are you doing that?" Almost more than anything, it explains why the mind is alive. We can easily go through the steps. We begin with seeing Lucy skipping rope, while explaining *what* she is doing. Then comes Aristotle's wonder in our as well as in Rerun's eyes. We just want to know, even when things seem obvious or foolish. We constantly encounter things that puzzle us, like jump ropes, or a smart girl's explanation of things. But we also want to know *why* things are as they are. Why bother? What is jump rope? Why do we do it? The next step is undoubtedly the effort to respond to the question. We must distinguish things, this thing from that, this thing is not that. We see if maybe a feasible explanation might exist after all. And finally with some persistence and method, we find answers, or at least beginnings of answers, both to "what" questions and to "why" questions.

Rerun's "why?" is not, in fact, entirely unanswerable. Lucy is explaining a common game or a contest that we have all played. It need not have a reason beyond itself. We in fact can understand the point of jumping rope, though it is also, like all games, something done for its own sake and need not be. Especially when we do not know the "why?" of things, we inquire about them. Answers are usually built on a long articulated series of "whys." We are, indeed, wrong not to inquire about things that perplex us. And we delight in pursuing inquiry as much as in finding answers. We suspect from our metaphysics, if not from our theology, moreover, that it is not quite possible, for us at least, to know everything about anything that actually exists. We are privileged to know what we know and wonder about what we do not.

The three pithy epistemological principles that Maritain, in a passing inquiry, gave to the young Yves Simon in 1921 about the relation of sense experience to knowledge are not bad guides, even yet, to the intellectual life. Our ideas, at least their content, do not originate with our minds but do come to be in them because of the *what is* we actually, from outside of ourselves, encounter, see, hear, touch, smell, or taste. What we know is that something is out there. Nor is there any thought without an image. But the image is not what is thought about. Rather it is that by which the thing we are curious about is known.

In brief, though I have an image of you, I do not know this image, but I know you. Our mind reaches reality, not just itself or its images. If the latter were the case, that what we knew were images and not existing things, none of us would live in the same world. As it is, we have a million minds knowing the same world. Contrariwise, if all we knew was our own images, we should have a million minds knowing a million worlds with nothing common in between. And if we did not live in the same world, why is it that we can all understand that a little girl is jumping rope? It is unimaginable that we all concoct the very same thing at the same time from separate minds not dependent on *what is*. It seems a remarkably remote coincidence if the little girl is not actually jumping the rope that causes Rerun to ask her why she is doing it.

But if there is something wrong with our sense organs, we will not have reliable avenues to things. We can be tricked. There are optical illusions, though we can come to know both the tricks and the illusions. This summer, some friends of my brother's brought over a charming little seven-year-old granddaughter for the afternoon. The girl was bright and delightful. She obviously wore very thick glasses, which she had only recently acquired. The grandparents evidently had noticed that when she watched television, she would walk right up to the tube to see it. They naturally inquired "why?" It turned out that she had severe astigmatism. Being very close was the only way that she could see at all.

We live in the same world for two reasons. First, the little girl knew that there was something to see that she could see more clearly close up. Secondly, the thick glasses when acquired enabled her to see from a relatively normal distance what she formerly saw only close up. After we correct the problem, we judge correctly about things that we see. We might still ask the skeptical question: "Are not, perhaps, all of us are deceived, by our senses or by Descartes' devil, so that none of us sees anything as it is?" But we could never ask the skeptical question unless we were pretty sure everyone did see the same things. Rerun asked Lucy, "Why are you jumping rope?" while he was watching her jump rope. He knew what she was doing. He did not ask her, "Why are you eating ice cream?" when she was actually jumping rope. All skeptics still open the door before they walk through it. The intellectual vocation includes the defense, as Maritain saw, of our senses and their connection to our knowing what is there for us to know, to what is not ourselves.

II.

Joseph Cardinal Ratzinger wrote a short Foreword to the 1988 Ignatius Press edition of Henri de Lubac's famous book, *Catholicism: Christ and the Common Destiny of Man.*[1] Following the papal election, I decided, after rereading Ratzinger's recommendation of this de Lubac thesis, that I had better reread the book itself. The following lines of Ratzinger about the nature of contemporary issues particularly interested me: "If previously there was a narrowing of the Christian vision to an individualism, we are now [1988] in danger of a sociological leveling down. Sacraments are often seen

1. Henri de Lubac, *Catholicism: Christ and the Common Destiny of Man* (1947; San Francisco: Ignatius Press, 1988).

merely as celebrations of the community where there is no more room for the personal dialogue between God and the soul—something many greet with condescending ridicule."[2] Evidently what many greet with "condescending ridicule" is the classic notion that the community, however good, is not everything, that there is no personal relation to God.

What was particularly significant about Ratzinger's remark in this context is that de Lubac's book was originally intended to counteract excessive early-modern individualism in theology, philosophy, and piety. De Lubac rather emphasized, following the Church Fathers, the social aspects of our lives both in terms of Trinity and Incarnation, Creation and Redemption. But in the end both de Lubac and Ratzinger became acutely aware that a counter danger had more recently arisen. It stressed the primacy of "social" or "political" in such a way that the relative personal autonomy within any true community itself disappeared. The "leveling-down" that concerned Ratzinger implies that nothing rises higher if the community is seen to be sufficient unto itself. As it turned out in the end, the problem was as much in the collectivism of Marxism as individualist classical liberalism, almost for the same reason. One is the flip side of the other. The building of the brotherhood, the Kingdom of God on earth, thus became the locus of all religion. By following Feuerbach's *Essence of Christianity*, religion was transformed into an almost mystical celebration of human brotherly community in this world as the real and only center of man. Justice and peace, not charity and wisdom, became its primary virtues. Any transcendent destiny was looked upon as an escape from and danger to the essential human task.

However, the community itself, both in classic thought and in revelation, has transcendent aims, but only in and through the metaphysical status of its individual members, who ground any community in *what is*, and in that to which all being, including each person, is pointed. "Thou hast made us for Thyself," as Augustine said in the *Confessions*. The community is always a relation among beings, not itself an independent being absorbing them all. This observation about both a liberal and collective danger struck me as pretty much on target, particularly the dubious notion, logically connected with it, that sacraments are merely "celebrations of the community" with no room for personal dialogue with God or relation to the sacrifice of Christ.

A conflict between community and transcendence thus became im-

2. Joseph Cardinal Ratzinger, foreword to ibid., 12.

possible in this new order. "Ideologized" politics would strive to eliminate any dissenters who thought that revelation advised anything different from what the autonomous community devised for itself in its absolute freedom. Instead of revelation becoming a check on the totalistic ambitions of worldly community, it, with all its enthusiasms, was absorbed into it and not allowed to disagree with it. With this background in mind, I reread the great de Lubac book. Indeed, it is through this path that I arrive at the idea of an intellectual vocation to which Maritain can be an impressive guide.

Near the end of *Catholicism*, de Lubac approvingly cites Jacques Maritain's *Humanisme intégral* (*Integral Humanism*) in the following words, which strikingly confirm Ratzinger's concern:

> There is in man an eternal element, a "germ of eternity," which already "breathes the upper air," which always, *hic et nunc*, evades the temporal society. The truth of his being transcends his being itself. For he is made in the image of God, and in the mirror of his being, the Trinity is ever reflected. But it is only a mirror, an image. If man, by an act of sacrilege, inverts the relationship, usurps God's attributes, and declares that God was made to man's image, all is over with him.[3]

This passage from Maritain is mindful of John Paul II's constant notion that sociology by its own methods could not directly detect grace and its activity in the world. The passage also contains one of the most concise definitions of that atheist modernity or humanism that we can find—that is, *God is made in man's image*. This description was made famous by de Lubac himself in his *Drama of Atheist Humanism*.[4]

In looking at Maritain's *Integral Humanism*, in its introduction, from which de Lubac cited, we find Maritain's famous definition of the person:

> A person is a universe of spiritual nature endowed with freedom of choice and constituting to this extent a whole which is independent in face of the world—neither nature nor the State can lay prey to this universe without its permission. And God himself, who is and acts within, acts there in a particular manner and with a particularly exquisite delicacy, which shows the value he sets on it. He respects its freedom, at the heart of which he nevertheless lives; He solicits it; he never forces it.[5]

---

3. de Lubac, *Catholicism*, 328–29.

4. Henri de Lubac, *Drama of Atheist Humanism*, translated by Edith Reilly (Cleveland: Meridian, 1963).

5. Jacques Maritain, *Integral Humanism: Temporal and Spiritual Problems of a New Christendom*, translated by Joseph W. Evans (1936; Notre Dame, Ind.: University of Notre Dame Press, 1968), 9.

This passage already reflects Maritain's famous, but difficult, distinction between the "individual" and the "person" that we find in *Man and the State*. In that book, he sought to explain how the individual could be "part" of the state and yet, as a person, be a whole and transcend it.[6] What ultimately was at stake was not merely the relation of human beings to one another in an ordered polity, but a complete inner life that was itself the locus of all relations both to other persons and to the divinity.

Maritain's comment in *Man and the State* is pertinent in this regard for what I want to suggest about his intellectual vocation, and with it, what an intellectual vocation is: "The human person is both part of the body politic and superior to it through what is supra-temporal, or eternal, in him, in his spiritual interests and his final destination."[7] Evidently, our "spiritual interests" and our "final destination" are themselves subject matter not merely of an objective order but of an effort to understand their dimensions. Such things are not directly what the political life is about, but the political life deals with human persons who have both these interests and this destiny. This understanding is something that Aristotle tried to get at in his notion of contemplation, toward which politics is indirectly ordained. Revelation itself, moreover, does not indicate that such a transcendent destiny or interests have nothing to do with each other. Revelation directly reminds us that we will also be judged by how we actually conduct ourselves to our neighbor. Many of the strictures about final judgment include knowing both what we should know, that is, the truth, and doing what we should do, the commandments.

In the definition of the person in *Integral Humanism*, Maritain insisted that the person is himself a whole and that he is free. Even God deals with man on these two bases, on his personal autonomy and his freedom. This understanding, of course, means that our pursuit of "why?" with both our questions and our answers to them is also tinged with the freedom to reject their serious import, even if we understand it as true. An intellectual vocation will thus normally include a thorough effort to appreciate and understand the arguments against truth and why they may be erroneous, no matter where they originate.

In the *Peasant of the Garonne*, Maritain asked, with regard to man's

---

6. Jacques Maritain, *Man and the State* (Chicago: University of Chicago Press, 1952), 148–50. See also Maritain, "The Individual and the Person," in *Social and Political Philosophy of Jacques Maritain: Selected Readings*, translated and selected by Joseph Evans and Leo Ward (Notre Dame, Ind.: University of Notre Dame Press, 1976), 2–9.

7. Maritain, *Man and the State*, 148.

worldly destiny, "Have we to say, too, that Christians should long ago have perceived that, along with their spiritual vocation, the ultimate end of which is eternity, they also had a *temporal* task with respect to the world, its well-being and its transformation?"[8] Maritain attributed this specific idea as formulated, the idea of complete temporal transformation, not to Christianity but to Marx. The Christian idea, he thought, had to be carefully distinguished at the deepest level: "The Christian can, and must ask for the coming of the kingdom of God in glory, but (he) is not entitled to ask for—not to propose as the end of his temporal activity—a definite advent of justice and peace, and of human happiness, as the term of the progress of temporal history: for this progress is not capable of any final term."[9] The reason that earthly progress cannot present any "final term" is precisely because each person's personal destiny is the inner life of God as freely presented to him by God on God's terms. The Kingdom of God, in the strict sense, can only be composed of those who have made this choice as their individual and thus common good. The aspect of Maritain's intellect that I think I admire most is this abiding awareness of the centrality of this issue.

III.

The condition of mind in the Church is graphically brought to our attention by the death of John Paul II and the election of Benedict XVI, both men of outstanding knowledge, men who worked together, yet with many different interests and emphases. It is not particularly useful to compare one to the other, since we realize that the multiplicity of minds is itself a good thing, provided these minds themselves choose to be intent on the truth and seek to know how it is to be acquired, preserved, and articulated.

We can speak of a "vocation" of the intellectual, both in society and in the Church. We sometimes hear the expression "public intellectual." We also hear the expression "the betrayal of the intellectuals or of the clerics." We recognize that ultimately all order and disorder in the public realm, and probably in our inner souls, stem from order or disorder in the souls and minds of thinkers whose ideas have fashioned the culture in which we live. In a famous passage, the economist John Maynard Keynes once said that we find out that what causes changes in our time is usually traced to some obscure thinker in past ages, to someone of whom we never heard,

8. Jacques Maritain, *Peasant of the Garonne: An Old Layman Questions Himself and the Future Time*, translated by Michael Cuddihy and Elizabeth Hughes (New York: Holt, 1968), 199.
9. Ibid., 202.

but whose thought shaped those who became major actors in a later era.

The Catholic Church is also a thing of the mind. What is peculiar about its understanding of revelation is that it is not, as Aquinas taught us, to be opposed to reason. Rather it is to foster reason, both in itself and, more interestingly, in the fact that revelation itself is addressed to reason. In the debate between Jerusalem and Athens, the Catholic chooses both. And in choosing both, he does not find either alienating, but reinforcing each other precisely in the line of truth. Catholicism, to repeat, is an intellectual religion. It is more than that, but it is at least that. And, even with his careful attention to mysticism, Maritain took pains to see its intellectual side. The minute any Catholic thinker or institution forgets this fundamental aspect of the Word made flesh, the whole Church is in trouble. "Peace and justice" in this world do not constitute what revelation is about, though it is also indirectly at least about justice and peace, even in this world.

Jacques Maritain, among others, represents, in a vivid and living way, the vocation of a man devoted precisely to the truth of faith in light of the truths of philosophy. We know from Aquinas that one of the major tasks of the intellectual, something that he can perhaps do better than anyone else, is to account for those seemingly plausible views that claim to explain the world in a way that is not compatible with the teachings of revelation. As Chesterton said, the truth of what we hold is not dependent on the time in which we live. If a thing cannot be held in the twelfth century, it cannot be held in the twenty-first century either.

We have need of those often few who are willing to spend their lives in the pursuit of some what often seem to be unimportant truths. Yet, sooner or later, that research, that thought-effort, becomes vital to the Church's defense. Suddenly it will be attacked and have no place to turn but to that obscure intellectual who was, in his honest way, pursuing the truth while nobody noticed.

The vocation of the man of intellect is and ought to be a humble one, however much academics are tempted to pride, to their own views, whatever they may be. One of the things the intellectual may be called upon to do, as Yves Simon remarked, is to give up his much cherished theory when it is proved to be wrong.[10] The vocation of the intellectual in the Church is the service of truth, articulated truth, a truth that is discovered not made by the man who thinks.

10. Yves Simon, *A General Theory of Authority* (Notre Dame, Ind.: University of Notre Dame Press, 1980).

If we look at the corpus of Maritain's works, we are astonished to see the range of things he addressed in a formal philosophic manner. He dealt with philosophy in all its forms, with ethics, art, metaphysics, mathematics, mysticism, psychology, science, education, physics, poetry, literature, politics, economics, theology, natural law, and history. He addressed his mind to what was there to be known, to what it is to know. And he let us know how he thought about such things. An intellectual vocation includes the effort to bring it forth into the world, to publish it in whatever venue seems fitting. Maritain's efforts were not always wise, though they usually were. I have never quite thought his endeavor to save Lucifer by his reassignment to Limbo was particularly successful or wise. I am still dubious about his natural rights theses. But he always had a point worth considering.

One of the things that is perhaps most admirable about Maritain's intellectual vocation is, as I suggested, its breadth. He was a man who knew that philosophy was above all the knowledge of the whole. He was aware that in understanding one thing, we need to pay attention to all things. And when we realize the extraordinary amount of time and hard work it takes even to begin such an enterprise, let alone the skills and languages needed to do it well, we again see Maritain's example of what it meant to have an intellectual vocation.

I am impressed with the short introduction that Maritain placed in his equally concise, An Introduction to Philosophy. "Philosophers," he begins, "were once called wise men."[11] He then cites Cicero's famous account of Pythagoras's concern that only the gods were wise. Human beings could only love or seek such wisdom. It is wise when a human being is aware of the difficulty in knowing "the highest truths."

Maritain then refers to Aristotle's famous remark in the Metaphysics that our nature is "in so many respects enslaved." This very remark of Aristotle is perhaps the closest that the great pagan philosophers ever came to an intellectual statement of the problem of original sin. But all of these cautions lead us to the sense that we ourselves are not exactly wise but, at best, "beggars at wisdom's door." We are but friends and lovers of wisdom. Undaunted by these historical worries, Maritain adds, "Nevertheless philosophy is nothing other than wisdom itself so far as it is accessible to human nature." To acquire this wisdom, Maritain devoted his life, but even here, it was in the service of an opening to a higher wisdom.

Yet, if we are lovers of wisdom and suspect that wisdom in a fuller

11. Jacques Maritain, An Introduction to Philosophy (London: Sheed & Ward, 1946), xiii.

sense exists, we should long for it, however it may come to us. "Nothing is more human than for man to desire naturally things impossible to his nature," Maritain wrote near the end of his *Approaches to God.*

It is, indeed, the property of a nature which is not closed up in matter like the nature of physical things, but which is intellectual or *infinitized by the spirit.* It is the property of a *metaphysical* nature. Such desires reach for the infinite, because the intellect thirsts for being and being is infinite. They are natural, but one may also call them trans-natural. It is thus that we desire to see God; it is thus that we desire to be free without being able to sin; it is thus that we desire beatitude.[12]

The mind is capable of knowing all things. We are indeed *"infinitized by the spirit,"* to repeat Maritain's felicitous phrase.

It is to be noticed, furthermore, that all three of these "desires" to which Maritain called our attention represent precisely what the wisdom we seek in philosophy cannot achieve by this same philosophy. Even when it suspects the human mind is open to receive such answers, it knows that they cannot come from itself. These are the questions of the vision of God, of the origin and nature of evil, and of the final content of human happiness, the very issue that de Lubac and Ratzinger were most careful not to let be subsumed either by individualism or a variety of collectivism, however designated. The vocation of intellect does not require that we all end our lives in a monastery as Maritain did. But it does, I think, require that we know that philosophy brings us to these final three questions, the "whys" of them, and the source of their answers as not, in fact, being in our politics or even in our philosophy.

Maritain once noted a common complaint that philosophers speak in an unknown or overly technical language. Why cannot they just simplify things? The complaint made him somewhat impatient. "To require that philosophers should use everyday language," he protested, "implies that their science is just an enterprising topic of conversation, idle armchair speculation after dinner."[13] Philosophers use the language they have to use to clarify what they are saying, but this is no defense of unneeded obscurity. "Their first requisite (of philosophers) is to know what they are studying, and to possess a sufficiently live and accurate notion of the problems of philosophy presented in their simplest form."[14] Maritain did not

12. Jacques Maritain, *Approaches to God,* translated by Peter O'Reilly (New York: Collier, 1962), 98 (italics added).
13. Ibid., vi.
14. Ibid., xiv.

forget the common man's need to know in ways he could make sense of.

As we recall in our first citation from Maritain in the beginning of this chapter, human intellects, "as God made them," are not easily prone to discursive or historical erudition. Most ordinary folks simply want to "see." They do not want or have the time or inclination to come to know in the technical way philosophers know. This need on the part of the common man, after all, was one of the reasons Aquinas gave (I-II, 91, 4) for the persuasive need of revelation, namely that ordinary folks, not just philosophers, could also "see." If these few "fundamental intuitions spring into our minds one fine day," as Maritain put it, still thinking of the common man, we are indeed "marked forever."

This marking too is what the life of the intellect is about. How do those who are not philosophers also know and live "the highest things?" This concern too is perhaps why Maritain devoted his intellectual life both to reason and to revelation. He wanted the common man to know that he is not excluded from the highest things. But he knew also that the philosopher too needs to be aware of answers he can not know by his own slow and laborious but worthy efforts. Too, there was Maritain's concern that common men are most often confused by philosophers whose philosophy at some point deviates from the truth. In this sense, the defense of philosophy is also the defense of the common man and perhaps explains much of Maritain's interest in political philosophy.

In conclusion, again thinking somewhat of the few insights and the advice that Maritain gave to Simon in 1921 to go to the *Summa theologiae*, let me cite the final bit of advice that Maritain gives us in his *A Preface to Metaphysics*. After having cited a number of pithy Latin first principles, including *operatio sequitur esse, id propter quod aliquid est, oportet melius esse,* and a number of others, he advised, "You will find in St. Thomas's *Compendium Theologiae,* a veritable treasury of such metaphysical axioms. It would be of great interest to draw up a methodical list of them. And we should do well to build up metaphysical axiomatic in the same spirit."[15] I might note that Josef Pieper, that model of philosophic clarity, has already done this compendium for us—in his *Human Wisdom of St. Thomas.*[16]

"Educators must not expect too much from education," Maritain told

---

15. Jacques Maritain, *A Preface to Metaphysics: Seven Lectures on Being* (New York: Mentor, 1962), 142.

16. Josef Pieper, *Human Wisdom of St. Thomas: A Breviary of Philosophy from the Works of St. Thomas Aquinas,* translated by Drostan MacLaren (New York: Sheed & Ward, 1948). Ignatius Press (2002) also has an edition of this book.

us in his book on education. Teachers can "engender" knowledge, so can virtue. But they can do so only as instrumental causes, not as efficient causes. That is, the intellectual vocation can only be ours if we choose to pursue it, to pursue the "why" of things, always suspecting there are answers, that we can even find many of them.

In the *Peanuts* on the day following Lucy's explaining to Rerun about jumping rope, we again see Rerun. This time he is intently watching the older Linus, who is bouncing a basketball. Linus says to him, "This is how we shoot baskets, Rerun." In the next scene, Rerun watches as Linus dribbles the ball, explaining, "See, we bounce the ball a couple of times to get our rhythm." Next, in a solo scene, Linus is tossing the ball at the basket. "Then we flip it through the basket." In the final scene, this time to a confused Linus, Rerun, not at all unexpectedly to us now, reaffirms his philosophical vocation, with the same question he asked Lucy, "Why?"

Yet, this persistent "why?" can be annoying. It can even be an excuse for not finding the answers. So on the following day, we see Lucy and Rerun sitting on the sofa in the front room. Lucy has a book. Again Rerun is looking suspiciously at her. "Rerun, I am going to read to you from this book," she tells him, "but if you ask 'why?' I will pound you." Undaunted, and aware of the power of coercion, Rerun, defending himself in technical legality, if not in nominalism, answers, "How come?"

Philosophy is not wisdom, but it is the love of wisdom. It is all right if the same question is asked again and again until the philosophers explain to the common man exactly the terms of the issue. The philosophical vocation does not mean that philosophers have all the answers, but it does mean that it is open to answers from whatever their source. It does mean that some things are not true and can be dangerous. Human intellects "as God made them," as Maritain put it, are not easily prone to discursive or historical erudition. "Most ordinary folks simply want to *see*." At their best, so do most philosophers.

3 CHESTERTON, THE REAL "HERETIC"

"The Outstanding Eccentricity of the Peculiar Sect Called Roman Catholics"

I did try to found a heresy of my own; and when I had put the last touches to it, I discovered that it was orthodoxy.

—G. K. Chesterton, *Orthodoxy*

I should regard any civilization which was without a universal habit of uproarious dancing as being, from the full human point of view, a defective civilization. And I should regard any mind which had not got the habit in one form or another of uproarious thinking, from the full human point of view, a defective mind.

—G. K. Chesterton, *Heretics*

I.

No one, I presume, wants to be charged with having a "defective mind," even if, perchance, he has one and knows it. However, as Chesterton implies in the chapter on "The Maniac," in *Orthodoxy*, probably the last thing a "defective mind" would know about itself is that it is defective. It takes the normal to see what is abnormal. In order not to have such a "defective mind," Chesterton tells us in *Heretics*, we need, as an antidote, the habit of "uproarious thinking." What, I might ask, does he mean by "uproarious thinking?"

Thinking, after all, seems to be rather a quiet, if not silent, activity. No one can tell, just by looking at us, whether we are thinking or not. Few "roars" or even murmurs come forth from our being when we are thinking. We usually want quiet, not noise. It is true that when we chance to come

This essay on Chesterton was originally presented at the Meeting of the American Chesterton Society, University of St. Thomas, St. Paul, Minnesota, in June 2005. It was subsequently published in *Logos* 8 (Summer 2006): 72–86.

across or concoct something that really inspires us or amuses us, we rush forth to tell someone about it, a sure sign that we are social beings, even in our silent pursuit of knowledge. But Chesterton, ever precise in his use of words, obviously intends "uproar" and "thinking" to go together. We can, however, easily imagine him laughing and even shouting in a lively debate in some London pub or university debating society.

But still, in Chesterton's usage, "uproarious" modifies "thinking," as if to say that what causes the "roar" is not the activity, *qua* activity, of thinking but what is thought about. The thought that causes the most "roar" is the one that is most unexpected, seemingly most outlandish by comparison with other thoughts. It may, for all that, still be the one that is most true. And in this sense, what causes the greatest "roar" in the modern world is precisely the unbearable public claim that Christianity, in its central positions about God, world, and man, is true—the claim that, in the end, it describes reality better than any contrary theory or supposition that is alive and flourishing in the modern mind. This very claim, presented simply as a truth to be calmly considered, is conceived to be so dangerous that a growing number of polities, and not merely Islamic ones, are devising ways legally to restrain its right to present itself in the public forum. Even Bible reading is suspect if it touches a tolerance topic.

Furthermore, what causes even more "uproar" is the further affirmation that the evidence for this truth is quite compelling both in logic and in the weight of probity that this evidence presents. If this truth is not accepted—and it is something of a fad not to accept it, whatever it holds—it is, in truth, more likely to be rejected through the influence of our own internal sins and disorders. We end up striving to protect ourselves from a reality to which we refuse to conform. No weight of evidence for the supposed "untruth" of Christianity is really brought forth. It is no surprise that the new pope, Benedict XVI, sees relativist intolerance to be one of the major problems of modern times.

No doubt, as we read *Heretics,* in which Chesterton systematically demolishes the alternate claims to truth that he found about him in his time, we have the impression that a century ago, more respect and attention were given to actual controversies about truth than we find today. What is characteristic of our more recent times is that we really do not debate anything, especially the truth of anything. Why? Ironically, we do not debate it for our fear that something actually might be true and therefore put demands on our minds, polities, and morals to change our ways. Thus, we only "tolerate" things. Most often this tolerance is but another way of admitting that we cannot or will not find the truth. It is not simply Socrates' knowing that we do not know.

A debate that presupposes that truth exists and is worthy of pursuit is itself a dangerous proposition, particularly politically. Our "debates" are power struggles and number countings, not attentive and logical examinations of evidence to arrive at true conclusions and reject the untrue propositions. By "tolerating" all truths, even the most contradictory ones, we imply that what is really true makes little difference about how we think and live. So we live as if there were no truth, except what we freely choose to call "our" truth, whatever it is. The "objective" world, it is said, supports no intellectual claim, especially in human things, that things are this way rather than that.

What is the reason for this situation? Today, as I have suggested, we are governed mostly by "tolerance" and "ecumenical" theory that, in many odd ways, prevents us from really debating the truth of things, ultimately the only thing really worth while debating. We do not really seek to change anybody's views for fear of being called bigots or fanatics. We only want to "understand" them while letting them be as they are, whatever the validity or consequences of their theories. "To understand all is to accept all." Thus, the "go forth and teach all nations" has little urgency if what we teach them is thought to be the cause of civil unrest, moral irrelevancy, and scientific stagnation.

Change would undermine the very premises of toleration. We do not want to "change" people's minds. We want to let them remain as they are so that we can "respect" them or observe them. The older notion of "respect" for ideas, however, meant doing them the honor of seeking to correct them if they were wrong. The greatest service one man could give another was to lead him to the truth, but by the route in which truth is known, that is, through argument and evidence, in courtesy and conversation. The mere claim to truth today is oftentimes considered itself to be intolerable and politically dangerous. We build our public order on the proposition that no truths can be held or claimed, self-evident or otherwise.

Tolerance does not just mean, as in its original sense, allowing other opinions to be accurately heard without intimidation, threat, or interference. Rather it means not allowing them to be heard or seriously to be considered on the basis of the evidence for them. Tolerance implies the intolerable. Tolerance theory means that nothing is intolerable, except perhaps the truth of things. Indeed, this attitude of tolerating everything because every idea is dangerous if claimed as true rapidly comes to mean that no truth is possible. We want to have no danger of any truth being claimed at all. This proposition becomes our politics and our culture. Tolerance passes from being a practical arrangement to a philosophic premise. The very claim to truth becomes a violation of the principle of tolerance.

This result indicates why those who insist that there is truth are more and more stigmatized as "fanatics." They threaten the very foundation of "tolerance," with the political and social institutions that follow from this idea. More and more, the only public crime is "intolerance," "bias," or "fanaticism," when these charges mean that truth is possible. Truth is the enemy of tolerance. We begin to see the consequences of this position increasingly in our courts both here and in Canada, where intolerance is becoming the instrument of preventing any serious discussion of the truth of things.

II.

Chesterton admitted a few years later, in *Orthodoxy,* that he actually did found a "heresy," one on which he had about put the finishing touches. The only trouble was, at this very point, he realized that his "private heresy" had already been invented long before his time. It was what used to be called "orthodoxy." And he was honest enough to admit that what he had figured out was in fact what was already understood to be true.

When we first read these startling words of Chesterton about inventing his own "heresy," we take them as something of a joke, a paradox, a pleasantry. We think that revelation is not something any human mind, including Chesterton's, could anticipate. This offhand remark of Chesterton's that he almost invented "orthodoxy" is, in fact, an extraordinary claim. Chesterton affirms, however, that he learned what was true not by reading the advocates of religion and philosophy, the apologists and the doctors of the Church, but by reading those who were vehemently opposed to the central religious and philosophical tradition of the Christian West. He learned, in other words, what was right by reflecting on the incoherence of what was wrong. What is wrong can itself point both to what is also wrong in another way or to what is right. *Ex bono, sequitur et bonum et malum,* as the scholastics put it. It is quite possible that what is good is rejected because it is good, though only in the name of some other good.

Of course, if everyone had this marvelous facility of straightening out the "defective mind" by "uproarious thinking," all might be well. Chesterton, to be sure, does not really claim that he invented Christianity all by himself, even if it seemed like a heresy. That invention would require rather a divine power or inspiration, which he did not claim to have. Chesterton is more useful to us, I suspect, if his claim to our attention is from logic rather than from inspiration. Were he "inspired," his opponents could only claim that they lacked the same inspiration. But since his claim is to be logical, he is truly dangerous because everyone can see the illogic that he points out in his opponents. He was humble enough to recognize that what he came to think corresponded to something that was already thought and thought to be true. Ultimately, this attitude will form the basis of Chesterton's wonderful appreciation of gift and gratitude as the foundation of our being. Yet, there is something always uncanny about Chesterton's ability to see the truth in the midst of error, though he thinks anyone can go and "do likewise" with a little effort.

Chesterton saw this truth not as a grim and antagonistic thing but as a kind of intellectual delight. How he must have enjoyed writing the following passage in the chapter in *Heretics* entitled "The Paganism of Mr. Lowes Dickinson":

All that remains of the ancient hymns or the ancient dances of Europe, all that has honestly come to us from the festivals of Phoebus or Pan, is to be found in the festivals of the Christian Church. If any one wants to hold the end of a chain which really goes back to the heathen mysteries, he had better take hold of a festoon of flowers at Easter or a string of sausages at Christmas. Everything else in the modern world is of Christian origin, even everything that seems most anti-Christian. The French Revolution is of Christian origin. The newspaper is of Christian origin. The anarchists are of Christian origin. Physical science is of Christian origin. The attack on Christianity is of Christian origin. There is one thing, and one thing only in existence at the present day which can in any sense accurately be said to be of pagan origin, and that is Christianity.[1]

Aside from being a kind of short summary of our history, the passage bursts with amusement about what the modern world does not know about itself, even its most cherished ideas. Even to be "anti-Christian" is a Christian idea. Only a real heretic could write such lines, I think, because he also knew that Christianity was not simply of pagan origin, even when it could accept what was good in paganism.

Chesterton, I suggest, is the real "heretic" of our time. If we approach this question statistically, we can ask, What is the percentage of people

1. *The Collected Works of G. K. Chesterton*, vol. 1, *Heretics* (1905; San Francisco: Ignatius Press, 1986), 124.

currently living on this planet who hold and practice as true the basic doctrines of Christianity and the philosophic bases necessary to defend it before reason? We would be lucky, I think, after we subtract all the Muslims, the Buddhists, Hindus, Jews, Confucians, skeptics, animists, atheists, agnostics, communists, Catholics and Protestants who deny this or that basic tenet of the faith, and whatever else we might come up with, if perhaps 5 percent of the world population of some seven billions are unequivocally "orthodox" in Chesterton's sense. And this number is arrived at before we make any distinction between sinner and non-sinner, the ultimate distinction on which our final destiny depends, be we Christian or otherwise.

It is true that some truth can be found in every heretical or unorthodox position. One cannot be wrong without being in some sense right. This basis of seeking to find the truth of things is the real foundation of every intellectual engagement with another philosophic or religious position. But the point I want to make here is that Chesterton himself, though he was relieved to find a whole tradition of orthodoxy that went before him, figured most of it out by himself through the sheer effort of examining whether the heretical positions were true or not on their own premises. Chesterton's "heresy," so to speak, was unusual or radical not merely in the fact that relatively so few held it, but that so few understood why the truth was truth in the light of the most persuasive alternatives presented to it.

III.

While we always find a delight in following the mind of Chesterton, we likewise find there something ominous also. He reminds us that our activities in the world are a function of the understanding of our place in the world, as if to say that we must suffer the consequences of what we choose, a consequence that we are often loathe to admit. To illustrate this point, I keep returning to the final paragraphs of *Heretics*, paragraphs that I consider to be simply prophetic for our time. Remember that these words were written in 1905.

One hundred years after Chesterton wrote, we see professors, pundits, politicians, and, yes, clerics all around us who embody, in one way or another, the "heresies" that he perceived. Chesterton invites us to go on a "long journey."[2] We are to embark on a "dreadful search." These are

2. Ibid., 206.

sober words. We are to "dig and seek" until we find our own, not someone else's, opinions. Our own real opinions may well be not our own unfet-
tered and contemporary thought but our acknowledging truth when we
find it, wherever we find it, even in orthodoxy.

Chesterton next tells us something of utter surprise. "The dogmas we
really hold are far more fantastic, and, perhaps, far more beautiful than we
think." It is to be noted that Chesterton uses the word "beautiful" as well
as "fantastic" in this context. Marriage, of man and woman for example,
turns out to be far more wondrous than any of the narrow alternatives proposed to us and lived out in the modern era. The currently popular "gay
marriage," with its mechanical ability to beget nothing, Chesterton would
probably call "fantastic" but not "beautiful."

Chesterton acknowledges that he has been hard on rationalism and
the rationalists. Rationalism is the view that we could explain everything
exclusively by our own reason. He apologizes to the rationalists for this
severity, even for "calling them rationalists." But the fact is "there are no
rationalists." Examine a rationalist and we will find something else really
motivating him. "We all believe in fairy-tales, and live in them." This comment, of course, recalls the wonderful chapter in *Orthodoxy* entitled "The
Ethics of Elfland," wherein we find that the fairy tales are more reasonable
than the ethical and scientific theories designed as alternatives to the central core of *what man is*. "Some hold the undemonstrable dogma of the existence of God; some the equally undemonstrable dogma of the existence
of the man next door."

Something can only be "demonstrated" if it is not already clear and evident. We cannot "prove" that the man next door exists. We can only see
him, affirm him, and testify to him. The difficulty with the man next door
is that he need not exist but does. The difficulty with God is that it is necessary that He exists, but He need not create the man next door, or us, for
that matter. We are always next door to somebody. God is not "next-door"
to anything, except to Himself. This is why God is Trinity, not, say, Allah.
The inner Trinitarian life of God means that He does not need the world.
It does not mean that world does not need Him.

Rationalism is a closed system that wants to explain everything by reason, including the existence of reason itself and its very reasonableness.
But the human reason that we know and possess did not create itself. It
was simply given with whatever it is we are made to be. When reason sets
out to explain its own reasonableness, it discovers that it is not the cause
of what it has discovered. The world is not made by human reason, but the

world does inform it. The first act of anyone's reason is not to know itself but to know what is not itself. Only then does it know itself, reflectively. Knowing something else, it knows that it itself knows what is not itself.

We sometimes wonder why "dogmas," clear, precise statements of what is true, come into existence. The very function of the mind is to make "dogmas," to seek to set down carefully, accurately what we understand to be true in the most precise way possible. Revelation, for its part, was a series of events, not originally a string of dogmas or ideas. Dogmas are efforts to state clearly what these events mean and how they relate to each other. We need to know this meaning and relationship if we are to know *what is.* The dogmas are needed to explain to us what the events were when they are encountered and testified to. (I might here cite a point of style by Chesterton's friend Belloc, in his essay on "La Rochelle" in *Places:* "If you don't like a sentence ending in a preposition, I do. It is the very genius of English.")

We may not know why our next-door neighbor exists, but we cannot doubt it without approaching madness. But how we deal with him depends on whether we understand what he is, a human being, an animal, a god, a nothing? We will deal with him differently according to what, in our theory of the cosmos, we decide he is. This is, after all, why we are now bent on aborting him, euthanizing him, cloning him, because we do not know what he is, or do not admit that we know. This is why Chesterton said, in a 1904 essay, that "theology is a product far more practical than chemistry."[3] Our lives depend less on chemistry than on guaranteeing that someone, claiming to use biology or chemistry, does not define us out of existence.

"Truths turn into dogmas the instant that they are disputed," Chesterton tells us.[4] In other words, dogmas are efforts to explain what we know to be true. "Thus every man who utters a doubt defines a religion. And the scepticism of our time does not really destroy the beliefs, rather it creates them, gives them their limits and their plain and defiant shape." A dogma is a "disputed truth" defined. Skepticism creates beliefs because it forces us to state what we mean about something we claim to know or observe. A definition of a thing is the intellectual effort to state its limits, its form, *what it is,* why it is this thing not that thing. The essence of philosophy is to distinguish this from that, to know why this thing is not that thing.

This understanding of dogma is what finally brings Chesterton to

3. G. K. Chesterton, "Why I Believe in Christianity," *Chesterton Review* 30 (December 2004): 265.
4. Chesterton, *Heretics,* 206.

his prophecy of what we might expect a hundred years from the time he wrote. "The great march of mental destruction will go on. Everything will be denied."[5] If we trace Western intellectual thought through the twentieth and still early twenty-first centuries, there is no doubt that "mental destruction" and the denial of "everything," particularly of our power even to know, is what post-modernism, deconstructionism, and liberal tolerance theories are about.

Next Chesterton does something of great perception. He reverses the usual shibboleths. In a series of remarkable paradoxes, he notes that it is only the believers who will know real things, while philosophers will deny them. "It is a reasonable position (say the philosophers) to deny the stones in the street; it will be a religious dogma to assert them. It is a rational thesis that we are all in a dream; it will be a mystical sanity to say that we are all awake," Chesterton thus began this last reflection in *Heretics*. Religious dogma not only talks of the Rock that is Peter, but of the fact that certain things have to be philosophically true if anything at all is to be believed. Faith "alone" depends on what is not faith. Evidence of whether Christ rose from the dead has something to do with a rock that closed his tomb. This very rock was rolled away. If we cannot affirm the existence of the rock, the resurrection becomes mute.

It was Descartes, the founder of modern philosophy, who, not surprisingly, wondered if the world was not a dream, so much so that he had first to prove the existence of God before he could affirm that a rock standing before him, or the man next door, really did exist. Once we reduce the existing world to a dream, we need not take it seriously. Whose dream is it? The first thing we do when we awake from a dream is to notice that things are solid around us. That is, we have something to check our dreams against, reality itself.

"Fires will be kindled to testify that two and two make four. Swords will be drawn to prove that leaves are green in summer," Chesterton continued. The great battles are epistemological because we contemporary thinkers need to defend our modern "rights" to make ourselves over into what we insist on being, whatever it is. We thus can tolerate no check on our thoughts and their "rationalist" plans from a nature we received but did not make. That would restrict our freedom of thought. We cannot admit the leaves are green, even though, as Chesterton said in *Orthodoxy*, they themselves need not exist and perhaps need not be green.

5. Ibid., 206–7.

"We shall be left defending, not only the incredible virtues and sanities of human life, but something more incredible still, the huge impossible universe that stares us in the face." Who is in fact defending the sanities of human existence, the child and the family? The "impossible universe" that stares us in the face is the one that, dogmatically, need not be. The great truth of our universe is that it need not be, but *is.* "We shall fight for visible prodigies as if they were invisible. We shall look on the impossible grass and the skies with a strange courage. We shall be of those who have seen and yet have believed."[6] In our time, it takes "courage" to affirm what the world that we see really is. We have seen and yet "believed" that what we see is real and needs no further "proof" but our own seeing and affirming.

These words are, as I say, ringing and "uproarious." They define the real "heresy" of our time, the "heresy" that can believe what it actually sees. This heresy was once called the *philosophia perennis.* In an essay in the *Common Man* entitled "The Outline of Liberty," Chesterton sought to explain the quality needed for the "spread of all truth, and especially religious truth."[7] Basically, we do not understand the full truth of a thing because we cannot see that position and its consequences against which it is originally formulated. The Catholic Church, Chesterton thought, is often seen only against the background of Protestantism, not against the background of Islam, or Hinduism, or Manicheanism, or Greek philosophy. Each of these positions brings out a different aspect of its truth against which it must define itself.

While there may be some optimists in the world, most people are pessimists over time. "The most general philosophy of men left to themselves, and perhaps the most practical illustration of the Fall of Man, is a vague impression of Fate."[8] This is a kind of deadened determinism or "fatalism" found in Buddhism, Brahmanism, and Theosophy. It means "an almost impersonal submission to an ultimately impersonal law." It was against this idea that Christianity was established. Pagans were not identified with optimism or pleasure. What is unique about Christianity, what is most extraordinary about it, however, is that "it proclaims Liberty. Or, as the only true meaning of that term, it proclaims Will."[9]

The essence of the Christian character tells a "strange story, of which the very essence is that it is made up of Will, or of a free divergence of

6. Ibid., 207.
7. G. K. Chesterton, *Common Man* (New York: Sheed & Ward, 1950), 233.
8. Ibid., 235.
9. Ibid., 236.

Wills." What seems to be such a heresy is that the modern world thinks that it is itself founded on Liberty, but not on a Liberty that makes any distinctions in things. In the Christian sense, "Will made the world; Will wounded the world; the same Divine Will gave to the world for the second time its chance; the same human Will can for the last time make its choice. That is the real outstanding peculiarity, or eccentricity, of the peculiar sect called Roman Catholics."

Before the Church came into being, this notion of liberty was not "especially emphasized." The breakup of Christianity in the Reformation again brought in a kind of determinism.[10] Fate or determinism is rejected whenever there is an understanding of Will at the heart of created things. The alternative is always a reappearance of fate, "whether desperate or resigned."

It is idle to talk to a Catholic about optimism or pessimism; for he himself shall decide whether the universe shall be, for him, the best or the worst of all possible worlds. It is useless to tell him that he might be more at one with the universal life as a Buddhist or a pantheist; for he knows that, in that sense, he might be more at one with the universal life as a turnip or a tree. It is his whole hope and glory that he is not at one with the universal life; but stands out from it, an exception and even a miracle.[11]

To put "will" at the center of things, however, is not what medieval and Muslim philosophy call "voluntarism." This latter position means that behind will stands nothing but more empty will. That is, there is no reason or nature or order with which to check or guide will. Rather, will is that power by which we decide whether or not we choose to live in the universe *that is,* in the redemption that is given to us, not the one we make for ourselves.

Ultimately, this understanding of the romance of will is what *Heretics* was about. It was about the glorious freedom we have to accept the world and its destiny, a world in which we find ourselves as free beings. Joseph Cardinal Ratzinger (Benedict XVI) put the issue well:

The creature, existing in its own right, comes home to itself, and this act is the answer in freedom to God's love. It accepts creation from God as his offer of love, and thus ensues a dialogue of love, that wholly new kind of unity that love alone can create. . . . This is how Christians understand God being "all in all." But every-

10. Ibid., 237.
11. Ibid. C. S. Lewis made a similar point in "On Living in an Atomic Age," in *Present Concerns* (London: Collins, 1986), 73–80.

thing is bound up with freedom, and the creature has the freedom to turn the positive *exitus* of its creation around, as it were, to rupture it in the Fall: this is the refusal to be dependent. Love is seen as dependence and is rejected. In its place come autonomy and autarchy: existing from oneself and in oneself, being a god of one's own making.[12]

This is as good a philosophic statement of what is at issue in the meaning of will and its relation to the universe as can be found.

Chesterton, in conclusion, had already sensed, in his own personal "heresy," that this Christian understanding of will, not "voluntarism," was at the heart of *what is*. Chesterton was right. All we have to do is read John Paul II's *Fides et Ratio* to realize that it is the faith in the modern world that is defending our obvious delight and duty to say of the rocks on the hills that they are rocks and of the grass on the lawns that it is green, to say of *what is* that it is, of what is not that it is not, as Plato also taught us to say. The greatest "heretic" of the modern era had to defy contemporary epistemology to affirm what every man knows. Every one of Chesterton's "common men" knows that rocks and grass exist, that we have minds to know them. And, yes, we also have wills with which to use or abuse them along with all Creation, including ourselves. That we have wills and can use them badly, for our own "autonomy," is not itself a bad thing. Our wills as such are gifts that make us what we are. But, as Chesterton saw, the most glorious thing about us is this very power to will. For, if we can use our wills badly, we can also use them properly. Surely this is the most "uproarious" and delightful thinking that we can imagine.

12. Joseph Cardinal Ratzinger, *Spirit of the Liturgy* (San Francisco: Ignatius Press, 1999), 32–33.

4 "THE VERY GRACIOUSNESS OF BEING"

Two things appear here as particularly appropriate to the element of risk and of adventure essential to the life of the Christian in the world: in relations with men: to recognize the central importance of friendship, in relations with God, to venerate the "sacrament of the present moment," and to expect a great deal from the manner in which divine Providence in the mysterious configuration of the destiny of each, arranges the chance meetings themselves that have cropped up all along the roads of the world.

—Jacques Maritain, *Notebooks*

I.

The phrase "the very graciousness of being" (156) is taken from Marion Montgomery, a man who has been a quiet mentor and inspiration to many, including John Hittinger. In a fundamental sense, the phrase comes as close as anything to describe the purpose of Hittinger's book *Liberty, Wisdom, and Grace*. The phrase suggests that something more than a closed world exists—"The seemingly trivial acts of graciousness may do much to preserve the dignity of persons" (160). No deterministic theory either of natural or social science really accounts for such acts. In fact, it makes them impossible And if there is more than a "closed" world, perhaps we can act in it.

Yet, if we can act at all, we must be, indeed we would want to be, free and responsible. The world is not totally, or principally, defined by veils of ignorance, rights, or even duties, but by something beyond, call it sacrifice or love or generosity or, yes, graciousness. It is rooted in what Maritain, following Aquinas, once called the "superabundance" of being.[1] When

---

This chapter was originally the foreword to John Hittinger's book, *Liberty, Wisdom, and Grace: Thomism and Democratic Political Theory* (Lanham, Md.: Lexington Books, 2002), ix–xx. Chapter 15 of this book is entitled "James V. Schall on Faith, Reason, and Politics." Hittinger is now provost at the University of St. Thomas in Houston. The numbers in parentheses in the text refer to pages in Hittinger's book.

1. See James V. Schall, "Law of Superabundance" (on Maritain), *Gregorianum* 72, no. 3 (1991): 515–42.

Aquinas remarked that the world is created in mercy, not justice, we know something more is at work in our own world than our own world (I, 21, 4). *"Et de plenitudine eius omnes accipimus, et gratiam pro gratia,"* as we read in the prologue to John. ("From his fullness we have all received, grace upon grace.")

John Hittinger begins his book with an account of his family's own colonial background—"My ancestors came to this continent in the 17th century for religious liberty." Members of his family, several of whom are buried in Arlington Cemetery, fought in the Civil War; his father was killed in the Vietnam War. He recalls fondly his own teaching in various Catholic colleges, his professorship at the United States Air Force Academy. "It is my goal to receive and understand, engage and develop, and make available and pass along, the riches of these traditions" (2). This engaging, understanding, and passing along are precisely what goes on in this penetrating book.

The book is unique because Hittinger knows, almost as an underground occupation, that the best of classical and Catholic thought has not completely died out. It has continued, often vigorously, if not in the Catholic or secular universities, though sometimes there too, then at least by isolated individuals seeking the truth of things, often within groups like the American or Canadian or Italian Maritain associations. If nothing else, this book is a guide to where that tradition is most alive. Hittinger affirms: "I consider myself ultimately a member of a tradition shaped by Thomas Aquinas. And it was thorough the reading of Jacques Maritain and Josef Pieper at Notre Dame that I first discovered the great adventure of liberal learning" (2). It is ever so, the preservation and growth of the deepest things usually commence with the unknown but attentive young student who chanced on the right book or teacher, whether it be at Notre Dame, Chicago, Oxford, Fordham, Dallas, Louisiana State, Christendom, or St. Mary's at Orchard Lake, where Hittinger himself was once located.

Hittinger ends the book with a chapter on Maritain's ideas on Church and State, with a special emphasis on the Vatican II Document, *Gaudium et spes* (*The Church in the Modern World*). This latter document, at the time intended in some sense symbolically to unite action and contemplation, intelligence and revelation, was presented to Pope Paul VI on December 8, 1965 by this same Jacques Maritain. Maritain was a French philosopher and diplomat, scholar and public intellectual. Though she only is mentioned in the last sentence of this vigorously argued book, Maritain's wife, Raïssa, and Maritain himself were among the most influential figures in intellectual life, not only in France and in the United States, but in the United Nations organization, in Germany, Latin America, Italy, Spain, and many other parts of the world.

We owe Maritain's coming to the United States to the fact that his wife was Jewish and from Russia. Though she was a convert, it was imperative that the Maritains leave France during its German occupation. The happy results of this exile are that Maritain taught in American universities and learned of the American way of life, which he praised in his *Reflections on America*, a book that the European Left did not like. He ended his career at Princeton, before he finally returned to France after his wife's death. There in Toulouse, he became a member of the Brothers of Charles de Foucault, among whose religious brethren he died in 1973.

II.

Fall of 1965 was when I began to teach in Rome. I well recall being present in St. Peter's square when the tall, white-haired figure of Jacques Maritain came forward to be greeted affectionately by Paul VI, who had, earlier in his career, translated several of Maritain's works into Italian. It was a moving, touching moment. What strikes Hittinger in this book—he specifically mentions the episode in St. Peter's square that I had witnessed at the time—is the irony of that scene. Just a few years later, Maritain published the *Peasant of the Garonne*, in which, while not repudiating the work of the Council, he at least expressed considerable worry about the direction of these reforms in practice, a prophetic position that cost Maritain much popularity at the time and still does. This was the same Maritain who, in his earlier days, was considered a man "of the Left" and, perhaps because of that, a remote cause of many of the confusions and problems that confronted the intellectual understanding of Christianity. One of the aims of Hittinger's book is a proper understanding of Maritain. In this worthy endeavor, the author is sympathetic but not uncritical.

The central figure of the book, then, is Jacques Maritain. He is central both because he discussed the issues of his day but also because he insisted on bringing up the issues that his day did not want to discuss. He is surrounded by a number of similar Catholic intellectuals, particularly Yves Simon and later Marion Montgomery, to each of whom Hittinger devotes an incisive chapter. Beyond this purpose, and in part because of it, Hittinger seeks to reestablish and deepen something that now seems obvious, namely, that Catholic philosophic thought was not, during the early and middle years of the twentieth century, in the disarray that many in recent decades have too easily assumed, often to justify later positions in fact at variance with the central core of Catholic inspiration. There is, no doubt, more intellectual disarray today than there ever was before 1970. Far fewer people proportionately read Plato and Augustine, Aristotle and Aquinas today than they did in Maritain's time. We are not better for it.

Indeed, Maritain, with Simon, Josef Pieper, Heinrich Rommen—Rommen's famous book *The Natural Law* was recently reissued by Liberty Fund with an introduction by Hittinger's brother, Russell—and a number of other thinkers led a serious intellectual endeavor to reappropriate the Thomist tradition as Leo XIII had advocated, a movement that itself predated Leo XIII. This movement required, as men like Maritain's friend Étienne Gilson or Christopher Dawson understood, a rethinking of Patristic and Medieval thought in all its forms, especially the thought that stems from the great St. Augustine. Gilson's essay "The Future of Augustinian Metaphysics" remains vital in our understanding that Catholic intellectual life includes both Augustine and Aquinas.[2]

Hittinger's book has three general purposes: (1) to recover and explain the central philosophic positions of Maritain, (2) to engage later philosophic and political positions that arose after his time but in the light of his premises, and finally, (3) to take up several positions of Maritain himself, such as human rights or his overly positive estimate of modern culture or world government, that do not themselves seem well founded. The work of Simon, who was a student and friend of Maritain and a profound thinker in his own right, often, as Hittinger shows, serves to clarify Maritain's own positions—on the common good, on subsidiarity/autonomy, and on authority.

One of the principal strengths of this book is Hittinger's own philosophical acumen, through which he is able to follow the wide-ranging Maritain in issues of natural science, politics, art, theology, metaphysics, poetry, history, and ethics. The chapter on Newman is of particular importance, as it addresses the whole problem of academic life, another area in which Maritain wrote extensively. Hittinger has the welcome facility of seeing where ideas go and who in the contemporary world embodies them. Following Gilson's guidance in *The Unity of Philosophical Experience*, Hittinger is able to address himself in particular to problems of Amer-

2. Étienne Gilson, *A Gilson Reader*, edited by Anton Pegis (Garden City, N.Y.: Doubleday Image, 1957), 82–104.

ican culture and the serious deviations now appearing within it at variance with basic classical or Christian positions.

In this regard, Hittinger devotes much attention to Locke, whom he sees rightly to be at the origin of many of the more recent political and cultural problems. Hittinger does not give much effort to Hobbes, but he is quite clear that the Hobbesian notion of rights is also found in Locke. Hittinger's polemic in this book with Rorty, Edward Wilson, and David Richards, not to mention Hawking and a number of others in other areas, about the nature of American founding is one of the best treatments I know for seeing just how perennial philosophical problems are related to movements in current American public life.

III.

Any reader of this book will quickly discover something already present in Maritain and the tradition out of which he comes; namely, that no single discipline is adequate to understand the complexity and far reaches of the human enterprise. This tradition is adamantly "anti-ideological," that is, it must take each reality for *what it is,* not claiming to know what it does not comprehend. It avoids imposing an idea on reality as if reality has no proper being of itself. On the other hand, it does not deny some unifying and transcendent things within this same order of being. What strikes one again and again throughout this book is that Hittinger and his tradition stand for philosophic openness. Oddly, it is the closed parameters of the modern mind that most characterize it, in spite of its own claim that it is open to all things. It is not.

The two core disciplines that come closest to grounding the whole human world as an order and not a chaos are metaphysics and theology, the two fields most shunted to the outskirts of modern academia. Chapter 12, "Maritain and the Intuition of Being," and chapter 14, "Newman, Theology, and the Crisis in Liberal Education," however, do serve to provide the order of intellectual and public things that is so characteristic of the Aristotelian and Thomist traditions. "The process of reasoning terminates in vision of what a thing is or the truth of some conclusion. Reasoning without some terminal insight, at least in aspiration, is non-intelligible in Thomas's scheme. All human knowledge, all human science, aspires to fruition in metaphysics" (146). This is well said.

In being also a defense of liberal education, *Liberty, Wisdom, and Grace* follows Aristotle, Aquinas, and Maritain. Hittinger has a deep appreciation of the contemplative order, that order in which we seek not to "do" something, but to know *what is*. In one sense, we can say that metaphysics points to action, for unless we understand the true nature of the world and the beings in it, we cannot act effectively. Yet, the end of action is not action, but knowing, beholding *all that is*, in its being and causes. It is this search in wonder that most awakens the potential philosophers, of whom Plato spoke, to devote their lives to knowing, and to knowing the truth. Hittinger obviously understands this basic point.

But metaphysics, though noble, is not complete in itself. It leads to questions it cannot, by itself, answer. This failure to itself have the capacity to answer all questions may, at first sight, seem to be a defect in human nature, a sign that it is not well made in the first place. Rather, this inability completely to account for the whole being of *all that is* properly describes the human intellect. It is truly an intellect, even if finite. It is not a divine intellect, which latter causes what is not itself *to be* and *to be what it is* by its own power and purpose. And if metaphysics, as well as politics, leads us to understand that, however good things are, they are not themselves everything or the cause of themselves, it must mean that there is an expectant, intrinsic, reflexive openness to human being within the very structure of its own intelligence. This is the ultimate grounding of the excitement that philosophy, at its best, generates. It is also the grounding of its humility. It realizes that, in the order of being itself, man is a receptive, not a creating, intellectual being.

It is precisely at this point that Hittinger brings in the figure, not of Aquinas, but of Newman. He does not imply that Aquinas would not have said the same thing. Newman is more immediately useful because he remains still the man who wrote the most incisive book ever written on what a university is. It does not take a genius to read Newman and compare his openness to all reality with the closed university curricula of more modern times. Hittinger delights in the blunt and carefully argued positions of Newman: "We should begin with Newman's simple beginning: 'Theology, I simply mean the Science of God, or the truths we know about God put into a system; just as we have a science of the stars and call it astronomy, or of the crust of the earth and call it geology' (3.7)" (169–71). Hittinger's point, with Newman, is simply that such a science exists with its own form and content, the denial of which is analogous to denying the existence of stars or the crust of the earth.

Newman and the medieval thinkers called theology, not sociology or politics, "the queen of the sciences." As Leo Strauss, a man whose worth

Hittinger recognizes, maintained, modern thought intimated that it has been an effort to depose this lovely queen, but the result is not only that we are not ruled by a queen, but that we wonder if there is any order or ruler at all.[3] Newman's case for theology as a necessary, indeed essential, part of the university was not based on some arcane desire to know obscure things from old books, but it was based on his understanding that theology did have something to say about the truth of things. The exclusion of theological considerations resulted not just in prejudice, but in an inability of the modern man to know as much as he could of the nature of the reality in which he finds himself.

This book often deals with matters that are called "practical," in Aristotle's sense, i.e., economics, politics, poetry. It was held by many that this is where Christianity was most at loggerheads with the modern spirit. One of Maritain's life efforts, beginning at least with *Integral Humanism,* was to seek to reconcile modernity with Christianity. Maritain himself had something substantial to say in each of these areas of practical life. But there is a habitual awareness that behind worldly questions, important as they are, there are prior questions of being and theology. The strength of the tradition within which Hittinger writes is that it takes metaphysics seriously and knows when a given author or school simply does not understand its meaning or importance, even to itself.

After a sympathetic effort to evaluate E. O. Wilson's famous "sociobiology," Hittinger finally concludes, forced by the evidence, that "in fact, Wilson stumbles through many areas in his attempt to make these (intellectual) connections. He presents an appalling lack of liberal education, try as he might to read his way into the broader view. His book contains errors in history, poor metaphysics, ignorance of theology, faulty logic. He would appreciate some evidence that Wilson had read and seriously considered positions which challenge his own (181)." These are strong words, even amusing ones, but they serve to emphasize how little capable the modern intellectual often is to understand a much broader philosophy than his own, which seeks to reduce reality to the dimensions of his own science.

IV.

Throughout this book, Hittinger refers to "the Philosopher Pope," to the thought of John Paul II. Both Maritain and the Pope were influenced both

3. Leo Strauss, *The City and Man* (Chicago: University of Chicago Press, 1964), 1.

by Thomas Aquinas and by certain strains in modern philosophy, Bergson in the case of Maritain, and Scheler in the case of Karol Wojtyla. This background is important because of the project of both the pope and Maritain of seeking to confront, and treat fairly and sympathetically, the intellectual movements of modernity. At the same time, both are acutely aware of the longer philosophic tradition of the West. In *Fides et Ratio,* the Holy Father explains that modern philosophy is often untrue to philosophy itself. Maritain's long reflection particularly on Descartes, the founder of specifically "modern" philosophy, show his awareness that something in modernity has broken with the basic realist foundations of classic and Thomist thought.

Hittinger devotes several chapters to Maritain's social thought—not merely Church and State, but also to liberal democracy, to equality, liberty, and rights. Hittinger is quite aware that the fault line of modern social thought runs through our theory of rights and hence our understanding of natural law and its foundations. Maritain is optimistic that the modern notion of rights and the classic notion of natural law or right can be harmonized. As a Frenchman, Maritain was quite aware of the French Catholic struggle with a kind of absolutist democracy stemming from the French Revolution. Many, not merely Burke, think that a good deal of modern ideology and totalitarianism arises out of a faulty understanding, first brought forth in the Revolution, of "human rights." Hittinger, to his credit, is very much aware of the problems arising from any rights theory. This problem as left by Maritain is still found in the works of the Holy Father and many Catholic apologists.

The modern school of "rights," stemming from Hobbes but going back to Gerson and nominalism, as Hittinger points out, is grounded in will, not in any being. Rights come to mean whatever it is that we enforce, no matter what it is. The classic notion of natural law or right, insofar as that was a classical or medieval term, was always related to duty, which in turn was related to the being of something in reality. The rhetorical problem, at least, of a vigorous defense of "human rights" leads to the dubious position of having to approve, on the grounds of mutually agreed upon "rights," of things that are quite contrary to the Christian or classical positions. Thus the "right to life," as Hittinger points out, for all its nobility is countered by the "right to abortion." As we cannot have it both ways, it seems clear that something is clearly amiss in the widespread use of "rights talk," as Mary Ann Glendon called it.[4] Hittinger does not think Maritain adequately solved this problem.

4. Mary Ann Glendon, *Rights Talk* (New York: The Free Press, 1991).

This book is not a biography of Maritain, nor is it a complete excursus on his general thought. What it is, I think, is a very perceptive and indeed critical reading of the leading Thomist thinker of half a century and more ago. I say "reading" because Hittinger is likewise aware that Maritain takes us back to Thomas, who takes us back to both the Bible and Aristotle. There are those who have constantly held that Maritain (or a number of other scholastic writers) were not "pure" Thomists, that it was better to go directly to the text of Aquinas. And while I have no difficulty with going directly to the text of Aquinas, I think that this Hittinger book shows us the value of also seeing the philosophic tradition of Aquinas as it engaged itself, through Maritain and his friends, in an actual period of time much closer to our own. It will ever be true that a direct reading of Aquinas will give us insights that not even a Maritain may have noticed. We may even find that Maritain's understanding of, say, the analogy of being or the proofs for the existence of God or the nature of modern psychology and psychiatry was faulty.

The fact remains that Maritain will have a lot to say that is true on each of these subjects and that he can lead us back to a reading and a tradition that, when done properly, can correct even itself, indeed correct Aquinas if need be. In other words, philosophy remains itself, even when we read the philosophers, however great. This was the meaning of the Pope's point in *Fides et Ratio* that, while there is no Christian philosophy as such, there is a genuine philosophy, and there are philosophers who have pursued it better than others. Not every philosophy can support revelation, something that becomes a major stimulation of philosophy itself in its own order. It is not an accident that those who pursue philosophy best are those, like Hittinger, who have read their Plato and Aristotle, Augustine and Aquinas, yes, Maritain, Pieper, Gilson, Marion Montgomery, and Yves Simon.

We are now passing a quarter of a century from the death of Maritain. The Philosopher Pope (John Paul II) is a very old man. As this book proves, the legacy of Maritain has been passed on to another generation, who in turn are engaged in passing it on to yet another generation. It is now argued by those who have reached intellectual maturity decades after Maritain himself flourished. Maritain's own work on education would ask about its being passed on again, this time in an intellectual and cultural world much more hostile to Thomism, Christianity, and to the classics themselves.

What a reading of this book suggests is the importance of keeping alive this tradition, in its integrity, even when the culture either refuses to consider it or rejects it implicitly by the way they live. Eric Voegelin, another major figure of the time during which Maritain lived, once remarked that "no one is required to participate in the crisis of his time. He can do something else."[5] It is within the spirit of this Voegelinian comment that this book of John Hittinger exists. That is, he is doing something else, something other than what the main line of the intellectual culture is doing. But since this book also falls within the tradition of St. Thomas, it will necessarily include a careful and sage consideration of the "adversaries," of what they hold and how they argue. This book does both of these things. It continues the tradition of the *philosophia perennis,* and within that tradition it accounts for what alternatives are presented as explications of the reality in which we all live.

The special feature of this book is "the political philosophy" of Jacques Maritain, as the title of the first chapter indicates. As I suggested earlier, Hittinger quite clearly understands that political philosophy does not stand wholly by itself. On the other hand, as Strauss indicated, political philosophy has a certain priority over philosophy. Why is this? Because in order to philosophize, there is at least some need of a polity that does not claim the whole of the human soul.

Maritain wrote in the heady days of the early formation of the United Nations. Indeed, Maritain was on the French delegation to UNESCO, in which the first drafts of the Declaration of Human Rights were proposed. Maritain valiantly sought a way to achieve some sort of "practical" agreement whereby men could officially and legally agree to respect the possibility to worship, marry, form a family, speak, participate in public life, teach, learn, and basically live in peace.

Even though during Maritain's lifetime, the Communist threat was the main political ideology that concerned him, after the defeat of the Nazis, we would be hard-pressed today not to acknowledge the lack of these human capacities in many cultures and countries, not excluding our own. Maritain was not naive. He did not think that "practical" arrangements would last long if there were no valid theoretical basis behind their existence. He was fully aware of the need of prudence and compromise in the practical political order. The general notions of secular modernity maintain that more democracy and more freedom, less fanaticism, less cult, will lead to a more peaceful world. But, as John Paul II frequently pointed out,

5. *Conversations with Eric Voegelin,* edited by R. Eric O'Connor (Montréal: Thomas More Institute Papers, 1980), 33.

there is such a thing as a "totalitarian democracy." It is every bit as dangerous as any other kind of totalitarianism.

And freedom oriented to nothing but itself has come to undermine any sense of a life of virtue or order based on nature. It seems that the notions of equality, democracy, rights, and freedom to which Maritain devoted so much attention have become rooted in unexpectedly dangerous intellectual flaws and notions. It is these latter ideas that are now being lived out in the political realm. What this book points to is the inadequacy of many of Maritain's noble initiatives.

Something else seems to have been at work within the cultures that, with intellectual bases of its own, have managed not to turn to the ideals that Maritain, with many others, thought mankind would accept after the experience of the wars of the twentieth century. Maritain lived in an era in which the civil governments of Europe and America still retained some connection with the classic Western heritage. They also lived in a time when armies and military force could protect Christians. The working of democratic theory, for better or worse, has now made it impossible for any connection between armies and religion, something that has not happened in Muslim lands or for that matter in China or even India.

The Catholic alternative to the Maritain proposal that theoretic questions are still vital to work out has been taken up by John Paul II, who has initiated, wherever he could, various commissions, colloquia, papers, and studies to try to resolve or mitigate, theoretically, the intellectual origins of political and cultural differences. This vital work of contemplation must bear fruit if the disorders of our time have any hope of moderate resolution.

The problem of political philosophy is twofold, as Hittinger recognizes. First is a question of the most workable form of the state, the problem of the "best regime," either, as Aristotle said, for this particular people, say, Athens or Sparta, or in general, granted the way most men in fact are. In modern times, the word "democracy" has come, however dubiously, to be a vague word intended to mean what the classics meant by "the best regime." The Aristotelian cycle of regimes, from best to least best, from worst to least worst, always was a sober reminder that any effort to change bad or tolerable regimes might produce a better regime, but often it produced a worse one. Regimes change when the population, customs, and principles of a people change. Europe and the United States are now flooded with new peoples as well as with philosophic ideas that seem far more dangerous than anything we had previously in our society. This too is a problem of political philosophy.

The second side of political philosophy is theoretic. It is not merely that of finding and founding or refounding a regime in which what it is to be a human being can flourish. It is also finding a regime in which the very idea of what this flourishing is can be discussed without excluding in principle the revelational responses to the perplexities of philosophy and the failures of virtue that appear in any existing society.

VI.

The strength of *Liberty, Wisdom, and Grace,* to repeat, is its very existence within the contemplative order that made its writing possible. In publishing this book, John Hittinger presents his argument to the world. If it is true that no one need to participate in the "crisis of his time," as Voegelin said; it is likewise true that no one, though at some cost, "need" to pay any attention to either reason or revelation, argument or metaphysics. Philosophy, Strauss remarked, seeks a "knowledge of the whole."[6] It is the peculiar virtue of this book of John Hittinger that his own philosophy is not closed to that whole that includes, as Newman said, the orderly understanding of what is revealed, not just as a curiosity, but as a furthering of philosophy itself when philosophy is most itself. Philosophy is most itself when it asks the right questions and honestly admits both that it does not itself create all answers and that it can recognize real answers when they are given, even by revelation.

Again, let me conclude with the notion of "the graciousness of being." In Maritain's *Notebooks* for May 6, 1911, is found this entry: "Saw (Georges) Rouault at the Moreau Museum. This man has a gift that few others possessed, a frankness before reality and *an immediate awareness* of things which nothing can replace."[7] In his philosophy of art, Maritain paid much attention to the work of Rouault.

With this phrase, I return to chapter 12 on the "Intuition of Being" in Hittinger's book. Here the author writes, referring to Marion Montgomery's book *Why Hawthorne Was Melancholy,* a book "I commend to you very highly," that "Hawthorne was quite aware of the issue of being and the tragic presumption of men who elevate their mind to a point of deny-

6. Leo Strauss, "On Classical Political Philosophy," in *What Is Political Philosophy and Other Studies* (Glencoe, Ill.: The Free Press, 1959), 92. See also Josef Pieper, *In Defense of Philosophy,* translated by L. Krauth (San Francisco: Ignatius Press, 1992).

7. Jacques Maritain, *Notebooks,* translated by J. Evans (Albany, N.Y.: Magi Books, 1984), 71.

ing the givenness of things and the common plight of humanity." To understand these notions within the tradition of political philosophy, we also
need metaphysics and revelation, and indeed all else that belongs to that
practical consideration Aristotle called not the queen of the sciences but
the "highest of the practical sciences," to politics and how we ought to live
that we may be free to know the truth and acknowledge freely of *what is,*
that it is.

PART II

RECKONING WITH PLATO

5 ON THE UNIQUENESS OF SOCRATES

*Political Philosophy and the Rediscovery
of the Human Body*

*To conclude, then, our discussion of the Republic, we suggest that the consideration of
the good city is meant to reveal how political life would have to be transformed in order
to admit of philosophic rule and why it is unreasonable to expect, perhaps even to desire,
such a transformation.*

—Christopher Bruell, "Plato's Political Philosophy"

*The sexual differentiation of the human body . . . suggests that . . . the human body is
not simply "one's own affair"; the body is a sign and, at the same time, the instrument
of a determinate and whole-seeking eros, rather than of a limitless and merely self-
indulgent appetite. Hence . . . the assertion of a purely private prerogative in sexual
matters is indicative of the failure synoptically to grasp the connubial significance of the
sexual character of the human body. Though we do not yet know the precise details of
Socrates' reformed nomos for sexual mating, we may expect that it will be intended to
combat self-centeredness by encouraging more attention to the connubial significance, as
distinguished from the physiological separateness, of the human body.*

—Darrell Dobbs, "Choosing Justice: Socrates' Model City
and the Practice of Dialectic"

I.

Near the end of his speech in the *Symposium*, Alcibiades affirmed that
"many are the marvels which I might narrate in praise of Socrates; most of
his ways might perhaps be paralleled in another man but his absolute un-
likeness to any human being that is or ever was is perfectly astonishing"
(221).[1] To describe the philosophic life simply as the imitation of Socrates

This chapter was originally published in the *Gregorianum* 76, no. 2 (1995): 343–62.
1. The translations of Plato used in this chapter, unless otherwise indicated, are from *The*

is both accurate and ironic. It is accurate because the life of philosophy, the erotic seeking of the knowledge of the whole, involves a lifetime of questioning, of personal sacrifice, of moral and physical courage, of discovering what we can about each topic—be it the soul, the city, or the cosmos—that is presented to our curiosity and our wonder. "Knowledge is presumably dependent on what *is*, to know of what *is* that it is and how it is?" Socrates asks Glaucon in book 5 of the *Republic*, as if the answer were self-evident, which Glaucon agrees that it is (477).

And yet Socrates does not like imitation, even imitation of himself. Imitation stands too far away from *what is*. He worries about the poets and the musicians for this reason, imitations of imitations. The potential young philosophers in the *Apology*, moreover, the very ones Socrates is accused of corrupting, do him a disservice, when, after enjoying in the streets his free performance in questioning their fathers to see if they are wise, they go home to imitate him before these very fathers. The fathers as the leading politicians become angry and plot against Socrates for corrupting their youth. Socrates, to be sure, took no money for his philosophy. He never claimed to be a teacher. He was merely following his daemon, wondering what the Oracle meant about his wisdom in comparison to others. If the youth were corrupt by imitating him, it is their own fault. He did not teach them.

If Socrates is wise, it is only because he knows what he does not know, though his gradual examinations of what others do not know do produce a genuine knowledge to replace a real ignorance. When he is imitated in a less than serious manner, even by people he likes and spends time with, however, genuine philosophy is not being served. The philosopher spends his serious time discussing the serious things. And in the *Laws*, we discover that God is the only really serious thing and that our own affairs, politics and the like, by comparison, are not really serious. This view of the unseriousness of human affairs is not meant to denigrate politics and human affairs, but to liberate them so that they will be properly located in the order of things. They are not themselves the highest things. Political philosophy was designed primarily to explain how political things could be arranged so that the philosopher would not be killed, would be able to devote himself to the highest things.

The irony in describing the philosophic life as the imitation of Socrates follows from this less-than-sincere imitation of his methods by the potential young philosophers, the direction of whose souls we by no means

Dialogues of Plato, translated by Benjamin Jowett (Chicago: Encyclopedia Britannica, 1952). The standard references to the Platonic text being cited, for instance (221), will be placed in the text.

yet know, nor do they. The dialogues of Plato are continual examinations of differing souls and the ways of life they might choose, of those few who choose the philosophic way, of those many who get lost thinking that other ways are better. The reading of Socrates that Plato gives us is a self-reflective examination of the direction of our own souls. It leads to self-awareness and self-illumination; it leads to the sometimes frightening prospect of knowing ourselves. The way of life of the philosopher did cause some astonishment in Athens, and not just to Alcibiades, the most volatile and most dangerous of the potential philosophers whom Socrates encounters. Indeed, Socrates himself maintained that he lived as long as he did in Athens, until he was seventy, because in a democracy, where all opinions are by law equally inconclusive, it was difficult for the many citizens who held the power to tell any difference between the fool and the wise man.

The wise man, when he appeared in the democracy, was taken to be as outlandish as the demented man. Normal folks avoided them both except for their curiosity value. Besides, who is to tell the difference between the one and the other, between the philosopher and the fool? Distinctions in democracies are all political, not natural. We are not allowed to acknowledge natural distinctions. Since it requires a certain amount of virtue even to recognize virtue, the philosopher will be largely invisible in most existing polities in which the highest virtue is statistically rare. The one who is most capable of recognizing the philosopher's worth is paradoxically the one who sees him as the most dangerous threat to his own way of life. No one praises Socrates more perceptively than Alcibiades. No one is more careful to refuse to listen to him. No one is, ultimately, more corrupt and more dangerous. The drama of the relation of Socrates and Alcibiades in the *Symposium* is the ultimate drama because it directly concerns which way a talented and handsome potential philosopher will choose in his own soul to live his life.

II.

Clearly both Callicles in the *Gorgias* and Alcibiades recognize in Socrates a danger to their own chosen paths in life. When they were young, like Glaucon and Adeimantus, they studied philosophy. But they did not want to hear justice praised for its own sake. Distinctly unlike Plato's two brothers Adeimantus and Glaucon in book 2 of the *Republic*, Callicles and Alcibiades do not want to understand the force of the arguments against justice, since they live according to these arguments. Callicles and Alcibiades suspect what effect philosophy would have on their souls. Thus they decide that philosophy is a threat to what they want to do in life, how they want to live.

Callicles and Alcibiades, when challenged, refuse to listen to Socrates because they cannot meet his arguments. But they implicitly understand his arguments and where they lead. Their rejection of philosophy is not un-philosophical in the sense of its being unknowing. They do not wish to change their lives, so there are things they do not wish to know, at least in public. They are first committed to the demos in their loves. Their politics is preferred to philosophy. Popularity is preferred to truth. They do not wish this love of the demos to be tested except by the demos. Their lives, and through them, their polities become closed to philosophy, to the imitation of Socrates, the gadfly who keeps his city alert so long as he is allowed to live in it.

In a philosophical and moral sense, both Callicles and Alcibiades were more dangerous to Socrates than the five hundred and one jurors and the prosecutors—Meletos, Lycon, and Anytos—at the actual trial that condemned him to death in a relatively close vote. Socrates knew this more subtle peril. Though he let Socrates talk on, Callicles simply refused to converse with Socrates, a refusal that sealed the philosopher's death. But Callicles was content to kill Socrates if he had to. That was the logic of his position. That is what the power of politics was about, in his view. Except as a kind of nostalgic and dilettantish affair in college, Callicles never gave philosophy a second thought. He held, without quite realizing the irony involved in his view, that death would silence the philosopher, the very philosopher who said that philosophy is a preparation for death. It is only because of Plato's remembrance of the philosopher Socrates that we remember the politician Callicles. Death does not silence philosophy, especially the political execution designed precisely to silence it. This is the paradox of politics when it is held to be the highest science.

Alcibiades was more shrewd and more capable of seeing the danger latent in philosophical discourse with Socrates than Callicles was. Callicles was content to let Socrates talk, knowing he had power of life or death over him in case Socrates' talk caused civic disruption. Callicles supposed this was a great power, something Socrates was not so sure of, as he did not know whether death was an evil. Alcibiades, on the other hand, was clearly attracted to philosophy even while choosing to reject it. Consequently, in one last desperate attempt, Alcibiades both admitted the charm of philosophy and simultaneously sought to corrupt Socrates, the philosopher. Alcibiades wanted to be sure that there would be no living example of virtue to stand against his own sordid record of betrayal and self-indulgence. Had he succeeded, there could only be, for the philosophers, the imitation of Alcibiades, not of Socrates, as a viable way of life. Politics would have been superior to philosophy.

III.

Christopher Bruell, in his essay on Plato's political philosophy, has suggested that the purpose of this philosophy was not to be put into effect in some existing constitutional order that could be described as perfect or ideal. We are not to seek to set up the best regime as it is so elaborately described by Socrates. The very effort to do so is a misunderstanding of the intent of Socrates. Aristotle, likewise, did not want this Socratic best regime to exist in practice, as he relates in book 2 of the *Politics*. He also objected to Plato on the grounds of the impracticality of some of Plato's proposals, notably, the communality of wives, children, and property. Wives, children, and property, Aristotle thought, are all better taken care of if they are held in private, if they belong to someone, not to everyone. This objection makes it look like Aristotle, at close range, thought that Socrates was serious about this proposal, even though Socrates, in book 5 of the *Republic*, recognizes that it is a most delicate subject and one that has to be broached with the greatest caution. Aristotle never would have said, however, that the purpose of Plato's political philosophy was itself to warn us not to attempt this actual transformation from existing state to perfect state. It was Aristotle who warned us, not Plato, in this context. Aristotle objected because he did not think the plan would work. He objected on practical grounds, on the grounds of existing human nature, on the grounds of its wretched tendencies.

But if Plato did not intend that this extraordinary proposal about political institutions was to be taken at face value, what good was it? It is a distinguished view, one that Bruell clearly elaborates, that book 5 of the *Republic*, and indeed the whole of the dialogue itself, is the greatest anti-utopian document ever written. Few have ever understood it this way, no doubt. Needless to say, when this thesis first appeared with Strauss it was a provocative novelty.[2] It still retains some of its heady paradox. If philoso-

2. Leo Strauss, "Plato," in *History of Political Philosophy*, edited by Leo Strauss and Joseph Cropsey (Chicago: University of Chicago Press, 1987), 33–89; Strauss, "On Plato's Republic," in *City and Man*, 50–137. See also James V. Schall, "A Latitude for Statesmanship? Strauss on

phers really examined the logic of justice, the argument went, they would see the fact that these extraordinary Socratic proposals about the communality of women, children, and property would have to be accepted in order that the real roots of disorder in the polis be ferreted out and corrected.

Considering them "in speech," however, makes this logic of justice, and therefore the limits of justice, clear. In agreement with Aristotle, we see how contrary to actual human nature these proposals are, the human nature that we all know familiarly in ourselves, in all existing cities. We should thus become immediately suspicious of any theories that claim to solve mankind's problems by proposals for radical changes in existing institutions—most notably, those of institutional rearrangements of family, property, and government that constantly reappear under various forms in modernity even today. On this reading, the *Republic* prevents totalitarianism, not causes it as the famous, or infamous, thesis of Karl Popper intimated. Knowing that social engineering was dangerous, what Socrates intended, it is held, was that we positively reject the temptation to put these proposals under any form into effect. We could only do this rejecting of these proposals if we understood their charm and the logic of the proposals themselves. The Straussian understanding of book 5 retains its force because it understands how attractive the proposal to reform human nature really is. Unless we understand this charm, we will not understand how important it is to reject its spell over us.

IV.

How do we go about thinking of these questions? Though I maintain that reason and revelation are distinct and both to be reckoned with, especially where they touch on the same subject matter, I suggest that they do sometimes, as here, shed light on each other in a way surprisingly pertinent to the abiding questions in political philosophy.[3] Not unmindful of Strauss's careful articulation of the first books of Genesis, I have argued elsewhere that book 5 of the *Republic* is illuminating when read in the con-

St. Thomas," in *Leo Strauss: Political Philosopher and Jewish Thinker,* edited by Kenneth L. Deutsch and Walter Nicgorski (Lanham, Md.: Rowman & Littlefield, 1994), 211–30; and Schall, "Reason, Revelation, and Politics: Catholic Reflections on Strauss," *Gregorianum* 62, no. 2 (1981): 349–55; no. 3 (1981): 467–98.

3. See James V. Schall, *Reason, Revelation, and the Foundations of Political Philosophy* (Baton Rouge: Louisiana State University Press, 1987).

text of the scriptural account of Creation and the Fall.[4] I do not mean, of course, that Plato somehow read Genesis, nor that the origin of Genesis was purely philosophical. But there is a fascinating correlation of teachings in the two accounts. I have no hesitation, in other words, in finding Augustine one of the greatest readers of Plato. The *City of God* is more than Platonic, but it is Platonic, and it is more than Platonic because it is Platonic.

The Fall evidently took place in a situation in which there was perfect conformity between man and nature. The best regime, in other words, existed in the beginning, not at the end of time, a sentiment we also find among the Roman philosophers. God was not accused of not having provided a sufficiency of material goods. Rebellion was not rooted in scarcity. This, to us, unexpected situation indicated that revolt against God or against the order of the world is not rooted primarily in some dire deprivation, clear injustice, or sexual disorder. We might likewise point out, in this context, that when Socrates does get around to discussing the decline of regimes in book 8 of the *Republic,* we are given no real reason why anyone in the best regime might find anything to complain of. We are simply told that "all things change." The Genesis account merely adds to this Platonic principle the one thing in Creation that can change for no apparent or determined reason, namely, the human power of choice itself.

We likewise wonder what Adam and Eve had to murmur about in these conditions of abundance. In Eden, things go along, as it were, swimmingly. Creation as such, including the creation of man, is good. The Genesis account seems rather to indicate that the ensuing disorder was rooted in the human will, not in things. The human will (the angelic will is in the same condition), as a constitutive part of man, is itself good, is itself will, is what it is. It is free. Its presence in Creation necessarily implied that something could go wrong, because it also implied that something could go right. It implied that *what is,* existence, needed to be itself affirmed as good on the part of the finite creature. Creation at its highest reaches was, for this reason, a risk. Things did not necessarily go right. Adam and Eve attest to this variable condition from the beginning. The risk, the possibility that things could go wrong, is itself a good.

The First Parents were commanded, in an amazingly insightful image,

---

4. James V. Schall, "The Christian Guardians," in *The Politics of Heaven and Hell: Christian Themes from Classical, Medieval, and Modern Political Philosophy* (Lanham, Md.: University Press of America, 1984), 67–82; Schall, "On the Neglect of Hell in Political Theory," *Politics of Heaven and Hell*, 83–106; and idem., "Regarding the Inattentiveness to Hell in Political Philosophy," *Divus Thomas* 92, nos. 3–4 (1989): 273–79.

not to eat of fruit of the Tree of Knowledge of Good and Evil. Evidently, the fruit of this particular tree, so to speak, was not itself poisonous to them. No one is tempted to eat rotten apples. The first pair were not being forbidden to eat the fruit for their physical health, as it were. The point was not, analogously, that God said to Adam, "Oh, by the way, watch out for the rattlesnakes." What this prohibition in the light of the name of the tree seems to mean is that man can claim, over against God, to be himself the source of the distinction between good and evil, a divine prerogative. The Tempter told them in fact that they would be "like gods." This information seemed to be a real temptation, not just for Adam and Eve. In classical philosophy, this distinction between good and evil is also recognized to exist. The subject matter of ethics, as Aristotle often remarked, is those things which deserve praise or blame. The most basic human distinction is that which entails good and evil human actions. And these actions reveal the soul that puts them into reality. This distinction between good and evil actions is discoverable by reason, but not made by it. In revelation, the distinction between good and evil is not made by the first pair. They learn of it after the manner of a command, but a command that they still must choose to obey and understand. Adam and Eve display some of the willfulness of an Alcibiades, though it seems to take expulsion from the Garden for them fully to understand what they had been forbidden to do. In this sense, it might be implied that there can be genuine philosophy in obedience, that obedience and reason are not simply contradictory. There is no reason to suppose that either Adam or Eve was stupid. It is not the simple who are tempted to pride, to the claim that what is good and what evil are the results of our own determining. There is reason to suppose that the first pair, like Alcibiades, chose to close their ears lest they would have to change their ways.

Moreover, the consequences, not causes, of the Fall are described as related to external disorders in work, in childbearing, and, later writers added, a disorder in rule; that is, coercive government was not from the beginning. The body was not the cause of evil, but it was involved in its consequences. Evil, in its intelligibility, was the result of precisely this claim of autonomy, the claim to locate the distinction between good and evil in the human soul, in its power to make and choose. It was located in the spiritual, not material, side of the rational being. Subsequent Gnosticism has its roots in the denial of this location of evil in the will. If we take a look at these consequences of the Fall, it seems evident that, in this system, no amount of rearranging property, family, or polis will ever result in a perfect rule, in the best regime. Why? The roots of disorder are not exterior to man himself.

The being of the exterior order is itself open to man's own actions that proceed from his reason and will. Thus, in the best regime we can expect to have disorder, and we can, in the worst regime, expect that real good might (or might not) appear. The reason for this possibility is that the human will remains external to the regime's order and to its instruments of law and coercion as well as external to the structure of family and property. Nazareth can happen even in the Roman Empire. Both human and divine will stand outside the laws of social and natural science, without denying the reality of secondary causes and an order of nature.

V.

A second series of reflections is perhaps pertinent to coming to terms with book 5 of the *Republic*. It can be suggested, without irony, that even when Plato is wrong, which is rarer than we had first thought when we began to study him, he is very close to being right. The famous proposal for communality of wives, children, and property is one of these places where Plato has hit a mark so close to the truth, and yet one which, if taken literally, is so very dangerous, that we must continue to marvel at him. Our age, indeed, might well be called the age of taking book 5 of the *Republic* literally. The proposed absolute equality of men and women, with the eugenic engineering this proposal "in speech" entails, is working its way out in practice by people who have not restrained their enthusiasm for changing human nature by themselves. The separation of marriage and children is in law and practice nearing completion.

The position paper for the Cairo Population Conference (1994) took precisely this position of talking about children and sex with no relation to family. The only sexual activity that interests the modern state, however, is that which results in children. Children begotten can efficiently be eliminated through abortion. When they succeed in being born, the conditions of their lives fall under the surveillance of the state. The state becomes the prime substitute parent and more and more the immediate parent through its control of subsidies, day-care centers, and education, particularly sex education, at all levels. The description of the lives of women, children, and property in the *Republic* is in many ways what we have or are seeking to bring into being after our own fashion. Sexual activity that does not result in children, however, has no political, moral, or biological purpose other than a kind of useless pleasure, something allowed or provided in order to keep the populace quiet.

Often the slightest adjustment of Plato's position, as I indicated, makes his point luminous. The Church, for example, has proposed that for a certain type of its internal "guardians," three vows are to be provided—poverty, chastity, and obedience. If we compare these vows to Plato's proposals for the communality of wives, children, and property, we will be struck that the same issue is addressed in both proposals, namely, what is the condition of life of those who devote themselves fully to the common good? By removing wives, children, and property as concerns of these guardians, which are instruments of divine not human law, if the monks might be called that, the very point that Plato was seeking to establish is met in another way that does not entail the harsh consequences, if actually tried, of Plato's proposals. On the other hand, for those who do not follow this giving up of wives, children, and property, the marital centrality of *eros* and the family, with its necessary property, the Aristotelian solution, is restored as another proper way of living for other sorts of guardians, indeed for all. Thus, Plato's finger is very close to the heart of any matter.

Moreover, if Bruell is right, Plato is not even wrong in the first place about his best regime, since his purpose was to warn us not to attempt establish it except in speech. Modern times have suffered under the scourge of philosopher-politicians seeking to remedy all evils by rearranging property, family, or government, only to end up creating even more awesome tyrannies. Plato has described this tyrannical process and how it can come about through democracy rather accurately. In Bruell's view this understanding of the possibility of horrendous tyranny is precisely what the reading of Plato teaches us to expect will come about. If we do not read Plato with care and attention, then, we will miss this irony in his proposals and mistakenly attempt what should be left only in speech.

Plato's extreme proposals, thus, can be saved in one of three ways: (1) We can take the Straussian view that the communality of wives, children, and property is not intended to be put into effect as it is too contrary to human nature. (2) We can take the monastic view that, in agreement with Plato, there is a conflict between some vocations and family life but that there is a dignified and sacrificial way to achieve Plato's ends without his means. Or (3) we examine the chaotic results of modern times that have left *eros* without discipline or morality and tried to deal only with the empirical and chaotic consequences. The theoretic result in all three instances is the same. Plato realized that the conditions of begetting were central to political philosophy.

VI.

If we look at the condition of Plato's guardians, then, we will see that Plato is especially concerned with their education, with what might corrupt them. We were first to look at where disorder came into the polis. It did not come through economics, or politics, but through the literary or poetic education of the guardians, of those who were potential philosophers and politicians. Thus, if we are to find just where disorder comes into the polity we build in speech, it comes in through the education of the guardians, especially through an examination of Homer and his accounts of the gods and the heroes as the poetic and primary source of the tales and models of how to live. As we look at the initial city that is constructed in speech, we notice the principle of specialization. We see that we need ultimately specialists of the whole. These are the philosophic guardians.

Initially, in book 4, we are surprised to note that these guardians were given families and houses. However, such was the concern of Socrates, these houses were just the opposite of what we might expect for political leaders. No one in his right mind would want to live in them. Every city, Socrates knew, was divided by how it dealt with wealth and honors. Greed and envy were the two most common and most corrupting vices. The parsimonious conditions granted to the guardians were in the name of the happiness of the whole, not the happiness of each individual guardian. The guardians were supposed to be those who identified their own personal happiness with the happiness of the whole.

This sacrificial aspect of their vocation explains Socrates' reluctance to give them the normal mansions and adulation that we have come to expect in ordinary regimes. Socrates wanted to keep his guardians safe from their own passions and temptations caused by wealth and honors. At first he did this by giving them Spartan living conditions and a modest, but very cautious, appreciation of their own worth. They were to know how easily human beings were corrupted. They were given examples to be followed in the revised poems of virtue and honor both among gods and men.

This proposal to establish the intellectual guardians in a Spartan existence, except for a discussion of the decline of regimes, would seem to have ended the *Republic* after book 4. At that point, we have now found a proper definition of justice, that is, each doing his proper task. We have located in the false tales of the poets, especially Homer, wherein disorder comes into the city and into our own souls. We have identified the source of disorder in greed and envy. We have disciplined the guardians externally and internally against them. But at the beginning of book 5, Adeimantus and Polemarchus whisper something. Something still upsets them. Socrates wants to know what bothers them. They recall Socrates' earlier remark that "friends have all things in common," a famous if enigmatic phrase that makes us realize that we have not really had a proper discussion of families, of wives and children and property.

It is at this point that Socrates becomes cautious about further discussion of the matter, so delicate it is. But Polemarchus, Adeimantus, Glaucon, even Thrasymachus, get into the discussion as they realize they have not heard, as we said, the arrangements about "the begetting of children . . . and of the whole community of women and children" (449). "We think it makes a big difference, or rather, the whole difference, in a regime's being right or not right." The peculiar structure of the *Republic* is designed to force attention to this volatile topic. This topic is the one that must be handled most cautiously. Socrates' arrangements recall Aristophanes' the *Parliament of Women*. This is the parody of Socrates' proposals. Socrates must be careful not to leave himself open to ridicule. But at the same time, he is serious about the family arrangements. Why is he so serious? Is it because of something deeper than the question of begetting itself?

VII.

Socrates' proposals, it is often said, simply eliminate normal *eros* from the *Republic*, at least in the city in speech for the guardians. Eros is replaced with a clear, even cold reason that cannot be corrupted even by *eros*. Eros appears to have an intrinsic selfishness about it. This view makes us wonder just what in *eros* is corrupting, since we also know about the *Symposium*.[5] The question is, again, why is Socrates so concerned with this elimination? We need to recall that Socrates himself had a wife and three children. Except for her appearance in the *Phaedo*, Xanthippe, Socrates' wife, does not much appear in the dialogues. We have no dialogue called *Xanthippe*. Are we to assume that he never discussed the highest things with Xanthippe? But, as I just mentioned, we do have the *Symposium*, in which Socrates is taught the secrets of love by Diotima, the lady from Mantinea, who is said to be "a woman wise in this (love) and in many other kinds of knowledge" (201). It is his conversation with Diotima that adds begetting to the

---

5. See Josef Pieper, *Enthusiasm and the Divine Madness: On the Platonic Dialogue* Phaedrus (New York: Harcourt, 1964).

speeches on love that we had heard up until the time of her appearance. Agathon had praised beauty for its attractiveness, for its uncanny ability to call us out of ourselves.

What true lovers seek, however, is the possession of the good. They are not just seeking their other halves, as Aristophanes held in his speech. Love wants both union and otherness. Diotima says to Socrates that she "will teach" him about love (206). "All men are bringing to the birth in their bodies and in their souls," she explains to Socrates. The analogy of physical and spiritual begetting is central to her discourse. Furthermore, both forms of begetting constitute a continuum. Physical begetting itself is seeking something beyond itself. Even what is begotten, the child, points to the fact that *eros* is not for itself alone. When the lovers are most closed in on themselves, they are pointing back to the world and to how the world came to contain these relationships that pointed beyond themselves.

Thus, Diotima explains to Socrates that "there is a certain age at which human nature is desirous of procreation—procreation which must be in beauty and not in deformity; and this procreation is the union of man and woman, and is a divine thing; for conception and generation are an immortal principle in the mortal creature" (206). *Eros* that begets is itself a divine thing. We are startled to see that it is "an immortal principle in the mortal creature." This teaching would mean that we are not dealing with fleeting things. What seems most fleeting, the pleasure itself, because of its presence "in the union of man and woman," in the mortal creatures, is itself symbolic of immortality. Begetting itself is a sign of immortality even on its physical side.

Diotima had already explained that "the happy are made happy by the acquisition of good things. Nor is there any reason to ask why man desires happiness" (205). Begetting in the body and begetting in the soul are aspects of the same *eros*. Both seek immortality. We do not need to ask why we seek happiness in all of our actions, especially these that relate to begetting. We do not ourselves make the good things we receive that make us happy. Diotima tells Socrates that love is not just love of the beautiful, which, to recall Agathon's view, has a kind of sterility of it. Beauty must be seen as good, as desirable, as something that moves. "To the mortal creature, generation is a sort of eternity and immortality... and... if love is of the everlasting possession of the good, all men will necessarily desire immortality together with the good. Therefore, love is of immortality" (206–7). And this love is a sacrificial love, as the case of Alcestis showed. She alone was willing to die for her husband. But Diotima explains that the cases of begetting or of searching for the beautiful even in poems and laws and other places are the "lesser mysteries of love, into which even you, Socrates, may enter" (210). Diotima has some doubt whether Socrates himself can attain the highest reaches of love.

But Diotima, as if at least to give Socrates a chance to know what she is talking about, proceeds to explain the way to Socrates. This is the great ascent from a particular beautiful thing to beauty itself.

The true order of going, or being led by another, to the things of love, is to begin from the beauties of earth and mount upwards for the sake of that other beauty, using these as steps only, and from one going on to two, and from two to all fair forms, and from fair forms to fair practices, and from fair practices to fair notions, until from fair notions he arrives at the notion of absolute beauty, and at last knows what the essence of beauty is. (211)

Again we are not wrong to catch here similar words of Augustine echoing in our hearts, of his last conversation with Monica before she died in Ostia. Neither are we wrong to see Plato's ascent grounded in an initial reality, in an initial particular thing, in a concrete beautiful thing.

VIII.

Darrell Dobbs, in his analysis, has understood that Socrates' proposals about the communality of wives, children, and property in the city in speech refer to our capacity to choose the best regime in our souls. The city in speech, in essence, is a kind of "therapy for comprehending constitutional polity as a whole."[6] Dobbs does not think that Socrates is merely proposing a kind of metaphysical reality check by turning our attention to *what is*. Metaphysics, Dobbs seems to imply, is not enough. We also have to attend to our ideals, for these, perhaps even more than a failure to turn to reality itself, can prevent us from really devoting our attention to *what is*. This is what the reading of the *Republic* requires us to do, to examine our souls at the most fundamental of levels. We are indeed to join Socrates "in making a model city." However, "Socrates' political proposals are not meant, then, as a blueprint for public policy; nor is it their principal intention to critique or to parody political idealism."[7] This position thus rejects both the notion that Plato was trying to establish an actual constitu-

6. Dobbs, "Choosing Justice: Socrates' Model City and the Practice of Dialectic," *American Political Science Review* 88 (June 1994): 275.
7. Ibid.

tion and the Straussian view that it was intended to ward off this utopian program.

What then was Plato trying to suggest? He was trying to counteract those desires and distractions that might arise from the body taken as a purely private self-interested affair. The noble lie was a medicinal exercise to help us see ourselves clearly, objectively. "Socratic communism address-es certain tendencies toward self-indulgent individualism which are root-ed in the separation of one's own body. The inappropriateness of private possessions of lands, houses, and money by civic guardians is indicated first of all."[8] It is clear that this sort of prohibition does not apply to every-one in the polity we build in speech, only to the guardians.

Hence we have the curiosity that while the farmers and craftsmen lead normal family lives, the guardians, because they are so much more close to the spirit and therefore more in danger of being more subtly corrupt-ed, need to have these things, as sources of potential temptation, removed from them. These criteria are, we might observe, essentially the same rea-sons for monastic or clerical vows whose purpose is to enable the monk not to be distracted from the one thing that is necessary and important. The careful attention to the least deviation from the good is something a Plato and a Benedict have in common.

In a remarkably subtle analysis, Dobbs notes what he calls Socrates as-sault on "erotic idiosyncrasy." This assault is described precisely as the re-jection of that notion of the body and pleasure that were seen in Callicles and Alcibiades, in the theory of tyranny that Socrates had explained in the *Republic*. The counterassault of Socrates, though this is veiled, is a theo-ry of friendship—"Friends have all things in common" (449). Friendship properly looks to the good of the other, not the self, even though it in-volves the self. Even though each individual is complete and independent as a human being, still this very being is, even on its physical side, not or-dained primarily or only to itself. "The intelligibility of the human body it-self depends upon an appreciation of its connubial significance in procre-ation." The body is not just a machine or a bundle of responses. The body "which bears unimpeachable evidence of the complimentarity of male and female, is only mistakenly regarded as a private affair."[9]

These same issues have been argued in a similar and brilliant fashion by Denis de Rougemont in his famous *Love in the Western World*. Here too

8. Ibid.
9. Ibid., 275.

eros in isolation is seen as a dangerous pole between a kind of transcendent death wish and its proper resolution or its reality in marriage.[10] The response to the dangers of *eros* is not the death wish of a Tristan and Iseult, a wish parallel in its own order to the search for the perfect regime. "But the troth of marriage is . . . a pledge given for *this* world," de Rougemont wrote.

Inspired by an unreason "mystical" (if you like) and, if not hostile, at least indifferent to happiness and the vital instinct, fidelity in marriage requires a re-entry into the real world, whereas courtesy meant only an escape from it. In marriage the loving husband or wife vows fidelity first of all to *the other* at the same time as to his or her true self. And whereas Tristan showed himself constant to a steadfast refusal, in a desire to exclude and deny creation in its diversity and to prevent the world from encroaching upon spirit, the fidelity of the married couple is acceptance of one's fellow-creature, a willingness to take the other as he or she is in his or her intimate particularity.[11]

These remarks of de Rougemont react precisely to the logic that sees no form or nature in material things, including human things. Presumably, this position conceives *eros* to be something so pure and so exalted that it cannot exist in and through the order of being. Death was the only alternative to the fear of mixing it up with normal things. This form of *eros* corresponds to the purity demanded of the intellectual guardians in the book 5 of the *Republic*.

In Dobbs's position, the objective of Socratic communism for the guardians is "to counter this mistaken tendency" towards an *eros* that is independent of a concrete object and "to illuminate the connubial (and thus the civic and even cosmic) significance of the body."[12] This is a position very similar to ideas that John Paul II made for some time about the spousal relation of Christ and the Church, of cosmos to God, of marriage to *eros*.[13]

Leon Kass has also from another angle sought to restore the thinking about the body and its functions to a more natural and harmonious function.[14] Socrates' perception of the unexpected dangers latent in marriage and pleasure, and therefore his proposals about the communality of wives,

10. Denis de Rougemont, *Love in the Western World*, translated by Montgomery Belgion (New York: Schocken Books, 1990). See also Josef Pieper, *About Love* (Chicago: Franciscan Herald, 1974).

11. de Rougemont, *Love in the Western World*, 309.

12. Dobbs, "Choosing Justice," 275.

13. John Paul II, *Theology of the Body*, 3 vols. (Boston: St. Paul Publications, 1981–86).

14. Leon Kass, *Toward a More Natural Science: Biology and Human Affairs* (New York:

children, and property as remedies, are designed not to eliminate marriage itself, but to isolate just what it is that can cause the deviation in the souls of the guardians from the good. Dobbs's statement of the issue is to the point:

> Socrates' assault on this form of (erotic) individualism thus aims to orient his interlocutors toward the wholeness of the connubial partnership and any other partnerships, such as the political community, to which the connubial partnership belongs. As long as the connubial significance of the human body is neglected, the dialectical examination of questions such as whether the just or the unjust are happier will only endanger the excellence of the human soul.[15]

The later Christian response to Plato, namely, the legitimacy both of guardians who do not have wives, children, and property and guardians who do have faithful and fruitful marriages, is itself an effort to take into account both sides of Plato's concern about the sources of disorder in the souls of those most ordered to the highest good, to family, polity, cosmos, and God. The asceticism of the sacrament and the vow were designed to take account of precisely this "erotic idiosyncrasy" without denying the ever-present possibility of sin or disorder precisely arising out of free will, even in the various guardians.

The point of Dobbs's analysis of Plato's city in speech is, as he says, therapeutic. That is, he wishes to foster the sort of general overall view of man and the cosmos needed "to the deliberate and reasoned adoption of a polity in one's soul." Before we decide how we should live, that is, the structure of our own soul "writ small," we need to grasp the true reaches of selfishness and to realize its consequences in our own understanding of human life. Is this city in speech in the manner presented here the best regime? Dobbs responds to this famous question in this judicious manner, "If the function of the political community is to assist persons in achieving virtue, then it seems that it could count as such—though it never see the light of day."[16] Thought, or the city of speech, in other words, is itself a reality and has its effect on the world through its illumination of our perceptions of ourselves, of the city, of the cosmos.

Whether this city actually exists, then, is irrelevant once its real purpose is seen. This purpose is to face that potential disorder of every soul that comes both from a misunderstanding of the body and of its relation

---

The Free Press, 1985); and Kass, *The Hungry Soul: Eating and the Perfecting of Our Nature* (New York: The Free Press, 1994).

15. Dobbs, "Choosing Justice," 274.

16. Ibid., 276.

to the city and the cosmos. What the *Republic* teaches is the order of soul. It does this through a philosophical exercise, a necessary exercise for all those whose souls would be ordered, that is, through the reading of Plato himself, a reading that can take place in any society that leaves men free enough to encounter him. Whether Plato's responses can be considered definitive can itself be wondered about. What is curious is that Plato, when carefully read, does abidingly bring to mind responses to transcendent questions that are found in revelation. This odd coherence does not necessarily imply a revelation to Plato, as some philosophers have cautiously posited.[17] But it does create a remarkable correspondence between two spheres too absolutely separated in modern thought.

IX.

Modernity, so to speak, has more and more argued that the disorder of soul is initially and primarily to be met by a reorganization of property, family, and polity. The soul itself is incapable of being touched by philosophic forces. Man is said to be moved only by passion and impulse. Politics is only a balance of forces. This modern view is to be seen as diametrically contrary to the classic view that was primarily and first interested in the reform of one's own soul. What this reform in the classics implied was that the understanding of the soul in its deepest meaning first required attention to those drives such as selfishness, pride, and the opposites of each of the virtues. It needed to know whatever, in short, would introduce disorder into the soul of the guardian and through this disordered soul into the family, the polity, and the world.

The therapy of Plato, in conclusion, is to enable us to examine our souls vicariously, as it were, in examining steadfastly the arguments in the various dialogues of Plato, particularly in the *Republic*. Plato's proposals about the life of the philosopher, the life of the politician, and family life were directed at real sources of order and disorder in the guardians. Moreover, Plato, through his attention to these sources, was himself ordained to the highest things, to that seriousness that alone is related to God, as the *Laws* eventually make clear (803). The things that could prevent us from these higher orientations arise in the soul as it is erotically drawn to objects that can deflect us from the good, from the beautiful. The New Testament, as if

17. See Eric Voegelin, *Order and History*, vol. 3, *Plato and Aristotle* (Baton Rouge: Louisiana State University Press, 1957). The Louisiana State University Press subsequently issued *Plato and Aristotle* as a separate paperback text, now available from the University of Missouri Press.

to reinforce this very point, admonishes us that the individual is not only not to perform definite actions that are disordered but not even to desire them—the point that St. Thomas made about the limits of civil law and the scope of divine law (I-II, 91, 4).[18]

Political philosophy rediscovers the body through a careful examination of that very tract in classical political philosophy that seems, at first sight, most alienated from the body. It is no coincidence, therefore, that what appears in late modernity and post-modernity is not a proper appreciation of the body but precisely a denial of its intrinsic connubial orientation. Joseph Cardinal Ratzinger perceptively arrived at a conclusion that is beginning to be presented in political philosophy itself: "The new esteem for woman which was the justified point of departure of modern movements ends then soon in contempt for the body. Sexuality comes no longer to be seen as an essential expression of human corporeality, but as something external, secondary and ultimately meaningless. The body no longer reaches what is essential to being human, but comes to be considered an instrument we employ."[19] The body seen as a mere instrument means that man's will is not itself ordained to the reality of the body and its particular being. A kind of Gnosticism takes political form to treat the body as containing in itself no principles or structures that need to be respected.

The value of these recent reflections on Plato is precisely that they allow us to re-propose to ourselves in thought, in speech, the right order of human and civil things, a right order that begins by coming to terms with the extraordinary proposals of Socrates in book 5 of the *Republic*. Socrates tells Glaucon there that "to speak knowing the truth, among prudent and dear men, about what is greatest and dear, is a thing that is safe and encouraging" (450). But if we are in doubt about where these things go, as Socrates cautiously admitted he was, the case is more perplexing. Socrates thought, however, that it was "a lesser fault to prove to be an unwilling murderer of someone than a deceiver about fine, good, and just things, in laws" (451). The uniqueness of Socrates, thus, remains, to use Alcibiades' word, "astonishing."

18. It is worth noting that John Paul II in *Crossing the Threshold of Hope* has referred to the deaths of Christ and Socrates: "Christ is not simply a wise man as was Socrates, whose free acceptance of truth nevertheless has a certain similarity with the sacrifice of the Cross" [(New York: Knopf, 1994), 42]. See my discussion on the relation of the deaths of Christ and Socrates in *Politics of Heaven and Hell*, 21–38, and in *At the Limits of Political Philosophy* (Washington, D.C.: The Catholic University of America Press, 1996), 123–44.

19. Joseph Cardinal Ratzinger, "Limits of Church Authority," *L'Osservatore Romano*, English ed., June 29, 1994, 6.

6 ON THE DEATH OF PLATO

Some Philosophical Thoughts on the Thracian Maidens

But there is another sort of old age too: the tranquil and serene evening of a life spent in peaceful, blameless, enlightened pursuits. Such, we are told, were the last years of Plato, who died in his eighty-first year while still actively engaged in writing.

—Cicero, *On Old Age*

I.

In volume three of his *Order and History,* Eric Voegelin reflects on the central importance both of Plato and Aristotle.[1] His treatise on Plato is an extraordinary analysis of Plato's life and abiding philosophic importance. When I ask a class to read this volume on Plato, I insist that they do not read the last short paragraph of this book until they have read the rest of the book. I do not want them to miss the astonishment that I myself experienced on first reading it. Too often, of course, such is human nature, this admonition not to read a designated passage has the effect of tempting most readers to read first what is not to be read until last. This reaction is not necessarily a bad idea in reading any book, except perhaps a detective story or Voegelin's book on Plato.

The last paragraph of Voegelin's treatise is a poignant account of the death of Plato. The charm of this passage matches the spell that Plato himself sought to cast in his writings. Plato invoked this very literary charm to incite us to pass to the higher things or at least to render us benevolent to them. Indeed, it was his answer to Homer. He realized that if his own style were not as intriguing as that of Homer, his philosophy would not be read

This essay was published in the American Scholar 66 (Summer 1996): 401–15.
1. Voegelin, *Plato and Aristotle.*

by anyone except the philosophers. And it was precisely those who were not philosophers who most threatened the life of the philosopher.

In violation of everything I have intimated in the previous paragraphs, however, I am going to begin this consideration by citing precisely this last paragraph of Eric Voegelin on the death of Plato. I can think of no justification for this procedure except that it is the only way I know to reflect with some care upon a certain extraordinary line of thought that Voegelin's ending can kindle in us about the ultimate meaning of Plato. In considering the death of Plato, moreover, we are naturally and rightly prepared to compare it with the death of Socrates as Plato himself recounted that famous death in his own dialogues, in the *Euthyphro*, the *Apology*, the *Crito*, and the *Phaedo*.

We wonder which of the two deaths was the more profound, granting that the death of Socrates was infinitely more memorable and graphic. Plato perhaps had no Plato to account for his own death, though Cicero recalled its serenity. Could this missing philosophical account of the death of Plato be what Voegelin, in the sparest fashion, belatedly tried to supply? The life of Plato subsequent to the execution of Socrates, no doubt, is consumed by the question that the death of Socrates had left Plato as a young man to resolve; namely, whether there is a city in which the philosopher will not be killed. Evidently, Plato in the end found, or perhaps even founded, such a city. He was not killed. In the city he founded, we still read about Socrates.

Plato's own famous pupil, Aristotle, to be sure, had once remarked, after an anti-Macedonian movement in Athens, that he himself had fled Athens, lest it be "guilty of the same crime twice." But Socrates himself did not choose flight or banishment to another city to avoid the same crime once. Surely, we do not want to suggest that Aristotle lacked bravery. Did Aristotle mean rather that there was nothing philosophically to be gained in making the same point twice? Aristotle knew the lesson of the end of the *Republic*, that if we do not choose our daemon rightly the first time, we shall not likely choose it rightly a second or third time. Was philosophy already safe then because of what Plato had established to replace Athens, that is, his philosophical Academy in which the memory of Socrates would remain alive? When Aristotle subsequently found himself in Asia Minor or in Pella, was he actually in the same city that he had left, the one within Athens that Plato had bequeathed beyond his own death? Does the antagonism of politics and philosophy remain in all existing cities? Do philosophy and politics both point beyond themselves?

II.

No doubt, we sense a distinct "ominousness" in the later dialogues of Plato, especially in the *Gorgias,* a dialogue full of foreboding, of war and strife, as its first lines intimate. The philosopher attempts to deal with the shrewd politician who has the power to kill him. When the politician chooses not to participate in the philosopher's sole protection for his life, namely, in the continuation of honest discourse about what "true politics" really are, we know the philosopher is dead (521).[2] His only safety is found if the politician will examine the issues with him. Already in the *Republic,* the philosopher who returned to the Cave and told his experiences to his former companions was in danger of his life (517). The prisoners did not want to hear that their life was not the real one.

Does Plato's serene death mean rather that philosophy has been rendered harmless, that Plato died still writing in peace because philosophy no longer threatened the order of existing regimes? Do the politicians now control philosophers by threat of death? Plato himself, in his dealings in Sicily, came close to death a couple of times in his efforts to educate the tyrant. We have no reason to assume that Plato was a coward. He did not dispute Socrates' courage and strength. Plato's death seems to portend something else, however, something on a par with the noble death of Socrates. Thus we would be surprised if the death of Plato, in some other way, did not also match the death of Socrates in philosophic profundity. How are we to think about these things?

The following passage about Plato's final day in 347 BC is the conclusion to Eric Voegelin's *Plato and Aristotle:* "Plato died at the age of eighty-one. On the evening of his death he had a Thracian girl play the flute to him. The girl could not find the beat of the *nomos.* With a movement of his finger, Plato indicated to her the Measure."[3] What is to be noted about this riveting passage? First of all, we observe that Plato died in his own bed. He was some eleven years older than Socrates at the latter's death. Plato did not drink hemlock by order of the laws of the democracy. To be sure, he did die in the evening, like Socrates. Athens could have let Socrates die of old age, but it chose instead to execute him at seventy. Athens, however, did let Plato die of old age. Old age was the first topic of discussion in the *Republic.* Socrates said that he liked to talk to old men as they had been down a path we all will follow. Plato went further along this path than Socrates.

2. The numbers in parentheses refer to the classical numbers of the Platonic text.
3. Voegelin, *Plato and Aristotle,* 268.

Socrates' last day in jail, we recall, was announced by Xanthippe, who told Socrates that this day would be a sad one for him as it would be the last time in which he could converse with his friends. All of Socrates' days, he hoped, were spent examining life, to see if it was worth living. He had spoken with those who were said to be wise because he wondered about the Oracle, who said that he was the wisest man in Greece. No one else proved to be wise except in his limited specialty. Socrates' days were spent in talking to his friends, something he enjoyed doing.

Socrates' last day is best described as his second trial. His first trial before the jury at Athens left certain things unsettled. The friends of Socrates were quite unhappy with it all. Socrates' life could not end without completing his conversations with the potential philosophers examining him about what he was doing. Socrates' conversation did end on his last day. He finished what he had to say. The potential philosophers had only tears, not refutations. Socrates took the hemlock calmly.

For an older friend like Crito, the death of Socrates initially represented a defeat, a slurring of Crito's public reputation. For everyone in the city knew that a rich man, as Crito was, could easily afford to bribe Socrates out of jail. But Socrates debated with Crito about why Socrates should remain in jail and suffer, though the execution could not be called a punishment since nothing can hurt a good man. Clearly such an extraordinary decision of Socrates to obey the laws needed explication.

But this jail and the sentence were not merited punishments for Socrates, as he had done nothing wrong, though he had upset the order of the existing city. He did not know whether death was evil in the first place, so he could not act as if it were the worst evil, to be prevented at all costs. He did know, however, that doing wrong was not open to him. These public arguments at the trial, of course, did not satisfy the young potential philosophers gathered around Socrates on his last day. In this last conversation, Socrates spoke of subjects not easily addressed in public, yet topics that had to be faced in a complete life.

Some of these friends, like Apollodorus, who was to recount the *Symposium* from Aristodemus, were already weeping. They showed thereby that they had not learned Socrates' lesson that philosophy was a preparation for death. When death is present, the philosopher is present. Was Plato ultimately the one follower of Socrates who understood this? If anything, the young listeners were very annoyed with Socrates, so that they subjected him to a second, more critical, trial, the trial before the potential philosophers about why he could face death so calmly. His apology at the public trial had not satisfied them, nor had it convinced a majority of the jury.

Socrates, by objective standards, may indeed have performed brilliantly at the public trial in handling the accusations of corrupting the youth. Many of these youths, sons of the leading citizens of Athens, were sitting before him on this last day in jail. Many of these same youth had annoyed their fathers, Socrates' accusers, by going home and playfully imitating Socrates. This semi-jesting imitation was why the fathers thought Socrates was undermining the city. This bothersomeness is what brought Socrates, from his hiddenness in his private life, to their public attention. Socrates indeed may have convinced some jurors and potential philosophers at the trial that he did believe in the gods, even if not quite believing in the gods of the city. No doubt, in the minds of these young men, among whom, though he was ill on this last day, was the young Plato, Socrates was not guilty as charged in the public trial. But there seemed to be another sort of guilt, even more grave, of which he could be accused. Was the absence of Plato at the death of Socrates related to his own very different death, the death of Plato? Do all real philosophers die in the same way, whether with hemlock or with the sounds of the flute?

III.

From the minute they heard of Socrates' discourse with Crito about how he was bound to Athenian law, the friends knew he was certainly going to die. He had already explained in his *Apology* that he did not want to drift in exile from one city to another and have the same thing happen over and over in any well-ordered city. Nor would he cease to philosophize. But as often as he had told them that philosophy was a preparation for death, something further was needed before they would be satisfied. Of course, the last day of discourse concerned the long and intricate discussion about the immortality of the soul. Socrates' calm before death had intelligible roots that the potential philosophers had not previously understood. The power of the state to kill Socrates always remained. But if it did execute him, it was not a defeat of philosophy. In fact, when the state kills the philosopher, it may strengthen philosophy. The only philosophy that is weakened is that whose teachers yield to the state seeking its own will.

Rather, Socrates' execution was the judgment on the state itself. No state was to have legitimate power before philosophy if it conceived itself, on its own standards, to be an alternative to philosophy. The philosopher who is willing to accept death cannot be threatened by the politician who, as we see in the *Gorgias,* loses his power over the philosopher who is unaffected by the politician's most dire threats. Callicles, Meletos, Lycon, and Anytos do preserve the democracy they love. In so doing they demonstrate the danger of democracy, a danger that Socrates evidently considered to be the most subtle danger a philosopher could encounter.

Philosophy, in Callicles' view, is set aside in the politician's youth as something interesting, but not for use as an adult. Philosophy asks questions that the actual state, because of its own disorder, cannot bear. It is better to silence Socrates than to change the regime. The sons of the politicians and craftsmen are expected to follow their fathers, not Socrates. Socrates had called the youth to another life, not to the traditional ones. This was his danger. But the real struggle was not with the fathers but with the sons, with their choosing which life to follow. Socrates seldom talked to those who had already decided, who had already definitively revealed their souls as upholders of the polis, of the ways of life of wealth, pleasure, or power. Socrates only talked with those who could still change their souls.

When students read the *Apology,* I ask them to indicate in the text just where they are in fact themselves present. At first, one catches in their eyes a look of amusement or polite skepticism. What sort of a question is it? How could Plato have included each of them in his dialogue? Yet, each is there, almost by name, certainly by spiritual reaction. On some reflection, suddenly a student will understand. To be sure, they all might have been there as members of the jury. Some of these very students, no doubt, will sit in similar trials some day and analogously vote to kill Socrates, even though most in their schools would sympathize with Socrates when they read him. Others will be there as one of the three accusers of Socrates, or as the potential philosophers whom Socrates was accused of having corrupted. It is not a bad idea, of course, to place oneself within the dialogues of Plato, to find one's own personality somehow shining through the characters he so memorably describes.

But the immediate answer to the question is that each of us is present when, on reading the trial account, we too accuse this same jury, now alive before us in Plato's account. Plato the philosopher, because he wrote of the trial of Socrates, makes us all participants, whether we like it or not. Socrates, with some amusement, had proposed that his punishment be free room and board at the town hall. He had done nothing but keep the citizens alert to the need to examine themselves daily, itself a good service to any city. He was the gadfly. He kept the citizens from being dull. Socrates then turned to the jurors to single out those who had voted for his condemnation and death. With sudden seriousness in contrast to his previous-ly playful mood, he spoke to them with gravity. He told them that from now on, whenever the story of this trial is told, these jurors will be condemned in the minds of any reasonable man as those who killed the philosopher.

The students clearly recognize, in reading the trial, that they too had agonized over those 281 jurors who voted to kill Socrates, that they too, as Socrates said, would join down the ages those vast legions who have again and again condemned that now immortal and deplorable Athenian jury and, through it, the politics that killed Socrates in a legal trial. Most of to-day's students, on reading this result, want to go out and change the world, not themselves. They want to become lawyers and doctors. They do not re-member what Plato said in book 3 of the *Republic,* that a society filled with students of law and medicine is already a sick society. Many students con-tinue to think that more law and more medicine will cure what can only be cured by a reform of their own souls. Again by contrast, we recall that Pla-to died calmly, at first sight undramatically, in his bed.

IV.

On reading of the death of Plato, do we, down the ages, also become present at his death? Of course we do. Again we see Plato, in his eighties, a man who has mostly finished the *Laws* in which Socrates as such does not appear. Plato was given enough life to complete his projects, to consider all sides of the death of Socrates. He graphically delineated the souls of each of the major and even the minor characters we find in the sundry di-alogues—Theages, Meletos, Cebes, Thrasymachus, Pausanias, Alcibiades, Polemarchus, Cleitophon, Laches, Gorgias, Ion, and many others. Each had his part. Plato understood the complexity of character, of life.

And who is at Plato's death? He does not have a room full of follow-ers seeking to copy down the final revisions of the *Laws.* No conversation seems left to complete. Aristotle is not there. Nor is Dionysios. His older brothers, Glaucon and Adeimanthus, are not there. No Xanthippe is there. No three sons. No potential philosophers. Who is there is a young flute-player, a Thracian girl. She is not there in any erotic capacity. Plato evident-ly wanted her to play the flute, that special instrument about which he so carefully discoursed in the *Republic* (399).[4] That is to say, the philosopher

---

4. The word for flute was *aulos.* It was apparently a double-reed wind instrument, more like an oboe than a modern-day flute.

dies to the sound of music. The music is not a therapy, but a pleasure. Aristotle had remarked that the gentleman should know music but should not be able to play a musical instrument too well. He knew that to play music well required a lifetime of study and practice, a lifetime that would prevent the gentleman from knowing the higher things, however much music might be related to them, as it intrinsically was.

Plato, of course, does not call in an accomplished flautist, as, presumably, he might have. He calls in the maiden who cannot find the measure. He can still teach her the measure. He moves his finger indicating the beat and rhythm. We are not told whether she picks it up correctly, but we assume she does. We assume that Plato died having heard the right measure, that he died listening to the flute as it should be played. His death would not have been complete had he not heard the correct measure. Thus Plato hears the flute with the proper measure.

Who is this flute-player? We note she was a Thracian. We can remember in the *Symposium,* when the banquet was about to begin, that a flute-girl entered the room ready to play. The diners at Agathon's house discuss drinking, as the three old men also do in the early books of the *Laws.* The guests at Agathon's table had all been drinking heavily the evening before. So they decide not to drink, or at least not to drink in competition or in excess. If someone might want some wine, that was quite all right, but if he did not, that was all right also. The banquet was convivial, pleasant. Even Socrates had dressed up for the occasion—"fresh from his bath and sandalled" (174). But when this conversation, or rather when the speeches began in earnest, the wine was moderate and the flute-girl left, only to return at the end when Alcibiades unexpectedly roared into the room.

The flute-girls at Plato's death and at Agathon's banquet are mindful of the Thracian maidens. The Thracian maidens are those very normal and delightful young women who tell us better than any one else what most people think of philosophy, think of what Socrates does with his days. Aristotle, it will be recalled, remarked that the philosopher Thales proved the usefulness of philosophy by gaining a monopoly on the oil and wine presses so that when the bumper season arrived, having himself studied all the signs of nature, all the unlearned growers had to pay him handsomely to use his presses. But as he did not want the money, being a philosopher, he was just illustrating that the philosopher was poor because he chose to be, because his time was better spent in other things. The philosopher knew something about music and about business, but he was not a musician or a businessman.

However, when two famous philosophers were walking down the road one day learnedly discussing the stars and other exalted things, one of them fell into a hole that he unfortunately did not see because of his absorption in philosophy. Seeing this, to them, absurd incident, the Thracian maidens began to giggle and laugh at the philosopher. Most of the human race, subsequently, would side with the Thracian maidens. One might suggest from this famous tale that the Thracian maidens ultimately also needed to be attracted to philosophy. Is it too much to suggest that, in Voegelin's account, this Thracian flute-girl at the death bed of Plato, fumbling with the measure, hints at a possible resolution?

But Plato's death has a further implication. The flute-girl did, evidently, when taught, catch the measure. She was not unteachable. Philosophy seeks the eminently teachable. Plato himself knew the measure. That is to say, Plato died, to borrow Josef Pieper's felicitous phrase, "in tune with the world."[5] Plato did not make the measure. He discovered it. He knew it. Protagoras in a famous phrase had affirmed that "man is the measure of all things." In his *Laws,* Plato had argued rather that we are the puppets of God, that our works and days, even our highest human sciences, even politics, are not serious, at least not in comparison with God. "God is the measure of all things" (716). We are to spend our days "singing, dancing, and sacrificing" because this is the only response we can make to the good *that is* (803).

Thus, when Plato dies, he dies according to a measure that he knows but does not constitute. The Thracian girl picks up a beat that she imperfectly blows into her double-reed flute, but she does not quite know how it works. Plato teaches her the measure. Those who do not know the measure can learn it from the philosopher. The redemption of the flute-girls and the Thracian maidens for philosophy finds its source here, in the measure that Plato in dying does not himself constitute but that he knows and knows can be learned by the flute-girl. The last person who sees Plato alive is the Thracian maiden, as she plays according to the measure he teaches her. Her flute is the last thing he listens to. Plato dies with philosophy reconciled to the Thracian maidens and the flute girls. The Thracian maiden who plays for him does not laugh at him, the philosopher dying. She does not think it mockingly amusing that this dying philosopher should call for her so that he might listen to the flute as he leaves this world. The philosopher is not laughed at. He is attended to, having taught the measure.

5. Josef Pieper, *In Tune with the World: A Theory of Festivity* (Chicago: Franciscan Herald Press, 1973).

V.

Socrates, as he left this world, himself on his last day had wondered about music. Before his conversation on immortality in the *Phaedo,* Socrates confessed that perhaps he had misunderstood the Oracle. Perhaps the Oracle meant that he should actually compose music or poetry, cultivate the arts. So he did set some passages in Aesop's fables to verse and some hymns to the festival gods. And Cicero also recalled that in his old age, "Socrates learnt to play that favourite instrument of the ancients, the lyre."[6] Plato realized in the *Republic* that the only way to counteract Homer would be to write poetry and music that outcharmed Homer. Plato's music, as we learn each time we read him, was beguiling. Even Callicles was trained in his earlier days by reading with amusement the philosophers, so that there seems to be some missing link between the philosopher and the politician. What had gone wrong in the life of the master politician Callicles? He found the image of Socrates in mature age, still conversing with potential philosophers quietly in corners, to be ridiculous and a waste of time. He had lost the charm. Socrates was unintelligible to him, though he sensed him still to be dangerous and thus would not answer his questions. Callicles, the statesman, was unwilling to test his own reasoning. He lacked music. He was unaware of the relation of music and philosophy.

But both the Thracian maidens and Callicles needed to be redeemed by true music and true politics. That is to say, we could not have a city composed only of philosophers, only of shepherds, only of craftsmen, only of politicians, only of flute-girls. Harmony required more. Specialization meant that not everyone could be expert in everything else, that is was all right if everyone did not do everything. The philosopher was a specialist in the whole. It was all right that Plato, the philosopher, did not himself play the flute well, but not all right if he did not know anything about it, did not delight in listening to it. Philosophers enjoy music in part because they know it, in part because they know that life is more than philosophy. All things have their harmony in the philosopher who is to know the parts, even the measure of the laws of music. Plato did not ask for a flute so that he could himself play. As he lay dying, he did not act, he listened, until he heard what was not in tune with the measure. Music and *nomos* were reconciled. The Thracian maiden played. Plato listened. Plato did not die in silence.

6. Cicero, "On Old Age," in *Selected Works,* edited by Michael Grant (London: Penguin, 1971), 233.

At the end of the banquet in the *Symposium,* the "sound of the flute is heard" (212). Alcibiades, unlike Callicles, has felt the charm of philosophy all his disordered life, even though he had to shut his ears against it. Astonishingly, he compares Socrates precisely to a flute-player.

And are you not a flute-player? That you are, and a performer far more wonderful than Marsyas. He indeed with instruments used to charm the souls of men by the powers of his breath, and the players of his music do so still: for the melodies of Olympus' are derived from Marsyas who taught them, and these, whether they are played by a great master or by a miserable flute-girl, have a power which no others have; they alone possess the soul and reveal the wants of those who have need of gods and mysteries, because they are divine. But you produce the same effect with your words only, and do not require the flute; this is the difference between you and him. (215)

The melodies of Olympus have a measure. Whether they are played by Marsyas or a miserable flute-girl, they have power. They possess the soul and reveal the "wants of those who have need of gods and mysteries." Those who have need of gods and mysteries are those who are not the philosophers. The philosopher has no need of being a musician, but he loves music. He has no need of the mysteries and the gods, but he loves them. What is missing in the cosmos is someone to praise *what is* for what it is, for its own sake.

VI.

The words of Socrates, Alcibiades tells us, are like music. They have a divine origin. Chaerephon, we recall, had gone to the Oracle at Delphi. His brother Chaerecrates was at the trial and could testify to it. Alcibiades, whose life Socrates had saved at the Battle of Delium, is the most talented and handsome of all the young men of Athens. Socrates loves him in his potential virtue but not in his corruption. Alcibiades stands at the threshold of ruining the city because he rejects philosophy. He goes on to betray Athens, Sparta, and Persia. He admits that Pericles speaks well, but when Alcibiades heard Socrates, he explains, "I felt as if I could hardly endure the life which I am leading." Alcibiades realizes that if he did not "shut his ears" against the words of Socrates, "and fly as from the voice of a siren, my fate would be like that of others—he would transfix me, and I should grow old sitting at his feet" (216). Alcibiades does not grow old sitting at Socrates' feet. Plutarch gives two accounts of Alcibiades' death (404 BC). He is murdered by darts either because he debauched a maiden or because he betrayed Lacaedaimon and Persia.

Xanthippe, his wife, is not present when Socrates drinks the hemlock, though she has been there in the morning. The potential philosophers and the good jailer are there. Socrates remembers to offer a sacrifice to the god of healing, for he is being healed in his death. Socrates entrusts this sacrificial mission to his old friend Crito, who could not get him out of jail with his money because Socrates had forbade him. We realize already at the banquet of Agathon (415 BC), however, that Socrates, in undergoing a more severe test than that of death, will not be corrupted by Alcibiades. He will not do wrong for the sake either of Callicles' demos or Alcibiades' own ambitions, or beauty or love, or pleasure, or popularity.

Why must Alcibiades at the banquet close his ears to the siren voice of Socrates? "For he makes me confess that I ought not to live as I do, neglecting the wants of my own soul, and busying myself with the concerns of the Athenians; therefore I hold my ears and tear myself away from him." Alcibiades knows perfectly well why he acts as he does. In this explanation he is more revealing than Callicles, though both of them do the same thing in refusing to listen to Socrates. "For I know that I cannot answer him or say that I ought not to do as he bids, but when I leave his presence the love of popularity gets the better of me. And therefore I run away and fly from him" (216). Alcibiades takes the only escape possible. He refuses to listen, and he immediately seeks to corrupt Socrates so that Socrates will not be superior to him in virtue.

When Alcibiades fails, he admits to the others that "I could not help wondering at his natural temperance and self-restraint and manliness." Alcibiades wonders about this virtue, but to no avail. Aristotle had said that wonder was the beginning of philosophy. Socrates, in fact, not Alcibiades, was the only one "with any real powers of enjoyment" (219). Alcibiades is thus the model of the opposite of the philosopher-king, more so than Callicles who is not a philosopher. Alcibiades not merely refuses to listen to argument. He also takes positive steps not to know. He does everything in his power not to acknowledge that he is wrong, even though he does know it. He tries to corrupt the only source of virtue he admires so that he will have no model testifying to his corruption.

The worst tyrant, as we recall from book 1 of the *Republic,* is the one who does evil or whatever else he wants. But this same tyrant not merely wants to do the evil that he desires, he also wants to be praised by everyone for what he does. This praise is crucial, for it implies that even evil needs rational approbation. Otherwise, as Socrates shows us in the *Gorgias,* the tyrant is utterly alone and in the worst possible position. The story of the ring of Gyges is found in book 1 of the *Republic.* It is the original invisible man who could do what he wanted if only he were not seen, and who corrupted also the people in defiling the shepherd who found the ring and corruptly became a king. In the *Gorgias,* the worst tyrant is the one who thinks that to do evil is better than to suffer it. He is the one who refuses punishment for his evil rather than freely accepting it and therefore acknowledging a good he did not make.

VII.

At the end of *Alcibiades I,* Alcibiades seems to have decided to follow Socrates; he has shown that he could follow the highest arguments of virtue posed by the philosopher. "I shall begin at this moment to take trouble over justice," Alcibiades explains. To this happy thought, Socrates responds, "And I would wish you to continue doing so. Yet, I stand in dread, not because I do not have trust in your nature, but rather because, seeing the strength of the city, I fear that it will overcome both me and you" (135). In a sense, we have here the preview of the young Augustine, the two loves and the two cities. Socrates lived a private life because he expected he would have been killed long ago if he did not. However ready for death he was, he did not seek it, but would suffer it if it came along. The *Symposium* revealed that Alcibiades, not Socrates, was the one seeking the beloved. What ultimately attracted Alcibiades, in spite of himself, was philosophy, the love of wisdom and truth. Socrates, for his part, realized that Alcibiades could also corrupt him, the philosopher, as well as himself. How? Because of another love, the love that Alcibiades confessed that he was attracted to whenever he left Socrates' presence. Politics, when it did not feel the charm of philosophy, remained the most serious opponent to philosophy.

If Socrates is the real flute-player, as Alcibiades said, is it not of some interest that Plato dies alone, in old age, of a natural death, with the sole consolation of a flute player, a Thracian maiden who does not know the measure? "God is the measure of all things" (716). Plato knew the *nomos.* His death was in tune with everything that was in the cosmos, the measure. Plutarch said that, as a young man, Alcibiades "obeyed all his masters fairly well, but refused to learn upon the flute, as a sordid thing." If we recall the Thracian maiden who played the flute for Plato when he showed her the measure, on the evening of the day on which he died, isn't that refusal of Alcibiades an extraordinary thing? In the *Crito,* Crito himself remarked that Socrates could also have been exiled to Thessaly, another wild place like Thrace. Crito's friends there would give Socrates complete protection, and there they would make much of the philosopher. But of course, Socrates realized that in a Thrace or a Thessaly, the philosopher would be merely an oddity, a showpiece. He would have had no one with whom to speak. Socrates tells Crito that their long years of "serious discussion" have taught them both that "to do wrong is in every sense bad and dishonourable for the person who does it" (49).

In his last words in the *Apology,* Socrates spoke of death, of going to the Isles of the Blessed, where he would meet the gods and the heroes, where he would even meet Homer; the old quarrel between poetry and philosophy could be resolved. Even Socrates wanted to continue his conversation beyond death to find out who really is wise. When Plato dies, however, he does not, like Socrates, seem to anticipate this further conversation. What he seems to anticipate rather is the music, that is, the praise. We should spend our lives "singing, dancing, and sacrificing" (803). Plato does not, like Socrates, seek among the gods and heroes to find him who is "really wise" and him who "only thinks that he is" (42). Plato understood the Alcibiades who refused to learn the flute. Plato did not refuse to listen to Socrates, the master flute-player.

Plato taught the Thracian maiden the *nomos,* the measure. Plato knew the flute. He taught her this measure the evening he died. The Thracian maiden did not laugh at him. He heard her play the flute. He knew the measure, that he was not the measure himself. "God is the measure of all things" (716). The Thracian maiden learned the measure. Philosophy, poetry, and politics are reconciled. In the Academy of Plato, we can still catch strains of the measure, even in any existing city, but only if we worry, like Socrates, about the demos, about the love that has no order.

In book 10 of the *Republic,* after mentioning the "old quarrel between philosophy and poetry," Socrates admits that

"If poetry directed to pleasure and imitation have any argument to give showing that they should be in a city with good laws, we should be delighted to receive them back from exile, since we are aware that we ourselves are charmed by them. But it isn't holy to betray what seems to be the truth. Aren't you, too, my friend (Glaucon), charmed by it, especially when you contemplate it through the medium of Homer?"

"Very much so."

"Isn't it just for it to come back in this way—when it has made an apology in lyrics or some other meter?" (607)

Eric Voegelin was charmed by the death of Plato. Philosophy, Voegelin thought, had fled to the Academy—Plato's Academy, not ours—wherein poetry and the pleasure of music are received back no longer tainted by the polis using them for its own purposes. The apology in lyrics and in meter, in measure, are present in the music of the Thracian maiden playing the flute with the *nomos* that the dying Plato gave her. Plato died in full tune with the world and with its measure.

VIII.

A friend of mine happened to be in the Stanford University chapel at the memorial service of Eric Voegelin. My friend did not know who Voegelin was at the time, but he made a tape of this moving service. At this world-famous university only about forty people attended the service for Voegelin. Philosophy has fled even the academy. Voegelin seems to have chosen the music, Schubert, and the readings, from Ezekiel, from the First Letter of John, and from the Gospel of John. In his lovely eulogy of Voegelin, Ellis Sandoz remarked that the last time he saw Voegelin, a couple of months before he died, he had just ordered a new edition of Shakespeare's works, as the one he had been using was worn out. Voegelin tried to read the complete works of Shakespeare every year. The day before he died (January 18, 1985), Voegelin spent his time correcting some page proofs of his essay, *"Quod Deus dicitur,"* a proposition, he remarked, whose "specific form" comes from Thomas Aquinas.[7] The very last word Voegelin ever wrote was "Plato."

On the day of Voegelin's death, a Psalm was read as he passed into unconsciousness. The Psalm was the Twenty-fifth. "Oh, keep my soul, O Lord, and deliver me: let me not be ashamed, for I put my trust in Thee." Voegelin died peacefully while this Psalm was being read. As his wife was too weak and anxious, the Psalm was read to Voegelin by his American Indian housekeeper whose name was, with splendid paradox, Hiawatha.

All true philosophers, when they die, die the same death. All true philosophers when they die, die in the same city.

7. Eric Voegelin, *"Quod Deus dicitur," Journal of the American Academy of Religion* 53 (December 1985): 568–84.

7   WHAT IS PIETY?

Just acts occur between people who participate in things good in themselves and can have too much or too little of these; for some beings (e.g., presumably the gods) cannot have too much of them.

—Aristotle, *Ethics*

I.

The four dialogues on the trial and death of Socrates—the *Euthyphro*, the *Apology*, the *Crito*, and the *Phaedo*—were not written at once or in the chronological order of the events themselves. Time-wise, the Euthyphro comes first. It depicts a rather amusing scene. Socrates has just been indicted for impiety by the young and arrogant Meletus. On his way to the court, Socrates comes across a younger "prophet" who is also going to court to prosecute his own father. The whole scene is rather delightful and quite playful.

However, the dialogue has serious overtones. It is about "piety." It is, to follow Leo Strauss, a "what is?" question. Thus, the great questions we ask are "What is good?" "What is true?" Since Socrates has been accused of being impious, he figures to confound the accuser, the annoying and unpleasant young man Meletus, whom we see more of in the *Apology*. Indeed, Meletus is the principal accuser of Socrates in the trial.

It is always important to get some sense of the character of the personages who appear in Plato's dialogues. What was Glaucon like? What about Adeimantus? Apollodorus? Theages? Even Plato himself? It is a fascinating study. No doubt in one or other, we will recognize in these characters something of ourselves or of the man next door.

Socrates wants Euthyphro to teach him what "piety" is, so he can defend himself against the accusation of being impious, an accusation the es-

This essay originally appeared in the *Fellowship of Catholic Scholars Quarterly* 29 (Summer 2006): 2–5.

sence of which Socrates naturally does not understand. So, as he does in the *Apology*, he hastens off find out answers to his questions. Who is better to tell him about this issue than someone like Euthyphro, whose profession is precisely to teach piety. He is a "prophet" and is concerned about the gods. In the end, of course, Euthyphro turns out to know very little about what he is talking about. He finally buzzes off on other business rather than continue the conversation of a persistent Socrates about what piety is. It is all quite amusing, really.

There may even be some overtones of Oedipus here. Or at least, Euthyphro is in court to accuse his own father of murder in a very bizarre case. Here, the son accuses the father of murder because he has bound up a slave, who had murdered another slave, and tossed him into the ditch while he goes to the authorities to find out what to do with him. The slave, meanwhile, dies before they can find out. So being a very strict moralist, Euthyphro, to protect his own piety, decides to prosecute his own father. Socrates finds it quite odd that a son's piety toward his own father would allow him to do this.

II.

Initially, it might be useful to spell out the meaning of piety in general, much of which, if we pay attention, will be found in the dialogue. Piety is an aspect of justice. Generally, we speak of two forms of piety— to our parents or ancestors and to the gods. The reason why piety is an "aspect" of justice, and not justice itself (the subject of the *Republic* and book 5 of the *Ethics*), is because it cannot be requited either proportionally as in distributive justice or mathematically as in commutative justice. Piety is something of a paradox, something "owed" when nothing specific can be determined about the content of what is indeed owed. Thus we can never adequately "repay" what we owe to our parents or to the gods, what they have given to us in life.

This question of what we "owe" to the gods is related to what is said in the *Symposium* about why the world needs rational creatures within it. The world is not complete in its Creation if it does not have within it someone with the power to praise it from the side of Creation itself. But in what does this praise consist? How do we "calculate" the debt? Or is it even something that can be calculated? This perplexity is what piety is about.

Within the *Euthyphro*, it is to be noted the number of times that "sacrifice" and "prayers" come up in relation to the debt of piety. Obviously, the gods do not "need" anything, or else they would not be gods. They cannot really be "paid back." In the highest things, there is, strictly speaking, no "need." This "un-neediness" is the consequence of the abundance within the Godhead. In Christian terms, not yet known to Plato, the Trinity is the only real doctrine that explains satisfactorily this factor of why God does not require anything but Himself. What is not God does not exist because God "needed" it. Neither does it exist as self-caused.

Euthyphro, in his effort to explain what piety is, keeps arguing in circles—is a thing pious because God loves it? Or does God love it because it is pious already, that is, it possesses something from within itself to be attractive to others? Socrates wants to find something objective that calls forth piety from within him. If we say, however, that a thing is pious because God loves it, then anything can be pious. This alternative implies that there is no objective order. Euthyphro, under grilling, does not want to teach Socrates, as it turns out, because he (Euthyphro) does not himself know what piety is. And of course, typically, neither does Socrates claim to know what it is, even as he is engaged with Euthyphro to find what it is not.

Yet, piety has some exalted status. It is "beyond justice." What can this mean? In practice, it means what we do to acknowledge the superiority of the gods, even when we can, strictly speaking, "do" nothing for them. Obviously, nothing we can do can really satisfy them. If they are not already satisfied, they are not gods. Likewise, to do nothing does not satisfy them either. What about prayers and sacrifices? In the *Laws,* Plato says that we are to spend our lives "singing, dancing, and sacrificing" (803e). What we are looking for is something that does not imply that we have the power to satisfy the gods. Otherwise, in logic, we would be gods ourselves. This is why philosophy is the "love" of wisdom, not wisdom itself. The gods are wise and need not philosophize. It is perhaps not an accident that Christ did not come as a philosopher, while Socrates appeared precisely as one.

Socrates is accused of impiety, that is, of not worshiping the gods of Athens, of the city. He denies the accusation. But he does not exactly worship the Homeric gods of Athens either. He is cautious. He is concerned with spiritual things, as he will say in the *Apology,* and if so with a source of spirit. This emphasis on spirit is why philosophy transcends the civic religion in Plato.

The religion that Plato has available to him can only allow such a solution. Plato does not have revelation; that is, he does not have available an explanation of the inner life of the Godhead that is itself Trinity. Nor does he have a doctrine of Incarnation, wherein God is also revealed as a specific human being, God and man, one God, but two natures. Nor does he have such a thing as Mass, a sacrifice that itself includes the notions of prayer, expiation, and the suffering of God. This latter also recalls Sophocles and his theme that "man learns by suffering."

III.

Euthyphro wants to be pious by prosecuting his father because of a crime that is not unlike the guilt of Oedipus, that is, unknowing. Meletus says that Socrates is a "maker of gods" (3b).[1] The theme of worshiping false gods is, to recall, at the heart of the relation of Yahweh to Israel. Or to put it positively, the Old Testament revelation deals with exclusiveness, with not worshiping false gods. Strictly speaking, these false gods would also apply to the gods of the Greeks.

What, we wonder, is so terrible about worshiping false gods? And what does one do to perform such worship? The Hebrews made golden calves. Obviously, there is nothing wrong with gold, or calves, for that matter. What is wrong with such worship? (This is the first commandment: "Thou art the Lord God who shall not have strange gods before Him.") And why is there a problem with worship anyhow? Is there something about the very nature of the intellect that would see a connection between getting it wrong about God and, as a result, getting it wrong with everything else?

Obviously, in worship, as the Euthyphro states, we cannot give anything to the gods that they do not already have. The relation of man to God is not to be based on the idea that God "needs" something from us that He does not have already. If this is so, what is the problem? It is because there are things beyond need. (This is what my *On the Unseriousness of Human Affairs*[2] is about.) A man does not "need" to tell his wife that she is beautiful. But if she is, and all wives are beautiful in their own ways, but he does not acknowledge it, it is worse than depriving her of what is best about her. For she is worthy of praise, but only freely. Nor can God "command" piety. A wife cannot "demand" praise. It must arise freely, but about something that she really is. So piety means a response that is "due" without justice, that is, without being able to say exactly what is owed.

1. The citations from the *Euthyphro* are from *Plato: Complete Works,* edited by John Cooper (Indianapolis: Hackett, 1997). Reference numbers to the Platonic dialogue cited are placed in parentheses the text.

2. Schall, *On the Unseriousness of Human Affairs* (Wilmington, Del.: ISI Books, 2001).

In some sense, the ultimate answer to piety has to come from the side of God. We need to be told what is best to do, or what would be the highest way to praise or acknowledge the Godhead, since we really do not know how praiseworthy it is in itself. This is what liturgy is about. The *Euthyphro* itself is filled with notions of gods that have no definite plan for us. "According to your argument, my good Euthyphro, different gods consider different things to be just, beautiful, ugly, good, and bad, for they would not be at odds with one another unless they differ about these subjects, would they?" (7e). This problem of the good and beauty is why Socrates, in the *Republic*, will have such a time with the Homeric gods. They approve of things that the philosophers know to be wrong.

Euthyphro says, "I would certainly say that the pious is what all the gods love and the opposite, what all the gods hate, is the impious" (9e). Is there such a thing that all love and hate among the pagan gods? If not, as some gods praise one thing and others its opposite, Socrates' view of philosophy as what transcends the gods makes sense.

Socrates says: "Then the god-loved is not the same as the pious, Euthyphro, nor the pious the same as the god-loved, as you say it is, but one differs from the other." Euthyphro: "How so, Socrates?" Socrates: "Because we agree that the pious is being loved for this reason, that it is pious, but it is not pious because it is being loved" (10d–e). That is, there must be something in it worth loving in the first place.

Euthyphro continues: "I think, Socrates, that the godly and pious is the part of the just that is concerned with the care of the gods, while that concerned with the care of men is the remaining part of justice." Socrates: "You seem to me to put that very well, but I still need a bit of information. I do not know yet what you mean by care of, for you do not mean the care of the gods in the same sense as the care of other things, as, for example, we say, don't we, that not everyone knows how to care for horses, but the horse breeder does" (12e–13a). The man who cares for horses knows what to do about horses. He has a standard.

Socrates adds, using another example, "Could you tell me to the achievement of what goal service to doctors tends? Is it not, do you think, to achieve health?" (13d). We recall in Aristotle that the doctor is ordained to health as its end or purpose, but the doctor does not have anything to do with what we do when we are healthy. Obviously, our care of the gods cannot be designed to making them healthy, as they are already complete. So what can "care of" the gods mean?

Euthyphro (recall what was cited above from the *Laws*) responds: "I say that if a man knows how to say and do what is pleasing to the gods at prayer and sacrifice, those are pious actions such as preserve both private houses and public affairs of state. The opposite of these pleasing actions are impious and overturn and destroy everything." But to this Socrates replies: "If you had given me an answer, I should now have acquired from you sufficient knowledge of the nature of piety. As it is, the lover of inquiry must follow his beloved wherever it leads him. Once more then, what do you say that piety and the pious are? Are they a knowledge of how to sacrifice and pray?" (14b–c).

Incidentally, I must confess that I love this line: "The lover of inquiry must follow his beloved wherever it leads him." It is indeed a worthy motto of a philosopher.

The problem, however, is whether the gods need anything from us. Socrates observes: "And to give correctly is to give them what they need from us, for it would not be skillful to bring gifts to anyone that are in no way needed" (14d–e). Of course, gifts are not given just because what is given is needed, in the sense that the receiver lacks something. That comes closer to justice. A friend of mine, the other day, gave his wife some flowers after they had lunch together on a rare occasion. The flowers were not "needed."

The "ancestor" of Socrates, Daedalus, the man who is mentioned in book 1 of the *Politics* as the example of the possibility of eliminating slavery by making statues that could weave, comes up here because of his "flying" ability, that is, arguments with Euthyphro go round and round. Euthyphro never manages to settle the issue about *what piety is*. "Do you they not realize now that you are saying that what is dear to the gods is the pious? Is this not the same as the god-loved?" (15c).

Since Euthyphro cannot define what piety is, he cannot teach Socrates what it is. Finally, at the end of this short dialogue, Euthyphro tells Socrates that he is in a "hurry" (15e). Socrates tells him that he had hope of an answer to escape the indictment of Meletus that he (Socrates) was impious. He hoped to acquire knowledge of "wisdom in divine matters" from Euthyphro. This wisdom would prevent his "ignorance" to "cause him to be careless and inventive about such things, and that I would be better for the rest of my life" (16a).

Already here, we find intimations of Socratic wisdom; that is, he knows that he does not know. He is accused of impiety because he is "careless." But in his search for what piety is, he has found no teacher in Euthyphro, who is supposed to be the expert. Hence, we are subtly led to believe that

Socrates is really more of an expert in piety than Euthyphro. Thus, Meletus can accuse Socrates of impiety because the experts do not themselves know what piety is.

Yet, on concluding the dialogue, we do know something more about piety. We know it is related to justice and involves the perplexing question of what exactly is it that we "owe" to the gods. Socrates does not deny that something is at stake here. From the point of view of revelation, we would probably say that "what is owed" cannot adequately be resolved on the human side by human means. Hence the unending pursuit of Socrates for "What is piety?" is justified and opens us to wonder about what is implied here.

Socrates will be accused of being impious and not praising the gods of the city. The irony is that the gods of the city are not worth praise as they do things that are wrong, hence the problem with Homer. Socrates' impiety, his passing to philosophy to find the answers, thus betrays a kind of logic. *"The lover of inquiry must follow where his beloved leads him."* We might restate what is at stake in this way. If Socrates did find the adequate answer to "What is piety?" he would have already had to have revelation, as the question cannot, as such, be answered on the human side. This is what the *Euthyphro* is about.

PART III

THE ABIDING IMPLICATIONS
OF FRIENDSHIP

8   ARISTOTLE ON FRIENDSHIP

Things that cause friendship are: doing kindnesses; doing them unasked; and not proclaiming the fact when they are done, which shows that they were done for their own sake and not for some other reason.

—Aristotle, *Rhetoric*

I.

Two of the most beautiful treatises from the ancient world are on the same subject—friendship. One is by Aristotle in books 8 and 9 of his *Ethics;* the other by Cicero. It should not go unnoticed that Thomas Aquinas commented not only on the whole of the *Ethics,* including the treatise on friendship, but that his discussions of charity as a theological virtue are also extensions of the analyses of friendship found in the classical writers, especially Cicero and Aristotle.

"Friendship is something everyone ought to think about," Cicero wisely affirmed.[1] Yet, like all things ethical—like laughter itself—one cannot really think adequately about this topic unless one has experience of it. Aristotle insisted that because true friendship was rare, we must begin with the imperfect sorts of friendship—those of the young, of the old, and of the imperfect—so that gradually we might make precise what true friendship is. Moreover, it is always possible to learn something of a virtue from the vice opposite to it. Vice perhaps cannot know virtue, but virtue can know vice. Vice itself, or the corruptions of the various sorts of relations that human beings might have with one another, hint at the glory of the

This essay was originally published in *Classical Bulletin* 65, nos. 3 and 4 (1989): 83–87.

1. Cicero, "On Friendship," in *Cicero: On the Good Life,* I, 3, edited by Michael Grant (Harmondsworth, England: Penguin, 1979), 176. See James V. Schall, *Redeeming the Time* (New York: Sheed & Ward, 1968), 65–96, 213–41; idem., *Reason, Revelation, and the Foundations of Political Philosophy,* 93–128; idem., "Unknown to the Ancients: God and Friendship," in *What Is God Like?* (Collegeville, Minn.: Michael Glazer / Liturgical Press, 1993), 140–70; idem., "Friendship and Political Philosophy," *Review of Metaphysics* 50 (September 1996): 121–41; and idem., "Justice: The Most Terrible Virtue," *Markets and Morals* 7 (Fall 2004): 209–21.

real virtue. Likewise, as Aristotle again insisted, we do not know anything fully in the area of human action and passion unless we know both the best and the worst with the range of their movements.

Perhaps on mere statistical grounds, we could suspect that Aristotle's commitment of two books of the *Ethics* to friendship but only one to justice is intellectually provocative. We hesitate to suggest that friendship is exactly twice as important as justice on such a basis. But we can certainly conclude that friendship is a critical good of human life. Without it, the highest questions never arise in their fullness, nor will happiness as such be achieved without it. Aristotle almost laconically remarks that "friendship seems to hold states together, and lawgivers to care more for it than for justice.... When men are friends, they have no need of justice, while when they are just they need friendship as well" (1155a11–24).[2] What constitutes the clear superiority of friendship to justice in Aristotle without denying the necessity of justice? Why is friendship "needed"? Why is justice not enough?

Students in universities, on first encountering Aristotle in his methodical, careful manner of proceeding by definition, experience, example, argument, never expect to find in him anything like the treatise on friendship. They are usually at an age when this topic is flourishing in, or perhaps confusing, their lives. Exactly as Aristotle described it, they change friends frequently; they seek pleasure; they reject utilitarian friendships even while they know the elderly who need them. Thus, there is a disarming warmth in Aristotle. We expect this perhaps in Plato, but we are surprised by it in Aristotle. But this should not dismay us. In this treatise, Aristotle is deadly serious. He is engaged in the culmination of his ethical reflections where he is constantly running up against questions that cannot, apparently, be resolved within this system, even though they appear to arise legitimately within his argument (1156a22–b6; 58a6–9).

To his credit, Aristotle never failed to state what the problems are that arise from the experience of friendship. He was a practical man. And the discussion of friendship fell within the realm of his considerations of the practical sciences, even though the question of what it is that friends do together seems to reach directly into the contemplative regions. Thus, book 10 of the *Ethics* seems to be the fitting book to follow the treatise on friendship. In book 10, we find that there are two kinds of happiness, political

---

2. For Aristotle, I cite from the *Basic Works,* edited by Richard McKeon (New York: Random House, 1941).

and contemplative; that we ought to have both; that both are necessary in themselves, while political friendship, by being what it is, is still preparatory to contemplative happiness.

It is to be noticed that the treatise on friendship comes after Aristotle has discussed the whole range of the moral virtues, of happiness, of the voluntary, and of the mean. Likewise, he had discussed the nature of the theoretic and practical sciences in book 6 with a needed discussion of how it is we can do evil to be found in book 7. In other words, by the time we reach books 7–9, we have apparently decided already what it is for a human being to be virtuous. We are surprised that anything could be missing or might need to be added, while we are aware that the magnanimous and munificent man, who really is virtuous, actually does not have everything, though what he lacks evidently cannot be simply acquired wholly by his own efforts or fortune, as in the case of the other virtues.

Perhaps we can make this understanding clearer if we realize that the difference between friendship and justice is that justice, strictly speaking, does not concern itself with the uniqueness of the person with whom one enters into just dealings. Justice is concerned with the abstract relationship (1158b29–33). And this concern is what constitutes its danger, as Plato understood so well. Anything human added on to justice is to be encouraged, but this addition is not the essence of justice. Justice, in this sense, is depersonalizing. The very people who are only just to one another are not, therefore, friends. In a sense, the relationship of justice prescinds from the reality of friendship itself. Friendship, on the other hand, deals only with those for whom justice, while not being denied, is not the primary concern in the relationship. Justice does not take into account the very uniqueness of the persons involved in the exchanges of friendship. Justice is for those who are not friends. Strictly speaking, enemies ought to be just to one another, something exemplified, say, in the life of Robert E. Lee. At a minimum, there is justice between friends. But this is not its essence or especially its perfection.

II.

In these reflections, I propose to look at Aristotle's analysis of friendship not from the point of view of politics, where he saw it rightly as the crucial bond holding any real polity together, but from the aspect of its theoretic incompleteness. This approach will seem paradoxical. After all, if

Aristotle did not complete his own treatise, who did? On the other hand, within Aristotle's discussion, he himself brought up a number of problems which he apparently recognized as valid, but which he felt have no manageable answers or procedures to cope with their resolution.

Aristotle justified including friendship in the *Ethics* by suggesting that the virtues need to be put into effect in our very lives (1166a23–b3). Not only do we need to be courageous or prudent or just or generous or temperate or liberal, but we need to be so in the presence of others. Definitions of virtues are not themselves virtue, a lesson Aristotle learned by disagreeing with a famous position of Plato. Yet, if we look upon friends as mere tools or occasions to put into effect our own virtues, this view becomes, even in theory, somewhat self-serving. This attitude would hardly be a virtue or considered so. Friendship, moreover, has the peculiar quality of being exceedingly limited (1158a10–17). And this limitation is one of the most perplexing aspects of Aristotle's discussion on this topic. The whole world is full of potential friends we will never have, a fact which makes us wonder why it is that we have the friends we do have.

Aristotle did not doubt that we can have many friends, but only if the communication or exchange for this sort of friendship is pleasure or utility. Ironically, having too many friends in the highest sense is a sign of no friends. Friendship is maddeningly restricted in theory. Friendship is exalted in proportion to its restriction, something G. K. Chesterton meant when he remarked that there is more difference between two and three than between three and three million. Why is this? First of all, true friendship needs a kind of stability of character in the friend and in ourselves. Aristotle did not think that this sort of stable character normally arose before what we would today call middle age. Life up to this time is preparation for friendship, not friendship itself, since we ourselves are changeable, as are our potential friends (1156b24–32). In other words, some successful effort to acquire the virtues is necessary for friendship.

Aristotle, of course, recognized the notion of honor among thieves. And he was quite familiar with Plato's realization that even to do injustice, there needed to be a kind of bond of perverted justice or friendship among the robbers (1159b8–10). If they too were divided among themselves, as Scripture said also, they could not stand. Likewise, also from Plato, Aristotle understood that friends should know what things are against virtue and truth. The identification or exchange of untruth, that it be seen as "untruth," is after all one of the great acts of friendship. Truth and its pursuit is indeed a bond of friendship, yet truth, as such, is universal. At first sight, it would look like the discovery and holding of the same truths would be more alienating than unifying. Yet, Aristotle's doctrine of knowledge maintained that the intellect of each individual is intended to know all things and seeks to know them.

The bond of knowledge between men, then, is a spiritual thing. One of the extraordinary insights into the Aristotelian theory of knowledge is his realization that the acquisition of knowledge does not, by itself, change the world. Knowledge of itself only changes the knower. Everyone gains. This understanding means that friends can indeed gain knowledge or truth which is not, by its very nature, threatening to another. The communication of the highest things in which friendship primarily consists is the search for and exchange of truths that reach the nature of *what is.* These truths will also include how we ought to live our lives. Friendship seeks permanence. That is, it recognizes that the pursuit of reality, of *what is,* will never cease. The Greeks did not believe that it would end, even in death, because the soul was itself a spiritual power. If it is asked, then, "What it is that the human soul or human being does forever?" the answer is that it seeks to know the whole of truth in itself, of each part, of the whole, but in such a way that the truth it knows can be spoken, exchanged with another human being, capable of both receiving and giving (1156a6–12).

III.

What were the more specific problems Aristotle had with friendship? Perhaps one that seems more contemporary was the question of whether husbands and wives could, in the highest sense, be friends. The long discussion from book 1 of the *Politics* about the nature of authority in the family, namely, that for the most part, the husband is the natural ruler, must be see in the light of Aristotle's discussion of friendship between spouses. Aristotle had held that the husband rules the wife with what he called a constitutional rule. This is a technical term that means that, unlike the case of those within the family who could not rule themselves for their own good, so that they needed an adult or normal reason to guide them, the wife could rule herself. Consequently, the natural analogate for constitutional rule in the polity was, in the family, the rule of husband and wife, and, in the individual, the rule of reason over the passions.

The family differs from the polity, however, because in it, there are only two members capable of ruling themselves. In cases of conflict, one must decide if the family's good or end as an abiding unit is to be achieved.

For Aristotle, this was a perfectly obvious and logical problem that, as such, had nothing to do with the intelligence or capacity of either member. Indeed, if there was a problem with capacity, the one more capable should rule in Aristotle's view. True, one could propose a kind of rotation in which one would rule on Tuesdays and the other on Thursdays, but Aristotle thought it sufficient to suggest that the two-membered "polity" of a family ought to rule itself by reason in practical things dealing with the good of this same family. For various reasons, it was most normal in experience that the husband exercised this rule, which was a rule of reason, that is, the decisions were reached by reasoned exchange. But in conflict, someone had to decide. There was no avoiding this reality.

The rule of the husband, however, was precisely a "constitutional" rule, that is, a rule in which the ruled contributed its reason to the decision:

The association of husband and wife seems to be aristocratic; for the man rules in accordance with his worth, and in these matters in which a man should rule, but the matters that befit a woman he hands over to her. If the man rules in everything the relation passes over into oligarchy; for in doing so he is not acting in accordance with their respective worth, and not ruling in virtue of his superiority. Sometimes, however, women rule, because they are heiresses; so their rule is not in virtue of excellence but due to wealth and power. (1160b33–39)

This agreement of excellencies is, for Aristotle, the only solid spiritual reason for two to stay together on divisive issues.

However, Aristotle's more profound discussion of marriage is in the treatise on friendship. We must understand that Aristotle did not think every marriage was a relationship that always involved the highest friendship, but he recognized that this could happen. Indeed, in one sense, since friends are to remain together throughout their lives, marriage seems, in Aristotle's thinking, to provide the most permanent form of friendship, with a common sharing of life. If the partners in the marriage were virtuous and intelligent, then they could indeed be friends in the highest sense.

Human beings live together not only for the sake of reproduction but also for the various purposes of life; for from the start the functions are divided, and those of man and woman are different; so they help each other by throwing their peculiar gifts into the common stock. It is for these reasons that both utility and pleasure seem to be found in this kind of friendship. But this friendship may be based also on virtue if the parties are good; for each has his own virtue and they will delight in the fact. (1162a20–27)

Aristotle does not deny that there is a difference between man and woman but acknowledges it and argues rather that the differing gifts are intended for a common good. What is to be noted is that a marriage can also between virtuous couples, which he acknowledges as delightful, but like any other relation, he presupposes the content of virtue and truth to be in each of the partners.

Marriage, then, is one sort of union, capable of the highest form of friendship, but in some fundamental respect quite unique because its mode of normal communication deals with the practical life of the family and its demands. The diversity of man and woman is good in itself and not to be jeopardized. No friendship of virtue except marriage will really have certain sorts of good in common, and the good that is truly existent in such a relationship will be the subject of exchanges in friendship.

Perhaps it is well to recognize that for Aristotle, friendship in the highest sense is rare. Indeed, as has been mentioned, this rarity presents something of a theoretical problem. Aristotle observed that we are fortunate if we have two or three friends in our lifetime. He recognized that chance and the rarity of true virtue and knowledge make the odds against this quite high. Still, the main reason for this rarity, and this is a fundamental point for Aristotle, is that we simply do not have time for many friendships. Friendship requires a lifetime. The variety of opinion and virtue and character will be such that the exchanges of friendship will be restricted. The bearing of one's soul to just anybody is not the mark of the friend, but rather the mark of the tyrant in his desire to protect himself from friends. The desire for many friends then can indeed be a sign of having no friends or of not knowing what is entailed in friendship.

On the other hand, the exclusiveness and intensity of friendship with one or two throughout a lifetime, precisely in order to have friendship at all, leaves open the wonder, at least about our relation to all other human beings who exist either in our lives, in our time, or in the whole history of the world. Surely, there is something sadly ironic about the fact that we are limited here, yet we recognize that without this very limit, we would have no friends at all. This very fact, which Aristotle does not discuss directly, does, nevertheless, on his own principles, foster the question of whether or not ultimate friendship with everyone who is good can come about. If not, the universe is incomplete in principle, whereas Aristotle constantly states that nature never made anything in vain.

This question leads to the question of friendship with God (1159a3–5). Aristotle held that we could not be friends with someone who is too exalted over us. Aristotle's denial of a friendship with God is rooted in a kind of pious understanding of the nature of the First Mover, whom Aristotle likewise recognized to move by love and desire. However, Aristotle was uneasy here, as it seems that if friendship is in fact the highest perfection of the rational creature, then it makes the First Mover something less exalted if it cannot have this perfection. Aristotle simply left the question unresolved, thinking the problem insoluble.

IV.

Finally, Aristotle desired to know if we would want our friends to be gods or kings or extremely virtuous (1158b33–36). He was extremely cautious here. The problem had to do with who it was we wanted to be loved or to be happy. If we had a friend whom we loved, we did not want our friend to become someone else (1166a20). Nor would we want ourselves to become someone else. Yet, if we were not virtuous, we would want to become better. We would likewise want our friend to become better. In either case, we would want at the same time to remain ourselves and to become good (1156b7–24; 58a33–37). The realism of Aristotle is very perceptive here, for this is the ultimate defense of finite being, that it is all right to be what it is. Men need not be gods, but they need to be better than they are.

But how is it possible for men to remain what they are, that is, men, not God? Moreover, what is to be done with our efforts to become good in the highest sense? Aristotle himself left these questions open. Indeed, he seems to suspect a metaphysical rebellion against *what is* to be possible in the human heart because of this sense of incompleteness (982b29). He merely insisted, however, that we would not want to be someone else even if that meant full happiness. Nor would we want that for our friends. Further, we would want to remain precisely what we are, that is, human beings. Aristotle did hint at the immortality of the soul in this context, but he realized that somehow this did not meet the demands of full friendship of the whole human being, which for Aristotle necessarily included body and soul.

The Aristotelian treatise on friendship, in conclusion, is full of questions that arose out of his ethical reflections. These questions are based on the real nature of man and do not arise simply from Aristotle's imagination. They have metaphysical implications of the deepest sort grounded in *what is*. The reading of this treatise, then, will ever remain unsettling because, when read with care, Aristotle brings us to confront certain things we might like to be true, even if, like him, we cannot see how they might be true. Aristotle, in other words, remains a teacher of the profoundest sort, one who raises questions that must be considered without trying to answer them in a false or ideological manner.

No one can finish reading Aristotle's treatise on friendship without a deep sense of consolation about where it is that the highest things among us are found, in our communication and living with other friends. However, we are also left with a curious perplexity of having discovered questions bravely and profoundly asked. These questions naturally arise in our pursuit of virtue and happiness, in our exchanges with friends. Yet, they seem unfinished, somehow, by one of the greatest philosophers to have lived among us, possessed of a wife whom he loved and friends with whom he conversed.

9   THE TOTALITY OF SOCIETY

From Justice to Friendship

The principal intention of human law is to create friendship between man and man.

—Thomas Aquinas, *Summa theologiae*

Comradeship and serious joy are not interludes in our travels, but . . . rather our travels are interludes in comradeship and joy, which through God shall endure for ever.

—G. K. Chesterton, *Charles Dickens*

I.

Human society has become for the modern world a complex reality, far too intricate for the mind of any one man to know thoroughly. Rarely do we understand it in its totality and unity. The basic structure of society can be grasped. Man can reflect on his experience and know the means and ends of his life in the city. Many ways enable us to discover the basic totality. The clearest way is to analyze the various aspects of law as it was set down and understood by St. Thomas Aquinas. We might also begin with justice, or the common good, or friendship, but these problems are one; the starting point alone is different. The striking thing about St. Thomas is that, within the context of the problem as he saw it, he implicitly, if not actually, uses the political definitions and distinctions between state and society and their functions that have become familiar to us.

In treating of law, Aquinas's ideas and terms serve as our basic approach. We accept Aquinas's definition that law is "an ordination of rea-

This essay was part of a master's thesis in philosophy at Gonzaga University in 1955. It was published in *The Thomist* 20 (January 1957): 1–26. The extensive citations from Aquinas in both Latin and English are here modified. This essay is reworked and shortened. Standard references to Aquinas will be placed in the text. The *Summa theologiae* is cited as (I-II, 87, 2); the *Commentary on the Ethics* cites the paragraph number (#1002). This early Schall essay contains themes that have long remained with me, which is why I include it here.

son for the common good, made by him who has care of the community, and promulgated" (I-II, 91, 4). We wish to inquire about law as it exists in a society, what it commands, what ideas, what effects it has. Human law deals only with external, human acts (I-II, 98, 1). These external acts must be ordered in such a way that the temporal peace and tranquility of society be maintained. This purpose is accomplished by regulating and prohibiting anything that could disturb the conditions of concord in society. St. Thomas calls this peaceful order *the end of human law* (I-II, 98, 1).

When dealing with the essence of law, Aquinas maintains that the end of law is the "common good" (I-II, 96, 4). The principle according to which external acts are regulated is the objective order of just relations without which a society cannot exist. Consequently, when speaking of the end of the law as the common good, he means the common good as a final cause by which particular external acts can achieve their end. "Actions are indeed concerned with particular matters: but those particular matters are referable to the common good, not as a common genus or species, but as to a common final cause, according as the common good is said to be the common end" (I-II, 90, 2, ad 2). St. Thomas identifies this common good in other places as the intention of the legislator. He means that it is the end or purpose for which the legislator acts (I-II, 100, 1; *In Eth.* #1666). However, the end of law in the sense of temporal tranquility refers to the effect actually achieved by the order of just relations in an existing society.

The first and minimal requirement of society, then, is the *de facto* order of men such that their actions with respect to one another are at least just. Law will command the acts of those virtues which have either directly or indirectly an effect on the external order. Those acts which have a relation to another in the external order are the acts of justice (I-II, 58, 2, 5). The precepts of law, therefore, will embody the external acts of virtue (I-II, 107, 1, ad 2). Virtues other than justice are embodied in law only insofar as their acts have an effect externally so that they can be considered as relating to justice (II-II, 58, 8, ad 3). If any given society establish and keep established this minimal order, it will have the basic requirement for a healthy society. The organization or institution directly concerned with this order is the *state,* or in Aquinas's terminology, the prince. The state, therefore, is that section of a society that has the external order of just actions and relations as its direct end. "For a prince is ordained to this purpose that he keeps justice, and, as a consequence, equality" (#1009).

The state, however, will be more or less perfect; it can progress or regress in its duty, for there is a whole range and hierarchy of just actions.

"The intention of law is to make all men virtuous, but in a certain order, namely, by first of all giving them precepts about those things where the notion of duty is most manifest" (II-II, 122, 1, ad 1). All problems of the external order may fall within the competency of the state in some sense at least, but it may well be that in any given body of men few of the factors that really constitute the good life will be realized.

This total order of just relations in society is called the common good of the multitude, and it will be the end for which all civil laws are primarily intended (#1030). Laws get their meaning and proportion from this end. This is not to deny that states in fact seek different ends. Thus, they establish different laws according to the way different peoples set up different goals or understanding of the common good, which, in practice, they define as virtue, wealth, world domination, or pleasure. However, as a matter of fact, the only legitimate understanding of the common good is the one that aims ultimately as virtue.

II.

Human law deals with the precepts of the virtue of justice. But how is law related to justice in reality? A man becomes just by performing just acts. That is, he decides what he is to do, then, he wills to act according to this specified or understood reason. This means that a man must see the objective *justum* (what is right) in any of his acts. Now these objective *justa* (right relationships) are in part determined by nature, that is, by reason itself, and in part by positive ordination of society. These right relations that man recognizes to be existing and operative are facts. He knows that he did not make these relations solely by himself. He must, therefore, take them into consideration in his every action so that the action will be proportioned to its end. By seeing and acting according to these just relations, he will be able to become a just and good man.

Law is just the other side of this same reality. It looks to what man should do, not from the side of the individual person himself but from the side of the legislator who established these *justa* (right relations) and *debita* (things due) for the common good, which man in his turn discovers to be factors in his every action. What a man can discover from reason therefore, namely, that there are natural limits and guideposts for his actions in reason, he, ultimately, comes to see as commands of a lawgiver, either human as in the case of civil law or divine as in the case of natural or revealed law. In other words, a man can see from reason *that* there are ways for a human being to act. He can discover in large measure just what these ways are. He may not know why this is so, but he cannot escape the fact that it is so.

However, when man progresses and discovers that these limits were not just accidental or arbitrary (assuming for the moment just human laws) and further, when he has come to see that they are commands of a lawgiver who in the case of natural law not only made the law but also the man himself; the he sees fully that the moral law is not simply a restriction or impediment. It is a definite order to man's end, a road by which he travels and not a pit into which he has fallen. Consequently, law commands an act be done which, from his point of view, man sees is in accord with his nature to perform. This formal cause of the human act is the dictate of reason which at the same time is the law as received in the subject and the *ratio juris* (reason of or in the law) that man sees must be maintained in the act. The *ratio juris* and the law, then, are the same thing, except that the law as such refers to the lawgiver (II-II, 57, 1, ad 2).

The order of strict just relations, therefore, will include the multiplicity of just human actions required for the exterior of society and the basic laws by which these acts are enforced and ordered (I-II, 100, 2). The principle or end according to which these acts can be denominated just and good will, then, is the objective common good of the multitude. The effect of this order will be concord, the external peace (I-II, 98, 1). And concord is the result of the effective establishment of special justice, i.e., commutative and distributive, among men (I-II, 180, 2, ad 2). This is why the principle of revolution is found precisely here, in the failure to establish justice, for men do not long endure their unequal lot.

We might ask at this point about the actual content of the order of *justa,* what exactly does it embrace? The general terms that St. Thomas and Aristotle use for this order are *justum politicum* or *simpliciter justum* (#1004). These terms are used to designate the order of justice in a perfect and self-sufficient community, a community looking to the fullness of human life. Such a community, however, can only be found among free and equal men so that the primary function of justice and law must always be the establishment and protection of equality and freedom. That is, the end and purpose of the justice that the law effects. Law is the dictate of reason by which the problems of what is just and what is right are settled, as it were, outside the contingent and turbulent exchange of ordinary human intercourse; it is the attempt to apply pure reason, reason abstract from passion concerning human affairs.

Justum politicum, however, is a complex notion. It is a complex genus referring to all the just actions in the community, no matter how these acts obtain their *ratio* of justice. Now these actions are subject to various divisions according to the various ways this same reality taken as a whole can be considered. Thus we can consider the range of actions according to how the rightness in each action is determined. Some will be proportional, some arithmetical, some will find their rightness measured in other ways, as in the instances of the potential parts of justice. The first two of these, the *justa distributiva* and *justa commutativa,* pertain to society as such (#1005). But we can also consider these self-same actions according to their cause or origin. Then some will be just because they are naturally reasonable (*justa naturalia*); others will be just only because the particular community established them as such (*justa legalia,* #1018). The legal *justa* (right relations) are always determinations of the natural precepts. Therefore, some *justa* can be *distributiva et naturalia,* others *distributiva et legalia,* etc., but always *justa legalia* must be in accord with the natural *justa.*

III.

In the *Summa theologiae,* St. Thomas makes a division of the Old Law with proves valuable in this regard. He divides the Old Law into moral, ceremonial, and judicial precepts according to the type of *justa* they contain. The moral precepts are the reasonable principles and their strictly reasonable conclusions, both of which necessarily flow from the nature of man (I-II, 100, 1). These *moralia* in turn can be divided according to the difficulty with which they are known. Some are known by most men (the Ten Commandments), some are known only by the wise (no divorce), and some only to God. These precepts embrace man's relations both with God and with other men. Those that deal with man's relations to God are very general and must be determined by society to give unity and coherence to the acts of worship. Such positive determinations are called *ceremonial.* These sorts of *justa,* then, will be positive in cause, either by society in the natural order or by God Himself in the case of revelation. The determinations that deal with man's relations with one another are called *judicalia* (I-II, 101, 1).

Four types of relationships of men to one another are possible: (1) prince to people, (2) citizens to one another, (3) people as a whole to another people, and (4) the domestic relationships (I-II, 104, 4). The *justa* that deal with these relationships, insofar as they are determinations of natural principles or conclusions from them, are positive in character; that is, someone decides their content.

If the sole meaning of the order is that there be only just relationships, however, it would produce a barren and rigid society. The order of *justa* is, as it were, the foundation or basis of something far richer and more significant. When a legislator commands, he primarily and initially commands an external act of justice. The order of just relations refers to the external order and unity of objectively right relationships that exist because of the efficient actions of men. This suffices to maintain and define the objective and minimal order of justice. But the legislator—either of the natural or the positive law—has in mind not simply this act of a virtue. He intends that virtue itself, the habit, be implanted in the citizen. This does not mean that every lawmaker must recognize this truth and have it in his mind when making a law. Aquinas is speaking about the nature of law as such, what it must do from its very nature and what the legislator must do as a simple consequence of making the law. That about which the law is given is an act of virtue, which is at the same time the rule of society. The act of observing a law is capable of inducing a habit in the man.

The end to which the precept of the law is directed is not simply that the citizen performs the act of virtue, but that he acquires the virtue (I-II, 100, 9, ad 2). Under the strict precept of the law will be the virtuous acts that a man does, whether he does them willingly or not. The principle intent of the legal structure of society is that a man does these acts virtuously, that is, because he sees their worth and not because they are commanded by coercion (I-II, 96, 3, ad 2). In this sense, the realm of virtue is very definitely a matter for society.

Thus, the existence of habitual moral virtue in the citizens is itself a common good, the common good of the many (*Contra Gentiles [CG]* III, 80). This common good of the many is something that each one personally possesses, but its operation and effect is shared by many (I-II, 100, 8). The effect and end of the whole order of just relations is to make men good. St. Thomas puts it this way: "He who seeks the common good of the many as a direct consequence must also seek his own good" (II-II, 47, 10, ad 2). For it is in and through the order of external just relationships that men can become good, but their goodness is their own perfection. They cannot become good by being not good.

Activities occur within society, moreover, that do not fall under equality and debt due in justice. These activities have a correct measure, but it is a relative one, or at least one that cannot be legislated accurately. For instance, we cannot actually give back to God, or to our native land, or to our parents, all that is due to them. We must do something, but the return is never equal. Most of these relationships, in addition to the natural obligation, have further determinations of the divine or positive law according to which certain definite acts must be placed. They do in this sense fall within the pale of the legal and just structure of society, but the acts as such never fully repay the obligation really due (II-II, 80, 1).

Some human activities cannot fall strictly under justice for another reason. The thing due is only due from a certain "goodness of virtue," or better, from the exigencies of virtuous intercourse. Here we must see that some things are absolutely necessary for human life on the part of the individual, such as the virtue of truth in man's words and actions. The thing due in this case is not something that can be measured or determined by a specific law, except perhaps in the case of civil contracts. Yet society cannot exist without this honesty. Liberality and affability, while not absolutely necessary, nevertheless are the perfections of human communication without which society could not last. Still, what is due must be left to the individual determination (II-II, 80, 1).

IV.

We still have not penetrated to the depth of Aquinas's social position if we content ourselves with making the good man, or better, if we permit the man, through his actions, to make himself good. If men are good, they have reached their natural perfection in the sense that their lives are well ordered, naturally speaking, should death come. But in societal philosophy, we look to the true perfection that society itself effects. Something exists beyond virtue, and that is friendship. The principal intention of the law, as opposed to the intention of the lawgiver, is friendship. This is, ultimately, the most beautiful and most powerful gift that God has granted to men. When we pass beyond human society, we find that Aquinas conceives of charity as nothing more than friendship with God (II-II, 80). Nothing is nobler or more humbling than this (I-II, 99, 1, ad 2). As Christians and as human beings, we cannot find a more truly profound and gratifying truth than this fact that our whole social and personal lives are ordained to friendship. Even from our own limited experience, it is clear that friendship is the perfection of human living; and, as we believe, of divine living as well.

Human law, in the mind of St. Thomas, has as its ultimate intention the friendship of men one to another. "The principal intention of human law is to create friendship between man and man" (I-II, 99, 2). The relationship between the establishment of the order of just relations, the common good of the multitude, and the existence of human friendship is a causal one. Friendship presupposes justice even though it passes beyond it in its own sphere. The purpose of justice is primarily to establish equality, either proportional or arithmetical, among the members of society. When this equality is established the function of justice ends, but that of friendship begins (#1632). Both justice and friendship deal with the same reality, that is, human communication. Where there is justice, there is the possibility of friendship. "Justice and friendship are about the same things. But justice consists in communication. For every sort of justice is to another (*ad alterum*). . . . Therefore, friendship consists in communication" (#1658). This must mean that the perfection of human social communication is not justice but friendship.

This conclusion shows that the philosophy of friendship and love is at the root of society. It is the goal of any real human life in the city (the Aristotelian city). Aquinas with Aristotle distinguishes the kinds of friendship according to two principles of logical division: (1) "according to the kind of communication the friendship is based upon," and (2) "according to the end of friendship, that is, utility, pleasure, or virtue" (II-II, 23, 5). Friendship based upon virtue is the highest of these, but we should not fail to understand the importance of friendships of business relationships or of pleasure.

Suppose, for example, a clerk in the store sees the customer coming and greets him with a smile and shows a real interest in the man about to make the purchase. The two have a pleasant exchange over the purchase or about any of a million other things. The customer then leaves and the two never see each other again. Yet, that exchange was a fine thing. It made something otherwise distasteful a pleasant and human thing. Society as a whole benefited, as did both men, because there was a real friendship, based on utility surely, but still a friendship that lessened the tensions among men. Also such friendly communication can form the starting point for a more perfect type of friendship and a more real union among the members of society. In a higher order, Christian charity gives depth and meaning to such friendships (#1700). This is not to deny, of course, that men are naturally friendly with one another in some sense, but it is difficult that this be more than passing, given human nature as it is since the Fall.

Philosophically, utilitarian friendship is called by St. Thomas *"affa-*

bilitas" or friendliness. It is a potential part of the virtue of justice, having an object distinct from the other forms of justice, namely, the external requirements of human order and communication. "And it behooves man to be maintained in a becoming order towards other men as regards their mutual relations with one another, in point of both deeds and words, so that they behave towards one another in a becoming manner. Hence the need of a special virtue that maintains the becomingness of this order and this virtue is called friendliness" (II-II, 114, 1). There is a very definite distinction, of course, between friendliness and the friendship following on virtue. This friendliness is not the friendship of virtue that stands at the very summit of societal life, but it has a very vital part to play in our daily lives.

V.

The perfection of all human communications is friendship based on virtue. This perhaps sounds a bit unusual, but the truth of the matter is clear. A man who, theoretically, is perfectly good is an unhappy man without the friendship that follows on virtue. For as we know, man's true happiness is not simply in the possession of a good number of habits but in virtuous activity and indeed in continuous and pleasing activity. "But to be happy consists in continuous life and operation. For he would not be virtuous who would not delight in the operation of virtue" (#1894). And the peculiar and distinguishing thing about friendship is that it consists in the communication of virtue; that is, of all the highest powers of man: "Friendship ... consists in the communication of virtue" (#1894). Thus the scriptural phrase that it is not good for men to live alone is not solely pertinent to the man-wife relationship. In its own way, it is the nature of every human relationship including the divine one (#1891).

From the communication of virtuous activity is established and secured a society of friends (#1899). The communication of true friendship is principally the one wherein man lives most fully, since he operates according to the highest faculty, reason (#1902). Thus in one sense, to exist (*esse*) for man in this life is to understand *"intelligere"* (I, 18, 2, ad 1). Friendship implies the fact that we come closest to the being and life of a friend precisely when we communicate thought and ideas; for being is what we naturally love. "This, however, is natural; namely, that each one should love his own being" (#1846). If the being of a friend is good; that is, if he is a good man, the highest manifestation of his being, his thoughts and his

loves, will be most delightful to us (#1909). Aquinas adds, "If his own being is of its very nature a thing to be chosen by a happy man, insofar as it
is naturally good and delightful, since, then, the being and life of a friend
are in one's affections the next best thing to one's own life, it follows that
a friend is also a thing to be chosen by a virtuous and happy man" (#1911).
We do need our friends for our very highest endeavors.

The principal act of friendship is what St. Thomas calls *"convivere,"*
which consists in the communication of human ideas and ideals. Hence,
it is the primary human stimulus to contemplation as well as the basic
source of the new and vital thinking required for the continuance and development of a people. Such exchange happens by "living together according to the communication of words and the consideration of the mind.
For in this manner men are said properly to live together, namely, according to the life which is proper to man, and not simply according as they
eat together; as happens in the case of animals" (#1910). The joy and comradeship of friends are, then, found in their intercommunication with one
another. There is a profound truth in the old observation: "The supreme
and ultimate product of civilization . . . is two or three persons talking together in a room."[1] Society is absolutely dependent for its vitality and existence on its ability to bring about adequate friendships among its people. Jacques Maritain, following a suggestion of Gerard Phelan, said that
friendship is society's "life-giving form."[2] Friendship cannot be commanded. Yet it remains that it is the perfection and beauty of society. St. Thomas beautifully remarks about law: "All precepts of law, especially those ordered to the neighbor, seem to be ordained to this end, that men love one
another" (I-II, 105, 2, ad 1).

The love of friendship is the love required by society because it alone
of its very nature makes a society, a real relation between persons.

Friendship adds two things to *amor:* one is a certain society of the one loving and
the one loved in love, namely, in order that they might have mutual love for one
another and that they might know of their mutual love; the second is that they
work from choice and not from passion. . . . Friendship is the most perfect of those
things which pertains to love, for it includes all the foregoing (loves, that is, desire of presence, *dilectio,* benevolence, *beneficium,* concord, *amatio*). Wherefore in
this category we must place charity which is a certain friendship of man to God
through which man loves God and God man; and thus there is effected a certain
association of man to God. (III *Sentences,* 27, 2, 1, ad 1)

1. George Herbert Palmer, *Self-Cultivation in English* (Boston: Houghton Mifflin, 1909), 6.
2. Maritain, *Man and the State,* 10.

Friendship extends to the persons involved so that the terms of the relations are real persons and not accidents. This shows that the nature of the real communication must be a mutual sharing of love and life among rational creatures. The ultimate and most perfect meaning of society, then, will be the acts of men who are friends with one another (III *Sentences,* 28, 1).

Even in material things, friendship is necessary that society be perfected. We have already noted how business friendships are most valuable. Friendships cause the material welfare of society to be better achieved. They provide for the immediate relief of citizens in distress so that the humiliation and degradation that may come from public and therefore impersonal relief is avoided by the love and aid of friends.[3] Thus, the need and existence of so much public aid in our society is an indication of a lack of real friendship. Aquinas reveals his recognition of these problems when he remarked that the intention of one of the Old Testament Laws was "to accustom men to its precepts, so as to be ready to come to one another's assistance," and he then adds "because this is a very great incentive to friendship" (I-II, 105, 2, ad 4). Society should have laws that command men to aid one another in their necessities both in order that friendships may arise from such natural aid and in order that society will not have to burden itself with an excessive amount of works that in this life would be much better provided for by human beings in their own small circle of life.

Aquinas makes a distinction between what he calls political friendship and the true friendship of virtue. The problem concerns the number of friends a man can have and the basis of communication on which the friendship is founded. Obviously, men are not friends in the strict sense with everyone in a society. Sheer human limitation prevents this, for they neither know all of them, nor know them well enough to be true friends. Citizens of a given state can be said to be friends nonetheless. Insofar as all the citizens of a state agree about the form of their government and the nature of the society and culture in which they dwell, they can be called friends. The best examples of this are when two men totally unknown to one another sit down together on a train, both completely diverse in occupation, religion, or place of residence. Yet, both find themselves staunch democrats, and as a result, they find it easy to be friends. The same thing happens when two men of the same nation chance to meet on a foreign soil; they become as long-lost brothers. Such agreement throughout soci-

3. This consideration is the essence of the second half of Benedict XVI's 2005 encyclical, *Deus Caritas Est* (San Francisco: Ignatius Press, 2006).

ety St. Thomas calls concord (#1836). Concord or friendship is something without which no society can long exist.

All political friendship is a part of the potential part of justice previously called friendliness or affability. It is the part, namely, that is concerned with the particularly political relationships. Friendliness includes all relationships. Concord, when not used as a simple substitute for political friendship, is a term generally attributed to the whole of society or people, designating the effect of political friendship among the people. It also refers to the existence of friendliness in general. The term "peace" adds the additional note of personal internal peace and order to external peace or concord.

VI.

St. Thomas, in his understanding of the law, shows his deep and penetrating grasp of the societal problem by revealing the necessary distinctions that modern theories have often come to find in society. He shows, following Aristotle, that society, the life of the city, is the area that depends on human friendship. The state, the area of authority and justice in the city, aims at the external order of human actions. Law is the font out of which these orders are both kept distinct and ordered to one another.

In conclusion, Aquinas relates the Gospel of Christ to societal systems. Natural justice and friendship, even of the highest sort, are not sufficient to the race of men as they exist under the present dispensation. Any intelligent understanding of ourselves and of our fellows tells us that something needs to be added to human beings to overcome the insufficiency of the motivation and the lack of universal love we find at the root of societal friction. Here, however, there is no intention of treating the Christian dispensation from the aspect of eternal salvation and ultimate friendship with God. Rather we treat it from its effect on society, although it would be vain to try to divorce totally the two considerations.

The three major failings of natural society appear to be (1) the inability to make men good, (2) the inability to extend effective love and friendship to all men, and (3) the inability to order rightly men's interior intentions as well as his exterior dispositions. All societal evils can ultimately be placed under one or more of these points. Now the Christian law does not cease at the external act, but it passes beyond to order correctly man's interior acts and ideas, placing order at the very root of the matter (I-II, 91, 4). Also since man is a social animal needing other men, the relationship is most adequately attained by a mutual and sincere love that binds all men to one another (III CG, 117).

The divine law (revelation) is meant as a help to the natural law, which latter also demands that men love one another (I-II, 100, 1).

> The divine law is offered to man in aid of the natural law. Now it is natural to all men to love one another: a proof of which is that a man, by a kind of natural instinct, comes to the assistance of anyone even unknown that is in need, for instance by warning him, should he have taken the wrong road, by helping him to rise, should he have fallen, and so forth: *as though every man were intimate and friendly with his fellow-man* (VIII *Ethic*, 1, 3, 1155a). Therefore, mutual love is prescribed to man by the divine law. (III CG, 117)

We must also notice that the contemplation of divine things presupposes peace and tranquility which are destroyed by a lack of love (III CG, 117). The highest effect of order on earth is true peace out of which springs true contemplation of God (I-II, 29, 1–4). It can be truly said, therefore, that a society of Christian men will come the closest to a perfect civil body on earth, since among them the sources of friction and hatred are most completely recognized and controlled, while the sources of human and divine love are most effectively encouraged and in operation.

Friendship and its perfection in the communication of thoughts and ideals, of dreams and hopes, can sometimes confuse and deceive us. We live our lives as if these friendships were mere incidents or side issues to the main problems of human existence. Yet, the reality is quite otherwise. We live our lives for our friendships. They are the goals, not the means. Sometimes I think that the only modern man who really saw this truth as St. Thomas did was G. K. Chesterton. In this, as in so many things, he reflects conclusions that Aquinas propounded in a more philosophical, though certainly not more interesting, way.

Indeed, Chesterton's book on Charles Dickens is perhaps the best societal analysis ever written. It may be permitted to use the concluding lines of this masterpiece for our own summation of the perfection of friendship in human life:

> The hour of absinthe is over. We shall not be much further troubled with the little artists who found Dickens too sane for their sorrows and too clean for their delights. But we have a long way to travel before we get back to what Dickens meant: and the passage is along a rambling English road, a twisting road such as Mr. Pickwick traveled. But this at least is part of what he meant: that comradeship and serious joy are not interludes in our travel; but that rather our travels are interludes in

comradeship and joy, which through God shall endure for ever. The inn does not point to the road; the road points to the inn. And all roads point at last to an ultimate inn, where we shall meet Dickens and all his characters: and when we drink again it shall be from the great flagons at the tavern at the end of the world.[4]

And again we see that Christianity has not been wrong in proclaiming that the friendships of men are the very means to the friendship with our God—"He who loveth his neighbor hath fulfilled the law."

So too, when Christ Our Lord wished to show to his Apostles his deep love for them, he could only say to them, "No longer do I call you servants. . . . But I have called you friends, because all things I have heard from My Father I have made known to you" (John 15:15; I-II, 65, 5). And here we have it! God shares his ideas and ideals with men. This is indeed the highest and most perfect act of friendship possible to us, his creatures.

4. *The Collected Works of G. K. Chesterton*, vol. 15, *Charles Dickens* (1906; San Francisco: Ignatius Press, 1989), 208–9. This passage will often recur in these pages.

10   THE TRINITY

God Is Not Alone

We acknowledge the Trinity, holy and perfect, to consist of the Father, the Son and the Holy Spirit.
  —First Letter to Serapion, St. Athanasius, d. 373 AD

A little knowledge of the most sublime things, even though it is poor and insufficient, is a source of the highest joy.
  —Thomas Aquinas (d. 1274 AD), *Contra Gentiles*

The intimacy of God himself . . . he is not infinite solitude but communion of light and love, life given and received in an eternal dialogue between the Father and the Son in the Holy Spirit.
  —Benedict XVI, Angelus, Trinity, Sunday, June 11, 2006 AD

I.

Questions about the meaning and destiny of man constantly arise in modern literature and in modern societal thought; the hope for redemption and the longing to hear the voice of God in the world are realities of our times. But the modern world has had the greatest difficulty in understanding the reality of God, which Christians feel is the answer to questions that all modern men are asking. It is, therefore, of some importance to present, in a manner as clear and as simple as possible, the meaning of the Christian God, to see why it is that precisely the Christian view of God can provide the key enabling us in some sense to unlock the mysteries of God as they are related to man in the world.

Christians agree with Moslems and Jews that God is one. "Yahweh, there

---

This essay originally appeared in *Redeeming the Time* (New York: Sheed & Ward, 1968), 63–96. *Redeeming the Time* was my first book, published while I was teaching at the Gregorian University in Rome.

is no one like you!" (Jeremiah 10:6). "Listen, Israel, Yahweh our God is the one Yahweh. You shall love Yahweh your God with all your heart, with all your soul, with all your strength" (Deuteronomy 6:4). This is the legacy that Christians have received from Israel. It is something they must believe in order to be Christians. Christians can, moreover, agree with the Greeks and the Romans that God transcends the cosmos yet is everywhere present in the world. They can even agree, in some part, with those oriental traditions that exalt God by teaching man to abandon himself to the All, rejecting too much confidence in passing things. Christian tradition in the best sense has wisely sought to be universal in outlook, seeking to accept all that is true and valuable in the beliefs and values of other men.[1] To respect and accept the truth contained in other religions is not just a practical expedient but a fundamental aspect of the Christian's openness to reality. The Christian must accept what is true wherever it may be found and from whomever may be discovered holding it. The unity of truth ultimately means at least this.

Yet, in reflecting on the long-term consequences of this willingness to accept the truth wherever found, we cannot ignore the fact that often in modern literature and thought it is the Christian who seems to inherit the task of defending what may be termed the "minimal" God, the God specifically shorn of all distinctions and unique characteristics, a kind of common entity in which as many men as possible can believe without violence being done to anyone's intellectual assumptions. The Christian is thus expected to be the man who can "prove" that God exists, that he is all-powerful, all-knowing, the ruler of all.

When the Christian has completed this task, which is, in its positive sense, surely a vital part of his mission, he is often tempted to relax in the hope that now he has done what he can for the cause of God. But this approach (very laudable in itself) of searching for and accepting whatever element of God may be found anywhere among men has one very unfortunate drawback. In the Epistle to the Hebrews (11:6), a useful and famous passage describes the minimal doctrines that a man must believe about God, namely, that he exists and that he rewards the good and punishes the evil. In discussing this minimum requirement, theologians add that, ideally speaking, the doctrines of the Trinity and the Incarnation should also normally be believed.[2]

---

1. The Vatican Council Documents on Ecumenism, Non-Christians, the Missions, and the Church in the Modern World are especially pertinent to this point.

2. The tradition of the Church on this point can be found in Denziger (*Enchiridion Symbolorum* [Friburgi: Herder, 1955]), #75, 2164, and 2380.

Yet when we compare the content of the doctrine of the Trinity and the Incarnation with those minimal beliefs found in Hebrews, it becomes quite evident that the Trinity and the Incarnation describe something distinctively Christian, while the fact that God exists as a rewarder and punisher is a belief that can be shared by many non-Christians. In other words, the full Christian vision includes, indeed requires, the Trinity and the Incarnation in addition to whatever else might be accepted about God from reason or tradition. The Trinity and the Incarnation are *the* realities about God, about his internal life, about what he does in the world, about his relation to human society. The Trinity and the Incarnation are the realities that govern any Christian discussion of God and the world. In treating reality, Christianity finds its greatest richness in reflecting on these two unique aspects of its faith. Christianity gazes at the world through the eyes of these distinctive doctrines of the Trinity and the Incarnation.

There is, however, a certain paradox here of more than ordinary significance. The evolution within Christianity of its own willingness to accept and encourage the truths and development found outside itself, of its ability to use pagan philosophers and to accept the spiritual insights and customs of other religions, its gradual openness to science and art, its growing sympathy with the faith of all men of good will, its effort in Vatican II to understand even the atheist—all these have made possible, almost for the first time, its own full comprehension of itself and of its belief in the Trinity and the Incarnation in the light of the vastness of the cosmos, of nature and man. Yet, as the early creeds recall to our minds, everything distinctive in the Christian faith is included in these two doctrines of the Trinity and the Incarnation.[3]

With the recent thought of Christianity again focused upon its theoretic basis and upon its significance in the world, there is, therefore, some value in setting forth the long-range implications of these fundamental Christian beliefs as they are reflected in and projected upon the universe and man. We must see in what sense, for man also, the beginning is also the end; in what sense the meaning of the universe stems from and ends in the life of God, in eternal life. For the Christian, the richness and fecundity of the life of God is the explanation and the justification for the glorious, bewildering complexity discovered everywhere in history, in the cosmos, in life, in society, in man himself. Moreover, the life of God, eternal life, is properly man's destiny, his destiny as the total group of men—the city, as Augustine called it, of persons sharing this divine life. In some fashion, we

---

3. These creeds can be found in Denziger, #2-150.

must recognize the unity we have with other men in our common relation to God, in our common presence before him and before each other.

II.

What men think of God permeates what they think of everything else. Historically, and even metaphysically, men have always encountered one primary embarrassment in thinking of God. God is believed to be one; as we have just seen, there are to be no gods like unto him. Even in polytheist concepts, there always seemed to be a place for a king-god, one unlike the rest. The idea that God is one seems almost of necessity to suggest the further, less easily acceptable, implication that God is also alone; that God, like man in modern literature, is also lonely. And no mater how man grapples with this conclusion that God is alone, no matter how rigidly inevitable it may seem, man finds, nonetheless, the aloneness of God quite unacceptable psychologically; indeed he finds the idea just a bit frightening. Even supposing that this one God is Love, with infinite tenderness toward all that is, still the very notion of God having no other, equal to himself, with whom to communicate is repellent. In this respect, God would seem to have been created, if it might be put in this way, just a little lower than man. Hence, we suspect, the primary reason for the many gods of polytheism is precisely this difficulty in believing in one, isolated, majestic God.

Nevertheless, God is one God. The argumentation for this truth seems unassailable. Whatever the lines of reasoning we might take to arrive at the fact of God, all converge upon one God. The hypothesis that two Gods exist simply cannot coherently be thought. The logic of every man takes this for granted.

However, not all explanations of the one-God concept are equally fortunate. Men are model-builders; they conceive their worlds and their gods in some manner after their own experience of life. It is right that they should do this, of course, for their sensory experience does constitute their primary avenue to reality. But we are in control of our models; we can in a very real sense fashion them according to what we choose to see. The almost inevitable effect of this thinking with respect to the one-God concept, however, if it is understood in terms of man's experience, is that the subject-ruler relationship that he finds everywhere in the Creation is applied to God, so that aloofness and dominance become for him the natural images of God's reality. Such images can strongly color our view of God without our realizing it, and may even distort it. It might even be argued, therefore, that the importance of the image we have of God can be judged by the fact that God himself revealed how men were to conceive him. "Philip said, 'Lord, let us see the Father and then we shall be satisfied.' 'Have I been with you all this time, Philip,' said Jesus to him, 'and you still do not know me? To have seen me is to have seen the Father.'" (John 14:8–9).

In looking at the teaching of Christ in the New Testament, we quickly discover that he did affirm that God is one; he did accept the Hebrew notion of God (Mark 12:29). Yet the Christian God is triune. The term "trinity" was of course, coined several hundred years after the death of Christ, probably by Tertullian. Neither Christ, nor the Apostles, nor Paul, nor the Evangelists used it. Christian theology and tradition have come to use it to define the sense, revealed in the New Testament, in which God is triune. In the Gospels and Epistles there is, strictly speaking, no formal treatment of the internal life of God as such. Everything that we know about the vast riches of God's proper life comes through the New Testament, to be sure, but it comes indirectly from examining and explaining what is related in Scripture concerning the Son of God's incarnate life and mission. The Father, the Son, and the Spirit are manifested as participants in the process of redemption. Furthermore, the more profound passages about the life of God, those of John and Paul, are usually the reflection of these writers, more penetrating illuminations about the simple phrases of the baptismal formulas or the utterances of the Lord.

We might almost maintain with some justice that the central teaching of Christianity about God, namely, that regarding God's Trinitarian life, was not Christ's first concern. Yet, even though we accept that the New Testament teaches primarily about the way to salvation rather than about the inner life of God, which in its fullness we can only begin to know in the Beatific Vision, we still feel our need to understand something about the latter. We are aware that the New Testament speaks of the Holy Spirit as a person: he is sent, he sanctifies, he teaches. We are taught that all men are redeemed in Christ by the Father through the Spirit, but we are not really satisfied intellectually by what we can learn in Scripture about the Spirit's exact significance.

All this is but another way of saying that the inner life of God is a mystery, which cannot be fully open and comprehended to men. It is something only God himself can comprehend fully: "After all, the depths of a man can only be known by his own spirit, not by any other man, and in the same way the depths of God can only be known by the Spirit of God" (1 Corinthians 2:11).

Nevertheless, though the mystery will remain, we can learn from the New Testament that this life of God is one of a community of love between three persons. They are distinct: the Son is not the Father but receives the divine nature from him; the Holy Spirit is not the Son but receives the divine nature in the love poured forth from the Father and the Son. Each is constituted a person by his relation to the others in the Godhead. Each fully possesses the divine nature: each shares a community of life in one divine reality.

That God is triune is, therefore, the great Christian truth about God in himself. Later on we shall explore more fully this sketch of the doctrine. Here we wish to stress only that aspect of its meaning: that in the Godhead there is "diversity," since each Person is "another." "This is the statement about the Holy Trinity: it ought to be spoken of and believed not as triple but as Trinity. Nor can it be rightly said that in one God is Trinity, but rather that one God is Trinity."[4] The revelation of the Trinity, even in this imperfect manner, is the ultimate truth of the Christian faith. The Trinity confirms our feeling that it is not good for God to be alone; our instincts are right about the inadequacy of a solitary God.[5] God is unity and community. The Christian vision, therefore, must begin with the Trinity. For if we fail to grasp this truth about God, all else will be of little real value when it comes to understanding the nature and destiny of the world and of ourselves.

It is customary in theology to make a division between those truths about God which can be derived from nature by reason and those derived from revelation. Truth itself demands that such a distinction be maintained; it is important to establish the category to which the knowledge in question belongs. However, to whatever category a specific truth belongs, when we are dealing with the inner life of the living God, it is imperative that we see it within the whole structure of reality. We should recall what God is, what man is, and what the world is.

God did not first create man and then, after some lapse of time, "elevate" him to a higher state. On the contrary, he created the universe for

4. This formula is found in the Eleventh Council of Toledo, Denziger, #528.

5. "We believe in one God the Father Almighty and in one Lord Jesus Christ the Son of God and in one God the Holy Spirit. We worship and confess not three Gods, but Father, Son, and Holy Spirit as one God. Thus there is not one God who is, as it were, solitary; nor is the very one who is the Father also himself the Son, but the Father it is who begets, and the Son who is begotten, and the Spirit is not begotten or un-begotten, neither created or made, but proceeding from the Father and the Son, coeternal, coequal, and co-operator with the Father and the Son." From the Formula "Fides Damasi" (about fifth century), Denziger #71. For fuller discussions of the doctrine see Denziger, #167, 367, 415, 441, 501, 525, 531, 542, 545, 616, 610, 2669.

man called from the beginning to live the divine life as a gift. This does not make God's action in giving man a share in his Trinitarian life any less gratuitous; what it does indicate is that the whole of human life along with the cosmic reality ordained to it will be reflective primarily of the Trinitarian life of God. Hence, if man and nature are to be understood in their Christian fullness, we must meditate with all the powers of our mind on the Trinitarian life that is the source and model of all reality. This need to relate the life of the Trinity to the rest of reality is one of the great challenges of modern thought. It will not mean trying to "deduce" human and cosmic foundations from the life of God; rather, it will mean an effort to see the implications of the fact that God's inner life is both that which reality itself reflects and that to which man, and through him the cosmos, is destined. So revolutionary is the import of the revelation of the Trinity that a vision of reality in its light is required. For this truth transforms all others in a most startling and transcendent manner.

III.

God is Trinity. If we accept the idea of God as creator, we can logically assume that whatever begins and ends in him will somehow be like him. The Creation itself does not, of course, reveal the difference of persons in God. The fact that God is triune and the highest creatures have a special relation to the Trinitarian life is something we know by revelation.

Scripture and theological reflection have provided some precious insights into the inner life of God. Perhaps the very first notion that comes to mind is the fact itself that it is a *life*, a complete life. One of the classical difficulties with the one-God or monistic concept (and a perennial source of doctrinal deviation in Christian history) has been the conjecture that God must somehow need the world because he would be incomplete without it. This notion has often been grounded in a seemingly legitimate and laudable effort to exalt the dignity of man and Creation. The idea was that God was incomplete without man and Creation, so that through his need for them they necessarily participated in the dignity of the divinity. The ironic aspect of this is that the universe and man are really more exalted if God does *not* need them. The problem is: "Why does not God need them?" And the ultimate answer is the Trinitarian life.

We can progress somewhat more deeply into this problem by reflecting on the notion of worship. Contemplation carries with it the idea of receptivity, of being given what is not possessed. Worship is based on contemplation, but the concepts of rejoicing and praise are added when it is applied to the contemplation of God. Worship is the act of man rejoicing in the simple fact of God—"Let God be God!" to use Luther's wonderful phrase. God is transcendent; he is what he is, who he is. God, in other words, is not subject to change. He is complete life in himself, he requires no intrinsic assistance outside himself. God is absolute, complete, and total in himself. When man worships God, he means precisely to accept this truth: that the reality of God, his life and activity, are in and for God himself. The relation between God and all else is such that God *requires* nothing but his own life. This completeness of God does not minimize the realities outside God. Quite the contrary, it indicates the primary truth about God, namely, that his Trinitarian life really is complete in itself, and this truth, as we shall presently see, is the essential and magnificent foundation of the dignity of creatures.

From the New Testament we know that God so loved the world that he sent his only-begotten Son (1 John 4:9). God is concerned with the world. At first sight this seems to be an enormously consoling doctrine. But is it? To maintain that God is concerned with the world is by no means reassuring if that concern is a deterministic thing in God. In such a case, any degree of warmth or support that could flow out of God's concern would vanish, since it would merely be a function of an organized system. Right at this point, the issue of the Trinitarian God arises in its most meaningful form. A God with no diversity of persons, a monolithic God, must seemingly look outside himself to the world as the primary arena of his activity. And by hypothesis, this relationship to the world must necessarily be one of inequality such that the relation is primarily, as we have already suggested in another context, one of mastery and dominance.

This superiority could express itself as a fate in which all events are in fact predetermined or as a caprice in which all set order is capable of being set at naught. In any case, since the life of a monolithic God would be difficult to explain by and of itself, it would apparently have to find its primary meaning in relationship with the world. The Trinity, of course, cannot be "demonstrated" from reason. It is possible to conceive of God as infinitely one, with infinite power, knowledge, love, and wisdom. Yet, such a God is aloof, and almost by default we are led to presume that the essential activity of such a God is concern for the world, since both knowledge and love seem to imply otherness, even otherness of persons.[6]

6. See Aquinas, *Summa theologiae,* I, 32, 1, and ad 2.

Such a consequence, then, brings us back to the Trinity. The doctrine says that the Godhead is manifested in and completed by three distinct persons who equally possess, but in different ways, one divine life. God is not some fourth essence apart from the three; three persons are one God.[7] In other words, the three persons have an inexhaustible love and life in themselves. Let us note what follows from this. Since the Trinity have a complete life within the Godhead, all that is outside their life is related to these persons *not* by necessity but by love and choice. The world thus exists because of the independence and freedom of God. This is made possible by the prior fullness and completeness of the Trinitarian life.[8]

We can take many attitudes towards the world in which we dwell. What we must now recognize is that, at bottom, it is a *chosen* universe; it is the product of a supreme, transcendent freedom, not coerced by any internal deficiency or exigency within God himself. As a result of the completeness of the internal life of God, everything else in the universe is the consequence of a free choice. Wherever we look, we ultimately see freedom, not necessity. And the contingent necessity we do see is thus rooted in the more basic freedom that brought reality outside God to be in the first place.

IV.

From the ideas of life, worship, and the freedom of Creation, the reality of God's own life manifests itself as something whole and complete in itself. But why is it whole and complete in itself? In God, three persons exist. As we have already said, each of these three persons is distinct, one is definitely not the other, and each is different because of his relationship to the others. Theology describes this aspect of Trinitarian life by affirming, as we have noted, that the persons in God are "relations."[9] This means that person in God is wholly unique and irreducible. One person is what he is, he cannot be other; yet his total reality is "toward" the other. Person, in its very essence, then, is "other-oriented." There is and can be no person who is simply for and by himself alone. A person, in order to be a person, therefore, must be totally himself, yet wholly oriented toward, open to, other persons.

---

7. "Thus in God there is only a *'trinitas,'* not a *'quaternitas.'*" This expression is found in the Fourth Lateran Council, Denziger, #804.

8. See John H. Wright, *Order of the Universe according to St. Thomas* (Rome: Gregorian University Press, 1957).

9. See Denziger, #528, 532, 570, 800.

The inner life of God contains diversity and community within itself, both of which imply order. And in the relations that are persons in God, there is a definite, irreversible order of Father, Son, and Spirit.[10] The Father from all eternity begets the Son, from the Father and the Son proceeds the Spirit.[11] In the Holy Spirit, the internal life of God finds its completion in a person who *receives* all that he is from the others, but who is still a person who is God. This means that order and reception are not in their very essence opposed to freedom and diversity, since all three persons are God who is one.

Historically, Augustine, in his book *De Trinitate,* was the thinker who suggested that a diversity of life in God could be best understood after the model of intellection and volition. In his masterful analysis, Augustine suggested how it might be possible for there to be three persons, yet one God with one intellect and one will. Intellection and volition, he pointed out, are aspects of the human life of man. They are not outside him. Yet, by them the otherness and diversity of reality become man's to know, and through knowledge become man's to rejoice in, to go out to. These faculties clearly make man something more than a static being concerned solely with himself. They imply that man's destiny is to be open to the knowledge and love of all things.

In the Prologue to the Gospel of John, it is said that the Word, whose glory was as that of the only-begotten of the Father, was made flesh. Generally in the New Testament, the Incarnation is conceived in terms of fatherhood and sonship. Since the essence of fatherhood is to beget a son to whom the father gives his own nature, and the essence of the generation of a word—or a thought—is the perfect expression of the mind that conceives it, we can see how the concepts of the second person as Son and as Word combine. In God is realized perfectly the desire to give to another all that one is, to have another as the perfect object of one's love.[12] The Son has received perfectly what the Father can give of himself. But the Father remains the Father and the Son remains the Son. The Son is the Godhead as originating from the Father who has no source, who from eternity is. This is part of the intimate life of the one God. The Son possesses the same nature as the Father, but He possesses this divine nature as received from someone, from the Father.

10. Ibid., #573, 805.
11. Ibid., #2–150, 800, 803.
12. See A. Brunner, "Vater und Sohn," *Geist und Leben* 32 (1959): 26–33.

The Son loves the Father as the Father loves the Son. The gift of their love is what both share and wish to return. The Father, therefore, is pure origin, the Son both receives and gives. The Son receives the divine nature from the Father; together with the Father he gives it to the Spirit. The Spirit is pure reception within the Godhead. Yet the Spirit is the starting point, as it were, of what is outside God. This is why all Creation is essentially rooted in choice, gift and love, why it is rooted in the Spirit (Wisdom, chapters 7 and 8).

Within the Godhead, the Spirit completes the life of God. He provides the final element of diversity in God's inner life. He is God as pure gift. What the love between Father and the Son yields is the Spirit. In human terms the value of a gift lies not so much in what it is as in what it represents. What any gift is in its essence—what we intend to give in it—is precisely ourselves. This does not mean that we shall cease in any sense to be ourselves or in any way deny the creative power of the other. On the contrary, both the giver and the one who receives rejoice in the acceptance implied of what each is. There is a perfection in the reality that we are, an acceptance in it which suggests the final excellence of any communication, namely, the return of what we are in the hope that this is the greatest of all gifts. In the Trinity, there is in some higher sense the perfection of this human analogy. The Spirit is precisely God as gift, God as total acceptance, the perfect reception of the divine nature as received personally from the Father and the Son.

The Father as un-begotten origin of the divine life, therefore; the Son as the reflection, as the perfect Word and Son of the Father; the Spirit as gift, the perfect reception of the divine life from the Father and the Son, all indicate that the divine life of persons, the one Godhead, possesses an otherness and a vitality within it that fully contains itself. Personal being in God is *societal*. And since this giving and receiving is mutual, complete, and between persons, the life of God is fundamentally a friendship. The Trinity is friendship. All human life proceeding from the life of the Trinity, then, originates and ends in friendship. In other words, the fact that there is otherness in God, that three persons are related to one another in God, means that the perfection of personal life, its metaphysical as well as its theological perfection, is friendship.

The Trinity, again, is friendship. And friendship requires that its members remain distinct. It is absolutely necessary that friends remain themselves while giving or receiving the new life of the friend whom they choose to love. Failure to perceive this exactly defines the great theoretical problem in Plato's *Symposium,* in which love ends up by destroying the other.[13] Put in Trinitarian terms, the Father is the Father, but begets the Son. The Son is the Son, but is the Word of the Father. The Spirit is the Spirit, but he is the gift of the Father and the Son together. God is only God in otherness, in a distinction of persons. For Christians, the God who does not possess otherness within himself is not their God, since God is love, and love requires equality in diversity, order in unity. And it is this that has been revealed in the Father, the Son, and the Spirit.

Is God free? Is it possible, for example, for there to be such a radical freedom in God that the Father might choose to be the Son instead, or the Son the Spirit? Notions of freedom such as these questions imply presuppose that the freedom of the highest reality cannot be stable. God, the argument goes, should be free to be a rock, or a fish, or the whole universe. Of course, it seems quite obvious from the outset that if God should really choose to become a stone, for example, and should on this supposition proceed really to become one, he would cease to be God.

Freedom in God, then, and consequently in all being, cannot suggest the possibility of annihilation. God is; the persons are. Freedom finally refers either to a goal or reality not as yet achieved outside oneself or to the firmness and persistence of a choice already made. The choice to be something else, some other real being, is equivalent to self-annihilation, which is impossible.

Knowledge, of course, is, in one sense, the choice to be something else; love is the choice to share the life of someone else. But neither of these admits the possibility of annihilation, rather precisely the opposite, the stability and growth of the reality that is known and loved. Knowledge and love are the paths by which we become what we are not, by which we share what is outside us without destroying it. The freedom of God, therefore, refers to his possibility of creating outside himself and loving what he as created, but this Creation outside himself cannot mean creating another God.[14] God simply is not free to create another God. But he is free to create other beings who can share His life. The volition in God itself is the perfection, the absolute rest in the goodness and completeness of God's being itself. The importance of this is that God is ultimately God. This means that there is the possibility of an ultimate choice, of a final, permanent love that need not always be seeking for something else. In that end, because God is love, to love is to keep.

13. This is the tale of Aristophanes (189d–193d). Plato has it mostly right in the rest of the dialogue.

14. See Aquinas, *Summa theologiae*, I, 19–24.

The divine life is one. This life is possessed by three persons, each in his own way. The relationship of those persons to each other is not temporal—the Father is not older than the Son—though it is spoken of in this way out of the exigencies of our human conceptual framework. Rather, as we have seen, it is a question of different ways of possessing the same divine life. These three persons so complete in themselves the potentiality of divine life that there can be no other persons in God.[15] Since each of these persons truly differs from the other, since each acts as a person within the Godhead, and since all else but each other they possess in common in the divine life, the whole reality of what it is to be a person is openness to and reception of another person. The life of God is of its very nature one life, but it is one life which is also a *koinonia,* a communion, a fellowship, a society at its very heart. God is not alone.[16] The ultimate perfection of person, therefore, is not independence and isolation, but rather society and commitment to others, communion with others in a common life and task.

Furthermore, since persons as such are permanently themselves, always radically retaining their distinction from others as independent lives, irreversible and unique—the Father does not become the Son, the Son does not become the Spirit—the diversity of persons is an integral part of personal communion.[17] Hence, any theory that involves the possibility of the merging of the person—be it the human person into God or the persons of God into each other—must be rejected. It follows from this that a society tends to diversity as well as to unity. The Trinitarian foundation of this principle is the three persons in one nature. The model of the perfect society, therefore, is not a monism, a being without distinction. The Trinitarian life of God, then, reveals to us an unexpected richness.

V.

Previously, we mentioned that the New Testament is not primarily concerned with expounding the inner life of the Trinity, but with the Trinity as a factor in the Incarnation. The Incarnation is a means to the salva-

---

15. See Denziger, #804.

16. "We believe and confess the most holy and omnipotent Trinity, Father, Son, and Holy Spirit, one God only but not solitary." Sixth Council of Toledo, Denziger, #490.

17. "Nor do we say that just as there are three persons, so there are three substances, but rather one substance and three persons. For what is the Father is not *ad se,* but relative to the Son, and what is the Son is not *ad se,* bur relative to the Father; likewise the Holy Spirit is not *ad se,* but is referred relatively to the Father and the Son in that the Spirit is predicated of the Father and of the Son." Eleventh Council of Toledo, Denziger, #528.

tion of men that offers to man the ultimate possibility of sharing in the life of the Trinity. Now in the light of what we have seen of the Trinitarian life, just what is the Incarnation and how does it relate to the Trinity? To introduce this subject, we can, perhaps, do no better than to recall the words of the devil in his discussion with Ivan Karamazov just before the trial of his brother Dmitri for the murder of their father. "As soon as men have all of them denied God," the devil muses to Ivan,

the old conception of the universe will fall of itself . . . and what's more the old morality, and everything will begin anew. Man will unite to take from life all it can give, but only for joy and happiness in the present world. Man will be lifted up with a spirit of divine Titanic pride and the man-god will appear. From hour to hour extending his conquest of nature infinity by his will and science, man will feel such lofty joy from hour to hour in doing it that it will make up for all his old dreams of the joys of heaven. Everyone will know that he is mortal and will accept death proudly and serenely like a god. His pride will teach him that it's useless for him to repine at life's being a moment, and he will love his brother without need of reward. Love will be sufficient only for a moment of life. But the very consciousness of its momentariness will intensify its fire, which is now dissipated in dreams of eternal love beyond the grave.[18]

This passage, which we have quoted at some length, is important for many reasons, but primarily for the way in which it points up the problem of the man-God and who he is. Dostoyevsky's devil has here described the alternative to God in classic terms.

We would be imperceptive if we did not recognize in this passage much that is relevant to the belief of many of our contemporaries. Indeed we can even see our own temptations here. This vision of man as essentially and primarily dedicated to the transformation of this earthly life belongs, it seems well to note, to Christianity. Since this mission of world transformation is a true task of man, this charming devil of Dostoyevsky's can isolate it and pretend that it is man's whole vocation. It is, of course, the sole practical alternative to the Trinitarian life as man's ultimate destiny. God does indeed command the transformation of the world by knowledge and science and service, but this effort is not to be conceived as something divorced from the next life and alien to it—a frequent temptation for Christians. The Christian vision of the world is precisely that in which the reality of the world and its tasks comes to share through man in the life of the Trinity.

18. Fyodor Dostoyevsky, *Brothers Karamazov*, translated by Constance Garnett (New York: Halcyon House, 1940), 628.

In the light of the Incarnation and the Trinity, then, the first thing we must recognize is that the very existence of the Trinity—the fact of an everlasting life independent of Creation, and consequently of ourselves—must always undermine and render impermanent any satisfaction or content man may have with the things that are merely of this world. Man has two very real and powerful hopes, so basic that they constitute what he is. One is for the transformation and humanization of the earth on which he lives; the other is for everlasting life, the life that is identified with the life of the Trinity. For it is to share this life with other creatures that God has created us in the first place. In Christianity, these two goals, as it were, the sharing in eternal life and the humanization of Creation, are one vision. Historically, man's humanity has often enough been truncated by an overstress of the next life, to the exclusion or minimization of the significance of his human or earthly mission. Today, however, the opposite temptation seems to be becoming more prevalent—that is, the temptation to follow the suggestion of Ivan's devil to forget God in pursuit of man in this world. The important thing to note here is not that one or the other of these poles has been too much stressed at one time or another, but that both are essential to man. To be man is to neglect neither.

VI.

The problem remains. How is this possible? How can eternal life be combined with the fleeting historical existence of man in the world? The first truth of Christianity is that God is triune. The second is that one of the Trinity, the Son, became man.[19] Who is God? God is the Trinity. But this must seem abstract and vague even after we have seen some of the importance of this revelation. Our thought about God will always tend to be nebulous until we clearly realize that the second person became man. He took on the conditions of finiteness in his very person. The second person, in assuming human nature in addition to his divine nature, by this very act bridges the gulf between the inner life of the Trinity and the life of man on earth. God has appeared among men. In his birth, living, dying, rising again, and ascension, Jesus Christ, that person of the Trinity who without setting aside his divinity took on our humanity, is *forever* in the form of God-man. As the Epistle to the Hebrews so beautifully puts it:

19. "We believe in his Son, our Lord Jesus Christ." St. Augustine, Denziger, #21.

Since in Jesus, the Son of God, we have the supreme high priest who has gone through to the highest heaven, we must never let go of the faith that we have professed. For it is not as if we had a high priest who was incapable of feeling our weaknesses with us; but we have one who has been tempted in every way that we are, though he is without sin. . . . Then there used to be a great number of those other priests, because death put an end to each one of them; but this one, because he remains *for ever,* can never lose his priesthood. It follows, then, that his power to save is utterly certain, since he is living forever to intercede for all who come to God through him. (4:14–15; 7:23–25)

Where Christ is, there is also the Father and the Spirit.

What does it mean that Christ became man? We have seen that the life of the Trinity is complete in itself. It has no need of anything beyond itself; it is itself the end, the perfect life. We have seen also that as a result of this perfect life, everything else in the universe is the product of divine freedom. We noted, further, that the nature of person is such that it can be associated with others in society; that the essence of person, its very structure, is to be open to, related to, the other. Now if there is to be an expansion, as it were, of the life of the Trinity whereby other persons (finite ones, necessarily, as there cannot be two Gods) share in its inner life, the only meaningful way this could happen would be if these finite persons freely chose such a life with the Trinity. The whole of the material and spiritual Creation outside God—a Creation modeled on the Son, as the prologue to John's Gospel tells us, on that person in the Trinity whose reality is the divine life as received and as giving—exists to make such a choice possible for men, to the end that their choice should be truly free, without the necessity that would arise if man were directly placed before the vision of God.

VII.

The first choice that man had of accepting life with God was rejected by him. This rejection, however we conceive it, we call original sin.[20] We often hear complaints about this doctrine, admittedly not an easy one to comprehend. How is it just, it is asked, that we should be affected by an ancient ancestor? Yet, original sin is the dogma of the physical connection of all men to one another in their origin and destiny.[21] However original sin is conceived,

---

20. See Denziger #1512.

21. The encyclical *Humani generis* of Pius XII held that in the present state of our knowledge, the transmission of this sin seems to demand one pair of First Parents. The problem of how this is to be interpreted is much discussed today. In general, however, it would seem that any theory of

it is the doctrine that men are together in some sin or alienation that only God can ultimately overcome. In a sense, we can perhaps understand this doctrine somewhat better if we realize that men do have the chance, and indeed duty, of influencing others. The parents cannot ask their child if he wants to be born; the child cannot oppose the beginning of their profound influence over him, for better or for worse. All men are what they are in large part because of the choices of their immediate and remote forebears. Original sin suggests that this situation was true for the whole human race. In this sense it is the direct result of a true freedom given to finite, material persons to influence for good or ill all human life that originates within mankind.

Nevertheless, original sin and the transmission of it did not deflect God's purpose in regard to man. Man's original choice was, to be sure, a rejection. But the finite will in this life is not something that need remain fixed. It can choose again since it exists in time, in a constant condition of growth. For this reason, another means was initiated that sought to achieve God's original purpose of associating other persons with himself in the life of the Trinity.

By an utterly free and mysterious decree of His own wisdom and goodness, the eternal Father created the whole world. His plan was to dignify men with a participation in His own divine life. He did not abandon men after they had fallen in Adam, but ceaselessly offered them helps to salvation, in anticipation of Christ the Redeemer, "who is the image of the invisible God, the firstborn of every creature" (Colossians 1:15). All the elect, before time began, the Father "foreknew and predestined to become conformed to the image of his Son, that he should be the firstborn among many brethren." (Romans 8:29)[22]

This new plan of God, then, is the cycle of the history of salvation leading from the promise to Adam, to Abraham, to Moses, to David, to the Jewish people, to Christ, and the passing on of this mission through the Apostles to all nations.[23] With the coming of Christ—true man and true God, with his life, death, and resurrection—the possibility of again choosing to live with God was offered to men. Salvation was to be achieved in associating mankind with Christ, our brother, to follow the path through death that Christ himself followed.

---

original sin, no matter how it is thought to be transmitted, will involve and connect the whole human race. See Pierre Smulders, "Evolution and Original Sin," *Theology Digest* 13 (Autumn 1965): 171–76; and Denziger #3895–8.

22. "The Dogmatic Constitution on the Church," in *Documents of Vatican II*, edited by W. Abbott (New York: Guild Press, 1966), 15.

23. See ibid., 111–28.

Christ, in accepting all the consequences of sin, transformed and redeemed all the suffering, all the finitude, and all the limitations of man in this passing world. Even death, the last barrier, was breached. "Death, where is your victory?" Paul asked (1 Corinthians 15:55). In Christ's life, in the fact of the incredible event of the Incarnation, that event whereby finiteness and infiniteness of reality merged into one another, all things proper to man as we know him were recreated in the blessing of the Lord's presence. And although sin, the last alienation from God, remains what it is, a free choice of man, still in Christ this choice too is forgiven and redeemed. "He looked up and said, 'Woman, where are they? Has no one condemned you?' 'No one, sir,' she replied. 'Neither do I condemn you,' said Jesus, 'go away, and don't sin any more'" (John 8:10–11).

No choice against God can remain permanent for the man who is free to choose again in the grace brought by Christ. The act of sin reveals how truly we are bound up with all things, how all things are interconnected, and how all is related to God. Sin is, then, a powerful negative witness to the importance of things. But sin is a choice that is always of something finite, as if it were in isolation from all else. Thus sin is always for itself, indeed, for the self and against God, as God is found present in all the things he has created. Because Christ as God and man is himself concretely connected with all reality, the image of all Creation and the firstborn among men, the damage of sin as it happens in the world can be repaired and transformed in him.

The destiny of mankind is to be saved by the Father through the Son in the Spirit. Mankind is to become Christ's brother; that is, it is to share the life of the Trinity, eternal life, as the Son shares it.

Something which has existed since the beginning, that we have heard, and we have seen with our own eyes; that we have watched and touched with out hands: the Word, who is life—this is our subject. That life was made visible: we saw it, and we are giving our testimony, telling you of the eternal life which was with the Father and has been made visible to us. What we have seen and heard we are telling you so that you too may be in union with us, as we are in union with the Father and with his Son Jesus Christ. (1 John 1:1–2)

But, as we have seen, the life of the Son in the Trinity is a life that both gives and receives.[24] Man, therefore, to be truly like the Son, must receive the divine life, which he does in the gift of Creation and grace, but he must pass

---

24. See Denziger #800.

this life on to others in the Spirit. This is man's mission in the world, his mission of meaningfulness and choice, wherein he actually decides in the concrete historical order of his temporal life whether he elects an eternal life with the Trinity in an openness of love and community. Here theology meets the hints and the agonies of man as we have seen him in modern literature and society. The Christian dispensation is such that this choice of eternal life with the persons of the Trinity is decided by man's openness to his brother in the tasks of this world, but to his brother who is so loved by Christ as to be identified with him. "In so far as you did this to one of the least of these brothers of mine, you did it to me" (Matthew 25:40). "Saul, Saul, why are you persecuting me?" (Acts 9:4).

From these observations on Christ and the Trinity we can see that the Incarnation is God's effort, as it were, to conform to human nature and to assume human destiny, with all material Creation and all human history, into the Trinitarian life. And yet this action is so supremely conformed to man's dignity that it is ultimately an invitation, not a demand, not something coerced. The life of the Trinity is a personal life of love and freedom. None can participate in it on any other terms. And this invitation does not come to man from some place in outer space or from somewhere in the obscure depths of the inner self; rather it comes through the new commandment that we shall love one another as Christ has loved us. We shall live our lives in this gift of mutual openness and friendship. If we reflect deeply on the significance this teaching has for Christian theology, we cannot help being moved by the truth that it means a constant transformation of the earth by the fullest use of our minds, hearts, and hands for the complete human fulfillment of the brothers in whom Christ is incarnated as his body, as Paul tells us (Colossians 1:22).

VIII.

We have, then, in Christianity, in its doctrines of the Trinity and the Incarnation, a simultaneous acceptance of the world—its demands, sorrows, and hopes—and eternal life, an eternal life of persons in society, in community, which through Christ unites mankind to the Godhead. We should ponder the meaning and relevance of these basic Christian truths. The kind of God we believe in tells us what we are. We have seen how we must look on the world as something chosen by God in freedom and love; how Creation is the basis for man's ability to make a free choice of God; how

God in himself is a Trinity of persons; how society and openness to other persons lie at the very heart of both ourselves and God; how the union we seek always retains the reality that we are.

What category or mode of thought is best to sum up what we as Christians are and have as a result of our common faith? What is the outlook on life and the world that best describes our faith? Somehow, the most precise description of this seems simply to be one of utter, complete surprise. This experience of surprise is one we should advert to most often, in any case, but what is of importance here is that we will never be able fully to grasp that the Trinity and the Incarnation are really true until we can fully open ourselves to their abiding freshness and wonder. We need to be open to the astounding and mysterious relationship they have to what we are in our own lives. Indeed, our capacity for being surprised by these things is part of our capacity for being surprised at all that surrounds us everywhere, both in the world of things and in the world of persons.

We can see some of this surprise in facing the vastness of the physical world itself. We cam begin to sense the incredible wonder that things like ourselves should exist at all. When we see the miracle, as it were, that the world itself is, then we can better understand that it is the reawakening of this sense of surprise that will lead us most surely to that state of mind and heart whereby we can again look upon the Trinity and the Incarnation as the astonishing truths they are. They are the truths of the inner life of God. This truth is the foundation of all society that is the Trinity, of the total material and historical life of man with God in Christ.

PART IV

THE MEDIEVAL EXPERIENCE

11   THE POINT OF MEDIEVAL
POLITICAL PHILOSOPHY

The framework of "Christian philosophy"... is that in Christ man received an intelligence which relates to the whole of the universe and of existence, and therefore by definition concerns anyone who engages in philosophizing—and which, moreover, is valid by virtue of a superhuman claim to truth. Should anyone reject this premise, he must in consistency regard "Christian philosophy," however one defines it, as meaningless. The whole of medieval philosophy must remain inaccessible to him, as far as its sole underlying motif is concerned.

—Josef Pieper, *Scholasticism: Personalities and Problems of Medieval Philosophy*

For the Jew and the Moslem, religion is primarily not, as it is for the Christian, a faith formulated in dogmas, but a law, a code of divine origin. Accordingly, the religious science, the sacra doctrina, is not dogmatic theology, theologia revelata, but the science of the law, halaka or fiqh. The science of the law thus understood has much less in common with philosophy than has dogmatic theology. Hence the status of philosophy is, as a matter of principle, much more precarious in the Islamic-Jewish world than it is in the Christian world. No one could become a competent Christian theologian without having studied at least a substantial part of philosophy; philosophy was an integral part of the officially authorized and even required training.

—Leo Strauss, "How to Begin to Study Medieval Philosophy"

I.

In 1973, the Spanish philosopher Salvador de Madariaga received the International Charlemagne Peace Prize in Aachen, in Germany. The city of Aachen, he pointed out, the ancient seat of the Holy Roman Empire, of Charlemagne himself, has its own name in most European languages—Aken, Aix la Chapelle, Aquisgrán. This variety of name implies a spiritual unity that predates the formation of modern European languages and states. At the conclusion of his remarks, de Madariaga recalled the com-

This essay was originally published in *Perspectives on Political Science* 28 (Fall 1999): 189–93.

mon heritage of Europe, its diversity within its unity. He made a suggestion that sums up, perhaps better than any similar proposal, what is at stake when we speak of medieval political philosophy and its legacy, both with regard to the classics that preceded it and to modernity that followed it.

"Our faith would therefore have to rest on something beyond and above the Common Market or even common defence," de Madariaga reflected,

and so we return to the two rivers of spirit on whose confluence Europe is born. Now, precisely here, we meet a dangerous paradox. We want to set up a European State, but we are dying of too much State about us. We must instill into our youth the feeling of individual responsibility for individual destiny. . . . We should . . . formally receive as European citizens every new generation, at an adequate time, and during the ceremony present to each youth a copy of a book bearing the text from Plato describing the death of Socrates, and from the Gospels, describing the death of Christ, not merely because they are the two spiritual fathers of Europe but because they both perished at the hands of the state.[1]

Must the state, killer of its philosophers and of the Savior Himself, continue to strangle also its citizens? Is medieval political philosophy the peculiar locus, the point, at which we see most clearly what the political order might be because we see there most clearly that it is not itself "the City of God," to recall Augustine's famous expression?

Such is the double heritage, Socrates and Christ, Athens and Jerusalem, about the meaning of which the medieval thinkers asked themselves. That is to say, they became vividly aware of their own order because they understood and made their own possession the traditions and positions that came to them from other times, from, so they held, that "time" beyond time they designated as eternity. Unlike modernity, they did not think it permissible or even scientific simply to ignore or actively to oppose the tradition of revelation when considering political things. Nor did they deny that reason and experience had something legitimate to say about political things.

All medieval thinkers had read their Augustine, who told them not to be surprised if such dire events as the killing of Socrates and of Christ should happen again and again in this world, in their very midst, in their very cities. Boethius, who was killed by an emperor, and Sir Thomas More, who was killed by a king, at the far ends of the middle ages, can be said to

---

1. Salvador de Madariaga, "Europe of the Four Karls," *The Tablet* (June 23, 1973): 530–31.

stand as proof of this possibility. The Augustinian heritage of "political re-alism" has prepared us for what ought not to happen but still does happen among us. "Augustine believed . . . that he had uncovered the lowest com-mon denominators of human existence in the *saeculum:* a need for social life, hence for peace and order; a divided will easily traduced by a lust to dominate and to possess; a world of insoluble estrangements, perils and shortcomings. But this was a man who loved and hoped."[2] Augustine thus understood in advance the data of a Machiavelli at the beginnings of mo-dernity, but he did not conclude with it. He did not think that understand-ing the worst in us justified our ignoring the best. We should ignore nei-ther the best we can understand by our own power nor the best to which we might be called.

Medieval men came later to read Aquinas, who told them that the state, while it could indeed be ruled by wicked men and be configured in distorted regimes, also, as Aristotle maintained, had something positive to accomplish, by and for honorable men, in and about this world. Man was a political animal, even in the Fall, even before the Fall. The polity was not simply or primarily the result of original sin, even though that sin had plenty to do with how it appeared among us and why there were recur-ring disorders that the state could not seem effectively to remedy. Through reading the very text in John's Gospel in which Pilate, with jurisdiction in the case, questioned Christ about His "kingship," all medieval men knew that the functionary of the Roman province was told that even his author-ity was from God. It was not, as such, denied legitimacy in the accounts of revelation.

II.

The standard texts discussing the history of medieval political philos-ophy—the McIlwanes, the Sabines, the Dunnings, the Carlyles, with their more recent followers—do not hesitate to see specifically medieval origins for modern constitutionalism, for representation, for elections, for limited monarchy, for guilds, for civic organization and beauty, for universities, for legal systems, for commerce, for business, for the mitigation of slavery, and for the idea of submitting the war power to political rule.[3]

2. Jean Bethke Elshtain, *Augustine and the Limits of Politics* (Notre Dame, Ind.: University of Notre Dame Press, 1995), 91.

3. George H. Sabine, *A History of Political Theory,* 3rd ed. (New York: Holt, 1965); Walter

"The main questions of that scholastic thought of the thirteenth century seem to have been these," J. W. Allen wrote,

What is the nature of obligation as between man and man, and, in connection with and dependence on that, what is the nature of political obligation? What is the purpose which justifies us to reason all that we mean by government? Or, in other words, what is the true function of government? And, finally, what is the character of that state the realisation of which will satisfy man's needs and aspirations? This last is the question Plato had asked in the *Republic*. These questions, though not exactly in the form I have given them, are raised at every point in the writings of the twelfth and thirteenth century. The question of the extent of civil authority and law-making power was wholly bound up with the question as to moral obligation in general. The controversy as to the relations between Pope and Emperor, stripped of its non-essentials, was a controversy as to the end and purpose of life on earth.[4]

That is, it makes considerable difference if man is the highest being and hence political science the highest science. This is what Aristotle had observed would be the case if, contrary to fact, there were no transcendent order.

If the "end and purpose of life on earth" turn out to be nothing but life on earth itself, then politics becomes not just the highest moral discipline but the highest science itself. This "highest" science then defines what is right or wrong within the polity. It determines the basis on which

Ullmann, *Principles of Government and Politics in the Middle Ages* (New York: Barnes & Noble, 1961); A. J. and R. W. Carlyle, *Mediaeval Political Thought in the West*, 6 vols. (Edinburgh: William Blackwood & Sons, 1903–36); F. J. C. Hearnshaw, ed., *Social and Political Ideas of Some Great Mediaeval Thinkers* (New York: Barnes & Noble, 1967); William Y. Elliott and Neil A. McDonald, *Western Political Heritage* (Englewood Cliffs, N.J.: Prentice-Hall, 1949); J. B. Bury, H. M. Gwatkin, and J. P. Whitney, eds., *Cambridge Mediaeval History*, 8 vols. (Cambridge, England, 1926–36); W. A. Dunning, *A History of Political Theories, Ancient and Medieval* (New York: Macmillan, 1902); Mulford Q. Sibley, *Political Ideas and Ideologies: A History of Political Thought* (New York: Harper & Row, 1970); Otto von Gierke, *Political Theories of the Middle Ages*, translated by Frederick William Maitland (Boston: Beacon, 1958); Heinrich Rommen, *State in Catholic Thought* (St. Louis: B. Herder, 1945); Charles Howard McIlwane, *Growth of Political Thought in the West* (New York: Macmillan, 1932); Christopher Dawson, *Religion and the Rise of Western Culture* (Garden City, N.Y.: Doubleday Image, 1958); Bede Jarrett, *Social Theories of the Middle Ages* (New York: Frederick Ungar, 1966); R. W. Southern, *Western Society and the Church in the Middle Ages* (Harmondsworth, England: Penguin, 1977); Henri Pirenne, *Economic and Social History of Medieval Europe* (New York: Harcourt, 1937); J. H. Burns, ed., *Cambridge History of Medieval Political Thought* (Cambridge: Cambridge University Press, 1988); and Arthur P. Monahan, *Consent, Coercion and Limit: The Medieval Origins of Parliamentary Democracy* (Montréal: McGill-Queen's University Press, 1987).

4. J. W. Allen, "Politics," in *Mediaeval Contributions to Modern Civilisation*, edited by F. J. C. Hearnshaw, with a preface by Ernest Barker (New York: Barnes & Noble, 1967), 260–61.

man stands over against the counterclaim that man has no authority higher than himself. The modern conflation of metaphysics into politics has
its origins in an erroneous understanding of precisely "the end and purpose of life on earth." Medieval political philosophy is the effort to think
properly about politics when man, in his one given being, both belongs to
and transcends the *civitas,* the civil community. The medieval people were
aware that something is at work in the world that is not wholly explained
by the world itself. For medieval thinkers, politics had a place within overall intellectual order. But it did not form the intellectual order itself. To
know the truth of things included knowing the truth of political things,
knowing where politics stood in the ranking of other things.

III.

Classical political philosophy, post-Aristotelian political philosophy,
medieval, modern, and even post-modern political philosophies are not
merely or primarily descriptions of politics within the historic time in
which they were written and formulated, even though this description is
a worthy academic endeavor. Philosophy itself is the effort to understand,
by the unaided power of the human intellect, *what is,* in its causes and
its wholeness. Philosophy includes what the various philosophers have
thought it to be. The errors of the philosophers are, ironically, an essential component of philosophy itself. Such errors live, and should live, as
Aquinas taught us, in our active intelligence precisely as considered errors.
Philosophy arises within an embodied intelligence that finds itself already
existing within things that it did not make but toward which its mind is directed in order to understand. The philosopher as an existing being and as
an existing this-kind-not-some-other-kind of being, that is, a rational animal, begins from within an order he did not make but to which he is open
through his intellect. His mind is a *tabula rasa,* but not the world to which
his mind is directed.

The need to add the term "unaided" to the normal power of the human
intellect implies, to be sure, a whole philosophical effort and tradition. The
adjective "unaided" never occurred to Aristotle to qualify reason; yet, as
St. Thomas was to demonstrate, it was very pertinent to Aristotle, to understanding even the truth of the great Greek philosopher. This addition
refers to the tradition of revelation that suggested that, for its highest efforts to know the meaning of man and the order of the world, the natural intellect was, in its own terms, insufficient, but not wholly helpless or

deceptive. But this very insufficiency, as Aquinas again shows (I-II, 91, 4), is solidly grounded in things that the intellect, by its own unaided power, acts on and seeks to know. Revelation appears to reason, thinking properly on itself, more as a curious harmony related to some whole than as a contradiction absolutely separating one realm from the other. The famous "two truth theory" in Arabic and late medieval theory sought to propose a workable solution for any problems between revelation and reason whereby the two could "contradict" each other; that is, though contradictory, both could be true. This move, however, split the integrity of the human mind in two. Medieval theory, including medieval political philosophy, at its best, however, found enough reason in revelation and enough perplexing lacunae in reason to lead it to suspect that the whole includes both in some coherent order.

Perhaps it is not wholly proper to speak of political philosophy as merely a "branch" of the whole that is philosophy, though it is that also. Political philosophy has the added burden of convincing the politician to permit philosophy to happen, at least in public. The conflict of politics and philosophy is, no doubt, an ancient one, as is the conflict of both with poetry. The medieval thinkers knew something of Plato, if only through Cicero or Augustine. The politician can use his coercive powers against the truth of the philosopher by threatening his life in exchange for accepting theories compatible with going civil theology. All medieval people, unlike most moderns, knew what happened to Christ. However, this coercion exercised by the politician on the philosopher or prophet works for the politician only so long as the philosopher ceases to prepare for and to accept death. The philosopher who simply supports the regime is never a threat to the regime. When the politician kills the philosopher or saint, what he does is to immortalize the reason why the philosopher opposed the state. This very act of political force against which the philosopher objected served to define the limits of the political order.

One could, perhaps, define modern political philosophy as that philosophy that does not consider it necessary, whether justified or not, to ponder the pertinence of revelation to reason. Medieval political philosophy, in a sense, arrived after medieval revelation and after the communities it built. Ralph Lerner and Mushin Mahdi point out that there were two ways to deal with this representation of classical philosophy within the order of life erected around the various Christian, Jewish, and Muslim revelations. The Muslim and Jewish revelations were presented primarily as "laws." This meant that the pious member of the community defined his standing before God insofar as he did or did not observe the laws. In varying degrees, the civil order itself was constituted by the order of revelation.

Broadly stated, theology was the paramount science in Christianity. The Christian community was constituted, not by a single divine Law that comprehensively prescribed opinions and actions of every kind, but rather by a sacred doctrine. The custodians of this doctrine were apostolic successors, the hierarchy, and the theologians, not the jurists. In Islam it is the all-embracing Law and its study that are supreme. Theology occupies a prominent, though subordinate position. Judaism, like Islam, is constituted by a comprehensive revealed Law.[5]

This meant that the pious member of the community defined his standing before God insofar as he did or did not observe the laws. In varying degrees, the civil order itself was constituted by the order of revelation.

It is perhaps well to notice that in Christianity, "sacred doctrine" is not what is directly revealed. What is believed is that from the inner life of the Trinitarian God, the person of Christ, true God and true man, came to dwell amongst us in a certain time and place. This basic belief is reflectively and authoritatively spelled out in sacred doctrine in order that we can understand it as accurately as possible. Sacred doctrine, however, was not the revelation itself, but a careful explanation of it. The mind seeks to know and state the truth of who Christ was. The sacred doctrine is not the direct object of belief, but rather the human effort to reflect on and state clearly what this revelation meant. In this sense, it is a work of reason stimulated by a revealed teaching.

IV.

What is the point of medieval political philosophy? Let me cite two passages I recently found in the local newspaper. The first concerns a liberal Anglican Christian bishop commenting on the fact that the African and Asian bishops at the Lambeth Conference upheld the sixth commandment ("thou shalt not commit adultery") as an essential part of Christian revelation. The Bishop of Newark accused African bishops of being "superstitious" in upholding the classical form of Christianity. John Paul II himself recently affirmed in his encyclical, *Veritatis Splendor,* the same principle that the African and Asian bishops did. The reason the bishop gave for his modern view of the sixth commandment was that it was "ignorant of modern

5. Ralph Lerner and Mushin Mahdi, "Introduction," in *Medieval Political Philosophy: A Sourcebook* (Ithaca, N.Y.: Cornell University Press, 1978), 12.

science."[6] The logic of this view is that Christian revelation has no rational basis in human experience itself. The faith is now judged solely in terms of a "higher" criterion, namely, modern science, whatever that is at a given time.

Needless to say, this position that the commandment is "unscientific" makes science a more absolute faith than revelation ever was. There is, in fact, no "science" that decides that the sixth commandment is counter to reason, and every evidence that it protects human life. Or to state the issue in terms of medieval philosophy, revelation is not against reason but addresses itself to reason, in this case the proper relation of the sexes, precisely in a manner that guides reason to be more reasonable. The argument is not whether there is a "reason" in error or sin, but in whether this reason, this statement of what it is, corresponds with a reality that the reason itself did not originally constitute in its intelligibility.

The second issue was from the review of a book on Islam. This is the passage: "One of those blocks (that prevent the 'Middle East from entering the mainstream of modernity') is the orthodox tenet that the Koran and the scriptures contain all the knowledge required to deal with the problems of contemporary society."[7] For Christianity, revelation is not a substitute for experience or for the books of the political thinkers about the proper rule of the city. The Koran, on the other hand, is conceived to be a description of the best city or regime. All regimes not embodying its strictures are held to be inferior. That is, revelation is a law. However, from the view of the medieval Islamic political philosophers, this prophecy needs to be judged by a higher science. Thus, it is possible to allow the public order to be ruled by the law for those who have not risen to philosophic excellence. Inasmuch as it is dangerous to manifest one's philosophic questioning of the law, the philosopher is left with "two truths." He can acknowledge that the best existing regime is the one given by the Prophet, but in his seclusion he still reflects on its truth in terms of a philosophy that might indicate the superiority of some other regime at least in speech.

Taken together, these two passages reveal the abiding pertinence of medieval political philosophy not just as an antiquarian interest but as something found in the daily press. For some, even for some Christians, science has replaced revelation. For some Muslims, the law has replaced

6. *Washington Times*, August 8, 1998, A12.

7. Review by Arnold Beichman of Milton Viorst, *In the Shadow of the Prophet: The Struggle for the Soul of Islam*, in *Washington Times*, August 9, 1998, B6.

politics, so that the philosopher has to become a strictly private man in order to survive. Unlike Socrates, the philosopher is not killed by the state;
rather he is simply reduced to silence or irrelevance. For both the Christian who takes his "revelation" primarily from "science" and the Muslim
who does not protest the law in public, the active interrelation of reason
and revelation, the medieval reality, are reduced to a practical monism.

E. B. F. Midgley, writing of the problem of modernity seen in the analysis of Eric Voegelin, sets down the essential framework of the medieval
position on faith and reason as seen in Aquinas. That is, an effort is made
to know and to state the truth taking into consideration both reason and
revelation. "Voegelin rightly sees that the natural order is incomplete and
that it needs to be open to that which is divine and transcendent," Midgley writes.

He [Voegelin] also rightly insists that divine revelation is mysterious and that
the divine truth cannot be fully comprehended or mastered by man in this life.
If Voegelin had confined himself to statements such as these, his teaching would
have been reconciled with the teaching of St. Thomas Aquinas. Departing drasti-
cally from Aquinas, however, Voegelin makes the unjustified supposition that the
mysteriousness of the divine revelation precludes the definitive definition by the
Church of the articles of faith. Voegelin insists that "uncertainty is the very essence
of Christianity." He wants the constancy of a tension between truth and untruth
as if the persevering attempt to find truth and to separate it from untruth would
somehow tend to destroy the reality of human existence. Indeed, he even writes of
the "murderous possession of truth," as if there were something evil in seeking to
find it unalloyed with error.[8]

The "reality of human existence" does not exclude but demands the effort
to state the truth as clearly and as accurately as possible. The fact that the
propositions containing such efforts lead to and indicate a reality more
penetrating than the formulations themselves is itself included in any understanding of Christian teaching.

V.

The point of medieval political philosophy is not merely Augustine's
"City of God" and "city of man" but their mutual relationship and difference within existing polities. It is true that one of the sources of cultural vi-

8. E. B. F. Midgley, *Ideology of Max Weber: A Thomist Critique* (Aldershot, Hants.: Gower,
1983), 4.

tality in the West has been precisely the two sources of authority and their mutual addressing themselves to man and to the condition of man in the world. But the hypothesis of this relationship was that truth and knowledge had a common source or origin, that they did not contradict each other, as Aquinas said. Medieval theory did not consider the human mind ever to match or comprehend the divine mind and its relationship through eternal law to the order of things. There was a certain contentment with mystery, but a mystery that was bathed in light and not confusion. All intelligence, including human intelligence, was able to know after its own manner.

Insofar as political philosophy recognized the limits of the city, and thereby let the drama of the highest things take place with a freedom and order that did not substitute the political authority for the divine authority, it made possible the free consideration of what was not political.[9] The politicization of the speculative order is what is characteristic of modernity wherein will, specifically human will, is found at the center of both nature and human nature. Indeed, human will interposes itself in a manner that makes it divine will. The transition from William of Occam and Marsilius of Padua to Hobbes marks the end of medieval thinking. The divine will, presupposed to nothing but itself, presupposed to no divine reason in Occam and Marsilius, becomes political will in Hobbes, again a will presupposed to nothing but itself. In a sense, the late medieval treatises on the divine will and the early modern treatments of the sovereign are the same treatise.

Do we still need medieval political philosophy, if not to clarify our polities, at least to clarify our minds? Pierre Manent concluded his *City of Man* with these rather enigmatic and remarkable words:

The emperor of the visible empire, "sol invictus," the invincible sun, has as his opponent and successor the vicar of the invisible empire, "servus servorum Dei," the servant of the servants of God. Some other time we shall study the cause that resides in the separation of the two Romes. We must prepare for a second and altogether different crossing. We never understand more than the half of things when we neglect the science of Rome.[10]

9. See James V. Schall, "What Is Medieval Political Philosophy?" *Faith and Reason* 16 (Spring 1990): 53–62.
10. Pierre Manent, *The City of Man* (Princeton, N.J.: Princeton University Press, 1998), 206.

The point of medieval political philosophy, in the scope of academic things, is that we have busily produced generations of scholars who never have understood "more than half the things."

The "inaccessibility" of medieval philosophy, to use Josef Pieper's term, has remained among us as an active absence. That is, what is lacking in a people who have known the elevation of grace but who have neglected to account for its effect is an elevated expectation devoid of any grounding except in the human will. The lack that Strauss saw in the Jews and the Muslims has become endemic to the moderns also. It manifests itself in political philosophies that substitute themselves for the metaphysics of being, of *what is*. In a strange way, stranger than we might admit, this is the story of our academic and, all too often, of our personal lives. We are a people who contemplate only ourselves, a people who are aware of only half of the things that count. Such is the point of medieval political philosophy. To the readings from Plato and John that de Madiaraga offers to each new citizen of our culture in which we seek to know "all things knowable," to cite Dante, it is incumbent to add a longer work. This work, as its author says in its very beginning, is also intended for young students, in the belief that they too can know the truth of things. This book is the *Summa theologiae* of Thomas Aquinas, the philosopher and theologian of the Middle Ages, the absence of whose presence has defined our modernity.

12   "POSSESSED OF BOTH A REASON AND A REVELATION"

If . . . we learn from medieval theologians what is faith in an objective truth and what is an objective philosophical knowledge, we shall find ourselves possessed of both a Revelation and a Reason. There then will be something to harmonize, and anyone attempting to do it will end at last in meeting the real problem.

—Étienne Gilson, Richards Lecture, University of Virginia, 1937 [italics added]

The Church has no philosophy of her own nor does she canonize any one particular philosophy in preference to others. The underlying reason for this reluctance is that, even when it engages theology, philosophy must remain faithful to its own principles and methods. . . . At the deepest level, the autonomy which philosophy enjoys is rooted in the fact that reason is by its nature oriented to truth and is equipped moreover with the means necessary to arrive at truth. A philosophy conscious of this as its "constitutive status" cannot but respect the demands and the data of revealed truth.

—John Paul II, *Fides et Ratio*

On this very morning, Monday, June 11, 1950, I returned to the writing of this article after reading in a current Parisian daily the following words: "The Church possesses a philosophical doctrine that is proper to her, that is to make Christians that are subject to her teaching, this is what the Church requires before anything else." No, the Church does not have a "philosophical" doctrine that is proper to her, but she has a faith that is proper to her.

—Étienne Gilson, "Wisdom and Time"

I.

In the summer of 1926, Étienne Gilson was invited to teach summer school at the University of Virginia at Charlottesville. This was his first visit to the United States. His friend, Professor Albert G. A. Balz, had invited him to give two lecture courses, one, "The Development of Thought

This essay was originally published in Peter Redpath, ed., *A Thomistic Tapestry: Essays in Memory of* Étienne *Gilson* (Amsterdam: Rodopi, 2002), 177–91.

from the Twelfth to the Sixteenth Centuries," the second, "The Evolution of French Thought since the Sixteenth Century."[1] Gilson, haltingly learning English at the time, seems to have enjoyed this visit and these students. His foreword to the Richards Lecture, which he gave in Charlottesville in 1937, specifically recalls these earlier summer school students, who "helped me through a difficult task." One can hardly overestimate the debt that American and Canadian scholarship owes to all those students and faculty who helped Gilson become familiar with academic life and language on these shores.

Balz had suggested that the theme for the Richards Lecture might be "Scripture and Authority in Medieval Thought." However, Gilson had something else in mind.

This subject (reason and revelation in the middle ages) allowed Gilson to return to the challenging theme of double truth associated with the much-maligned Siger of Brabant. He had dealt with the theme once before [*"La doctrine de la double vérité,"* in *Etudes de philosophie médiévale.* Strasbourg, 1931] and was anxious to try again in the light of his own the *Unity of Philosophical Experience* and especially of (Jacques) Maritain's *Distinguer pour unier,* which had made a strong attempt to bring faith and knowledge into organic unity.[2]

The Richards Lecture is startling in its scope and in its concise brevity. Indeed, in the light of its treatment of Muslim thought and of what happens to philosophy itself or to theology when either declares its own absolute autonomy, Gilson's book remains remarkably contemporary.

"You will not civilize a tribe of Bedouins by teaching them metaphysics," Gilson soberly quipped in 1937.[3] Needless to say, this very issue has not been completely resolved even yet. Presumably, Gilson had no objection to teaching metaphysics to natives of any sort, even academic American ones, if it were possible, but he was quite clear in practice that something more than pure metaphysics was first needed, a sort of *perambula metaphysicae.* One only needs to recall here the reason given in the *Crito* for Socrates' not accepting banishment to Thessaly, to an uncivilized kingdom, namely that one requires a certain sophisticated civilization to talk

1. Laurence K. Shook, *Étienne Gilson* (Toronto: Pontifical Institute of Medieval Studies, 1984), 143.

2. Ibid., 234.

3. Étienne Gilson, *Reason and Revelation in the Middle Ages* (New York: Scribner's, 1938), 43. (Henceforth, this book will be cited as RRMA.) It is of some interest that at almost the same time, Hilaire Belloc was writing on this same subject of the importance and nature of Islam, "Great and Enduring Heresy of Mohammed," in *Great Heresies* (New York: Sheed & Ward, 1938), 71–140.

metaphysics in the first place, otherwise the philosopher is a mere spectacle for the entertainment of the barbarian king and his companions (45c).

What Gilson brings up in the Richards Lecture is the very nature of metaphysics in Islam and, more particularly, since the Bedouins are not philosophers, though Avicenna and Averroes are, of the revelation of Allah, of the nature of this Allah expressed in philosophical terms. The problem of the "two truths," of a truth of reason and a truth of revelation that can contradict each other, remains among us as the background to our current worldwide political turmoil. Rereading the Richards Lecture more than six decades after it was originally given brings up in a graphic manner the often obscure relationship between the politician and the philosopher, a relationship that was, of course, at the heart of philosophy itself, as the life and death of Socrates continually teaches us. The problem of Christian martyrs in Islamic countries is not totally unrelated to this same question.[4]

And what may be an issue even more profound than that of the philosopher and the politician is the relation of revelation to theologians who seek to interpret revelation solely in terms of this world and its closed ideologies or philosophies. Indeed, the question is more to the fore in efforts to achieve all the ends of Christian revelation, i.e., salvation, without any influence of this same revelation, without any reference to its doctrine or practice.[5] Gilson understood what was at stake: "To any sincere believer who is at the same time a true philosopher, the slightest opposition between his faith and his reason is a sure sign that something is the matter with his philosophy."[6] If, by contrast, we can define theological "modernity," we might say that it is when the slightest opposition between faith and reason occurs, and we think that there is something wrong with theology or faith, not our reason.

"We are compelled to distinguish political philosophy from political theology," Leo Strauss wrote in 1959. "By political theology, we understand political teachings which are based on divine revelation. Political philosophy is limited to what is accessible to the unassisted human mind."[7] We are equally "compelled" to wonder, on reading these lines in the light of Gil-

4. See sections on Islam in Robert Royal, *Catholic Martyrs of the Twentieth Century: A Comprehensive World History* (New York: Crossroad, 2000); and Peter Marshall, *Their Blood Cries Out: Untold Story of Persecution against Christians in the Modern World* (Dallas: Word, 1997).

5. See Joseph Ratzinger, "Dominus Jesus," *The Pope Speaks* 46 (January/February 2001): 33–56. See James V. Schall, "On Being Faithful to Revelation," *Homiletic and Pastoral Review* 101 (March 2001): 22–31.

6. RRMA, 83.

7. Leo Strauss, "What Is Political Philosophy?" in *What Is Political Philosophy*, 13.

son, whether we are forbidden to compare, relate, and reflect, once we have brought them out, on the political teachings found in revelation with what "unassisted reason" comes up with? Surely, without violating the integrity of either revelation or reason, we are not "compelled" to let the two bodies of knowledge simply sit there unrelated? This bringing them together would involve two questions: "To what extent can we 'understand' what we do not believe?" And "why is what we do not believe sometimes, at least, in agreement with what we learn by our 'unassisted reason'?"[8] If we cannot ask such questions, why not? We are, in fact, "compelled" to ask them.

How one might confront these latter questions of faith and reason might well still have something to do with Aristotle, the "Philosopher," as St. Thomas called him. Indeed, in his discussion of Averroes, Gilson pointed out that philosophy was not necessarily to be identified as such with everything Aristotle held, as Averroes seemed to think. Averroes assumed this identity between philosophy and the literal Aristotelian teaching because he considered his own revelation, that of Islam, to be at best a myth for the guidance of the masses of Bedouins and others who could not be philosophers.[9] On the other hand, "Thomas Aquinas would follow Aristotle when he was right, but no further, and because he was right."[10] Since philosophy itself was not identical with Aristotle, even though Aristotle was the greatest of the philosophers and had it mostly right, it would be possible to learn at least some philosophical things indirectly from revelation when one came to consider the truth of Aristotle's propositions as they related or did not relate to this same revelation.

Moreover, as much of the modern world was built on a specific philosophical rejection of Aristotle, it seems incumbent to reconsider Aristotle precisely because of the relativism and skepticism that have come to dominate modern philosophy in his absence. "The very rise of so-called modern science and modern philosophy," Henry Veatch well observed,

was originally associated—certainly in the minds of men like Galileo and Descartes—with a determined repudiation of Aristotle: it was precisely his influence which it was thought necessary to destroy, root and branch, before what we now know as science and philosophy in the modern mode could get off the ground. Accordingly, could it be that as so many of us today are turning our backs so bitterly

8. See Ralph McInerny, *St. Thomas Aquinas* (Notre Dame, Ind.: University of Notre Dame Press, 1982), 145–65.
9. RRMA, 43–50.
10. Ibid., 79.

on all the hitherto boasted achievements of modern culture, we might find ourselves inclined, indeed perhaps even compelled, to return to the Aristotelianism
that both antedated and was considered antithetical to the whole modern experiment in knowledge and in living?[11]

Veatch too was "compelled." There is a double irony here. It is precisely
those things in Aristotle that needed correcting in order for the valid parts
of modern science to be discovered that came about because of the influence of revelation on our understanding of the world. The themes of a definite beginning, of a stable set of secondary causes, and of the need to in-
vestigate empirically that made science possible are ideas that owed their
origins to revelation.[12] Thomas's agreeing with Aristotle "when he was
right," and not just because he was Aristotle, serves in its own way to distinguish understandings not susceptible to ideology from those that are.

II.

Étienne Gilson was conscious of the real, though often difficult to
prove, relationship between the events of the mind and those of subsequent public order or disorder. The wars of the world are usually fought
out previously in the minds and hearts of the clerical and academic dons
before they ever appear in legislatures or on fields of battle. Incomplete or
erroneous ideas of the minds of one generation or era would be taken up
later in different places and in different ways. "Philosophers are free to lay
down their own set of principles," Gilson had observed the previous year
at Harvard, where he gave the William James Lecture at the 300th anniver-
sary of that university's founding:

but once this is done, they no longer think as they wish—they think as they can.
... It seems to result from the facts under discussion, that any attempt on the part
of a philosopher to shun the consequences of his own position is doomed to failure.
What he himself declines to say will be said by his disciples, if he has any; if he has
none, it may remain eternally unsaid; but it is there, and anybody going back to the
same principles, be it several centuries later, will have to face the same conclusion.[13]

11. Henry Veatch, *Aristotle: A Contemporary Appreciation* (Bloomington: Indiana University Press, 1974), 4.
12. See Stanley Jaki, *The Road of Science and the Ways to God* (Chicago: University of Chicago Press, 1978).
13. Étienne Gilson, *The Unity of Philosophical Experience* (1937; San Francisco: Ignatius Press, 1999), 243.

The traditional notion in popular opinion of the uselessness of the philosopher, of which Plato spoke in book 6 of the *Republic,* gains a sobering corrective in Gilson's careful words to the audience at Harvard University. We betray our culture, we do not know what animates it, if we are ignorant of the ideas, especially aberrant ideas, on which it is founded or by which it comes to act. But if error will not let us alone, unexamined, neither will the truth of things. The very articulation of an erroneous position is itself a challenge to some philosopher down the ages to get it right. This is the import of Socrates' praise of the two young philosophers in the beginning of the second book of the *Republic,* who could explain error so well but who knew that there was something wrong with their explanation and hence needed Socrates to explain things to them.

Philosophy and revelation have different origins. One of the attractions of particularly Greek philosophy is precisely that it has, apparently, nothing but itself to explain itself. It was not open or closed; it was itself. It dealt with whatever was at hand, including myths and stories. To many, it seemed, after they had been rediscovered by the various schools of believers in the Middle Ages, that Plato and Aristotle must have known, in order to say what they did, the contents of the Hebrew bible. The fact is, however, that they did not know this source. Certainly, someone like St. Paul knew of philosophical things, both to warn of their dangers and to prod the Romans for not knowing what they could know. But though there were certain universal elements in Hebrew revelation, still theirs was largely the affair of a small and obscure people in an out of the way corner of the world.

We might debate whether the "intent" of world history in some Hegelian sense is that these differing civilizations, Athens and Jerusalem, come into contact with each other. What cannot be doubted is that, after Alexander the Great and the Roman presence in the New Testament itself, they did confront each other. The first question for Christians was merely how could they live peacefully within the Roman Empire? When Augustine comes along, he is quite prepared to justify Christianity *because* its believers make good citizens and soldiers of Rome. While remaining "wayfarers and pilgrims" in this world, they do not alienate themselves, as later thinkers would charge, but provide the incentives whereby the world could be most itself.

What Gilson is concerned with in the Richards Lecture, however, is the history of efforts to relate revelation and reason in some coherent unity, one that does justice both to reason and revelation, one that explicates their exact scope. He suggests that in fact this coherent unity was worked out but rejected almost before it had a chance to flourish in the time of Thomas Aquinas—hence it is still waiting to be rediscovered. But at the time, this failure had something to do with intellect. To this point, Gilson writes in his Charlottesville lecture:

Had it been given to Thomas Aquinas to convince, if not his own contemporaries, at least his immediate successors, the intellectual and moral crisis would have soon come to a close, and the whole history of western thought would have been different from what it was. Unfortunately, the net result of Averroes' influence was to breed in the minds of the theologians a growing mistrust for philosophy. If that [Averroes' view] was natural reason, Revelation would be better off without its help than with it. Hence, in even the greatest among the late medieval philosophers and theologians, an increasing tendency to ascribe to faith alone, not only what Thomas Aquinas would call the articles of faith properly said, but even what we saw him define as rational preambles to matters of faith. It thus came to pass that the list of the revealed truths that can be either believed, or proved, was steadily growing shorter and shorter to the point of shriveling into nothingness.[14]

When this "nothingness" was reached, what was left was a pure fideism on the one hand, and modern science on the other.[15] From Machiavelli, Bacon, Descartes, Hobbes, and on to the present, we begin to see that no religion can be excluded from revelation and no religious position can be touched by science which is itself an arbitrary restructuring of the world according to human needs and wants with no restriction from a fixed human nature.[16] Indeed, a good part of modern science is concerned with the problem of whether there even is a world other than its thought about the world.

What Gilson set out to do in the University of Virginia lecture was, effectively, to reinvigorate reason by restoring revelation with its proper content and to its intended purpose. Whether reason "could" save itself by itself was a separate question, but Nietzsche's answer in *Beyond Good and Evil* that reason in fact did not save itself has haunted modern thought ever since.[17] The 1945 and 1989 rejection and defeat of the leading twentieth century ideologies that became powerful political movements, however, did not evidently return the culture to an openness to revelation. Rather it established doubt, the impossibility of knowing anything at all, at the heart of all intellectual things.

14. RRMA, 84–85.
15. See James V. Schall, "Protestantism and Atheism," in *Redeeming the Time*, 97–120.
16. See Strauss, *City and Man*, 7.
17. Nietzsche, *Beyond Good and Evil*, 42, 43.

The astonishing reappearance of Islam in 2001 as a militant factor, moreover, itself takes the form of an ideology based on nothing more fundamental than the arbitrary will of Allah and hence the impossibility of stable secondary causes and science itself. Indeed, the "fury" of Islam was often described as a kind of frustration at its own impotence before the West, before what it often called "Satan." The West was perceived as precisely corrupt and decadent so that all that was needed to topple it was zeal and shrewd use of arms and weapons that anyone with some training could handle. The struggle within Islam itself was about its truth, about the connection between its marginalization in the modern world and its religious beliefs, about the intellectual foundations that are claimed in its support.

III.

Gilson begins his examination with the first encounters of revelation and philosophy, those that suppose that revelation makes philosophy unnecessary, if not dangerous. We associate this initial position in particular with Tertullian, whose famous aphorism, "What has Jerusalem to do with Athens?" has itself become, in the hands of Leo Strauss, an instrument of restoring both philosophy and revelation to serious consideration, though within what must be suspected, at least at first sight, of bearing Averroistic overtones. Strauss, without denying the reality of either, seems to have denied any possible encounter or cross-fertilization between reason and revelation.[18] He "protected" revelation not, as Aquinas did, by recognizing at least some elements of revelation that could also be examined by genuine philosophy, but rather by setting the way of life of the philosopher and the way of life as the prophet or priest in radically different worlds. Whether this separation served to protect either revelation or reason can be questioned, since it admitted the possibility of two bodies of "truths" that had no means of contacting one another. On the other hand, to his credit, in an academic world that had forgotten the origins of its own meaning, Strauss at least enabled the question of revelation to appear as a legitimate, if perplexing, one.[19]

18. Leo Strauss, "Jerusalem and Athens: Some Preliminary Reflections," quoted in Susan Orr, *Jerusalem and Athens: Reason and Revelation in the Works of Leo Strauss* (Lanham, Md.: Rowman & Littlefield, 1995), 179–208.
19. See Thomas Pangle, "Introduction," in Leo Strauss, *Studies in Platonic Political Philosophy* (Chicago: University of Chicago Press, 1983), 18–23; Schall, *Reason, Revelation, and the Foundations of Political Philosophy*, 182–224.

The second great approach that began to realize the faith and reason might have more to do with one another than simple opposition was that of Augustine. Augustine was a seeker of truth, wherever it might be found. As a young man, he was almost a classical potential philosopher of the Platonic variety. Beautiful things in which he sought beauty itself deceived him until he found his way. "Augustine was never to forget," Gilson wrote,

that the safest way to reach truth is not the one that starts from reason and then goes on from rational certitude to faith, but, on the contrary the way whose starting point is faith and then goes on from Revelation to reason. By reaching that unexpected conclusion, Augustine was opening a new era in the history of western thought. No Greek philosopher could have ever dreamt of making religious faith in some revealed truth the obligatory starting point to rational knowledge.[20]

Augustine realized that belief was one of the things that led him to understanding, especially the understanding of what it was all about, of the highest things. Henceforth, there would be a constant effort in Christian thought to find that philosophy to which faith naturally led. The only problem with this sort of approach, in Gilson's view, was that if one did not accept the initial premise of faith, no matter how philosophic or logical everything flowed from the faith, it could not reach or have anything in common with a nonbelieving philosophy. The latter is now understood for the first time as being its own autonomous field. Hitherto, philosophy had been open to whatever is, from what ever source.

Thus the second type of relation of revelation and reason, typified by Averroes, was the view that philosophy was a higher science than revelation and indeed subsumed it into itself by explaining what religion was. A philosophy that could "explain" religion was higher than religion. The "truths" of faith were not "mysteries" but "myths" that could be explained by the wise man, by the philosopher. It followed from this position that the revelation of Islam, in this case, could not be seen as compatible with philosophy as explicated by Aristotle, who is now taken as himself literally explaining what the human mind by itself could hold, including religion. The Aristotelian positions that were contrary even to Islamic faith, say, the eternality of the world as opposed to Creation, were thus seen as philosophically determinative. Reason corrected revelation or reduced it to myth.

What happened in this system? Averroes developed a threefold relationship to philosophy. There were the great masses who did not under-

20. RRMA, 17.

stand it, there were the dialecticians who understood mathematics, and there were the philosophers who understood Aristotle. Nothing in the Koran could be taken seriously except that which had to do with an exhortation to live a good life, which Aristotle already understood and explicated long before the Koran ever appeared. The Koran thus became a kind of Platonic myth simplified for the good of those who could not understand. Submission to the Koran was a blind obedience that precluded any examination of what might be commanded in its name. No "natural law" had to be wrestled with.

The theologians who were in charge of this myth were to be left alone. The philosopher was simply to set them aside and not bother explaining what the real situation was. It could only cause problems, even persecution—Averroes himself died in exile. Indeed, it was perhaps best not even to write or speak of philosophy in public. Philosophy could not be explained to everyone, so it was not necessary to bother trying to do so. Religion served its purpose by providing a sort of substitute philosophy for the masses that served political purposes in keeping the masses in order. But none of the truths of philosophy could be confronted by those of revelation. They belonged to different orders.[21] The philosopher alone knew and understood. His way was a lonely way.

The Christian version of this system had vast ramifications. It was again a variety of absolute separation between philosophy and revelation. Aristotle himself did not develop a philosophy which was in "response" to some revelation, though he did, as did Plato, deal with the traditional gods and stories of the Greeks. In this sense, the Aristotle "as Aristotle" that Aquinas sought to encounter, the Aristotle not interpreted or explained by Arab philosophy, could still be "open" to a revelation that he did not know. Aquinas's Aristotle was not open in the sense of Augustine's searching for intelligence, though that too, but open in the sense of an open-ended philosophic reflection that could be right or wrong depending on philosophy itself, and not simply on the fact that Aristotle said it.

The case of the Latin Averroists, however, presupposed a philosophy that is closed in on itself, a rationalism, as it would be called. The line of nominalism from Scotus to Occam to Marsilius of Padua to Hobbes and into modernity is based on a break between *what is* and what we know. Ideas were not to be abstracted from real things. There were only words. Each thing was different. Gilson doubts if it is exactly fair to call Siger of

21. Ibid., 42–54.

Brabant, the most famous name associated with Latin Averroism, a pure model of the system itself. What happened, however, was that there was no link whatsoever between faith and reason. Faith did not search "reason." Reason was its own world. If its positions contradicted revelation, which they presumably did, that only meant that there were two separate spheres of reality with two separate systems of "truths." So long as there was still belief, philosophy could perhaps still be challenged, though with fewer points of contact. But with the loss of any belief, what is left is a reason not limited to its own truth, but an autonomous reason, a reason whose self-enclosed circlings had no other source but itself. It could not even be open to the notion that there was an order in things that itself revealed traces of mind, at least a divine mind.

Of this earlier form of rationalism's significance, Gilson wrote: "The existence of a medieval rationalism should never be forgotten by those historians who are investigating into the origins of the so-called modern rationalism, for indeed the Averroistic tradition forms an uninterrupted chain from the Masters of Arts of Paris, to the 'Libertins' of the seventeenth and eighteenth centuries."[22] Gilson even suggests that St. Thomas himself would not have been possible without the Averroistic challenge, since it was that challenge that incited him to clarify the proper relation of reason and revelation.

However, we might add, the unresolved philosophic problem in Islam itself is at the origins of many of our current problems, including the broader problem of the relation of Christianity to any classic religion to itself. If it is true, as Stanley Jaki has argued, that part of our present problem is the inferiority complex in Islam over the fact that it has not been able to enter into the modern scientific and political basis on the basis of its own theology, the reason for this is not due to some brain deficiency on the part of Arab thinkers.[23] Rather it is because of Gilson's principle that once we lay down our first principles, we no longer think as we want, but as we can. Averroes himself evidently attempted to protect philosophy not only from Islamic theology, by his distinction of three classes of people who have nothing to do with each other, but also from an Aristotle who was not closed in on himself.

22. Ibid., 65.
23. Stanley Jaki, "On Whose Side Is History?" in *Chance or Reality and Other Essays* (Lanham, Md.: University Press of America, 1986), 233–44; and Jaki, "The Physics of Impetus and the Impetus of the Koran," in *Absolute Beneath the Relative and Other Essays* (Lanham, Md.: University Press of America, 1988), 14–52.

If Allah is pure will and piety means submission to Allah, then it is absolutely impossible for there to be any such thing as stable secondary causes or even such a thing as a world itself, since God could make contradictories possible. It is sometimes argued that one of the strengths of Islam is its simplicity, its few precepts that almost anyone can obey. But if the world is not that simple, if God is more complex than Allah's absolute will, if Incarnation is possible, if secondary causes really can act, it follows that the argument with Islam is not simply about a goodly number of fanatics but its very understanding of its God.[24] The failure of Islamic philosophers to save the world, while sending armies on the mission of conquering it, turns out to have been of momentous contemporary importance.

IV.

Gilson then recalls that it might be possible to find an understanding of philosophy and of revelation that accepts the truth of revelation and its content while at the same time accepting the truths of philosophy as philosophy. But this position cannot avoid suggesting that not every philosophy is true. Indeed, faith seeks understanding, even in the order of understanding. The crucial issue is that of the order of things.[25] The importance of Thomas Aquinas is the ability to "handle philosophical problems as a philosopher and theological problems as a theologian."[26] Gilson explains that the conclusion that something is true on the basis of faith is due to the testimony of God. What I know as true in this sense is not the result of a rational analysis or understanding, by which I also may discover something as true. This dependence on faith also means that those truths that are specifically of faith are intended for every believer and not just for the intellectuals or theologians. "All believers, all Christians are in the same predicament, for all of them agree as to what they believe, and none of them has any scientific knowledge."[27] This is specifically what sets the Christian apart from Averroes and his school.

But is there then no contact between reason and revelation, granted the autonomy of both and the separate origins of their truth? Aquinas did not accept this "absolute" separation of reason and revelation, in part on philo-

---

24. See the discussion of Islam in James V. Schall, "Introduction: The Home, the Crown, and the Cross: On Explaining Humanity to Itself," in *The Collected Works of G. K. Chesterton*, vol. 20 (San Francisco: Ignatius Press, 2001), 25–27.

25. RRMA, 70–71. 26. Ibid., 72.

27. Ibid., 75.

sophic grounds. The good sense contained in revelation might indeed be persuasive and consistent, but it would convince only those who accepted the basis of faith and its authority.[28] The real problem was whether Averroes and his tradition understood Aristotle properly, and even more basically, whether they understood philosophy properly. If we consider Aristotle to be a great philosopher but that he might have erred, then we will need a philosophy, not theology, to show this error, even if our suspicion that there was an error did arise from theology. Aquinas could see that an idea could not be intellectually consistent but still not true. He could not be content with a divided soul, for that shattered the whole order of Creation, the whole order of things.[29]

Yet, because of Aquinas's particular awareness both of theological foundations and philosophical arguments, he realized that certain elements that appeared in faith also were open to philosophical discourse, the existence of God, the order of morality, for example. This affinity was peculiar and surprising if there was indeed an absolute separation of reason and revelation. Likewise, there were positions in revelation that, according to revelation itself, were beyond human reason, though they were part of the wisdom of God and hence not, ultimately, contradictory to being. Philosophic speculation could not "prove" that there was a Trinity in the Godhead, though it might examine arguments that maintained that it was impossible to show their own dubiousness.[30]

It is to be remembered that the purpose of revelation is very specific. It is not intended to answer all unanswered questions. Indeed, it is related to the question of whether everyone is a "philosopher." One of the ironies of Greek philosophy had been that the highest branches of philosophy could in practice be reached only by a few. In Islam, if the general believer only had an untrue "myth" to keep him politically settled, as Averroes seemed to maintain, then the presumed transcendent destiny of the believers was based on nothing at all. "For this is the proper aim and scope of Revelation to provide all men, philosophers or not, with such knowledge of God, of man, and of His destiny, as is required for their eternal salvation."[31] In this sense, it can be suggested that revelation is an "answer" to Greek philosophy. It does not replace philosophy or denigrate it in any way, but it does propose a possible solution to an enigma inherent in Greek philosophy, something still in another way in Averroes. Moreover, the salvation of real

28. Ibid., 79.
30. Ibid., 83. See Schall, *At the Limits.*
29. Ibid., 81.
31. RRMA, 82.

men in a real world does indicate the need of philosophical positions that can defend the world as existing and the real responsibility of those found within it.

The upshot of Aquinas's position that there were certain truths within the corpus of revelation that were also verified or found in philosophy hinted at the unity of the whole of truth. The source that contained some truths that could be verified is quite in a different status from one that holds an absolute separation of reason and revelation on ideological grounds. Revelation is indeed open to reason, in that it accounts for at least some reasonable things. A reason that is not able to answer all its own questions on its own terms is simply honest as a philosophy when it is stimulated by theology.

Gilson comments on the history of philosophy after Aquinas, beginning with Scotus, that because of the tendency to minimize the relation of faith and reason, both areas of knowledge were independent of each other, to the detriment of both.[32] "A bitter opponent of Duns Scotus, Occam always maintained that absolutely nothing could be proved about God in the light of natural reason, not even his existence. To him, as to Averroes, what reason can say concerning theological matters never goes beyond the order of mere dialectical probability."[33] Gilson, in fact, dates the end of the Middle Ages to that point when there is despair of reconciling in any way reason and revelation.[34] Gilson sees the mystic tradition in part to be an attempt to save realism. A'Kempis and Luther, however, both seemed to agree in the rejection of philosophy.[35] "After the Reformation and the Humanists, the men of the sixteenth century found themselves confronted with a theology without philosophy, the *positive* or *modern* philosophy of Fr. de Vitoria and of M. Cano; and of a philosophy without theology: the purely rational speculations of R. Descartes and Francis Bacon."[36] It was out of this background that the notions of the specifically "modern project" (Strauss) of a world of improving the human estate by human powers alone arose.

Gilson's conclusions are in two steps. The first is a reminder of his basic insight into the importance of the history of philosophy: "The history of ideas is determined from within by the internal necessity of ideas themselves."[37] The issues of reason and revelation will remain substantial-

32. Ibid., 85–86.
34. Ibid., 91.
36. Ibid., 94–95.

33. Ibid., 86–87.
35. Ibid., 92–93.
37. Ibid., 95.

ly the same. The second step concerns the substance of peculiarly Christian revelation that at point after point encounters legitimate philosophical questions unanswered by philosophy itself. The real issue is this:

Knowing...that He who is more than Prophet has spoken, what are we to do with this message? If what His message says does at times escape the grasp of natural reason, what is natural reason going to say about it? Once we have reached that point, God can no longer be conceived by us as a mere "wholly other" to which our *a priori* category of the "Numinous" bears witness; the Son also is a witness, and He has said who the Father is. That, at last, is a Revelation worthy of the name: not our own revelation of God to ourselves, but the revelation of God Himself to us.[38]

Gilson's point, it seems, is not merely that this is the "content" of revelation, this Son and Father, the general terms of which any serious reader might see to be there in revelation's documents, but that this revelation in its curious content, in its Trinity and Incarnation and all the teachings that go with it, does meet a genuine philosophy that has argued to the existence of God and his major attributes.

This approach is not "proving" theology by reason, which would be a heresy and a divine claim on the part of the human mind. Nor is it arguing to the genuineness of philosophy beginning with faith and dialectics. Rather it is preserving what is theology and what is philosophy in a mutual openness, typical of Aristotle's own philosophy, as Aquinas understood it. This openness would not reject any truth merely on the grounds that it did not come from reason alone. Reason is open to all truth, not just to its own procedures taken in the rationalistic sense. Faith remains a gift, but a gift also to reason that stands curious about itself, about its own questions, when it hears at least the outlines of what is said to be revealed to it, to reason. In wrestling with this unexpected source, reason strangely becomes more itself, more philosophical. And in this mode, it is, as Aquinas called it, a "handmaid" itself quite needed to prevent theology, without it, from inventing its own groundless ideologies.

In conclusion, it is perhaps in this context that we can reconsider Leo Strauss's enigmatic words in 1964, when he spoke in Jerusalem about "the Divine message of the City of Righteousness, the Faithful City." Strauss thought that to speak of this "city among the heathen," it was necessary to understand the "outlines" of this "city," as much as possible, by our

38. Ibid., 98–99.

own natural powers, a project Aquinas certainly would accept. To elaborate this description, political science in particular has, in Strauss's view, much less need of the "indispensable handmaid" of theology as of "political philosophy as the rightful queen of the social sciences."[39] The question is, of course, in the light of Augustine's "City of God," whether "the rightful queen of the social sciences" will retain its proper place as the highest of the practical sciences but not the highest of the sciences as such, in which case it would become itself a metaphysics.

In the light of these reflections on Gilson's understanding of reason and revelation, however, in the light of the history of philosophy as itself the presence of ideas that need to be resolved in the name of truth, we might suggest, as Strauss knew in his description of positivism and historicism, that social science itself is a product of this very modernity from Descartes and Bacon, indeed from Occam and de Vitoria, from Averroes and Tertullian, ideas that did not understand the proper relation of Athens and Jerusalem. One might well argue that the whole modern history of the West, the whole thesis of John Paul's *Fides et Ratio,* is to recommence that insight into reason and revelation that Thomas Aquinas hammered out but which subsequent generations, to their peril, did not pursue. Gilson's *Reason and Revelation in the Middle Ages* brings us back to these considerations, perhaps not a minute too soon, even though we have neglected it for lo, these many decades since Gilson was in Charlottesville, in Virginia.

39. Strauss, *City and Man,* 1.

13 AQUINAS AND THE DEFENSE OF ORDINARY THINGS

On "What Common Men Call Common Sense"

Not only the practical politics, but the abstract philosophies of the modern world have had this queer twist. Since the modern world began in the sixteenth century, nobody's system of philosophy has really corresponded to everybody's sense of reality; to what, if left to themselves, common men would call common sense.

—G. K. Chesterton, *St. Thomas Aquinas*

Omnes autem res humanae ordinantur in finem beatitudinis, quae est salus aeterna, ad quam homines admittuntur, vel etiam repelluntur, judico Christi, ut patet, Matth. xxv: 21. (All human things, therefore, are ordered to the end of happiness, which is eternal salvation, to which men are admitted or also repelled, by the judgment of Christ, as is clear from Matthew 25:21.)

—Thomas Aquinas, *Summa theologiae*

I enjoyed the luxury of our approach to London, that metropolis which we both loved so much, for the high and varied intellectual pleasures which it furnishes. I experienced immediate happiness while whirled along with such a companion.

—James Boswell, Thursday, March 28, 1776

I.

In 1964, Étienne Gilson, at that time residing at the Pontifical Institute of Medieval Studies in Toronto, gave the Fenwick Lectures on the occasion of the 175th year since the founding of Georgetown University. These lectures were subsequently published under the title *The Spirit of*

This lecture was published in *Fellowship of Catholic Scholars Quarterly* 27 (Winter 2004): 16–22. Originally, it was the Annual Aquinas Lecture presented at the University of St. Thomas, Fredericton, New Brunswick, Canada, January 28, 2003.

Thomism. In the first discourse, Gilson remarked, perhaps sadly, perhaps frankly, that "not all good Christians love philosophy."[1] We think of Tertullian's famous question, "What has Athens to do with Jerusalem?" Gilson himself mentioned, in this same category, Arnobius and Peter Damian, as well as the Abbé Lucien Laberthonnière, who thought one had to choose "between being either a philosopher or a Christian."[2] Actually, Leo Strauss seems to hold a somewhat similar position: one must choose between the way of the philosopher and the way of the rabbi. Even St. Paul at times suspected not a little "foolishness" in philosophers.

One wing of Christianity, however, has devoted itself to saving philosophy, even from itself, while another has suspected that with Christianity, philosophy is in fact more itself, more philosophy, than it would be without it. This was surely the thesis of John Paul II's *Fides et Ratio.* We might say of Thomas Aquinas that he was a theologian, and because he was a theologian, he was also a philosopher. Indeed, we might say that because he was a theologian, he was a better philosopher, and because he was a philosopher, he was a better theologian. Yea, more, we might even say that had he not been a theologian, he would not have found much interest in philosophy; and were he not a philosopher, he would not have seen much point to theology.

I trust that here in Fredericton, at a university named after St. Thomas, the good Christians do love philosophy and for its own sake, which is, as Aristotle implied, the only reason why we should love it. Or as Socrates put it in the seventh book of the *Republic,* "It is the nature of the real lover of learning to struggle toward what is, not to remain with any of the many things that are believed to be, that, as he moves on, he neither loses nor lessens his erotic love until he grasps the being of each nature itself" (490b). Philosophy is indeed a thing to be loved, a thing about which to be excited.

In fact, I might be so brash as to hope that even the "bad" Christians, should there be such, which I must piously doubt in these noble halls, might also love philosophy. *Intellectus quaerens fidem* (intellect seeking faith) is, I suspect, as much a reality in "bad" philosophy as it is in "good" philosophy, perhaps more so. And when we know about revelation, I think, philosophy becomes something even more to be loved. Revelation is not the death-knell of philosophy but its reawakening. It is philosophy that

---

1. Étienne Gilson, *The Spirit of Thomism* (New York: P. J. Kennedy, 1964), 10.
2. Ibid., 11.

first properly poses the questions that it cannot satisfactorily answer for itself. It also knows that it is philosophy that knows when its own answers are not adequate. Much of modern philosophy, I suspect, is an often desperate effort to "prove," on the basis of what is said to be philosophy alone, that revelation cannot happen, cannot be true. The more we see of these philosophic proofs of revelation's presumed "untruths," the more disturbingly accurate revelation seems to be in its understanding of the actual human condition and its perennial tendencies.

The great Augustine, moreover, remarks, in the first chapter of book 19 of the *City of God*, that *"Nulla est homini causa philosophandi nisi ut beatus sit."* "There is no reason to philosophize except that we might be happy." I am ever indebted to E. F. Schumacher's dedication to his *A Guide for the Perplexed,* a wonderful book, for causing me to notice a sentence that I had often overlooked in reading *De civitate Dei.*[3] Few more profound words have been written, and I find myself often citing it.

Moreover, it is all right if a great man reminds us of another great man, if, say, Cicero reminds us of Plato, or Aquinas reminds us of Aristotle, or Boswell reminds us of Johnson, or Chesterton reminds us of Aquinas himself. We go to the trouble of thinking—it is in fact mostly a delight—because we want to know where we stand among existing things. We want to know that our personal destiny is not "in vain," to use a famous phrase of Aristotle. We want to know that the *things that are* originate in gladness, not sadness. It is perhaps no accident that Scripture, in depicting the birth of children, speaks both of sadness and gladness, almost as if to say that our lot includes both, but in an order in which, in the end, the sadness is subsumed into gladness, if we choose to let it.

II.

James Boswell told Samuel Johnson in a post-chaise on the way into London, in 1776, that "high and varied intellectual pleasures" are to be found in that glorious city. It is Aristotle who teaches us that all human activities have their proper pleasures, including those of the intellect, the neglect of which latter pleasures, the intellectual ones, usually turns us to disordered pleasures. Ironically, there is a this-worldly penalty for not enjoying the delights of the mind. Pleasure, rightly considered, is always a

---

3. E. F. Schumacher, *A Guide for the Perplexed* (New York: Harper Colophon, 1977).

consequence of, or better reality within, doing what we ought. As Aristotle said, there are some things we would choose, even if they did not give us pleasure, like seeing, an observation that makes the pleasure and power of seeing even more mysterious.

Thomas Aquinas even suggests that literally all human things are ordered to a final beatitude which directly concerns ourselves, challenging us to accept or reject it, almost as if it is exceedingly important what we think, what we choose. The activities of our minds are not supernaturally indifferent. It makes a difference what we think about the *things that are*. In the end, Aquinas adds, we do not judge ourselves, which suggests that there is a reality we do not make, but only receive. Indeed, it suggests that what we do not make is, in the end, more what we want than that which we choose to give ourselves from the depths of only ourselves. Ultimately, we are receivers.

Charles Taylor made the same observation as Aquinas. "The point of things isn't exhausted by life, the fullness of life, even the goodness of life," Taylor observed at a lecture given at the University of Dayton in 1996. "What matters beyond life doesn't matter just because it sustains life. . . . For Christians, God wills human flourishing, but 'thy will be done' doesn't reduce to 'let human beings flourish.'"[4] The purpose of this life is not the eternal continuation of just this life. And Chesterton, that great admirer of Aquinas, was bold enough to speak of "everybody's sense of reality," as if it made obvious sense to say that we all live in the same world and know that we do.

Yet, intellectual things do not always allow us to be content with ordinary things. If we have but a breath of Plato in our souls, as we should, we know that no beautiful thing exhausts what it is to be beautiful in itself. Each beautiful thing, without denigrating its own being, its own *what it is*, is a reminder of what is luminously beautiful, even in what is ordinarily beautiful. Thus, it is precisely the ordinary that most often directs us to the extraordinary things and, paradoxically, it is the extraordinary things that are most needed to defend the ordinary, normal things. We underestimate God's grandeur, I suspect, when we conceive it to be quite an easy thing to save us, knowing, if we be honest, what we are. Just why it is all right to be an ordinary human being is, if anything, more puzzling than why it is all right to be a perfect one. Why, after all, should there be anything at all but

---

4. Charles Taylor, *A Catholic Modernity*, edited by James L. Heft (New York: Oxford, 1999), 20.

God? We suspect that Aquinas's little caveat, *"judicio Christi,"* has something to do with it.

III.

In a letter he wrote to a Thomistic congress in Rome in 2003, on Christian humanism, John Paul II, recalled, as did Chesterton back in 1933, how modern systems of philosophy do not allow us to see ordinary things. Between us and them there stand epistemological theories that obscure, if not totally darken, our vision of *what is*. And there are moral theories and practices that are perhaps even more blinding, more difficult barriers through which to see reality.

Modern man, the pope said, seems to be "in search of his own fulfillment." By this phrase, I take it, the pope means that modern man seeks to "define," exclusively by himself, what it is to be human. He is subject to no "natural law," even of himself. Then, recalling what he wrote in *Fides et Ratio,* John Paul II analyzed:

the factors that are obstacles in the process of humanism. Among the most common should be mentioned the loss of faith in reason and its ability to arrive at the truth, the refusal of transcendence, nihilism, relativism, the forgetfulness of being, the denial of the soul, the prevalence of the irrational or feeling, the fear of the future and existential anxiety. . . . Christian humanism, as St. Thomas demonstrated, has an ability to preserve the meaning of man and his dignity.[5]

We do not often enough, I think, consider the problem of precisely "intellectual obstacles," of the notion that ideas themselves can and do prevent us from knowing the truth of things. In *Orthodoxy,* Chesterton remarks that "there is a thought that stops thought."[6] We should have some sense that, often perhaps, we choose our ideas precisely so that we will not see a reality that would demand that we change our ways of living. How we think is not merely a frivolous exercise, such as the four hundred and first crossword puzzle that we halfheartedly fill in because we have nothing else to do with our minds, or like the television ads we watch because shutting the whole thing off is too much trouble.

The Holy Father's short list of intellectual obstacles here is quite interesting. The first one he stresses is a "loss of faith in reason." "What does it

5. John Paul II, "Message to the International Thomistic Congress," *L'Osservatore Romano,* English ed., October 15, 2003, 6.

6. Chesterton, *Orthodoxy,* 33.

mean to have 'faith' in reason?" we might ask ourselves. We like to think that faith and reason are separate, either one or the other. But we have here a man of incisive intellect speaking of a lack of "faith" in reason as itself an obstacle that might prevent us from knowing what humanism might be. A point comes when we must discover a ground, a first principle, that itself is too obvious to "prove" by something more clear than itself. Strictly speaking, this is not "faith," except in the sense that we must take as a given, that is, what invariably functions within us the way it does.

Chesterton, again, made much the same observation in almost the same words about the intellect's power over itself:

> The point is that the human intellect is free to destroy itself. . . . One set of thinkers can prevent further thinking by teaching the next generation that there is no validity in any human thought. It is idle to talk always of the alternative of reason and faith. Reason is itself a matter of faith. It is an act of faith to assert that our thoughts have any relation to reality at all.[7]

In practice, few who theoretically doubt whether the mind can know reality fail to open the door before trying to enter a room. Unlike Descartes, we do not normally think we have to prove the existence of God in order to know that something besides ourselves is out there in the world.

The word "humanism" itself needs to be further considered. The pope speaks of "Christian humanism," knowing that not all humanism is "Christian." Humanism has been considered, not infrequently in the modern world, to be implicitly "atheist humanism." That is, to be human, it is said, we have to be atheistic. We are said to be "alienated" from our own being if we do not give ourselves the total content of what we are, if we do not, simultaneously, destroy what outside of ourselves is said to cause us to be what we are. This sort of "humanism" does not want to be dependent on any *"theos,"* any god, for an explanation of what man is. But to have "faith" in reason means precisely to affirm that reason contacts a world we did not create ourselves out of our own minds. The kind of being we are is already given to us. We are, in a sense, given to be what we already are. The drama of life is whether we accept or reject the kind of being we are given to be.

The pope also speaks of the "refusal of transcendence" and the "forgetfulness of being" as intellectual obstacles. Notice that he does not say the "intellectual rejection" of transcendence, but rather its "refusal," even if, or especially if, there is intellectual proof for its existence. Charles Taylor, in

7. Ibid.

the Dayton lecture, made the same point: "In Western modernity the obstacles to belief are primarily moral and spiritual, rather than epistemic."[8] Our theoretic problems are designed often to cover our moral problems.

And the pope speaks of the "forgetfulness" of being. This is a curious word. How can we "forget" what is in front of us at all times? I think of the first response found in Aquinas's *de Veritate,* in which he says, simply, *"illud autem quod primo intellectus concipit quasi notissimum, et in quo omnes conceptiones resolvit, est ens. . . ." (de Veritate,* I, 1).[9] Something other than ourselves exists; it is most known to us. In its light, we also exist as the kind of knowing beings we are. To "forget" being means that we are so busy examining and explaining everything else in our own terms that we neglect what is in front of us, what is the most curious thing about us, what is most known to us, namely, that we are, rather than are not, that there are things that are not ourselves.

IV.

I am fond of citing a lecture that Eric Voegelin gave in Montréal in 1980. One of Voegelin's missions in life was to "recall being," if I might put it that way, to insist that we do not "forget" it but rather find its "ground." He spent his life urging us to get away from the constant going over ideas as if they were original sources and return to the experience of being on which they were founded. Those familiar with Plato, Aristotle, Augustine, and Aquinas already recognize this necessity, as we saw in the brief citation from Aquinas about being. Voegelin remarked that there are "no new ideologies in the twentieth century," only the working out of older ones. Ideologies, which are in essence explanations of the world that originate not in being but in mind, can last rather a long time if there is a vested interested in keeping them alive.

Voegelin then added that "the college teaching level is usually thirty, forty, or more years back of what is going on."[10] And is what is "going on," even if we do not know it, that which decides our intellectual agenda? By no means. We need not be advocates of that vague "philosophy of the future" that Nietzsche spoke of in *Beyond Good and Evil.* Indeed, Voegelin

8. Taylor, *Catholic Modernity,* 25.

9. "That which the intellect first conceives as that which is most known to it, and into which it resolves all conceptions, is being."

10. *Conversations with Eric Voegelin,* 16–17.

himself admonished the students in Montréal in 1980, "Nobody is obliged to participate in the crisis of his time. He can do something else."[11] And what is this "something else" in which he can participate? Socrates said in the sixth book of the *Republic*, "Let's agree that philosophic natures always love the sort of learning that makes clear to them some feature of the being that always is and does not wander around between coming to be and decaying" (485b). It is absolutely vital that we realize that the philosophic life is open to us even in the most corrupt of societies or universities. This is the grounding of Voegelin's admonition that we are not "obliged" to participate in the crisis of our time; we are not prisoners of our time because we have something else, a philosophy of being, of *what is*. But we must find it, choose it.

The final sentence in Nietzsche's *On the Genealogy of Morality* is the following: "Man would much rather will *nothingness* than *not* will."[12] Just what to will "nothingness" might mean is problematic. We recall that, in Christian theology, God creates the world *ex nihilo*, from nothing. This "from nothing" has never been understood, of course, to mean that the world is made of something called precisely "nothing." But it does mean that of itself, apart from God's being and will, nothing is but God himself. Nietzsche's urging us "to will" is contingent on the existence of a will that did not will itself to be what it is. Behind the "will to power" is a will whose power is given to it.

V.

In the *Protagoras,* we find a passage of rare humor. It concerns the significance of our conversations about *the things that are.* Socrates has just given his analysis of the poems of Pittacus and Simonides on the difficulty of becoming and being good. The young sophist Hippias offers to read his own analysis of these very poems, but Alcibiades, ever cutting, brushes him off deftly, "Yes, Hippias, some other time, though" (347b). "Don't bother us," in other words. Alcibiades, that most attractive and dangerous of all the potential philosophers whom Socrates ever encounters, wants Socrates directly to answer the questions posed by Protagoras. He wants philosophy, not speeches about philosophy.

11. Ibid., 33.
12. Friedrich Nietzsche, *On the Genealogy of Morality: A Polemic,* translated by M. Clark and A. J. Swensen (Indianapolis: Hackett, 1998), 118.

At this point, Socrates wants to stop talking about poetry and odes. "Discussing poetry strikes me as no different from the second-rate drinking parties of the agora crowd," Socrates bluntly remarks. He continues with a damning description of local intellectual life, a description valid for most all times: "These people largely uneducated and unable to entertain themselves over their wine by using their own voices to generate conversation, pay premium prices for flute-girls and rely on the extraneous voice of the red flute as background music for their parties" (347c–d). Clearly, Socrates implies here that conversation should arise out of our own experience— "philosophy exists in conversation," as Frederick Wilhelmsen once made the same point. The artificial experience of the night club with the latest music will not generate the deeper conversation to which we ought to turn our souls.

Then, in one of the finest descriptions of human conversation in all literature, Socrates continues:

But when well-educated gentlemen drink together, you will not see girls playing the flute or the lyre or dancing, but a group that knows how to get together without these childish frivolities, conversing civilly no matter how heavily they are drinking. Ours is such a group, if indeed it consists of men such as most of us claim to be, and it should require no extraneous voices, not even of poets, who cannot be questioned on what they say. When a poet is brought up in a discussion, almost everyone has a different opinion about what he means, and they wind up arguing about something they cannot finally decide. The best people avoid such discussions and rely on their own powers of speech to entertain themselves and test each other. These people should be our models. We should put the poets aside and converse directly with each other, testing the truth and our own ideas. (347d–e)

Socrates, be it noted, is not against drinking, nor is he opposed to singing or dancing, as we know from both the *Laws* and the *Symposium*. Indeed, these activities are in many ways our highest human expression of joy and gratitude before the *things that are*. They are our response to *what is*, that it is.

The burden of this passage from the *Protagoras* is one that teaches us where philosophy really exists, in conversation, in conversation generated by a desire to know the truth of things. The conversation is civil. It is friendly. It does not disdain drinking, but it requires sobriety. Things need to be decided. We do not rely ultimately on outside books, whose understanding Socrates often tells us, as in the case of the poets, is itself fleeting. We argue from a reality we know and confront. We should converse, seek the truth, even of our own ideas.

V.

Christof Cardinal von Schönbrun once remarked in a lecture in Austria that Thomas Aquinas was the first, and perhaps only, man ever canonized simply for thinking, as if it made a difference both whether we thought and what we thought about. We live in a culture whose basic proposition is that truth is dangerous, discriminatory. This context makes Aquinas doubly dangerous. He not only held that truth can be affirmed but that we can make the judgment in which it exists. Our grounds for living with others cannot be based on the proposition that there is no truth. They should be rather that we see and hold the same truths.

Josef Pieper, in his marvelous little book *The Silence of Saint Thomas,* remarked that we often overlook the fact that Aquinas was first a teacher and devoted considerable effort to teaching others precisely the truth. Though I think that they are not in opposition, when sorted out, we often praise Socrates for the honesty of knowing what or that he did not know, whereas in Aquinas there are something like ten thousand "articles," brief one- to four-page units of argument, each of which concludes to the affirmation of what is true and further states on what basis the conclusion is reached. "To lead a man from error to truth, this he (Aquinas) considered the greatest service which one man can render another," Pieper wrote. For those of us who are admonished also to give a cup of water or to clothe the naked, this passage deserves long meditation on the hierarchy of things to be done for our neighbor. It is not wrong to think that the men of our time need truth more than bread, to recall something in Dostoyevsky.

"Teaching, for Thomas, is something other and greater than to impart by one method or another the 'findings of research,'" Pieper continued. "Teaching is a process that goes on between living men. The teacher looks not only at the truth of things; at the same time he looks at the faces of living men who desire to know this truth."[13] This careful observation is, in a way, the same point we saw in the *Protagoras,* in which we needed to be in direct conversation, face to face. Teaching is a spiritual endeavor, both on the part of the student and the professor. Truth, as such, is not something that can be owned. If Schall has a truth that is peculiarly "his" own and no one else's, it is not worth having. The highest things are free in their very truth. It is possible that a teacher can take a student to something, to a text, to a reflection, whereby the eyes of the student are open. He begins

---

13. Josef Pieper, *The Silence of Saint Thomas* (Chicago: Regnery, 1957), 23.

to see, not only see but long. Every experience of truth takes us out of ourselves.

VI.

If the human mind cannot reach reality, if there is no mind in things, if the only world *that is*, is the world that we project from within our wills, it follows, it would seem, that there is nothing we can receive. We are, in that case, the criterion and content of our own existence. Our modern "humanism" is not based on the gift of ourselves from whatever it is that causes *to be*, but it is the self-definition of our own world, in which what is not from our own wills simply is not allowed to exist or be considered as part of our humanity. An old *Peanuts* cartoon shows Schroeder, the Beethoven lover, excitedly telling Lucy, after she asks, "This is a new recording of Brahms Fourth Symphony." With a disbelieving look, Lucy wants to know what he going to "do" with it. Schroeder tells her that he is going to "take it home and listen to it." She cannot comprehend this contemplative sort of answer. She wants to know if he is going to dance or march to it. "No, I'm just going to sit and listen to it." Lucy tries one more time, "You mean you're going to whistle or sing while you listen to it?" For the fourth time, Schroeder tells her that he is just going to "listen" to it. In the final scene, Lucy is standing alone gazing at the departed Schroeder. She concludes, "That's the most ridiculous thing I've ever heard."[14] Yet, Schroeder is right; we are essentially hearers and listeners before we are speakers and doers.

"There is no thinker who is so unmistakably thinking about things, and not being misled by the indirect influence of words, as St. Thomas Aquinas," Chesterton wrote.

That strangeness of things, which is the light in all poetry, and indeed in all art, is really connected with their otherness; or what is called their objectivity. What is subjective must be stale; it is exactly what is objective that is in this imaginative manner strange.... All ... the romance and glamour (of things), so to speak, lies in the fact that they are real things; things *not* to be found by staring inwards at the mind. The flower is a vision because it is not only a vision. Or, if you will, it is a vision because it is not a dream.[15]

---

14. In Robert Short, *The Gospel According to Peanuts* (Richmond, Va.: John Knox Press, 1965), 26.

15. Chesterton, *Orthodoxy*, 183–84.

The ordinariness and, at the same time, the strangeness of the very same things, this is what Aquinas has to teach us about *what is*.

Yet, it is the lesson of the history of philosophy that once we exhaust what we can know about the cosmos, we eventually turn to the mystery that is ourselves. Socrates had it right: "It's ridiculous, isn't it, to strain every nerve to attain the utmost exactness and clarity about other things of little value and not to consider the most important things worthy of the greatest exactness?" (504d). In the older translations, Ignatius of Loyola used to provoke the precious, intelligent, and charming young Francis Xavier, at the University of Paris, with these plain words, unsettling to any college student: "What does it profit a man to gain the whole world and lose the life of his immortal soul?" Some modern translations have it: "What does it profit a man to gain the whole world and lose his life?" If not losing our lives at any cost is our criterion, our principle, we are followers of Hobbes not of Christianity. There is something higher than the whole world. This is our tradition.

Let me conclude, in summary, with the following fifteen random propositions:

1. "Not all good Christians love philosophy" (Gilson).
2. "The things of the greatest importance are worthy of the greatest exactitude" (Socrates).
3. "Since the beginning of the modern world, nobody's system of philosophy has really corresponded with everyone's sense of reality" (Chesterton).
4. *"Omnes autem res humanae ordinanter in finem beatitudinis, quae est salus aeterna"* (Aquinas).
5. "I enjoyed the luxury of our approach to London, that metropolis which we both loved so much, for the varied and high intellectual pleasures which it furnishes" (Boswell).
6. "It is the nature of the real lover of learning to struggle for *what is*" (Socrates).
7. "The flower is a vision because it is not only a vision" (Chesterton).
8. *"Nulla est homini causa philosophandi nisi ut beatus sit"* (Augustine).
9. "The point of life isn't exhausted by things, the fullness of life, even the goodness of life" (Charles Taylor).
10. "What does it profit a man to gain the whole world and lose the life of his immortal soul?" (Ignatius).
11. "Man would much rather will nothingness than not to will" (Nietzsche).

12. "The teacher not only looks at the truth of things, at the same time he looks at the faces of living men who desire to know this truth" (Pieper).

13. Schroeder tells a frustrated Lucy that he is "going to take the new recording of Brahms Fourth Symphony home and listen to it" (Schulz).

14. "We should put the poets aside and converse directly with each other, testing the truth and our own ideas" (Socrates).

15. "There is no thinker who is so unmistakably thinking about things, and not being misled by the indirect influence of words, as Thomas Aquinas" (Chesterton).

PART V

IMPLICATIONS OF CATHOLIC
THOUGHT

14 THE "REALISM" OF ST. AUGUSTINE'S "POLITICAL REALISM"

Augustine and Machiavelli

Augustine's picture of fallen man, ridden by avarice, lust for power, and sexual desire, is a somber and pessimistic portrait, which calls to mind the views of human nature expressed by his followers at the time of the Reformation, Luther and Calvin, and by Machiavelli and Hobbes.

—Herbert Deane, *Political and Social Ideas of St. Augustine*

To the classical account, St. Augustine adds the insight of Christian pessimism. Like the author of the Prince, he tears away the veil of respectability that successful political regimes hang, or try to hang, over their origins. His purpose is not, however, like Machiavelli, to provide a manual of politically useful maxims for a new "founding father." He means to show how, with all the sweat, blood, and tears . . . , it is, nevertheless, not the will of men, but the will of God that is accomplished in history.

—Henry Paolucci, *Political Writings of St. Augustine*

I.

As a teacher in political philosophy over the years, I have become intrigued by the effect of reading with an average class of modern students both St. Augustine and Machiavelli, the archetypes of what is called in political philosophy "political realism." Often these same students are bent on saving the world, largely, as far as I can tell, by going to law school, itself something of a problem in political philosophy. For we can, in this context, recall St. Augustine's own sobering account of his early teaching career. In Rome, his own students failed to pay their bills. In Milan, he realized that preparing students for law and rhetoric would not lead either him or them

This essay was originally published in *Perspectives on Political Science* 25 (Summer 1996): 117–23.

to the highest things. Thus these youthful enthusiasms will not seem overly surprising or only confined to our own time and place.

Indeed, such suppositions about legal and political solutions to moral
and social problems form almost a recurrent phenomenon among those
many who want to find the City of God in places wherein it is not likely to
be discovered. Activism in our time seems so superior to contemplation;
politics seems superior to mysticism. Charity has become, in effect, compassion, a very different thing as it is used. The first, charity, means God's
love in everything; the second, compassion, implies that no one is judged
by any criterion but his own, whatever that be. Compassion has replaced
reason and obviated the need for forgiveness.

Within activism, and, probably as a consequence of the reversal of the
classical priority of contemplation to action, furthermore, fewer and fewer
intrinsic limits to politics and action are acknowledged or observed. The
scope of a freedom in modernity is defined, to be brief, not by nature or
by nature's God, but by a freedom itself subject to nothing further than
the self. In a sense, the heady freedom Machiavelli granted to the prince
is substantially granted to or subsumed by everyone. "Every man a king"
has come to have more sinister overtones in a world bereft handbooks for
kings that also teach them to be morally virtuous.

When contemporary students first encounter St. Augustine, moreover, they are usually disturbed. They find themselves unsettled by Augustine's pessimistic view of human nature, even if they suspect that he might
be right on the empirical side. They do not like to admit the legitimacy of
his experience even when they admit that he might be a realist; that is, he
just might accurately describe the dire things they see about them every
day. In the moral order, we are reluctant to admit how little progress we
have made, even more reluctant to relate this lack of improvement to ourselves.

To explain this instinctive dislike of the pessimism of an admittedly
fascinating man like Augustine always is to contemporary students, we
cannot forget that one component, conscious or unconscious, of any modern student's soul is always the Enlightenment heritage, itself not unrelated to the Pelagianism about which Augustine was so concerned. Thus, a
student presumes that no evil is connected with our lot, with our choices.
He assumes that improving the human condition is a relatively easy process brought about by changing a few political and economic patterns that
are, apparently, unduly opposed by a few bad men. Just how, on the same
presumptions, these same few came to be "bad" in the first place is not

altogether certain. Rarely is the necessary change in society first to take place in one's own heart.

Such views reveal a certain paradoxical individual powerlessness in these very students so insistent on structural changes or on the nonexistence of natural norms. They suspect, though they do not quite know why, that neither St. Augustine's pessimism nor his thought on predestination were somehow powerless. The drama of St. Augustine's *Confessions*, indeed, graphically affirmed that the real struggles of the world were not political at all or only reductively so. Thus to concentrate on external reform above all else implies a certain inner meaninglessness that is the very opposite of St. Augustine. Not unlike Plato in book 2 of the *Republic*, he maintained that we need not go too far from ourselves to find the real sources of disorder in the world. Those anxious to reform the world but unwilling to look at themselves revealed in their own souls the beginnings of that pride that St. Augustine found to be the greatest of the vices because it did not consider anything but itself.

On the other hand, when these same students, worried about Augustine's pessimism, first read the famous passage in Machiavelli's *Prince* in which the shrewd Florentine diplomat takes his position over against previous political philosophy, they become often unaccountably ebullient. "What is it they think they have read?" elderly professors wonder. After all their presumably careful reading with you, do they see no problem with the provocative author of the *Prince?* To them, evidently, Machiavelli seems so modern, so contemporary. He appears to provide a way to "liberate" politics and even human nature from religious or moral constraints.

This famous "unarmed prophet," Machiavelli himself, thus proclaims, with ringing words, his final exasperation over all previous political philosophy: "Enough of these ideal kingdoms! Previous philosophers have written about how men ought to act. From now on, we will write on how men do act. For if the prince acts as he should, as the philosophers and prophets have instructed him, surely he will be destroyed among so many bad men." When it comes to politics, then, there is little margin for error about the deeds of man or little use in moral exhortations.

Many students, not all, to be sure, find that they delight in this bluntness, this flamboyance, this daring of Machiavelli. Yet they instinctively, it seems, reject St. Augustine's very similar factual and verifiable remarks on what is to be expected in the human heart and in the human polity. Machiavelli, by contrast, is real, whereas Augustine has about him all this complicated philosophical and theological theory. Machiavelli corresponds to their experience or to their youthful iconoclasm. They admire the delicious irony of his praising bad popes while mocking good rulers who are so morally upright and so politically innocent as to get wiped out.

The classical authors thus limited the state too much. "Who is to say what is right and wrong, anyhow?" This is a very contemporary theme, to be sure. Politics needs a newfound "freedom." This freedom may be hard and productive of bitter fruits, at times. Certain "necessary" deeds will need to be performed for the "higher" political good. But at least harsh means get results. The politician needs the freedom to live "beyond good and evil," as Nietzsche was later to put it. The new prince needs to be able to be both a fox and a lion, to be loved or hated, to act according to law or force, whichever is most appropriate for his own ends. He is indeed to prefer good arms to good laws. The word "virtue" has come to mean not what Aristotle, Plato, Augustine, or Aquinas meant, but what Machiavelli advised the successful prince to do. The prince succeeds also by changing the meaning of the language, all the while keeping its formal words.

Freedom, pragmatism, and realism can now, in this approach, go together with a theory that justifies dire, extreme political actions. While St. Augustine had a pessimistic view of human nature, however, it did seem more or less to correspond with facts of observation; thus he was not utterly "unscientific" to detail moral facts. Machiavelli himself, for whom human nature was rather evil seems, likewise, almost scientific. This "scientific" aspect of Machiavelli's basic premises would become codified a century and a half later with Hobbes.[1] Machiavelli appears to open a way to human improvement that, paradoxically, is not too much hampered by the tenets of the old philosophy and old religion that placed certain specific moral restrictions on what a prince or republic could, or could not, do.

By following Machiavelli's pithy maxims, then, "new foundings" and unimagined republics were possible, provided we did not attend to the classical questions about good and evil in establishing or preserving them, provided we had the "courage" to act on the new principles. Machiavelli as a teacher sought to convince potential philosophers, and through them princes to replace Socrates' admonition to prefer death to doing wrong with the new "liberty" to choose between either good or evil means for the prince's own end, even if that end be called the public good. Augustine did not expect any political order to be free of evil, but he agreed with Socrates

---

1. See Leo Strauss, *Political Philosophy of Hobbes* (Chicago: University of Chicago Press, 1952); and Strauss, *Thoughts on Machiavelli* (Glencoe, Ill.: The Free Press, 1958).

that we could not actually do evil or violate the commandments for some princely purpose.

II.

Thus, Machiavelli has a certain malevolent attraction, especially to the better students who have not yet begun to work through the implication of this "new" philosophy. Frequently, the teacher has to stop a student. He has carefully to explain to him something Machiavelli suggested and ask the student if he understands this teaching. Does he agree with it? But Machiavelli continues to appeal to a sense of brutal efficiency while he implies that his method of politics will get things done in any era, in any place. Machiavelli, like classical political philosophy, claims universal address. My students from the Third World, I have observed over the years, are often also charmed by Machiavelli. They assume either that their country has been ruled in practice by the ideas of Machiavelli, so that now they understand what has been going on, or they hold that Machiavellian ideas will solve their current national problems. Thus he appears to be, as he claims, the harbinger of a new order. All the moralists and idealists, Machiavelli teaches, have had their chances, and what have they produced? They have only produced "more of the same."

The reason why the world has not improved, it is said, is because we have put too many ethical restrictions on the princes. Since the *Discourses* of Machiavelli are said to be written in favor of republican government, what modernity has provided is a way out of the Augustinian caveats about the location of the City of God and the weaknesses of human virtue and resolve. Machiavelli apparently wanted also to give the people the same "freedom" he gave to the princes. If we give republics and democracies the same power that Machiavelli gave to the princes, all the objections to the exclusively heavenly location of the perfect city disappear. That is to say, we can begin to think not just of a perfect city in speech, but one also in fact, in deed, though one established and ruled according to the norms of the new philosophy of order, the *novus ordo*. The "City of God" and the Prince's "new foundation," however, are very different.

Machiavelli, who seems implicitly to have wanted to teach the potential philosophers, turns out not to be as pessimistic as St. Augustine about the conditions of the world. Machiavelli "lowered the sights," it is said, only in order to get a handle on how most radically to improve things. Machiavelli, contrary to his own explicit words, was the one "unarmed prophet" who succeeded. He did this by teaching the new potential philosophers, who would in turn teach the princes, how they were to judge and act. He taught this new way of seeing with considerable subtlety, by the examples he chose to praise and by the corrections he made in philosophy. He was a very dangerous unarmed prophet.

III.

This essay is not an essay on Machiavelli. But the oft-repeated remarks by scholars over the centuries that there is something common between Augustine and Machiavelli leads me to ask the question: What is there in Augustine that might give rise to this observation? I have often been struck, furthermore, by the fact that there is nothing in Machiavelli, not one of the most horrible examples or of the cruel actions that he approves of or advises, that would have surprised either Thucydides, Plato, Aristotle, Augustine, Aquinas, or Shakespeare. We know of Plato's sophisticated tyrants, Callicles and Alcibiades. We know of Iago and Richard III. Aristotle actually has a famous discussion in the *Politics* about how tyrants can keep power, a discussion that Machiavelli must have known, as it gives much the same advice about how to rule that Machiavelli does. Yet, we are somehow loathe to think of Aristotle as a teacher of evil, as a teacher of Machiavelli. Aristotle's "practical science" rightly included a full knowledge of both good and bad, of truth and falsity, not so that evil might be done, but that it might be accurately known, and hence avoided and prevented.

Aristotle's worst tyrant, for example, advises us to lop off the heads of those who stand out in the polis. Aristotle's tyrant allows no private friendships; that is to say, implicitly, if he is to stay in power, he is not to allow the highest things to be lived in his polity. Such a tyrant is to know everything that goes on in both the domestic and public orders. He by public works keeps everyone exhaustively busy and distrustful of one another. The difference between the classical authors and Machiavelli with his influence in modernity is not that Machiavelli knew something more about the dark side of human nature than Thucydides, Plato, Aristotle, Augustine, or Aquinas did. Machiavelli is only shocking because, unlike the classical authors, in spelling out in graphic, often historical detail about what a "good" prince did to stay in power, Machiavelli approved of these means. It is this latter approval that we do not find in the classical authors' descriptions of tyrants and other forms of disordered rule.

IV.

Another way to approach St. Augustine and the City of God, of which he wrote in a title that goes back both to the *Psalms* and to the *Republic,* is again to recall Aristotle's discussion about regimes or constitutions. There is indeed something corporate both in our natural living and in our ultimate destiny. Aristotle maintained that most people, most of the time in history, lived under either an oligarchy or a democracy, both of which were, in Greek terms, disordered or bad regimes. Regimes, moreover, primarily reflected the internal order of soul of their citizens. Aristotle distinguished six simple forms of rule. He also contemplated "mixing" these regimes to counteract each other's defects. Life in Aristotle's best political regime was itself not the highest activity to which each man is open. But it was necessary to it and preparatory for it, something that was to make revelation and Aristotle particularly compatible.

Aristotle was most cautious, furthermore, about changing regimes unless we knew what we were doing, to what we were going to change. Change was always in a certain order, not always necessarily from bad to good. Sometimes it was from best to second best, or from the best of the worst to the second worst, to the absolute worst. Thus, it was not sufficient to identify the nature of bad regimes. We had to articulate a workable and moral way to change them to be better. Good intentions or naive meliorism was not enough, but inaction was better than change if our efforts led to something worse. All actual regimes in some sense stood over against the light of the best regime, even if it were discovered, by a long intellectual dialectic, only to exist in speech or in the mind. It was precisely this latter light that Machiavelli sought to dim and extinguish so that nothing could judge his new foundation except its own success.

Jacques Maritain, in a famous essay, put the heart of the problem in this way: "Machiavellianism is a philosophy of politics, stating that by rights good politics is supra-moral or immoral politics, and by essence must make use of evil."[2] Probably no passage reveals more graphically the difference between St. Augustine and Machiavelli about politics. St. Augustine was quite aware that many evil things were done in the name of politics. He was not surprised in the slightest by this incidence of evil. In fact, the early books of the *City of God* were a careful recounting of these

2. Jacques Maritain, "End of Machiavellianism," in *Social and Political Philosophy of Jacques Maritain,* 323.

evils as seen in ancient, particularly Roman, history. What St. Augustine did not do was to conclude that these evil things, however they happened, were not evil.

St. Augustine, consequently, was prepared to envision large numbers of our kind lost in damnation rather than to call what was evil good, rather than to lower his sights. His so-called pessimism was not the pessimism that would say that, since we are so bad anyhow, we ought to use evil so that we would stand above politics to create our own criterion of good and evil quite at variance with the classical standards. His pessimism was rather a practical sort of judgment that saw with a cold eye what most men actually did. He knew of these things because he could see himself, could see the reality and power of his own will and choices. Even with the possibility, through revelation, of repentance, he did not see many evident signs that this same repentance was a popular or frequent activity among sinful men. Augustine is like Machiavelli because he sees the deep resources of disorder in the human city, even when populated by Christians. He is unlike him because he knows himself, knows that the disorders arise from the human heart, from a heart such as that possessed by the actual Augustine.

V.

The evil that did occur nonetheless needed to be accounted for in terms both of the state and of divine providence. That is to say, the state for Augustine was occasioned by the Fall and its consequences. St. Augustine's theory about evil as nonbeing, a lack of good in what is substantially good, moreover, still needed to explain how God's providence resolved the paradox of a good God and these very unsplendid vices of human history. The doctrine of hell or final rejection has its roots in Plato and in the scriptural notion of the power of human free will choosing itself. Augustine was aware that a denial of a final place of punishment for the wicked implied that no human life, good or bad, made any ultimate difference.[3]

It is of considerable interest in this regard that St. Thomas, in his famous question about the existence of God, responds to the primary objection about the reality of evil over against God's goodness by citing precisely St. Augustine, who said that God could bring greater good out of

---

3. See James V. Schall, "Regarding the Inattentiveness to Hell in Political Philosophy," in *At the Limits*, 89–102; and Schall, "On the Neglect of Hell in Political Theory," in *Politics of Heaven and Hell*, 89–107.

any evil that rational beings might bring about.[4] In other words, evil, because it appears in being, which is good, cannot prevent God from bringing forth good consequences from the good that always remains in those beings that do evil actions. One of the goods that evil actions incite is precisely the occasion for repentance, which is essentially, on the part of the doer, the willingness to acknowledge the wrongness of what is done, or in Plato's terms, to accept the punishment for it. God could not, like Machiavelli, lower the sights, but He could forgive, provided the standards that distinguish good and evil are kept, which is precisely what forgiveness implies. Ultimately what is at issue here is whether it would be better for God not to have created at all rather than to create a free, finite being who could reject what is in fact good. The drama both of Augustine and Machiavelli revolves around fundamentally different answers to this question. If Augustine's position is wrong, then, obviously, Machiavelli is right.

VI.

St. Augustine, in his discussions about the Roman Empire, was confronted with the question from Cicero about whether the Roman Republic or Empire was indeed the best of states. Unlike Plato, Cicero wanted to find an actual best city and thought he had found it in the Republic of Rome.[5] Cicero, of course, rightly recognized that this best Roman Republic was disappearing before his very eyes. Indeed, his own murder was at the hands of those who would justify the claim for a new *Pax Romana*. Cicero would, however, consider this new regime of Augustus to be the worst of tyrannies. In Cicero, on this very point, we find a certain priority of action over practical philosophy, of justice over theoretic philosophy that is not found in the Greeks, especially in Plato and Aristotle.

For St. Augustine, his own analysis of the actual Roman regime in the light of Cicero's definition of the state caused him to change the famous criterion from Cicero's justice to love as the basic link or bond of actual states. Two loves built two cities. St. Augustine realized that we could in

4. "*Dicendum quod, sicut dicit Augustinus in Enchridio (C. II): 'Deus, cum sit summe bonus, nullo modo sineret aliquid mali esse in operibus suis, nisi esset adeo omnipotens et bonus, ut bene faceret etiam de malo.' Hoc ergo ad infinitam Dei bonitatem pertinet, ut esse permittat mala et ex eis eliciat bona.*" I-II, 2, 3, ad 1.
5. See James V. Schall, "Post-Aristotelian Philosophy and Political Theory," *Cithara* 3 (November 1963): 56–79; and Schall, "Post-Aristotelian Thought and Modernity," *Aufstieg und niedergang der römischen welt* 2: Principat, Band 36.7 (Berlin: de Gruyter, 1994), 4902–36.

201

IMPLICATIONS OF CATHOLIC THOUGHT

fact love what was not the best, and in fact mostly did so. The effect of this change of definition was to recognize that Aristotle's analyses of the bad regimes did in fact correspond to the political reality of history. That is, most actual regimes were in fact disordered, and the best regime was not the highest thing available to man.

The major problem that arises in Augustinian political philosophy in contrast to modern theory, then, has to do with means, though few would maintain that just any means are legitimate. Even Machiavelli worried about excessively cruel means, as in the famous case of Ramirro d'Orco, who was ordered to do cruel things to establish order in Cesena. But then Ramirro, for his obedience, was in turn executed for doing these very excessive deeds by the same man who ordered him to perform them in the first place. The purpose of this cruel execution—Ramirro was cut in two and hung on the city gates—was not to inspire justice or fear of the Lord, but to inspire fear and amazement in the hearts of the people, or better, to teach us how to rule.

It seemed clear to St. Augustine, however, that the classical moral virtues needed to be understood in the light of the Christian doctrines. St. Augustine did not object to the virtues found to exist among the Greeks and Romans. What concerned him was that even at their highest achievements, they did not point directly to man's destiny in the present order of salvation. They did not account for original sin and grace, even when they suspected that something radically and abidingly wrong remained present in the human condition. These Christian doctrines meant not only that man was in fact destined to something higher than that to which human nature could expect in its own proper order, but they also implied that even in achieving the natural virtues, there was some incompleteness, some natural inability to achieve what philosophy could understand to be proper and due to human nature.

St. Augustine, in other words, had a streak of optimism midst his pessimism that saw, through revelation, not merely the City of God as man's ultimate destiny but a possibility for some limited but real improvement in the world, provided improving the world was not taken to be man's only purpose.[6] With the Fall, something radically was wrong even in the natural order, which remained in itself good and to be praised. How is this situation to be both acknowledged and explained?

6. See Charles N. R. McCoy, "St. Augustine," in *History of Political Philosophy*, edited by Leo Strauss and Joseph Cropsey (Chicago: Rand-McNally, 1963), 151–59.

→202

"[Pagan philosophers] were the first to admit that their model of the most desirable society cannot be translated into action. It exists in speech or 'private discussion' only," Ernest Fortin has remarked in this regard.

De facto, one is always faced with some sort of trade-off, that is to say, with a choice among a variety of regimes none of which is superior in every respect to any of the others.... Augustine's critique ... reminds us of the one that would later be developed by Machiavelli and his followers, who likewise took issue with classical thought on the ground of its impracticality. The difference is that Augustine never thought of lowering the standards of human behavior in order to enhance their effectiveness, as did the early modern philosophers when they boldly tried to root all moral principles in some powerful but selfish passion, such as the desire for self-preservation. If anything, his (Augustine's) own standards are even more stringent than the most stringent standards of the classical tradition. As he saw it, pagan philosophy was bound to fail, not because it made unreasonable demands on human nature, but because its proponents did not know or were not willing to apply the proper remedy to its congenital weakness. That remedy consists in following Christ ... for he alone reveals the true goal of human existence and furnishes the means whereby it may be attained.[7]

These remarks of Ernest Fortin address head on the problem of the similarity and difference between Machiavelli and St. Augustine.

It is of some importance to spell out what is stated here. First, both Augustine and Machiavelli thought classical moral teachings to be "impractical," that is, that they could not achieve the admittedly noble goals that were fashioned in reflection on human nature by the classical philosophers. Both St. Augustine and Machiavelli agree in their descriptions of what men "do" do. Machiavelli took this inability of religion or ethics to bring about the virtue it proposed as a sign of the falsity of the position of the philosophers. The best regime for Machiavelli thus was that regime that could be brought about granted the impossibility to achieve the classical virtues and granted that the definitions of classical virtue no longer held for actual men. This position enabled vice or evil to become a legitimate and theoretically justified instrument of rule.

St. Augustine proceeded in a different fashion. He agreed with the classics, especially with Plato, that the existential status of the best regime is at issue. Plato's constant reminder that the best regime exists only in speech

7. Ernest L. Fortin, "Augustine and the Hermeneutics of Love: Some Preliminary Considerations," in *Augustine Today*, edited by Richard John Neuhaus (Grand Rapids, Mich.: Eerdmans, 1993), 41–42.

was, however, unacceptable to St. Augustine. This is why, among other reasons, he wrote the *City of God*. St. Augustine does not disagree with Plato about the need to think about and formulate the outlines of this city according to principles of reason. Here St. Augustine is in disagreement with Machiavelli but in agreement with Plato. Augustine did not think philosophy either useless or false. St. Augustine's solution is that the "City of God" does in fact exist and is the destiny of mankind. It is an "actual" city, though one unlike any existing political city.

But this City of God, the locus of what men really want and are really offered ("You have made us for Thyself, O Lord"), does not come about through man's own efforts alone. In fact, it is inconceivably better than the purely contemplative solutions hinted at by the philosophers. The City of God does not by itself denigrate the dignity of politics, but it does imply that politics is limited and circumscribed. This is why any theory of a limited state is very compatible with Augustine; indeed, such a thesis has at least one of its origins in Augustine. Augustine would also restrict or put in its proper place the activity of politics itself, even in a limited state. He thought that however important politics might be, there were more important things to do.

VII.

However, very few men, in St. Augustine's view, actually choose the "City of God," even when it was freely offered to them in their liberty. Human life in the world, even with grace, remains pretty much as Machiavelli described it. In other words, no one is to be surprised that we could find popes who were great sinners but who turned out to be, for that very reason, models of political shrewdness, yes, of political Machiavellianism. Machiavelli, on grounds of realism, did not oppose just Plato and Aristotle, but also Augustine and Aquinas. The force of his opposition was that, by empirical observation, neither rational means, that is, the virtues, nor graces, for the most part, "worked." Machiavelli's method, evidently, did "work," but it did so by sacrificing the virtues and the graces.

The resulting city ruled over by the prince was precisely what might be expected of those who refused to be bound by any of the higher virtues. Machiavelli, along with Nietzsche, came about not merely because classical virtues were too difficult but also because Christian grace, in the light of these virtues, was not obviously effective. Chesterton was right in observing that Christianity has not been tried and found wanting, but tried and found difficult. An Augustinian accepts this difficulty without denying the Christianity. A Machiavellian denies the Christianity in order to find an easier way.

What results from St. Augustine's view of grace and fallen nature in the political realm is what has come to be called "Augustinian realism." The state is indeed a divine institution, but it is not the location of perfection or grace. It is a remedy, an institution that must deal with disordered souls as they manifest their desires and degeneracy in public. It is a necessary evil. It ought not to exist but does exist because of the appearance of what ought not to be but is. The "City of God" is not a political institution, but it is the locus of happiness and destiny for those human beings who are conceived, born, and live in existing cities.

This "separation" between the two cities was seen by the earlier writers of the history of political theory, such as George Sabine, to be the contribution of St. Augustine to political philosophy. The *City of God* was written, Sabine observed,

> to defend Christianity against the pagan charge that it was responsible for the decline of Roman power. . . . [Augustine restated] from the Christian point of view . . . the ancient idea that man is a citizen of two cities, the city of his birth and the City of God. . . . Man's nature is twofold: he is spirit and body and therefore at once a citizen of this world and of the Heavenly city. The fundamental fact of human life is the division of human interests, the worldly interests that centre about the body and the other-worldly interests that belong specifically to the soul. . . . This distinction lay at the foundation of all Christian thought on ethics and politics.[8]

And yet, if we are to take this view about Augustine that his major import was to distinguish the two cities, we will find it difficult easily to account for his argument against the Roman philosophers with regard to the Fall of Rome.

For it was St. Augustine's view that the Christians, because they were Christians, in fact made better soldiers and better citizens. St. Augustine's argument with the classics and, if we can anticipate, with Machiavelli later on, was that the polity, the state, could be improved, though it was not and never could be precisely the "City of God." The correct description or definition of the highest things, in other words, was precisely what prevented any civil society from claiming to be something it was not and could not be. In this sense, Sabine was right to see the fundamental importance of

8. Sabine, *History of Political Theory,* 189.

the two cities. But the fact that actual states were not the "City of God" did not mean that nothing of those higher things was operative in them, nor did it mean that what was disordered in personal or civil life became legitimate because it was prevalent. Augustinian realism included the realism of those who in fact lived good lives under grace, even midst the many who lived bad lives rejecting the same grace.

As Augustine said, God could recognize these actual evils and still be so omnipotent that good could come out of the good that stays in any being lacking order. In this way, when this happens, there is restored to the social order, even to the state, something that counteracts the failures of the classical virtues to be easily practiced and of the more complete pessimism that must come if a Machiavellian ruler gains power on employing Machiavelli's own principles.

VIII.

What is being accomplished in history, to conclude, recalling Paolucci's words, is not will of man but of God. The meaning of "political realism" in St. Augustine addresses first the will of man. It does so through the experience, through the account of St. Augustine about what he knew in himself. It is in this sense, as Étienne Gilson points out in a famous essay, a realist metaphysics based on the reality of one man, Augustine.[9] Augustinian realism thus recognizes that at the root of what we see of disorder in the world is a personal will that is the good that God allows to exist even if it chooses against Him and His norms embedded in the being of man the rational being. God even with tender grace has no choice but to leave man in the radical freedom that allows him to choose between two things to love, himself or God and the good world that confronts man.

Machiavellian realism reveals a lack of willingness in the name of will. It accepts the consequences of its choices but refuses to name these consequences by their classic names. The city that the prince founds bears all the characteristics that Aristotle had already found in the tyrant's city. Augustine would have no trouble in recognizing the Machiavellian city, for he too wrote of it. But Augustine knew that grace was present even in the most disordered life, because he knew his own life. His realism included grace, and grace included a challenge to the classical virtues precisely in their own failures. Thus Augustine, unlike Plato, was not content merely

9. Étienne Gilson, "Future of Augustinian Metaphysics," in *A Gilson Reader*, 82–104.

with a city in speech, was not content to be merely a philosopher, though he was a philosopher.

Indeed, Augustine found the Platonists to be the best of the philosophers. But as he told us in the *City of God,* from them, from the philosophers' lofty analyses of justice and the good, he did not hear of the Word made flesh. The realism of Augustine found in each actual city citizens who mostly rejected grace, but some few who would accept it. Thus, it was not merely the City of God that interested him, but all actual cities. Augustine became a bishop, not a lawyer or a philosopher. In this choice, though he was in fact both lawyer and philosopher, there is much reflection for those who would see him as merely a pessimist or as merely a religious precursor for Machiavelli. "Two loves" did build two cities. They still do; of such is Augustinian realism.

15 "MYSTIFYING INDEED"

On Being Fully Human

It is a curious thing that human beings spend so much energy denying their own spiritual and rational nature. No other being tries with such effort to deny that it is what it is. No dog or horse would ever try to show that it is not a dog or horse but only a mixture of matter, force, and accident. Man's attempt to deny his own spirituality is itself a spiritual act, one that transcends space, time, and the limitations of matter. The motivations behind this self-denial are mystifying indeed.

   —Robert Sokolowski, "Soul and the Transcendent Meaning of Persons"

The serious discourse of Christ is now part of the life of thinking, but there still remain situations in which Socratic irony is appropriate. Christian revelation elevates but does not replace human reason, and it leaves intact not only reason's power to discover the truth, but also its dialectical and playful manner of doing so.

   —Robert Sokolowski, "Autonomy of Philosophy in *Fides et Ratio*"

I.

Every so often an event happens that causes us to stop, almost dead in our tracks. We say to ourselves: "This is really significant." This event is not ordinary, which is why we notice it, even though it may chance to happen in the course of an ordinary day. We want to explain why it is so striking. The event can be, and usually is, the meeting of a particular person (all persons are particular, "singular"), or it can be the seeing of a work of art, the hearing some music, or even the witnessing a good game or match. What happens to stir our reflections might even be a tragedy, natural, human, or artistic. But it can also be, as it is here, the reading of a newly published

This essay, occasioned by Msgr. Robert Sokolowski's important new book, *Christian Faith and Human Understanding*, was originally published online by Ignatius Insight (March 2006) in two parts. It is found at: www.ignatiusinsight.com/features2006/schall_sokolowski1_mar06.asp.

book, one that was sent to us from out of nowhere, something we did not actually buy. The event, I say, is the "reading," not the mere publication or possession of the book itself. Strictly speaking, a book does not "exist," or better "re-exist," until someone actually reads it, actually understands it.

Now the reading of books, I know, is relatively common, especially if you spend your days, as I do, in academia. It is part of the trade, even of the "tricks of the trade," of the regular "duty" of office, so to speak. If you read nothing, sooner or later you are fired, or should be. But long ago, you realized that no one, including yourself, can read everything. You read what you can, not all of which overwhelms you. The fact is, however, that some things are better than others. Some books, like those of Plato or Sophocles, we call "classics," and rightly so, because we find so much in them no matter how often we read them.

Other books, we notice, put things together, explain what belongs where and why; these are books, as I like to put it, that tell "the truth of things." They are not necessarily what are called "classics," which, as Leo Strauss said, often contradict each other. Philosophy, at its best, is about the whole of things. Philosophy exists before, within, and beyond books about philosophy. It is an openness to reality, to *what is*, wherever it is found. It wants to know how and *why things are* at all and why things are *as* they are. Nothing that addresses the mind and our being can be left out of our considerations on the supposition that it is not "philosophical." The very leaving out of anything makes the enterprise un-philosophical.

The reading of books enables us to be more than ourselves, to participate in things we never directly experienced or discovered by ourselves. However, even in the case of the relatively few things we may have figured out for ourselves, we are still blessed if we can know what others have thought and done, especially if we are dealing with the most important and fundamental of things, issues we too often fail to broach. The book I am here speaking of and have just read is that of Msgr. Robert Sokolowski. His *Christian Faith and Human Understanding*, just published by the Catholic University of America Press, is a masterpiece of good sense, clarity, profundity, and accuracy of expression.

Sokolowski is a friend of mine. Thus, I write these remarks to call attention to something particularly well done, particularly insightful. Aside from those four or five books of his I have not read, I have previously read various essays of his, his excellent *The God of Faith and Reason*, his *Eucharistic Presence*, and his *Introduction to Phenomenology*. These are heady books, as is this new volume. Sokolowski has a genius for making what otherwise would be abstruse points intelligible to ordinary people. He does not let philosophical language get in his way of explaining the truth of an issue. Indeed, at times, we find something almost "folksy" about his explanations. I do not, however, intend here to write a book review, but I do want to state how illuminating the book is both to ordinary people and to scholars. Sokolowski's clarity brings both into his argument.

Perhaps I could call what follows an "appreciation." I think it worthwhile to make some extended comments on *Christian Faith and Human Understanding*. At bottom, I want to recount something of what is found in this welcome book. To explain it, I do not want to be carried away to produce something three hundred pages long, as is this concise book. But I do want to say that this is not merely a profound book, but a very readable book. Any person to whom the book is implicitly addressed in its very subject matter—bishop, priest, seminarian, medical doctor, psychoanalyst, politician, craftsman, engineer, lawyer, soldier, businessman, housewife, public intellectual, college professor, graduate student, and yes, theologian and philosopher—can understand it.

Every man, John Paul II said in *Fides et Ratio,* itself the subject matter of the first essay in this book, is a philosopher. Everyone wants to know the truth of things. Professional philosophers do not have a monopoly on philosophy. Indeed, as St. Paul intimated, they are not infrequently themselves rather foolish in their explanations of things. But first, for anyone reading this book, his soul had best be prepared to be confronted and challenged by truths he quite likely never suspected, the essential truth that to be fully human one needs both philosophy and grace. Moreover, their relationship is, as Aquinas said, noncontradictory and, as Sokolowski shows again and again, is not in fact contradicted by anything that the modern mind really knows.

The book does not skirt the most profound of issues, such as the Trinity and the Incarnation. It deals with the questions: "What is philosophy?" "What is natural law?" "What is a person?" "What are the virtues?" "What is a soul?" "What is science?" Indeed, for the attentive reader, Sokolowski's habitual method of explaining things is itself extremely educative. The reader is taught as he reads in that very sense that Aquinas advised, that of showing what the order of the subject matter is, how it fits into the whole, how we know and speak of it. Sokolowski always gives brief, pithy examples of his point, again in the best Aristotelian tradition. The mind first and most easily sees general principles in particular instances. As Aquinas said, speaking of beginners in theology, they get tired and bored when things are not presented after the manner of natural knowing, when they cannot see what is going on in their own minds through the mind of the teacher or writer. None of this obscurity is found in Sokolowski.

Sokolowski writes so that the ordinary reader can follow him, but he never avoids the most fundamental of issues. This book is also, as I have indicated, directed to the scholar in his own domain. Nor does Sokolowski ever fail to confront the major points of opposition to what he presents. He knows the difference between mind and brain, together with their relationship to each other. His rejection of an error is always itself an understanding of "what the error means" in its own terms and why it is to be rejected, again in intelligible terms. He holds, without denying that some are more intelligent than others, that every human mind can know much of what is most important to know about reality, about itself. It can know the truth in its basic presentation. Indeed, Sokolowski defines the human person most simply as an "agent of truth." But what is argued, if it is to be seen and understood, has to be presented carefully and systematically.

Sokolowski, who did his higher studies in Louvain, is a philosopher both in the tradition of Aquinas and of modern phenomenology through the work of Edmund Husserl. He is very careful about words and how they are used in all disciplines from theology to psychoanalysis. But behind this attention to language, he is concerned to see how we know and identify things, including our speech about God, where it comes from, how it is used, what it means, why it means what it means. The book is divided into four parts. The first deals with faith and reason, the second with the Eucharist and the Trinity, the third with the human person, and the fourth with what he calls "faith and practical reasoning," wherein he goes into the nature and art of medicine, the professions, seminary training, and universities. His penetrating discussion of political things—Sokolowski is a careful reader of Aristotle's *Politics*—is found in the third section. Even a brief understanding of the variety of these topics will suggest the old principle that to know something, we have to know about everything.

II.

This book at first sight is a collection of sundry essays and lectures previously published in various journals or as chapters in books. The essays represent the quintessence of the work that Sokolowski has pondered over the years as he has taught in the excellent School of Philosophy at the Catholic University of America, where he remains a professor no student in the Washington area with even an inkling of intellectual curiosity wants to miss. What strikes the reader early on in reading this book is, however, that certain basic themes from revelation recur again and again, yet in ever new contexts. Sokolowski notes this recurrence and thinks it might be useful, which it is. Indeed, it is what gives a remarkable unity to this book.

Basically, what Sokolowski does is to show, in each of his considerations, how the content of revelation that we have received and had articulated in tradition—Creation, Redemption, Resurrection—does inform, develop, and, yes, "heal" reason when we reflect on what these truths might mean. These considerations are not merely pious insights but ones rooted in the very fabric of his immediate subject matter, which is first presented in its own philosophic depths. While the basic intellectual structure of revelation has its own inner coherence and articulated relationship with its own matter, it is itself directed to reason, a reason that must already be alive to itself to realize the implications of what is addressed to it.

Revelation thus in large part depends, for our grasping of its significance, on whether we also have gone to the trouble of articulating what we can know by reason. This is why we read the philosophers, to know what they claim to know. This implies that we know what reason and philosophy are about in their own orders. It also intimates that we know what "bad" or incoherent philosophy is and can account for its own deviation from the truth. Our relation to revelation does not depend solely on our relation to philosophy. But both human life and revelation have a direct stake in a philosophy that is true, granted that in knowing the truth we must *ipso facto* know what is not true.

Sokolowski is careful to distinguish and identify the exact meaning of the content of Christian revelation. In an earlier essay,[1] which does not appear in this volume, he described the philosophic method as one of "making distinctions," of the attentive and careful effort to state accurately what one observes and knows, to see that this thing is not that thing, but also to see how and whether this thing is related to that thing and if so, how. Initially, this is a deeply contemplative act that just wants to know, something that appears before any question of "doing" comes into the picture.

In this process, Sokolowski is willing to speak of the differences and similarities between knowing by using language and knowing by using pictures or gestures. He recognizes that man is the animal endowed with

1. Robert Sokolowski, "The Method of Philosophy: Making Distinctions," *The Review of Metaphysics* 51 (March 1998): 515–29.

mind and speech but that man also knows by his whole being. Sokolowski spends some time distinguishing between human speech and the sounds of animals, in a world that often thinks it cannot tell the difference. But he spends more time in addressing the question of divine speech, the Word and words, what exactly it is that we know that is addressed to our minds and to our being in revelation.

The theme or thesis that comes back in almost every essay in some form or another is that of the basic understanding we have from revelation about God, man, and the world. Sokolowski points out that for classical philosophy, a most worthy, if limited, philosophy in its own right, something we still need to know thoroughly and learn from, the world contains the gods or principles as the highest and most important part of its structure. God or the First Mover in this world has no personal relation to the lesser parts of the world which, along with the divinity, evidently always were. The best we ourselves, who have souls, can expect is perhaps an immortality of the soul. We are not pure spirits and, I think, do not want to be. At our highest level, we are devoted to the contemplation of this First Mover, who moves us by love and desire of itself, and by its relation to the cosmos as an order. Perfection, in the classical philosophic view, is to know this order that we did not make. Our action in the world is to put what order we can in our own lives and cities according to the level of being we possess, in imitation of the order we find in the world.

In revelation, both Old and New Testament, however, the world is not the result of chance, nor is it eternally in being. It does not cause itself or its own order. Basically, the world and all in it need not exist. God does not "need" the world, even if he be its source and cause. Why? The reason is internal to himself. He does not require the world because He is already complete in his own inner life, which is itself a social or Trinitarian life. What we can know of this Trinitarian life through revelation constitutes the highest of our intellectual exercises. We not only seek to know it but to know it "face to face," to use Old and New Testament words. It is for this that we come to be in the first place, but not of our own making.

God is not lonely, something about which Aristotle worried. God would be God even if he did not create the world. God does not change by creating what is not himself. If the world exists, as it does, it therefore must do so not because it had to exist. Sokolowski deals with those theories, evolutionism and determinism in their manifold varieties, which claim that the world is necessary or simply accidental, that it explains itself. What this book accomplishes is to enlighten every aspect of reality, once it is described and juxtaposed against the background of the Christian understanding of God as creator and redeemer. Literally nothing we know by natural reason alone is seen in the same light, once we understand its structure or understood meaning in the light of these truths. They explain why the world exists and how it reaches its end through the relation of God to the human persons within the world. Not only do we have a personal uniqueness and destiny before God—we are created, each of us specifically to be what we are—but we are to participate in the inner life of God. We are to be, in Christ, friends of God and of one another. The lofty Aristotelian consideration of friendship is included in and transformed by what we know of God in revelation. The greatest of the revelations as far as we are concerned is simply that we can, contrary to Aristotle's logical wonderment on the topic, be friends of God, as His behest.

Central to Sokolowski's discourse is the question of the redemption and the Eucharist. Sokolowski's discussion of what the Eucharist is becomes particularly important when we see how it relates to everything else, including Creation. He explains how a priest should understand the basic canon of the Mass as he says its very words. He explains the central Catholic teaching on what happens in the Mass, including trans-substantiation, its relation to the Last Supper, to the Crucifixion, and resurrection. There is only one Mass which is at the center of reality, something that is here clarified so that we can see both the human and transcendent dimensions to what is happening. This Mass is the central act of the Church. Indeed, the Church exists that the Mass can still be present among us, the same Mass. It is God's response to the human search for an adequate way to be "pious," to respond to the Godhead in adequate terms, something natural religions and philosophies could never figure out by themselves. Sokolowski is quite attentive to the relation of a decline in belief and practice, especially in the contemporary Church, to failure to understand what the Mass is and to say and participate in it after the manner of what it is. Indeed, this is the central thesis of this book.

Again to explain how this Mass is possible, something that we do wonder about, it is necessary to return again to Creation, its original purpose, which is to invite free and intelligent beings to choose God after the manner in which God is revealed to us, that is, in the birth, life, death, and resurrection of Christ. Thus, Sokolowski deals with the question of who and precisely what Christ is, what the meaning of the two natures in one divine person is. Christ reveals man to himself, so that he might know and choose to be fully what he is. This choice of his being fully himself is now within the context of Incarnation and Redemption. Sokolowski has a rather brilliant section on the history of the Incarnation in Church history. He argues that the central and recurring heresy in the Church over the centuries is that of denying, not the possibility of God, but the possibility of Incarnation and subsequent redemption through Christ. The affirmation of Christ as God causes much more hatred than the denial of God's existence. Most of the early heresies from Arianism to iconoclasm are an astonishing effort to avoid the significance of what the Incarnation means. Literally, it means that one of the Persons in the Trinity became man, true God and true man, and this for our redemption, for our return to the original purpose of Creation in the first place.

It is in this sense also that Sokolowski deals with the meaning of the human person, against the background of Creation and redemption. Not only is a person a rational substance, but it is an absolute unique and singular being in every instance of its appearance, human, angelic, or divine. Sokolowski's use of logic and precise thought in defining the meaning of person is one of the great presentations in this book. This centrality of the person too will found the discussions he develops on politics and natural law. He grounds in the person not only the life of politics in the virtuous and free development of human beings in various political regimes, but indicates why politics, as Aristotle had intimated, "does not make man to be man." Politics already assumes or understands man to be what he is, a certain kind of being, neither angel, god, nor beast, who, reflectively, can know what he is, but know also that he did not make himself to be what he is. And this rightly causes him to wonder why he is at all.

As a philosopher, Sokolowski is very attentive to the importance of the life of thought as a theoretical enterprise. Indeed, on reading this book, one might very well say that the very front line of defense of all human dignity is in the hands and minds of those who think things through. The vocation of the philosopher is, in this sense, often a humble one, however much it is also open to pride. Christianity has long understood, as Josef Pieper in his *Anthology* has remarked, that the political life needs the contemplative life.[2] Christianity must have within it those who are humble enough both to think and to think with the aid of what is known from revelation. Unless this thought is first carried out, the world of action will go on subject to other ideologies and systems that come up with ever more varied and dangerous alternatives to what man is. Conversely, revelation

2. *Joseph Pieper: An Anthology* (San Francisco: Ignatius Press, 1989), 121–23.

has within itself not merely thought but action, including, as Benedict XVI states in his recent encyclical, that which originates in charity, something not wholly accounted for by human reason, but something whose effects it can recognize and politically account for.

Hence we must know what human action is (a topic about which John Paul II wrote so well as a young man) and how it relates to thought. Aristotle is of course a good guide here, as is Aquinas. But the centrality of the person also indicates that the human being includes mind and body, hence concern for well-being of human beings. Indeed, revelation both tells us to believe that Christ is Lord and to give a cup of water, both. And the rendering of things to Caesar tells us that the polity is indeed necessary and natural to us. That the human person has a transcendent destiny is itself what limits politics but also contributes to its dignity. A correct and complete understanding of what a human person is depends, in part, on an understanding of what the divine persons are.

But the very drama of revelation includes this understanding of God, who needs not create, but who does so out of love and generosity. The world, Aquinas said, is created in mercy, not in justice, even though there can and should be justice in the world. But God does not "owe" us our Creation. As Sokolowski shows, this makes us greater, not less. But we can only see this if we see ourselves against the background of revelation which explains to us, in terms we can come to understand even philosophically, why we need not be, yet are.

III.

The last section of *Christian Faith and Human Understanding* deals with what is known as practical intellect, with doing and making. Again in each of these chapters, Sokolowski shows how the professions of law, medicine, business, the military, and education, both university and seminary, relate to intelligence. Previously, Sokolowski had a very direct chapter on, basically, what a bishop is and how to be one. No bishop can afford to neglect this chapter, I think, for Sokolowski's discussion of the difference between an intelligent bishop and a theology or philosophy professor is very insightful. And as in the case of an Augustine and a Ratzinger, it is useful at times to have bishops who are themselves also philosophers. Catholicism is a religion of the mind, but this relation comes from the content of revelation itself. Even though both Plato and Aristotle seem to have wondered about it, it is not something concocted by some thinker except under the stimulus of what is handed down in both Testaments. The bishop, like the pope, himself a bishop, is to teach, sanctify, and rule. All three belong together. But the bishop's main responsibility is to know and hand down what he has received. This principle applies also to the theologian. Whatever great insights bishops and theologians may have, their purpose in being is not to drum up something never heard before, except that which was never heard before through revelation.

Sokolowski in fact thinks one of the main problems that confronts the handing down of what is taught in the Church is the speed and thoroughness with which the Mass was changed after Vatican II. He is very careful to state this problem in accurate terms. He does not think that efforts to improve the Mass and its understanding were not legitimate, but he does think that the effect of such radical changes influenced every area of Catholic life and thought. They have left a heritage of confusion that needs to be corrected, something to which Benedict XVI seems carefully to be addressing himself. The heart of this issue again is what the Mass is and its proper understanding and correct celebration.

Sokolowski's studies on the relation between dogma and social practice are very insightful. He sees clearly that a downgrading of the centrality of Mass as a sacrifice results in an upgrading of the Mass as mainly an expression of a community. The priest begins to see himself as a kind of actor. What goes on is not the Cross but only brotherhood almost for its own sake. This section makes sobering reading.

Sokolowski's discussion of the art of medicine and the other professions is quite insightful. Following remarks of Francis Slade, whom he often cites, Sokolowski is careful to point out the difference between an end and a purpose. An end is something already within something and indicates what it is and what it is at its perfection. A purpose is a human choice. The end of medicine and of the medical profession, something on which all else depends, is the healing of a particular human being who is sick. The doctor does not invent the human being, or even the healing. What he does is to intervene for the healing. The professional standing of the doctor as someone to whom we can trust ourselves depends on his understanding of the end of his profession. If we think that he thinks it is all right to kill or impair us, we will not go to him. But the doctor can still have purposes that may or may not be in direct conformity with the end of the profession. He may want to be rich or famous. This in itself does not necessarily mean that the doctor is not also practicing what medicine is.

These same principles apply to other professions. Sokolowski's discussion of the professions of law and engineering, as opposed to craftsmen in the field, is most useful. And in all of his discussions, he always reflects on how the Christian understanding of man in his supernatural status improves our understanding of the professions. His discussion of psychoanalysis is much needed. What is it? What does it conceive itself to be doing? His basic principle remains that there can be no good profession without a proper understanding of what human persons are, of what the world ultimately is. This involves him with an ongoing discussion of those sciences which more and more prescind from this understanding and think that science in its formulae is what decides what a human being or the world is.

Sokolowski's discussion of the role of philosophy in a seminary education is the last chapter in the book. It is a gem of clarity, not merely in its concreteness, but in its scope of what a well-educated priest (and Catholic and human being) ought to know. The Catholic clergy do not need each of them to be geniuses, but they need intellect and common sense. I am always amused at the iconoclasm that I sometimes find in Sokolowski. For instance, it has been a standing joke in seminary and university education for many years that textbooks are an impediment to learning, that scholastic texts are dry and unhelpful. Not at all, Sokolowski replies. They are very useful. No doubt, they need to be done right—his book itself, I suspect, is the best book on the reform of seminary intellectual life I have seen—but they are definitely useful to go through a wide range of necessary and fascinating subjects. He even gives a suggested number of courses and subjects that need to be covered.

In his discussion of Catholic universities, Sokolowski pays considerable attention to theology departments as key to the whole enterprise. Universities, Catholic ones included, have become subject to the "disciplines" and their professionalism. This criterion presupposes a kind of rationalist ideology about what truth is and how to establish acceptable positions that can be taught within them. Any relation to Church or authority is looked upon as a threat to this kind of ideology. What needs to be seen is how the mind works when its very essence is to begin, not with what the mind is supposedly capable of learning "by its own powers," but what it can learn by accepting authority. He rightly refers to Yves Simon's great work on authority in this context.[3] But the point is illustrated in the whole of Sokolowski's works that seen against the background of revelation clear-

---

3. Yves Simon, *A General Theory of Authority* (Notre Dame, Ind.: University of Notre Dame Press, 1980).

ly and accurately understood, any discipline is better in its own order. It not only must use the mind to know things it never thought of, but it must see that its own mind is affected by the Fall and its own disorders, things that are not merely intellectual but moral attention.

Obviously, then, I like this book. I am in the habit of recommending books. My column in *Crisis* was entitled "Three Books."[4] In it, I suggested three books that, I think, go a long way toward explaining everything, that give that universal "scope" that is peculiarly Catholic. They are *Joseph Pieper—An Anthology*, Peter Kreeft, *The Philosophy of Tolkien*, and Ralph McInerny, *The Very Rich Hours of Jacques Maritain*.[5] Let me add a fourth book, *Christian Faith and Human Understanding*, as a book that will put everything together and give a new light to almost everything that we know.

In the beginning of this chapter, I cited a passage from Sokolowski that remarked on how odd it is, "mystifying indeed," as he picturesquely put it, that man would take such efforts to deny what he is. If anyone wants to know what modern man is most often denying, nothing will help him more than this book on faith and understanding. Sokolowski, referring to the German philosopher Robert Spaemann, also cited Socrates and Christ as if they both belonged to the same overall discourse. He intimates that the understanding of both Socrates, the philosopher, and Christ, the Word made flesh, is necessary for the wonder of our intellectual lives, for our knowing the fullness of *what is*. To be a theologian means to be able to describe the content of revelation as handed down in precise and accurate terms. John Paul II said in *Fides et Ratio* that one needs also to be something of a philosopher. And to be a philosopher means to be open to *what is*, including to the something called revelation as referring to realities we must confront if we are to neglect nothing in being. No one in academic life embodies these two aspects of what a thinker is better than Robert Sokolowski.

4. Schall, "Three Books," *Crisis* 22 (April 2004): 63.
5. Kreeft, *The Philosophy of Tolkien* (San Francisco: Ignatius Press, 2005); McInerny, *The Very Real Hours of Jacques Maritain* (Notre Dame, Ind.: University of Notre Dame Press, 2003).

16 · TRANSCENDENCE AND
POLITICAL PHILOSOPHY

And yet—do we not find ourselves somewhat caught in the modern world of work—faced with the increasing politicization of the academic realm and the ominous shrinking of the inner and outer opportunities for public discourse, and especially genuine debate? Where shall we seek the "free area" in which alone theoria (and by theoria, we mean concern, limited by no practical [political, economic, technical, sectarian] considerations, with "truth and nothing else")? We begin to understand Plato's academy had been a thiasos, a religious association assembling for regular sacrificial worship. Does this have any bearing on our time?

—Josef Pieper, *Scholasticism: Personalities and Problems in Medieval Philosophy*

I.

The primary task of political philosophy is to situate life itself in an intelligible context, in the whole, so that politics, as itself something essential to this life, to this whole, need not, however, function as a "substitute metaphysics." Politics, in its self-justification, when its intrinsic limitations are not intellectually understood, can become a spurious description of the order of reality, itself dependent solely on human projections. This awareness that politics can claim to be more than itself implies that the defense of politics is the allowing it to remain itself. It is the highest practical science, but not the highest science as such (1095a15–16). At some fundamental level, this requires the recognition that there are things "beyond politics."

The understanding of these things beyond politics constitutes the essential factor in limiting politics to be politics. Behind any given order, in other words, is the intelligibility of that order, the order of its parts, and the end of the whole. Things will not "act" as they should unless they are allowed to be *what they are*. This conclusion necessarily implies that many

This essay was originally published in the *Review of Politics* 55 (Spring 1993): 247–65.

quite legitimate spheres of human reality besides politics exist, even when we rightly grant that man by nature is a political animal. This explication was, in part, the burden of Aristotle's last book of the *Ethics* and the first book of the *Politics*. To politicize what is not political is to subvert or destroy it. The first line of defense for anything, then, particularly for politics, is theoretical. This position means that the contemplative order ultimately "upholds" the practical order by knowing what politics is in the order of things.

Socrates, at the end of the fifth book of the *Republic*, called philosophers those "who delight in each thing that is itself" (480a). But not all things are the same; each thing acts according to *what it is*, to its being, to its level of existence. Dogs act in dog ways, stars in star ways. What is peculiar about specifically "human" being is that it possesses activities that remain within it, as well as those that reach out to a world no human being made to be *what it is*. Through intellection, then, what is not intellect itself can, in some sense, come to exist in a limited, finite being, after the manner of intellect, not existence. Thus, it is not enough for human beings merely "to exist" to be *what they are* in their fullness. Nonetheless, they should exist in such a way that what is not their particular selves becomes also theirs, without ceasing to be the finite beings they are.

The order and cause of the whole is a legitimate concern of the human intellect. Man *is* a rational being. "Placing happiness in sheer naked existence," Yves Simon wrote,

is a metaphysical mistake of the first magnitude, and of great profundity—of such profundity, indeed, that the metaphysician at once recognizes in it the kind of error from which much can be learned. The plenitude that happiness implies is not found in naked existence but rather in the ultimate exercise of his (man's) best activity.[1]

In the classical philosophical tradition, this highest activity implied that, however interior its depth in the rational being, the reach of reason transcends itself to seek to know a *what is* that the human intellect does not itself constitute in being. That is, the very concept of happiness, with which Aristotle began his reflections on ethical and political philosophy, includes both (1) the self remaining the self, not a god or a beast (1253a29), and (2) the self reaching what is the highest cause in itself. The human intellect seeks to know what it can about the first cause because it knows finite

1. Yves Simon, *Philosophy of Democratic Government* (Chicago: University of Chicago Press, 1977), 265.

things that do not fully explain either their existing at all or their existing as this and not that particular kind of a being.

II.

Political philosophy at its best is ordered to understanding how this pursuit of the highest good and the highest knowing can come about through virtue, freedom, and ordered authority. At its worst, political philosophy seeks to identify itself with what it makes on its own authority. Political philosophy in this latter sense identifies the self and the "transcendent self," that is, the self that knows things other than itself, with what the mind constructs out of its own resources, particularly its highest resources in reason.

This latter possibility of a self-constructed reality not in conformity with *what is,* moreover, is the reason why specifically "modern" political philosophy is paradoxical, why it is itself a philosophic problem of the greatest moment. That is, the good polity must be constituted to allow nonpolitical or transpolitical reflections, actions, and institutions to occur and exist—from those activities of human love of the particular to those of prayer and voluntary good works.

This awareness that politics does not constitute everything is what Aristotle meant when he called politics the highest "practical" science, but not the highest "theoretical" science (1141a20–22). When, in Machiavelli's *Prince,* the theoretic kingdoms of the ancient and medieval philosophers are rejected in favor of what men do "do," the essential check on politics, the theoretical check, was undermined. Controversies about the place of Machiavelli in political philosophy essentially revolve about this consideration of giving to the politician the "freedom" to himself determine the distinction of good and evil.

Both in terms of their power and moral sovereignty, modern states in particular—those theoretic-practical entitles that only fully appeared in the sixteenth century—have the raw capacity, or at least desire, to prevent any consideration of truth other than the polity's own public version of the world. In the *Apology,* Socrates maintained that he owed his life to his remaining for as long as possible a private citizen (31). And while this privacy did not in the end save him, his death preserved the primacy of truth to politics. The modern state in its extreme forms, by contrast, demands both internal and external conformity with its, often democratically chosen, order. That is to say, the reason for Socrates' privacy, to pursue the truth, remains a problem in the modern state, perhaps in a form even more extreme than in the democracy at Athens. This is why the modern state is so much more dangerous, even when, or perhaps especially when, it claims it is founded, theoretically founded, on no specific truth, the claim of the modern liberal states.

In this sense, moreover, a true metaphysics, a valid science of *what is,* however difficult to come by in itself, presupposes a limited, or at least, an inefficient polity. This practically limited polity need not mean, of course, that the best philosophy, let alone the best art, is necessarily produced by or in the best existing states. We have examples of tyrants supporting good art and killing saints. It does mean, nonetheless, that the accurate description (or existence) of the best state is not exclusively what we mean when we describe or await the fullness of *what is.* This is why the philosophical description of the best regime ought to be a protection, not an undermining, of existing practical regimes without at the same time denying their function in pointing out disorders in existing regimes.

III.

Thus, a truly "limited politics" is justified only by a valid metaphysics that properly places the part within the whole, the part that is politics within the whole of *what is.* This "part" that is politics does not deny that it is itself in some sense a view of the whole, an architectonic science, that looks at how all practical actions relate to each other and to what transcends practical action itself (1094a25–b11). In turn, a valid metaphysics must account for the question of revelation, of a more comprehensive whole than what reason itself might grasp, whether revelation be understood in the Platonic sense or in that of Islam, Judaism, or Christianity.[2] The truth of any or all of these revelations, clearly, is itself a fundamental, unavoidable issue, obscured by the primacy of a theory of tolerance unquestioned in its own premises. The argument for transcendence in political philosophy is not an argument against the need to sort out the validity of the various claims of revelation to be true.

That is to say, normally legitimate questions arise from the human experience of living and living politically, wherever and whenever this experience occurs in human history. There are questions that arise in political

2. See Schall, *Reason, Revelation, and the Foundations of Political Philosophy;* Schall, *Politics of Heaven and Hell;* and idem., *What Is God Like?*

living that remain unsolvable by politics itself. Yet such questions are quite intelligible in themselves. Since Aristotle held that nature makes nothing "in vain," including human nature, this position usually causes us at least to wonder whether, in the case of the highest things, there is not something incomplete or even contradictory about the world or man.

The atheist's charge, be it mild or violent, of "ill-made" against the Deity on account of the conditions of the actual world is not altogether unintelligible. No doubt, there is a school of thought that calls such transcendent questions illusory. They are said to be the causes of wasted energies better spent on improving the world. The essence of humanism becomes, in this position, the exclusion of the highest things as distracting. But this conclusion only causes the issue to go officially underground, even in ourselves.

IV.

Moreover, if there be experiences of transcendence that arise out of politics itself, what are they? The most famous is perhaps the manner in which Socrates came to speak of rewards and punishments in the last book of the *Republic*. Justice required him to posit immortality and a place of final reward and punishment for goods and evils not adequately accounted for in the existing polity. Another issue would be the specific object of "contemplation" that Aristotle told us in the last book of the *Ethics* is the highest end of that consideration of happiness that ethical and political life within human experience requires us to ponder (1177b8–1178a5).

What then is the nature of the responses these unsettled questions that arise in political philosophy itself have received? Both metaphysics and political theology permit us at least to acknowledge that some of these responses of revelation belong to the same realm of discourse as philosophy does. But the key question, other than the accurate description of what such answers of revelation are stated to be, is whether such answers are addressed to the questions properly and necessarily posed by the political philosophers. "Political theology," in this sense, would specify the intelligible formulation of such responses as they were presented in the traditions of revelation.[3]

3. An accurate understanding of what Catholicism, for instance, specifically holds on a particular topic, thus, would today include the presentation in *Catechism of the Catholic Church* (Rome: Liberia Editrice Vaticana, 1994). Even a tradition of revelation, then, needs to clarify itself to itself in order for others to know what it holds of itself.

Political philosophy thus would be an aspect of theology and revelation, though not derived from either, if the content of revelation turned out to complete or resolve dilemmas left unanswered or unaccounted for by political philosophy. If such answers completed the meaning of the higher things in their comprehension and were, simultaneously, answers to questions arising in political life, it would be less than philosophical to conclude that no relation existed between the questions properly posed and the answered correctly formulated. This approach would be doubly meaningful for the philosopher, in particular, if there were also found in the tradition of revelation at least some positions that were also able to be reached by philosophy alone. This parallel appearance would suggest confirmation that both truth and cosmos in the light of the highest things are one in origin.[4]

Aristotle had observed, to recall, that if man were the highest being, politics would be the highest science (1141a20–22). That is to say, the political answers to the highest questions would be definitive were man the highest being. Thus, there could be no grounds for a conflict between philosophy—or even poetry, to recall the *Republic* (607b)—and politics, since politics as the master practical science would rule all other disciplines. Any opposition between the order of polity and the order of *what is* would be a delusion, since there could be in nature no order to which the human intellect was open that would indicate the limits of the city.

On this hypothesis, the *City of God* or the *Republic* in speech would not be able to justify itself against the city of man, the polity, whatever else that higher city turned out to be. This latter position was, in essence, the sophist position from book 1 of the *Republic*. It has many revivals in modern political philosophy when nothing superior to the will of the people or the prince can be conceived or admitted as operative in any polity.

In Aristotle's view, however, man was not the highest being, but the lowest of beings with intelligence as definitive of their form and existence, the *"microcosmos,"* to be exact. Aristotle advised rather that the very dignity of the human in its highest reaches depended upon human beings devoting at least some of their fundamental energies to the highest things as such (1177b31–1178a2). The philosophers especially were to consider what transcended human doing and making, to consider what was itself uncaused, what could not be otherwise, what was for its own sake. In this

4. See Gilson, RRMA; McInerny, *St. Thomas Aquinas;* McInerny, "Introduction," in Lerner and Mahdi, *Medieval Political Philosophy;* and Pangle, "Introduction," in Strauss, *Studies in Platonic Political Philosophy.*

sense, the "pull" of the higher things exercised upon each individual human being was the source of his liberty from things less exalted, while not at the same time denying the latter their limited goodness. The value of these latter things were not denied but enhanced by the philosophic recognition that they did not form or constitute *all that is.*

Eric Voegelin put the matter in this way: "'Reason' did not exist in language in the history of mankind until it was formulated in the Greek fifth century as a word denoting the tension between man as a human being and the Divine ground of his existence of which he is in search."[5] The very presence of this tension, this reason, is what limits politics most radically to guarantee that it be merely, yet nobly, an organized relationship in which each human being ought to be able to act according to his being. This resultant action or interaction we call politics did not itself, however, result in some sort of new substantial being.[6] What was attracted to the highest things, in tension with the Divinity, was not the polity itself, but each individual as such, no matter what his polity. Man's being was totally political, yet the political was ordered to what was beyond the political.

Thus, in Aristotle's words, "political science did not make man to be man" (125822–4), by which he meant that the *what is* of man was already intelligible, already a "given," because man did not cause his own existence and knew he did not cause it. By self-reflection within the very act of knowing something besides himself, some particular thing, some stone even, man also knew he existed, knew he caused neither the stone nor himself to be. So it is, neither the object other than man himself that he knows in cognition, nor the man himself known indirectly as the "I" who knows, was formed or created by man.

This understanding of how we know was what constituted the very first sign of the limited being of man, the realization that man was already man "from nature." This conclusion was the metaphysical grounding of the "moderation" that underlies classical and medieval political philosophy. Too, this moderation meant, in some basic sense, that the human enterprise was primarily one of discovery or "surprise," not one of self-construction.

5. *Conversations with Eric Voegelin*, 138.
6. See J. M. Bochenski, "Society," in *Philosophy: An Introduction* (New York: Harper Torchbooks, 1972), 93–101; and Schall, "The Reality of Society according to St. Thomas," in *Politics of Heaven and Hell*, 235–52.

V.

"The supreme adventure," then, as Chesterton put it, "is being born. ... When we step into the family, by the act of being born, we do step into a world which is incalculable, into a world which has its own strange laws, into a world which could do without us, into a world that we have not made."[7] The project of what man was "to do" or "to make," both perfectly human powers, originated in the prior reality of what man was in being by the very fact that he was conceived and born a human being, not something else, not a toad or an angel. It was on this latter fact, on the "given-ness" of our human *being*, that human freedom and destiny ultimately rested, even in the political order. Implied in this reality was the realization that the metaphysical and transcendent ends indicated by revelation, for which human being and freedom existed, were more exalted than any alternative or substitute ones that man might make or concoct for himself. The Nietzschean "death of God" and the modern revolutionary project to replace all natural and divine ends by man-established ones were, indirectly and by accurate comparison, testimony to the superior formulation of man by nature and its own source.

The importance of this position needs to be understood. The first step is the effort to replace man's natural "being" and its intelligible destiny by an artificial or humanly elaborated one. This replacement is the enterprise of modern political philosophy from Hobbes and Rousseau. It is the logical and expected alternative left to an intelligence that finds no order given in the whole or in the structure of its self. The only source of "rationality" that exists, on the hypothesis that no divine order can be posited as a first cause, is the human intellect. But this human intellect is now presupposed to no given form of its own. As a result, the task of the "highest" science—now politics, not metaphysics—becomes that of "creating" or forming man according to norms specifically opposed to what he was seen to be in nature.

In this connection, then, Eric Voegelin's remarks on "the death of God" are pertinent. "The murder of God is committed speculatively by explaining divine being as the work of man.... In order to appear the unlimited master of being, man must so delimit being that limitations are no longer evident," he wrote.

---

7. Chesterton, "On the Institution of the Family," in *Heretics*, 143.

It does not suffice . . . to replace the old world of God with a new world of man; the world of God itself must have been a world of man, and God a work of man which can therefore be destroyed if it prevents man from reigning over the order of being. The murder of God must be made retroactively and speculatively. . . . Historically, the murder of God is not followed by the superman, but by the murder of man: the deicide of the Gnostic theoreticians is followed by the homicide of revolutionary practitioners.[8]

Political philosophy, thus, presupposed to no limits, necessarily became itself the origin of the distinctiveness of things, including human things.

Both human and divine things were strangely intractable, however, to an absolute human power to refashion them into something better. In the modern project, on the other hand, we only know what we make so that all truth, including political truth, is in fact "artistic" truth. Artistic truth is conformity between what we make and what we intended to make. If politics is this sort of truth in its essence, if the polity "makes" truth because nothing higher than it exists, we lose our capacity, by right, to oppose any structure of the city except on the basis of another, more powerful will. Thus, nothing can, strictly speaking, be "wrong" with any polity as such, since its origin lies exclusively in will and political will dependent on no order outside itself. In this sense, Machiavelli could rightly suggest that the only bad prince was one who did not succeed. In this way, transcendence, of whatever form, has disappeared into politics. Hobbes's Leviathan is accountable only to itself when it comes to the validity of the truth in theology or politics or poetry.

VI.

Leo Strauss, in commenting on the nature of modern liberal education, noted how philosophy became subservient to political philosophy when political philosophy itself accepted the Baconian improvement of man's own estate as its very purpose:

According to classical philosophy, the end of the philosophers is radically different from the end or ends actually pursued by the non-philosophers. Modern philosophy comes into being when the end of philosophy is identified with the end which is capable of being actually pursued by all men. More precisely, philosophy is now

8. Eric Voegelin, *Science, Politics, and Gnosticism* (Chicago: Regnery-Gateway, 1968), 54–55, 64.

asserted to be essentially subservient to the end which is capable of being actually pursued by all men.[9]

This conclusion is, no doubt, the "lowering of sights" from Machiavelli that specifically means the personal incapacity of most men to be virtuous in the classical sense. The very notion of transcendence and a consequent distinction between good and evil knowable by the human intellect as given has disappeared. This difference between what men do "do" and what they ought to do is, in essence, the root of the difference between classical natural law and modern natural right.[10]

What followed from this position, as Strauss also perceptively observed, was not merely the abandonment of classical philosophy as such, but the incorporation of higher means and norms of revelation into this very scheme of a new political philosophy. Man's highest good became identified with a version of politics based on a projection of Plato's community of wives, children, and property, on Hobbes's primacy of "life," on comfort and compassion as the purpose both of philosophy and revelation. In this context, even "grace" and "mercy" were politicized.[11]

"Philosophy thus understood could be presented with some plausibility as inspired by biblical charity, and accordingly philosophy in the classical sense could be disparaged as pagan and as sustained by sinful pride," Leo Strauss wrote.

One may doubt whether the claim of biblical inspiration was justified and even whether it was always raised in entire sincerity. However this may be, it is conducive to greater clarity, and at the same time in agreement with the modern conception, to say that the moderns opposed a "realistic," earthly, not to say pedestrian conception to the idealistic, heavenly, not to say visionary, conception of the classics. Philosophy or science was no longer an end in itself, but in the service of human power, of a power to be used for making human life longer, healthier, and more abundant.[12]

What is particularly remarkable about this passage is that it describes rather accurately the theoretic framework by which the City of God was

---

9. Leo Strauss, *Liberalism: Ancient and Modern* (New York: Basic Books, 1968), 18.

10. See Alexander Passerin d'Entreves, *The Natural Law: An Historical Survey* (New York: Harper Torchbooks, 1965), chap. 1; and James V. Schall, "On Being Dissatisfied with Compromises: Natural Law and Natural Right," *Loyola Law Review*, New Orleans 38, no. 2 (1992): 289–309.

11. See Schall, "On the Disappearance of Mercy from Political Theory," in *Politics of Heaven and Hell*, 353–78.

12. Strauss, *Liberalism*, 20.

turned into the earthly city as its exclusive meaning, both in philosophy and in theology. Moreover, this earthy city, now seen as the intellectual end both of philosophy and of revelation, no longer has any transcendent check upon what this power in the service of a longer, healthier, or more abundant life might turn out to be. By gaining the freedom of human autonomy, we have lost a vision that did not arise from man himself.

Thus, we have "lowered the sights" from what we ought to do—the "visionary" conception of the classics—to what we do "do"—the "pedestrian" description of life as bereft of transcendental purpose. We have implicitly reduced revelation to philosophy and philosophy to politics. As a result, politics becomes a version of economics, as Hannah Arendt maintained, that consists in nothing nobler than keeping alive, no matter at what cost or for what purpose.[13]

VII.

If this line of reasoning be at all correct, Hobbes remains the one philosopher necessary to understand what has happened both to philosophy and to revelation. Indeed, a legitimate case can be made for the thesis that political philosophy is today, because of the peculiar nature of modern philosophy, at the heart of the struggle to retain the validity of even revelation. The reason for this relationship is that theology, by using more and more the concepts and terms of modern thought to explain itself, has indirectly embraced ideology as its own description of what it is about. To uphold classical theology today, the main burden lies not in philosophy but in political philosophy.

In this context, furthermore, it is not altogether inappropriate to recall Aristotle's reasons for rejecting the literal view of the best state as seen in Plato's *Republic:* "The extreme unification of a state is clearly not good; for a family is more self-sufficient than an individual, and a city than a family, and a city only comes into being when the community is large enough to be self-sufficing. If then self-sufficiency is to be desired, the lesser degree of unity is more desirable than the greater" (1262b11–15). This famous passage suggests why the project of Hobbes to stay alive at all costs was intellectually plausible. That is, all disparate being was reduced to the mere existence of one corporate being.

13. Hannah Arendt, *The Human Condition* (Garden City, N.Y.: Doubleday Anchor, 1959), 286–91.

On the positive side, Aristotle's remark also serves to ground the reason why the polity and the human person could have different ends yet remain essentially related. Man remained a social animal even though his reason transcended politics. The greater substantial unity and greater inner activity of an individual person was itself the basis for its own higher and transcendent destiny.

The meaning of this result is clarified in Aquinas's introduction to his "Commentary on Aristotle's *Ethics.*" Here, Aquinas wrote, "The whole that the political multitude or the family constitutes has only a unity of order, by reason of which it is not something absolutely one. Therefore, a part of this whole can have an operation that is not the operation of the whole." (#5). This reflection gives us the most profound reason why the polity cannot absorb all our being. Even when the polity is at its best, the wholeness of each individual requires and can be given an end proper to itself that is not that of a political relation or order based on human interaction alone. It is because of this position that the "ground" of being itself can "pull" each of us, to recall Voegelin's analysis.

Thus, any charter of absolute human liberty free of any limits must also begin here. Any philosophical endeavor to recreate or construct a "new man" solely in terms of autonomous human intellect must, in the name of existence and being, reduce man to a single corporate entity. For autonomous man, final existence of some perfect polity down the ages arrayed against nothingness is the sole human guarantee, whatever its consolation, against ultimate human and individual meaninglessness.

VIII.

In the context of modern philosophy and its weakness, then, is there any inner-worldly project for a "recovery of the transcendent"? Is it possible to contemplate a politics set over the endeavor of merely staying alive? The first step, as Charles N. R. McCoy wrote, is "a scrupulous care for the thread of tradition in political philosophy." That is, we first need to see how the extreme results within the history of theology and philosophy were in fact related to a natural order whose essential form was not self-created.[14] The denial of this given, natural order must be seen to lead logically to certain definable, even remarkable forms of counter-order that are proposed or imposed as alternatives to *what is*. The classless society, the general will,

14. Charles N. R. McCoy, *Structure of Political Thought* (New York: McGraw-Hill, 1963), 7.

secular liberalism, even ecology and newer forms of feminism and multi-culturalism seem to be attractive on precisely this basis of a free re-propos-ing of what it is to be human from a malleable raw material that has no or-der or form of its own.

But for this first step to be possible, we must have some source of lib-erty from the many all-consuming modern ideologies themselves. Both Professors John Senior and Alasdair MacIntyre have intimated that some form of revival of the monastery or the contemplative academy is neces-sary, assuming it is possible.[15] Josef Pieper, as we saw in the beginning of this chapter, hinted that this final openness to real being requires some-thing like a Platonic academy in which worship is a regular feature, since what distracts us most is the disorder we find within ourselves.[16]

Transcendence, moreover, implies the inadequacy, though not the cor-ruption, of human reason.[17] In Voegelin's terms, some tension exists where-by the human intellect recognizes that it does not itself constitute the ground of being. Thus, it had no other choice but to search for it, if it ex-isted—hence the efforts to "prove" God exists—or to be sought by it, with the capacity, because of its intellectual powers, of itself being found. The very possibility of revelation presupposes this latter capacity as an intrinsic feature of the human intellect itself.

In his *Notes toward the Definition of Culture,* T. S. Eliot set down the critical alternatives:

The dominant force in creating a common culture between peoples, each of which has a distinct culture [of its own], is religion. Please do not . . . make a mistake of anticipating my meaning. This is not a religious talk, and I am not setting out to convert anybody. I am simply stating a fact. . . . The unity of culture, in contrast to the unity of political organization, does not require us all to have only one loyalty: it means that there will be a variety of loyalties. It is wrong that the only duty of the individual should be held to be towards the state; it is fantastic to hold that the su-preme duty of every individual should be towards a super-state.[18]

15. John Senior, *Restoration of Christian Culture* (San Francisco: Ignatius Press, 1983); and Alasdair MacIntyre, *After Virtue* (Notre Dame, Ind.: University of Notre Dame Press, 1981). See also Christopher Derrick, *Rule of Peace: St. Benedict and the European Future* (Still River, Mass.: St. Bede's Publications, 1980).

16. This would also be the position of Schumacher, *Guide for the Perplexed.*

17. Interestingly enough, John Paul II, in *Centesimus Annus* (1991), remarked: "There can be *no genuine solution of the 'social question' apart from the Gospel,* and that the 'new things' can find in the Gospel the context of their correct understanding and the proper perspective for judgment on them" (#5).

18. T. S. Eliot, *Notes toward the Definition of Culture* (New York: Harcourt Brace, 1968), 200–201.

Eliot thought that the universities ought to acknowledge a loyalty to something higher than the state. Yet it has been precisely the incapacity of the universities to preserve a philosophy other than skepticism, historicism, relativism, or positivism that points to something lacking in the very natural enterprise of philosophy itself.[19]

IX.

"It is exceedingly rare to find in the academy a recognition of the importance of recovering to the individual mind," Marion Montgomery wrote, "the gifts to it in its ways of knowing. . . . It remains to the particular mind, then, to rediscover those complementary gifts, through which one recovers virtue in the self, and an ordinate deportment toward creation. In that pilgrim journey, the risks of one's own being are at issue."[20] What, we might ask in conclusion, are these "risks of one's own being"?

In modern political philosophy, the risk is the identification of happiness with a political order over time in which the elevated aims of revelation are reabsorbed into the highest practical science to propose a worldly solution to the question of happiness. This is the very question with which we all must begin moral and political considerations in the first place. Eliot had warned that "modern political thought, inextricably involved with economics and with sociology, preempts to itself the position of the queen of the sciences."[21] In the Greek tradition, however, metaphysics was the "queen" of the sciences, while for the tradition of revelation it was theology. The "risk" of political philosophy assuming into itself philosophy as such is then not merely a curious intellectual exercise, though it is that too. It is nothing less than turning over to the polity the definition of *what is.*

Leo Strauss, consequently, was remarkably astute in his *City and Man* when he set down his program: "But in our age, it is much less urgent to show that political philosophy is the indispensable handmaid of theology than to show that political philosophy is the rightful *queen* of the social sciences, the sciences of man and human affairs."[22] What is to be noted here

19. See Nicholas Lobkowicz, "Christianity and Culture," *Review of Politics* 53 (Spring 1991): 373–90.

20. Marion Montgomery, "Virtue and the Risks of Being," *Intercollegiate Review* 19 (Winter 1984): 26.

21. Eliot, *Notes toward the Definition of Culture,* 164.

22. Leo Strauss, *City and Man,* 1.

is that Strauss rightly called political philosophy the queen of the social sciences, not the queen of the sciences as such.

This restriction of Strauss meant that political philosophy itself was ordered to philosophy, whose own relation to theology or revelation at least required, in Strauss's view, an accurate knowledge of what was known by reason. The problem for philosophy was whether it could resolve all the questions that rightly and legitimately reason could pose to being, particularly human being. Aquinas was most perceptive in locating the "necessity" of revelation, of answers to questions rightly asked and initially formulated, within political philosophy (I-II, 91, 4). That is to say, transcendence and political philosophy, without denying the distinction of faith and reason, are, in some basic sense, part of the same discourse.

The second "risk" of being, therefore, is the temptation to ideology, to divorce the questioning power from all answers extant in reality. What is new is not Strauss's insistence on the social scientist's seeing the outlines of the City of Righteousness by his own powers, at least as much as he could. What is new is the co-option of so much of the tradition of revelation by the ideologies of the modern era. Not merely must we pay attention to those related to socialism or fascism, but also to those related to environmentalism, feminism, advanced liberalism, certain forms of conservatism, and deconstructionism.[23] The tension and openness to being that Aquinas stood for is but rarely and clearly proposed in the intellectual circles of revelation itself. This means that the autonomous forms of political philosophy have in practice nowhere to turn except to themselves once they decide that human will is the only basis of political reality.

The final "risk" of being, consequently, is what Voegelin called "the cheap answer." That is, a restricted description of what our being is. Its outlines are found only in man himself and this in direct opposition to the answers found in classical metaphysics and revelation. These ideological responses, because of the queen of the social sciences, take on exclusively political form. Any speculative rectitude to politics is denied in theory because no intelligible order exists except order based on human reason alone.

To the double-pronged question, "Why are things at all, and why are they as they are?" Voegelin wrote,

There is of course no answer, because the ground from which things are what they are, and are at all, is a transcendent divine ground; there is no answer except in

23. See Paul Johnson, "Is Totalitarianism Dead?" *Crisis* 7 (February 1989): 9–17.

the symbolism of theology or of a myth or of a metaphysics of transcendent divine being or something like that—which does not render any simple proposition for knowing about the matter. The question itself, you might say, implies its answer, because in raising this question the very nature of man who is in search of his ground, expresses itself in questioning to the last point, or to the last resort, what is the ground of everything with regard to existence and essence. In this question one keeps one's human condition and is not tempted to find cheap answers.[24]

What is clear, however, is that such alternate "cheap" answers abound. It remains very difficult to discover the real ground of being because of them.

However, the main "risk" with Voegelin's own position, it would seem, lies in the fascination of a transcendence that cannot, or did not, become definitely Word, flesh. That is, the caution to define what the consequences of transcendence are in philosophy itself and in political philosophy is not a guarantee of "openness" or a protection of the incomprehensibility of the divinity. In effect, it is a doubt that transcendence reaches each individual in an ordered way, which is the very notion of a "public" revelation, granted that its credibility presupposes intellectual "preambles," reasons, as Aquinas maintained (I, 2, 2, ad 1). These positions do not necessarily become merely "simple propositions for knowing about the matter." They are reactions of the intellect itself in its own order to what it has received. Each person transcends the polity because he is a whole, even in his most distinct powers, particularly in his intellect that seeks to know what it has experienced in propositional terms, without denying their origins in what is.

Clearly, it is true that no finite intelligence can by its own powers know and possess *all that is,* the highest things. The risk is that we conclude from this truth that distinctive revelation does not reach philosophy in terms of the seemingly insolvable positions already perplexing the philosophers. Strauss's worry that revelation was a sort of unfair tactic for philosophers must be counterbalanced by the sense of unity that results when political theology and political philosophy exist in the same person seeking *what is,* however presented from reason or revelation.[25]

The problem for the philosopher and the political philosopher in recent years is not the claims on intellect by the doctrines of revelation. Rather it is that revelation too often speaks in terms of those very political ideologies that the political philosopher recognizes as strictly human in origin. Liberation theology and environmental Christianity are obvious

24. *Conversations with Eric Voegelin,* 2–3.
25. Leo Strauss, *Natural Right and History* (Chicago: University of Chicago Press, 1964), 164.

examples in recent decades. Again, this awareness of the intellectual nature of ideology is why it might be held that political philosophy is today a necessary discipline for the possibility of receiving even authentic revelation.

Without transcendence, itself critically evaluated in the most rigorous terms of what we know of reason, then, political philosophy is "unlimited" in theory. Without political philosophy, transcendence will not be recognized as addressing individual human beings in their uniqueness, beings that are not exhausted by the city in their meaning or destiny. The "bearing" of the experience of Plato for our time, Pieper's question in the beginning of these considerations, seems to be that experientially, philosophy and worship cannot exclude each other.

The ultimate risk, therefore, for the city is the elevation of this exclusion of revelation from political philosophy not only to a principle, but to a principle of power subject to nothing but itself. The first task of intellectual freedom remains the articulation of how this conclusion was reached in the history of political philosophy. Without this history, it would seem, revelation will tend to explain itself in terms of a modern ideology that, in its origin, knowingly or not, is a denial of a metaphysics and revelation. Revelation itself will be posed in terms of the human project that has already excluded anything but man himself.

In the end, to paraphrase Leo Strauss in *The City and Man,* it is necessary for everyone to listen to the divine message of the City of Righteousness, the Faithful City, to see whether its outlines are proposed in terms of man left to himself. The intellectual alternatives to metaphysics and revelation are posed in terms of man's own powers that have replaced any freshness from *what is,* from the ground of being, from that source that caused man to be man in the first place.

"Man transcends the city," Leo Strauss maintained, "only by pursuing true happiness, not by pursuing happiness however understood."[26] What jeopardizes political societies today is not "to what extent man could discern the outlines of that City [of Righteousness] if left to himself," but rather, on finally knowing this extent, what is it that the Faithful City teaches to the questions posed by the political philosophers.[27] The crisis of political philosophy, in this sense, stems from a crisis in theology, a crisis caused by the imitation of the modern political philosophers by these same theologians who have prevented us from hearing of the true City of Righteousness.

26. Strauss, *City and Man,* 49.
27. Ibid., 1.

17 MYSTICISM, POLITICAL PHILOSOPHY, AND PLAY

Spiritualism seems to me absolutely right on all its mystical side. The supernatural part of it seems to me quite natural. The incredible part of it seems to me obviously true. But I think it so far dangerous or unsatisfactory that it is in some degree scientific. It inquires whether its gods are worth inquiring into. A man (of a certain age) may look into the eyes of his lady-love to see that they are beautiful. But no normal lady will allow that young man to look into her eyes to see whether they are beautiful. The same vanity and idiosyncrasy has been generally observed in gods. Praise them; or leave them alone; but do not look for them unless you know they are there. Do not look for them unless you want them. It annoys them very much.

—G. K. Chesterton, "Spiritualism"

God is being beyond experience, that is, the primacy of God over religion. If God is a being in Himself, independent of His being experienced by man, and if we know about this being from what is revealed in Torah and prophecy, then the theoretical exposition of that which is known is possible in principle, which means theology. To this extent, theology is the expression of simple and unambiguous piety.

—Leo Strauss, "The Holy"

I.

To link mysticism, political philosophy, and play together is, at first sight, rash. What could they possibly have in common, since they clearly are not the same? Mysticism relates to our contact, if we have any, with the *"mysterion,"* with the mystery that lies at the threshold or ground of all finite beings, among which we are. Religion is a natural virtue, *pietas,* an aspect of justice. It is our effort properly to relate ourselves to God as the origin of our existence in terms of what we "owe" for what we are and for

This paper was originally given at an Eric Voegelin discussion at the American Political Science Association Convention in Washington. It was subsequently published in *Modern Age* 48 (Summer 2006): 251–59.

what we receive, something obviously that can never be fully repaid. This latter fact, our inability adequately to respond to the reason of our being, is why the virtue of religion is related to, but not exactly the same as, the virtue of justice. Justice seeks to repay exactly what is due. Religion thus is conceived as related to justice, yet something beyond it, a kind of noble effort to do what we can for being what we are, an expression of our acknowledging that we exist as finite beings.

We do not exist in mere justice. If we existed in justice, it would mean that God, out of some deficiency in himself, "owed" us the "to be" that we possess and that keeps us out of nothingness, something that we are intuitively aware that we cannot do for ourselves. It would also mean that we could adequately "repay" the good of existence itself that has been granted to us by the cause of our existence. In this sense, it would imply that we ourselves are equal to the Godhead, a dubious proposition, however tempting to human nature. Already here is the sense that existence itself is something that is rooted in an abundance, or even "superabundance," as Aquinas noted, a realm of nonnecessity, yet of real spiritual and even material depth that may indeed have much to do with the strange vastness of the cosmos itself. Even natural religion hints in its sense of its own inadequacy that, for comprehension of this reality, what we deal with approaches love, something simply "given," not something that is "owed."

But as Strauss says, God is primary even over religion, over our natural understanding of how, with rite, mind, or discipline, to relate ourselves to what is not ours to establish or fully to define with our own powers. Natural mysticism is the experience of being taken up into the mystery of *what is*, whatever it is. Still, we cannot *a priori* exclude the possibility that the mystery we seek to know will first seek us, that it itself contains the plenitude of being that we call "person," or even "persons." As we read in Psalm 94:6, "Can he who made the ear not hear?"

This fact that God is "primary over religion" touches on the mystery that might explain the classical questions that we each must ask at the risk of not being what we are: "Why do I exist?" "Why am I not something else?" "Why does everything possible not exist?" The very fact of these questions brings up the Aristotelian questions of whether the world is made "in vain" and whether God is "lonely." If the world is indeed made "in vain," no further questions need be asked, nor are they even sensible. But if they are not "in vain," we must be alert, listen, consider what is proposed, even from revelation. And if God is "lonely," perhaps he needed the world to exist, but perhaps this is not the only explanation of why it exists.

Likewise, we need a criterion to be sure that that to which we orient ourselves is not diabolical, granted that there are both evil and good spirits to which we might be attracted. The fascination of evil, both the attraction to it and the naming of it, is not something that can be adequately account-ed for by the simple denial of its existence. Thus piety has the connotation of an orientation to the true God, an awareness of the fact that false gods and prophets can rise among us, even in political terms. This reflection brings up the further philosophical question, and I think it is a philosophi-cal, not theological, question, of whether there be any criterion by which we might be protected from making such a mistake of identifying what is in fact evil with what is good?

The historical function of dogma, I suggest, falls within this area. Just why isn't a "suicide bomber," who, in all sincerity, successfully kills himself and a hundred others in the presumed name of his Deity, not as noble and holy as any other witness to the divinity? The only real answer to this ques-tion is that there is a natural law and that grace presupposes nature. If our theology gives us a God who is pure will with no roots in being, what is good is simply arbitrary and can become evil simply by will.

The political order acknowledges that we are mortal beings whose ac-tivities in this world reveal our souls. The political life is man's proper life, though not his highest life. The political life, as such, by being itself, points to something beyond itself. It is adequate for what it is capable of doing, but not for doing everything related to human purpose and destiny. If man were the highest being, Aristotle told us, politics would be the highest sci-ence. But man is not the highest being. Yet, he is open through the very na-ture of his intellect to the highest science, to a reality that his knowledge as such does not constitute but does know.

As Aristotle also said, one of the candidates for the definition of hu-man happiness is political power and honor. Modern ideology in one sense is a mystical absorption into the vision of man-for-himself, autono-mous man who spends his energies on what it is to be human, even seek-ing to "reconstruct" it so that it would, supposedly, be "more human" than the being given by history, nature, or nature's God. When this sort of this-worldly mysticism occurs, the world is closed off from the divine, from the transcendent *what is.*

But the underside of politics, its normalcy and necessity, as it were, its fragility, as Thucydides taught us in the plague and the revolution of Cor-cyra, is seen most clearly when political order breaks down. Hobbes's *bel-lum omnium contra omnes* generally happens when a political order breaks down from natural or political causes. The coercive force of law is also needed for most people, for virtue, not as its essence but as its support. In a natural, political, or military disaster, when the infrastructure of a society is almost completely destroyed, we see astonishing things. Robberies, looting, killings, greed, and selfishness come to the fore. We usually also see acts of heroism and generosity, though often there is little criterion or willingness for distinguishing the two.

When the normal structures of a city are destroyed and the political leadership overwhelmed, corrupt, or incompetent, we realize that political order is a needed and welcome thing. But it cannot exit without its being created, maintained, and fostered. "Man is by nature a political animal" means at least that he needs to build a city, that is, a constitution, an order of law and procedure by which the necessities of life are provided for and maintained. We have no "right" to this order apart from our efforts to bring the city forth and maintain it. And some regimes in their structure, as Aristotle constantly noted, are better than others, both absolutely and relatively.

II.

Play, like Creation itself, indicates what before us is unnecessary yet fascinating. Aristotle said that play was like contemplation as it also was something "for its own sake," something beyond necessity. Nor everything is "for" something else. At the end of the game, we have time for praise and celebration, even for the honorable losers. The loser does not abdicate his humanity by losing but learns another side of reality, what it means not to win. The loser also plays according to the rules. He is necessary to the game. This realization suggests that the order of the universe contains what happens in it in order that the full scope of being may be manifest. At the heart of disorder is the reality of freedom, such that the freedom to reject the good must be contained within the whole's purpose and be ordered to it. Wherever the story was told, Socrates said to the jurors who voted for his condemnation at his trial, they would be remembered as those who voted to kill the philosopher. He was right, of course, and without their vote we perhaps should never have had Plato and all he brought into the world. Yet, it was a terrible but free vote.

Games are not played for the primary purpose of the exercise of those who play them. They are played for themselves. They are played to win. In their unfolding and completion, the games themselves are what is fascinating. They need not be, but are. Games belong to the realm of superabundance. We do not "need" them to keep ourselves alive, as we need food and water. Yet we delight in them because of what they are. The grass that grows on ball fields is not lawn, nor do sheep graze on their grasses, insofar as it is not today artificial turf! Half the world watches the Olympics or the World Cup. Most of the nation watches the NCAA basketball finals or the Super Bowl. The British watch the British Open and the Australians the Melbourne Cup. It is not because they have nothing else productive to do. The spectators are there to see what unravels before them; the players are there to see who wins, according to the rules. The referees are there to enforce the rules so that the game is the game.

Why is it, in Chesterton's happy phrase, that no normal lady will allow a gentleman to look into her eyes to see "whether" they are beautiful? But she will allow it because he "sees" *that* they are beautiful? Beauty, like thing-ness, one, truth, and good, is a transcendental affirmation of being. *Omne ens est verum et bonum* (every being is true and good). *Quod visum placet* (what is seen pleases). The predicate adds to the subject that already is a relation to mind or will. Nothing more is to be said of beauty than that it is beautiful, but still, that needs to be said. Even when we explain beauty's proportion, radiance, and form, we still recognize that what is there is beyond our explanation. Knowledge both limits by defining this thing to be not that thing and opens us to what is still there beyond our definitions. Beauty takes us out of ourselves simply because it is already there. We behold it. We are astonished that something we did not or could imagine is there, before us. We do not create it. We rejoice that what is not ourselves exists as it does and as do we, beholding it. And in so acknowledging, we admit into our being what is not our being. Our mind is capable of knowing all things. We can be more than we are.

Our games need not exist, yet they absorb our attention in their unfolding. They take us out of ourselves into their own time and place and drama. We are curious about this experience of our loving games almost as much as we are by our experience of loving beauty. Often they are the same experience: "What a beautiful shot!" "What a beautiful dive!" We are aware of more than simply *what is* when we can say of it that it is true, or good, or beautiful.

The industry of making football gear, football stadiums, even football rules and regulations does not exist before the game. They exist because of the game itself. The game causes them to be as they are. A great coach or manager knows the rules of the game; to his friends, he can talk them, recall them, or argue about them. But this theoretical knowledge by no means guarantees that he will win the game, as other coaches and managers also know the rules. We can have the stadium, the rules, the uniforms, the football itself, the coaches, the referees, but still not have the game until the teams are on the field, ready to play, hopefully according to the rules, seeking to win.

Man is a multi-experienced being. He works, he prays, he plays, he thinks, he laughs, he makes, he governs, he dies. Aristotle said that happiness included a "complete" life. He meant that all of these aspects of his given being ought to be exercised for him to be *what he is*. The purpose of the polity, Aristotle also tells us, is not just that we may live, but live well, not just that there be a good, but a common good. The "living well" is not apart from our own knowing and choosing what it might mean to "live well." By his very existence, man finds himself already human, a fact about which he had nothing to do. Man did not first conceive what it is to be man. His task then is not to make himself man, but good man. He is likewise free to make himself bad man. Not a few do. It is the mark of civilization to be able to tell the difference. The first concern of the legislator, Aristotle told us, is virtue.

Is what happens in the universe closer to games than it is to the workings of machines? What would this similarity between game and universe imply? C. S. Lewis used the happy image of the "Great Dance" to describe what goes on in the universe when if finally reaches its purpose. It is a "beatific vision," but it is also an overflow in being, in human being. What seems to be "necessity" may be closer to "doing something again," just for the delight of it. This latter experience was the great image that Chesterton used of the sun rising each morning. We may think that it is necessary and therefore uninteresting. Chesterton remarked that natural laws may well be more like a child wanting to be thrown into the air again and again simply because it was delightful.

Behind such images is the great theological truth that the world need not be, but is. This unnecessity brings us to the further question of the reason we have finite, intelligent being in a vast but finite universe. Is *what is* ultimately there to be beheld? "Celebrations," Aristotle said, "are for successful achievement, either of body or of soul" (1106b33). That is to say, celebrations are left to be begun when all else is done, when we have won. Is it not remarkable that the fascination of the game, when we do not know its conclusion, ends in celebration when we do know how it turns out? This is the arena of the "Great Dance." The definition of God is "I am who am." Only this existence can explain the "Great Dance."

III.

Augustine, in a famous passage in book seven of his *Confessions*, tells the Lord that he has loved Him "late," perhaps very late, even too late. He confesses to looking for God everywhere among those "beautiful things" that he found in his world. But these were not God. Yet, Augustine knew that they were beautiful. He later learned that they were also dangerous, or could be. That initial experience seemed enough for a while. Yet, they did not explain themselves either, the beautiful things. From whence is their beauty? Augustine tells us further that God had ever been present within him, only he did not notice it. He had been looking in the wrong place. He did not mean that he was God. Augustine was quite aware of his own personal finiteness, though it seemed to drive him constantly outside of himself, as if he himself lacked something even in being what he was.

We might wonder what on earth God was doing in Augustine's soul. Why would a self-sufficient, all-powerful being bother with turbulent Augustine and his striking vanities? Surely, if He were more clearly there, Augustine would not have had to look for Him elsewhere. Moreover, Augustine has to tell God what he has been about, not always edifying things. He thinks that even when he was enjoying the various and beautiful things, he found that they were not God. Still he was looking for Him. He was unaccountably "restless." Why? Not just because he was more greedy or unsettled than most, though he probably was, but because he was perplexed that he found himself looking for something in spite of himself.

Augustine's own experience, rightly considered, indicated that something in the actual being that he, Augustine, was did not encounter an adequate object or fulfillment or presence. He was, but he was not complete in being what he was. This was his reflection on his experience. The places he looked were fine enough, beautiful, in fact, but systematically, as he tested them with his own resources, they seemed curiously inadequate. The "is-this-all-there-is?" syndrome was very much uppermost in his mind. It is an experience that can easily lead to despair, to the suspicion of existing in a world with no meaning, but with a faculty that demands meaning.

Augustine can be called a Christian mystic in the tradition of Plato and Plotinus; the scene in the *Confessions* at the death of his mother, Monica, is proof enough of this. His encounter with things was real enough. Augustine was not a pantheist, nor was he a Stoic who wanted to identify himself with the all that was the world because the world was divine. His quest was not a return from a fallen state to the Paradise from which he had been expelled. There was the *via negativa* in Augustine—this is not God, nor is that.

Augustine implicitly knew that he would recognize what he was looking for when and if he found it, just how he was not sure. "Thou hast made us for Thyself, O Lord." Augustine dimly was aware that his search for God was posterior to God's search for him. His was not a lonely quest, or better, a quest for aloneness. He knew of pride. He also knew of the "City of God." The universe was not filled with God and Augustine, though evidently *everything that is* mattered, including Augustine. How a human being "matters" to God is evidently after the manner of what a human being is. The search was "face to face," as Paul put it, but both God and man remained what he was in the exchange.

However, the world itself need not exist. Hence, Augustine did not need to exist, nor his loves. Again to recall the play image, Augustine's "confessions" indicated to him that he had not been playing the game according to the rules inherent in human reality. One must want to be what one is. "Political Augustinianism" has ever stood for the fact that the most we can expect from the kingdoms of this world is not much. At best it is an effort to keep down the worst in us. Augustine did not expect too much of politics, but he vividly knew that some regimes were better than others. Augustine's is a clear and almost brutal description of what does go on among kingdoms and principalities and, yes, empires and republics too. We will not find in any actual polity anything that might be confused with Plato's *Republic* or the "City of God."

Yet, Augustine sought for what Plato alerted us to in his city in speech. Just because the kingdoms of this world, however necessary and real they be, were not the locus of this city in speech, it did not mean that the endeavor to describe it, anticipate it, seek it was in vain. Quite the opposite, one could easily lose himself in this beautiful city in speech. But Augustine was no mere Platonist in this sense. His realism was closer to Aristotle. Nor did he think that the mystery of human disorder was located in the fact that we did not know what it meant to be good. Our reason could and did tell us much of this *what it is to be good*. Rather the difficulty was in the fact that, knowing what it is to be good, we still are not good. Augustine is not the first great analyst of the will for nothing. The mystery was more in our wonderment about why we did not do what we knew we ought to do. This perplexity brought him to the Christian context of grace and redemption. What was to supply what was lacking?

IV.

Mysticism, political philosophy, and play serve to relate the transcendent to the human through the setting of the cosmos in which we find ourselves. Pope Leo the Great (d. 461 AD) in a sermon on the Beatitudes (#95), remarked, using words of St. Paul:

What mind can conceive, what words can express the great happiness of seeing God? Yet human nature will achieve this when it has been transformed so that it sees the Godhead "no longer in a mirror or obscurely but face to face"—the Godhead that no man has been able to see. In the inexpressible joy of this eternal vision, human nature will possess "what eye has not seen or ear heard, what man's heart has never conceived."[1]

I cite this particular passage because it is quite clear about the three aspects of mysticism—that we seek to see "face to face," that the mystical encounter is personal, and that to achieve this purpose, human nature must be transformed, something it cannot do by itself. The passage also understands the limitation and the purpose of words before mystery, their inadequacy and their necessity. All words point to the being to which they refer. No word is the being itself. This insight posits the paradox of "the Word made flesh" and curious desire to see "face to face."

Political philosophy, in its broad extent, accounts for what men do in the Cave, what they do during the revolution on Corcyra and during the plague in Athens. That is, it does not allow us to pretend that what men do "do" to each other, to use Machiavelli's famous phrase, is not a poignant fact of our historical record. If there is to be a redemption, it must be within this context of what has happened and does happen both through natural disaster and human initiative. On the other hand, once human and civilized living has been established because the city is ordered, human nature is brought to leisure. That is, the question arises, "What do we do when the necessities and amenities are provided, even with our own work and cooperation?"

Aristotle mentions the politician who has himself not learned anything of the intellectual pleasures for what is worth knowing and doing for its own sake. He said that such a political man would in all likelihood seek more base pleasures, something that can be easily documented in the biographical history of not a few politicians. Such an observation leads to

---

1. *The Liturgy of the Hours* IV, Sunday, 23rd Week, 222.

the less attended fact that perhaps the intellectual and theoretical failures are more dangerous to any polity than natural disorders and even what are usually called sins of the flesh. Aristotle had suggested that intellectual disorders are often the products of moral disorders. That is, intellectual theories are the result of efforts to justify our actions. This effort can be very subtle, and in one sense constitutes the history of philosophy. It is at this point where the question of the dogmas of *what God is* is most pertinent to the life of the city.

The polity itself is not a subject, not a substance, not a person, but a relation of order among beings, each of whom personally transcends the city's own order. The polity does not and cannot "see God" face to face or in any other way. What "sees," or at least can see, are the individual citizens who bear the reality of the polities of this world. In this sense, the polity is ordered to what is beyond itself without itself thereby becoming unnecessary to the human purposes of the mortals who compose it. The polity cannot survive without at least some who are devoted to things higher than the polity. The place of the mystic in the public order is but an aspect of the place of the philosopher. The politician can rid the polity of such a threat if the contemplative life is perceived as undermining the actual existing polity. This is what the state-sanctioned deaths of Socrates and Christ were about. This dire consequence means that the politician stands at the crossroads between mysticism and human things. The politician can be absorbed in himself, in false gods, in making the polity itself to be God. In each of these cases, he betrays both his own vocation and the city he is to serve.

But even in the virtuous politician, politics points beyond itself. We can hope to render the politician benevolent to the mystic or philosopher without making him (the politician) to be himself a mystic or a philosopher. But with the advent of the teaching that the purpose of authority is to serve and not to be served and that the love of neighbor is a direct consequence of the love of God, we can and do find politicians who reveal a kind of mystical service to those they serve and care for. Mysticism is not merely the participation in the outreaches of the Godhead as it can be known by men. It also relates to that relation the Godhead has to each of the members of the polity whose dignity indicates the kind of service sometimes required, a service that is both designed to care for the needy and provide order for those who are to take care of themselves. The purpose of government is not itself to care for everyone but to provide an order in which everyone can care for himself.

It is said by the philosophers that man's happiness consists in contemplation, especially as what is highest in him is "divine," that is, what connects him to the gods. That is right. The polity exists for itself, but in achieving what it is, a life of amazing abundance is fostered in which questions of the highest moment are to be considered and answered. In this context, the fascination of play seems at first to have an unimportant place. What I want to argue here, rather, is that play provides us with a better understanding of what is left to be done when the polity itself is what it is. The polity is not a claim itself to be divine, but the claim to be an order in which we can "live well" by our own powers in relation to others. We can have a true common good that will not exclude the highest things, including those addressed beyond religion, to those of revelation. Religion refers to human initiative; revelation refers to divine initiative.

Mysticism and philosophy are the logical and experiential ends of the human beings in their cities whereby they contact and understand the source and the end of what they are. The real motive for this effort, however, is properly and freely to respond to the gift of our existence. We are to respond to God, as Plato said in the *Laws*, by "singing, dancing, and sacrificing" (803). In the light of revelation, these are most interesting words. They recall ritual and sacrifice. They also make us wonder whether revelation itself is an indication of what has perplexed the human race from the beginning, namely, what is the proper way to worship God? And even more, would human beings be expected to be able to formulate this way on their own powers? The history of religions, in its incredible variety, can at some level be said to be a record of these human efforts in the order of religion. This multiplicity and variety is why, I think, Strauss reminded us that revelation transcends and directs religion precisely as "piety," that is, as the response of God as to how adequately to worship him.

Catherine Pickstock used the happy phrase that worship is the "consummation of philosophy." Eric Voegelin remarked that Christianity is "philosophy itself in a state of perfection." It is Pickstock's phrase that hints best at the relation of philosophy, mysticism, and play. For the spirit of worship, indeed, to use Guardini's phrase, "the spirit of the liturgy," a phrase taken up by Benedict XVI, concerns not merely the love of wisdom, but the celebration of wisdom given to us and accepted by us as that to which our minds are ultimately directed.[2] And there is a "dogmatic" framework

---

2. Catherine Pickstock, *After Writing: On the Liturgical Consummation of Philosophy* (Oxford: Blackwell's, 1998). Joseph Ratzinger (Benedict XVI) wrote in the preface to his own *Spirit of the*

in which we can formulate whether we are properly stating what we are about. The dogmatic structure is not itself God, but it points through itself to what is not yet ours, but is. Ultimately, what surprises is not that things do fit together, but how they fit together and our response to the order of things. The last words remain those of Chesterton: "Do not look for [the gods] unless you want them. It annoys them very much."

Liturgy that he was also writing in honor of Romano Guardini's book, with the same title, that was published at Easter 1918.

PART VI

THINGS PRACTICAL AND

IMPRACTICAL

18   SPORTS AND PHILOSOPHY

To be always seeking after the useful does not become free and exalted souls. Now it is clear that in education practice must be used before theory, and the body be trained before the mind; and therefore boys should be handed over to the trainer; who creates in them the proper habit of body, and the wrestling-master, who teaches them their exercises.

—Aristotle, *Politics*

I must repeat once again, the first principle of all action is leisure.

—Aristotle, *Politics*

I.

On February 15, 1983, *Vital Speeches* published an address of mine entitled, "On the Seriousness of Sports." This essay was later included in my book, *Another Sort of Learning*.[1] Originally, it was given at a Conference on Sports Journalism held at Harrah's Club in Reno, Nevada. This state, as you know, is a well-known arena for a certain kind of sports, namely, "gaming sports," as they are called. Last year, moreover, I published a book entitled, *On the Unseriousness of Human Affairs: Teaching, Writing, Playing, Believing, Lecturing, Philosophizing, Singing, Dancing*.[2] Note the words "playing" and "philosophizing" in the subtitle. They are not accidental or wholly unrelated to each other. And how they are not unrelated is the subject matter of what I wish to speak with you this evening.

At first sight, of course, to the attentive reader, it will seem that, in the intervening two decades, Schall has passed from calling sports "serious" to calling them "unserious," an obvious contradiction, something this same Schall, as a matter of principle, warns us to avoid at all costs. Yet, if we all be Thomists, as I hope we are, we are intellectually prodded by apparent

This address was presented before Delta Phi Epsilon, the foreign service professional fraternity at Georgetown University. It was published in the *Fellowship of Catholic Scholars Quarterly* 28 (Summer 2005): 29–34.

1. James V. Schall, *Another Sort of Learning* (San Francisco: Ignatius Press, 1988), 218–29.
2. Schall, *Unseriousness of Human Affairs*.

contradictions, such as that between serious and unserious, to examine things more carefully. We are taking a more careful look at something of obvious interest like sports to see what we can learn from what appears, at first sight, to be at odds and contradictory.

But first let me ask a prior question: Are sports at all worthy of attention, serious or unserious? If the answer is "no," then we need proceed no farther. Over Christmas one year, to put this issue in another way, I spent a couple of days with a cousin of mine and her husband. It happened to be the day of the Fiesta Bowl, the national championship game in college football, which game I definitely I wanted to watch. In fact, I delayed my return to Washington from San Diego, home of the Chargers and the Padres, for a couple of days just so I could watch that game. Most of the bowl games I had, with the benefit of popcorn, seen up to that time at my brother's were lemons. But the Fiesta Bowl between Ohio State and Miami that year turned out to be a wonderful game.

My cousin, for whom the Fiesta Bowl was not the epitome of existence during New Year's, several times suggested that watching football, even at New Year's, was a sheer "waste of time." She could not understand why aging gentlemen, like myself and her husband, found it worthwhile to sit around for four hours to watch a one-hour game between monstrous men violently smashing each other by trying to get an oblong leather ball across something called a goal line. Her skepticism about sports reminds me of Chesterton's quip, speaking of golf, that he could not understand why grown men, dressed in knickers, with sticks in their hands, walked around a green meadow avidly chasing a little white ball.

Now, I am the first to admit that pro football games, as are Bowl games, are too long, too contrived, because they make extra time for advertising. It does take some of the luster off watching a good game, the essence of which is what I want to explain here. In this sense, soccer, with its continuous time for everything but serious injuries, is a far better game, granting that the rhythm and flow of the two games is different. Time-outs are part of football, as is walking out of the batter's box in baseball. The extended TV pauses we presently have to suffer through, better than government ownership of communications, may not be so necessary. But like the two-minute drill at the end of a football game, you do have to admire the genius of advertising types who know that they have but thirty seconds to catch our attention to sell us a bottle of beer, a Ford truck, or a vacuum cleaner, before we block them out of our minds, screens, or attention.

How does one explain both that my cousin is right—watching football or other sporting events is indeed a "waste of time"—and, at the same time, that the games are still well worth watching, worth spending the time contemplating, preferably in person at the game itself, but also on television? I usually approach this matter by recalling the famous passage in St. Exupery's *The Little Prince* that reminds us that it is only the time that you "waste" with your friends that really counts.[3] You cannot be a friend with someone who is forever watching the clock to do something else. "Wasting time" means the capacity to enjoy the present, really to look at what is going on, at who or what is before us in this time and this place.

In a paradoxical sense, all the important things in time stand outside of time. When we are absorbed in a game, in a very real sense, we are "outside of ordinary time," the time we measure on our watches. The "time" measured by the referee's watches, though within cosmic time, is a different kind of time. This is game time, the frame within which the action takes place. Referees measure the time within which the game goes on. When we are on referee's time, we are already within the game action. Even "time-outs," controlled by the referee's watch, are part of the game. We leave our own time for the time of the game while we are beholding before us its unfolding, its action.

Indeed, Aristotle asks us to notice that when we are wholly interested in something, be it writing, playing, or loving, we do not notice the passage of time. He notes this phenomenon of not noticing cosmic time passing especially in the case of the theatrical drama, and it also happens at concerts. The initial point I wish to make here, then, is that watching a good sporting event of whatever variety, from the Rose Bowl, to the Preakness, to the World Cup, to the NCAA basketball finals, or to a good high school lacrosse game, has an effect on us. It causes us to stand outside of real time. And time itself is indeed real, as Aristotle and Augustine remind us. It is a category of the real.

II.

But this observation about time leads us to another question, as it should, namely, what is the relation between time and nothingness, or even more profoundly, between time and eternity? Aristotle already hints, I think, that game time is closer to eternity, *nunc stans,* as Aquinas called it,

3. Antoine de Saint Exupéry, *The Little Prince* (New York: Harcourt, 1943), 87. "The exact quote is, "It is the time you have wasted with your rose that makes your rose so important."

than to the time that keeps going on and on, as measured by our watches. The phrase, "time stood still," is well worth pondering, and hints at something Aquinas was getting at, that eternity is the "standing now," not the complete evaporation of time or its complete denial.

Where does this leave us? Schall has now established that "wasting our time" is quite all right. After the publication of my *Vital Speeches* talk, some journal, I believe it was *Sports Illustrated,* picked its theme up with the amusing comment that now Schall has finally and philosophically justified the dream of the common man, in his eternal struggle with his womenfolk, namely, with a clear conscience, to sit around with a beer and chips on Saturday or Sunday afternoon to watch a game, whether it be baseball, golf, tennis, football, basketball, sailing, diving, soccer, cricket, boxing, or auto racing, to mention no more. Actually, over the years, as I usually have my large classes read this essay, I have been struck by the number of young women who tell me that they have always wondered why they too like sports. Most women, I suspect, agree with my cousin, bless them. When they are reluctantly forced by the culture to watch the Super Bowl, they spend their time knitting, talking of the children, or admiring the half-time shows or the way the cheerleaders fix their hair.

The phrase "wasting time" generally has a pejorative meaning. It implies that we are not doing what we ought to do, that we have our priorities wrong. Surely, we think, no one wants his priorities wrong! This question of priority naturally brings up the question of what we ought to be doing and whether sports have any place in the scheme of things. And this is the question that brings us to Aristotle, whom Thomas Aquinas rightly called simply "the Philosopher." It also brings us to Aristotle's mentor, the great Plato himself, who was quite certain that the rules of games should not change but that we should all play them in our youth according to the rules our ancestors set down for how the game is to be played. Change the rules of games, Plato thought, and you change the polity. He said much the same about changing our music. Indeed, Plato even says that a young man should not marry until his top sprinting speed begins to decline. You might ask yourselves why he put it in that way.

In a way, this consideration even brings us to St. Paul, who told us that we run the race to win the laurel, the prize. That is, we run the race, we play the game, to win. If we do not understand this about a game, that it is about winning, about winning indeed according to the rules, then we have no idea what games are about, and probably not what life is about. Grantland Rice, the famous sportscaster of my youth, in a famous phrase

said: "It matters not whether you win or lose, but how you play the game."
He was quite wrong. The only thing that matters, as Vince Lombardi said,
is winning, but, again, winning according to the rules of the game. Without winning, there is no game. The real reason we play the game is to find
out who wins and the style with which they play to win. This is why games
are fascinating, why we play them, because that is the only way to find out
who plays better, who plays best of all.

In Aristotle, particularly in the last book of his *Politics,* we find passages that make several relevant distinctions about what we do in living and
playing—distinctions nowhere more clearly elaborated than in Josef Pieper's famous essay, *Leisure: The Basis of Culture.*[4] Again, we have to examine
what we mean by the words we give to the things we do and know about.
"Wasting our time" seems to be the other side of the Aristotelian phrase
about things existing "for their own sakes" or knowing something "for its
own sake." There are things we want because they are useful for something
else or simply pleasurable to us. There is nothing wrong with this, provided we do not think that there is no other reason for our fascination with
things.

I have already hinted that the phrase "wasting our time" may not be
all that bad. I do not in fact deny that what we do when we watch a game
is precisely "waste our time." What I do deny is that this wasting is a bad
thing, granted that other important things have to be taken care of. We
have to choose how we use or waste our time, the time given to us, the
only time there is. I do not, however, want my logic to be carried to the absurd conclusion that Schall justifies spending all his time watching games
or to the equally absurd conclusion that he believes we should spend all
our time in "significant" things of usefulness or duty.

To take the next step in understanding the fascination of sports—
and that word "fascination" is worth looking up in a good dictionary, as it
has some reference to the holy—I usually like to cite a passage from Allan
Bloom's *Shakespeare's Politics,* a passage to which I also call my students'
attention when we read it. The passage concerns, not the game, but the
"play,"—interesting word here—that is, the theater. It reads as follows:

What is essentially human is revealed in the extreme, and we understand ourselves
better through what we might be. In a way, the spectators live more truly when
they are watching a Shakespearean play than in their daily lives, which are so much
determined by the accidents of time and place. There could be a theater dealing to-

4. Josef Pieper, *Leisure: The Basis of Culture* (South Bend, Ind.: St. Augustine's Press, 1998).

tally with private life, the cares for providing for a living and raising a family. But men who never get beyond that life would be cut off from their fullest human development.[5]

Notice, that Bloom here is not speaking of actors, but spectators, just as in this discussion, with Aristotle, I am speaking primarily of the spectators, not the players, in a game.

Without the spectators, I think, there is no game, even though a game can go on with no spectators, with no cheering. For an understanding of what Bloom is getting at, we must return to Aristotle's *Poetics*. Aristotle understood that when we behold the plot of a drama unfolding before us, we are moved from within our very selves by fear and pity for the characters. We form our souls after the models of the virtues and vices we see before us. Games, likewise, simply draw us and have their own catharses in our souls as we behold them within their own time.

III.

What, you might object, does an exalted Sophoclean or Shakespearean drama have to do with the Super Bowl, the Masters, March Madness or the Penn Relays? Indeed, we might ask, what does it have to do with Aristotle's *Metaphysics* or Aquinas's *Summae*? The answer is that in a good game we see displayed before us not only the unfolding of a game to its unknown conclusion, but we see the excellence of our kind stretched to its best in a certain order. The very notion of the Olympic Games was designed to find out what human beings could achieve in the excellence of their physical being. Who could run or skate or ski or swim the fastest, who could jump the highest or the most distance, who could throw the shotput or the javelin the farthest? Who wrestled or boxed best? What team played best volleyball or soccer or hockey? These are the testing of our human limits.

Let me also say a word about cheating and refereeing. In a Breeders' Cup in Chicago a couple of years ago, one of the betting combinations known as the Pic-Six was rigged. By a slick change in certain tickets after the race was won, certain few tickets, partly because of an unexpected long shot, apparently won an enormous amount of money, some three million dollars. On investigation, it turned out that the winners were college fraternity brothers from Philadelphia, one of whom just happened to work

5. Allan Bloom, "Philosophy and Poetry," in *Shakespeare's Politics* (Chicago: University of Chicago Press, 1964), 9.

for Auto-Tote, the company that ran the betting mechanism. Thus, it is possible for games or races to be "fixed" or "thrown," as they say.

The question of gambling and games I will not go into here except to say that betting has long been considered to be part of games, particularly horse races. One of the purposes of referees or stewards is to make sure that the games are played according to the rules of the game. The rules of games are made up, they are arbitrary, but once they are set, they form the structure of the game and make it what it is. The referee is not a player in the game, but without him, generally, there is no game. He is responsible, not to the outcome of the game, but to the rules, so that the outcome, when achieved by the winners, is "according to the rules."

Thus, there is a clear right and wrong in games. Rules have penalties. If you read the sports pages of any newspaper in the world on any given day, you will notice that they are full of moral judgments about right and wrong, about fairness and unfairness, about honor and worthiness and about cheating and dishonesty. In this sense, sports are almost the last bastion of clarity in morals, though the slowness of baseball facing the steroid problem reminds us that sports figures are not always on the side of the gods. This awareness of the firmness of rules in sports is also why, as in the case of an incident in German soccer, there is something more corrupting about a referee who cheats than a player who cheats. As in the playoff between, say, the Patriots and the Steelers, a player may get by with an unnoticed penalty. His team may win as a result. No justice can be requited in such a case. We may not like this failure to notice, but the rules of the game, as such, are not being broken here. But if the penalty is not called because the referee is promised a huge financial reward, we clearly have a higher form of corruption.

As Thomas Boswell said in the *Washington Post* (January 10, 2003), there is a danger in trying to make the game so perfect, with so many rules and checks, that it is no longer playable. In this case, the referees, the replays, and the fine points of the rules become more important than the game. "A sport can reach a point where it has so many rules—which are amended so often and then enforced by officials who are repeatedly overturned by replay—that the game strangles on technicalities, loses its flow and exasperates our patience." As in life itself, place must be left for human error, even human corruption. Otherwise, our games are for angels, not men and women.

IV.

But let me come to the essence of what I want to say about watching and playing games, about sports. Not too long ago, I had an e-mail from a student who had read my essay on "The Seriousness of Sports." In it, he told me that it explained something to him about himself that he had never quite understood before, namely, what was it about good games that so absorbed his interest? He had heard a million times, even from his own mother, that he was, yes, "wasting his time" by watching various games. He almost believed there was something wrong with him. But the fact is that someone who finds no fascination in watching games is probably much farther away from what is highest in our human experience than someone who does experience this sense of interest, this "wasting of time," but does not understand what it is about.

Aristotle makes several perhaps enigmatic remarks on this score. The purpose of "recreation" is work, he tells us, while the purpose of "work" is leisure. We work so that we may have leisure. We have leisure so that we may have *all that is*. Aristotle says, in fact, that we are "un-leisurely" in order that we may have leisure. Work, or labor, or technology, or business is not what we are doing at games, even when we are playing them with great exertion. Indeed, the Greek and Latin words for what we call "business" mean precisely that we are "un-leisurely," that we are busy, devoted to producing or running useful things.

Aristotle suggests that there are things beyond use, indeed the highest things. The Greek word for these things is *theorein,* theory, while the Latin word is *contemplatio,* contemplation. Such words imply that we have things to do "for their own sakes." That is, we do not need some "useful" reason to do them. We do them simply because they are worthy, fascinating, delightful. They have no reason beyond themselves. Somehow they draw us into themselves.

What does this consideration have to do with sports? Aristotle, in his uncanny way, compares contemplation and sports, or more particularly, the watching of sports. Games themselves need not exist. They are technically artifacts, things made up. Yet, when they exist, when they are being played, they are "for their own sakes," they are, if you will, a "wasting of time." Aristotle does say that theory or contemplation is more "serious"— that word again—than games. His point is not to imply that games can replace the gods, but to suggest to us that what most of us experience about games, their fascination, their absorbing our time and interest, is analogous to our absorption in the highest things.

A similar thing happens to us when we hear a good symphony or see a play. We are taken out of our time to behold something for its own sake. Things like dancing and liturgy fall into the same category. They do something to our time because they give us something in itself worthy to behold, something, like ourselves, that need not be, but is. This is why on reading, say, Joseph Ratzinger's (Benedict XVI) book *The Spirit of the Liturgy*, we sense that what it says is analogously closer to watching games than it is to almost anything else we normally encounter.[6]

In conclusion, I do not know if your generation still remembers Charles Schulz and *Peanuts*, how Charlie Brown could never win a ball game, nor would Lucy ever let him kick off the football without pulling it out just before he kicked it, so that he fell flat on his derrière, much to her amusement. The cartoon series *Peanuts* was one of the great ongoing reflections on the relation, among other things, between philosophy and sports in our time.

In a collection called *If Beagles Could Fly* (New York: Topper, 1990), we see Charlie Brown returning home, still with his baseball hat on, glove in hand. He is obviously dejected. Sally, his sister, is stretched out on the beanbag chair watching TV. From behind her, Charlie says to her, "It was the last game of the season, and we lost it." In the next scene, Sally is off of the beanbag and walks away from a glum Charlie. She says to him, in shades of "wasting time," "So what does that mean?" Next, Charlie is standing alone next to the beanbag, hat now on sideways, with a sudden philosophical look on his face. To himself, in answer to Sally's question of meaning about losing, he reflects, "Well, in the long run, and as far as the rest of the world goes, it doesn't mean a thing." But in the final scene, we see Charlie with his head despondently buried in the beanbag. He simply cries, "But I can't stand it!"

That comes very close to what I want to tell you about sports and philosophy. Charlie's "can't stand it" is in defiance of a world in which losing the last game doesn't mean a thing, when in fact it means everything.

---

6. Ratzinger, *Spirit of the Liturgy*. See James V. Schall, *Far Too Easily Pleased: A Theology of Play, Contemplation, and Festivity* (Los Angeles: Benzigter/Macmillan, 1976); Johan Huizinga, *Homo Ludens* (Boston: Beacon, 1950); Hugo Rahner, *Men at Play* (New York: Herder and Herder, 1967); and Josef Pieper, *In Tune with the World: A Theory of Festivity* (Chicago: Franciscan Herald, 1973).

There are things worth doing for their own sakes, even worth doing "badly," as Chesterton said, and all of Charlie Brown's games were badly played. There are games to be won and games to be lost. We come closest to what the contemplation of the highest things might mean when we are drawn into watching a good game, when we forget about time and behold something just because it is there, because *it is*. These are, I think, ordinary, everyday experiences that, as in the case of my young friend, puzzle us because we are fascinated by them.

Sports, Aristotle tells us, are of less serious import than the contemplation of the highest things, than the simple joy and wonder in knowing the things *that are*. But this is not to denigrate them. It is merely to point out that games of our kind are given to us out of the abundance of things, wherein "wasting our time" spells out nothing less than the things that cause time to disappear for us into the timelessness we call, sometimes, eternity. The world itself, after all, in our theology, need not have existed. It is a colossal divine waste of time, but we are delighted that it is. This is what games are about and why we have philosophy to think about them.

19 THE REAL ALTERNATIVES
TO JUST WAR

If there is a great European war in the near future, it will not be a capitalist war for markets, but a war of creeds for the possession of men's minds. And each side will be firmly convinced of the justice of its cause.... The war-makers will not be capitalists and armament manufacturers but the idealists and propagandists, and principles will be as important as poison gas.... But any peace propaganda which shuts the eyes to realities is worthless and may even increase the danger which it sets out to combat. It has been the fault of both pacifism and liberalism in the past that they have ignored the immense burden of inherited evil under which society and civilization labour and have planed an imaginary world for an impossible humanity. We must recognize that we are living in an imperfect world in which human and superhuman forces of evil are at work and so long as those forces affect the political behaviour of mankind there can be no hope of abiding peace.... For war is not only the work of man. It is also willed by God as the punishment of sin and as its instrument by which the Divine Justice performs its inscrutable judgment.

—Christopher Dawson, "Catholic Attitude to War," 1937

While the effects of sin abound—greed, dishonesty and corruption, broken relationships and exploitation of persons, pornography and violence—the recognition of individual sinfulness has waned. In its place a disturbing culture of blame and litigiousness has arisen which speaks more of revenge than justice and fails to acknowledge that in every man and woman there is a wound which, in the light of faith, we call original sin.

—John Paul II, Address to American Bishops, May 14, 2004

I.

A calm and reasonable case can and should be made for the possession and effective use of adequate military and police force in today's world. It is irresponsible not to talk about and plan for the necessity of force in the face of real turmoil and enemies actually present in the world. No talk

This essay was originally published in *Policy Review* 128 (December 2004, January 2005): 59–70.

of peace, justice, truth, or virtue is complete without a clear understanding that certain individuals, movements, and nations must be dealt with in terms of measured force, however much we would like to deal with them in a more peaceful or pleasant manner. Without force, many will not talk seriously, and some not even then. Our human, moral, and poverty problems are greater today because of the lack of adequate military force or, more often, of its failure to be used when necessary.

This view, no doubt, goes against the rhetorical grain, but it is a fact that needs attention and comprehension. We are not in some new "world-historic" age in which we can "bypass" these "outmoded" instruments of power, however rhetorically fine it is to talk that way. Human nature has not changed, neither for better nor worse. Human institutions, either at the national or international level, have not improved to such a degree that they themselves cannot be threats to the human good. Who watches the watchdogs remains a fundamental, if not *the* fundamental, question of the human condition. It is an issue with philosophical, theological, and political dimensions.

This position is a countercultural position. It goes against much articulate liberal and religious sentiment. I consider these often ungrounded sentiments about abolishing war to be themselves part of the problem of war's dangers. General Douglas MacArthur's tomb is in the old city hall in Norfolk, Virginia. I once visited it. On the wall above his grave is a plaque with the memorable and eloquent words that this military commander spoke on the occasion of the Japanese Surrender in 1945. On reading them, I was struck that they now appear to me to be part of the problem, not the solution, as I once thought.

It is my earnest hope and indeed the hope of all mankind that from this solemn occasion a better world shall emerge out of the blood and carnage of the past—a world founded upon faith and understanding—a world dedicated to the dignity of man and the fulfillment of his most cherished wish, for freedom, tolerance, and justice. . . . We have had our last chance. If we do not now devise some greater and more equitable system, Armageddon will be at our door. The problem is basically theological, and involves a spiritual recrudescence and improvement of human character that will synchronize with our almost matchless advances in science, art, and literature, and all material and cultural developments in the past two thousand years. It must be of the spirit if we are to save the flesh.

Since MacArthur spoke these words some sixty years ago, we have had thousands of wars of varying degrees. We thought that we had founded a system to prevent wars, especially small ones. We talk about theological and spiritual problems. MacArthur seemed to assume that such a perfect system could be established. But, in this, he was something of a utopian, not a realist. As a result, the spirit and means whereby many small wars could actually have been stopped, the work of converting the whole world to a better "system," resulted in little being done when needed on a scale that would be effective, often a small scale.

My starting point, then, is rather taken from Maritain's phrase that "justice, brains, and strength" can and should belong together.[1] We need not collapse before tyranny or terrorism or those who sponsor either. But we must effectively do something about them. "Peace and dialogue" rhetoric do not work in absence of a force component. The more the reality of measured force is present, the more dialogue and peaceful, including religious, means are present. In practice, this "doing" peace must include adequate and intelligent force. The intense concern that the famous "weapons of mass destruction"—and how to make them, how to use them—not fall into the hands of Muslim or other leaders is not fanciful. Every holiday since 9/11, some e-mail arrives warning us of the possible use of "dirty bombs" in some American or world city. That they have not been used, I suspect, is more because those who would use them, and such people exist, have actually been prevented by force. Units who would blow up major installations, if they could, do exist. All they lack are delivery capabilities.

Further, I argue that our main problems are not too much force, but too little. A peaceful world is not a world with no ready forces but one with adequate, responsible, and superior force that is used when necessary. The failure to have or use such forces causes terror and war to grow exponentially. Unused force, when needed at a particular time and place, ceases to be force. But force is meaningless if one does not know that he has an enemy or how this enemy works and thinks. That latter is a spiritual and philosophical, not technical, problem. Many an adequately armed country has been destroyed because it did not recognize its real enemy. Neither is this an argument for force "for force's sake." It is an argument for force for justice's sake. I am not for "eternal peace," which is a this-worldly myth, but for real peace of actual men in an actual and fallen world. Peace is not a "goal" but a consequence of doing what is right and preventing what is wrong and, yes, knowing the difference between the two.

Justice and force require one another in the actual world. Too often

1. See James V. Schall, "Justice, Brains, and Strength: Machiavelli and Modernity in Political Philosophy," in Schall, *Jacques Maritain: The Philosopher in Society* (Lanham, Md.: Rowman & Littlefield, 1998), 1–20.

they are placed in opposition in a way that renders both unbalanced and ineffective. It is not a virtue to praise justice as if it need not be actually enforced or worthy things defended. The greatest crimes usually are grounded in a utopianism that is blind to living men, that does not see how to limit and control disruptive forces that continually arise in human life. Though I argue mainly about military force, the same argument includes police power. These forces are not substitutes for the virtue of justice, but this difficult virtue relies also on the existence and proper use of force for it effectively to exist. Contrary to much rhetoric, we do not live in a world in which diplomacy, dialogue, diversity, and law, however valuable, have replaced force. We can hopefully reach an adequate public order. But failure to understand that law and dialogue at some level also need the presence of reasoned force ends up creating not more peace but less.

II.

In late spring, in Baltimore, I walked to the end of Chestnut Street where it meets Joppa Road. On one corner was a large official-looking residence called "Mission Helpers Center." On both sides of its entrance gate were large blue and white signs that read, "War Is Not the Answer." These placards recalled the many too-simple slogans about war, often, like this one apparently, from religious sources. Here are some that I recall seeing in recent years: "War is obsolete." "War is never justified." "The answer to violence is not more violence." "War does no good." "No one wins a war." "Love, not war." "Diplomacy, not war." "Dialogue, not war." "Stop violence." "Only the U.N. can declare war." "Justice, not war." "No war is legitimate." "Everyone loses in war." "War, never again."

When I saw the "war-is-not-the-answer" sign, I said to myself, "But to what question is war *not* an answer?" Or is there a question to which war *is* the only sensible answer? Must we be pacifists and draw no lines in the sand? Does nothing ever need defending? Can we choose not to defend what needs defending and still be honorable? If war is not the "answer," what is? Without being naive or utterly innocent of the realities involved, how do we rid ourselves of tyrants or protect ourselves from ideologies or fanatics when they attack us with their own principles and weapons, not ours?

Machiavelli advised that a prince should spend most of his time preparing for war. The prince was not pious except when useful to his own end of staying in power. If we are this prince's neighbors, do we take no notice of his preparations? Do we give him the answer he most wants to hear from us, namely, "war is not the answer?" Those who practice this doctrine of no war make easy targets. The prince thinks war *is* an answer. It can help him in his goal of acquiring and keeping in power. We may have to suffer a defeat. We should not choose to bring one on ourselves.

Even though much carnage and chaos happen in any historic war, on every side, still we cannot blithely conclude from this fact alone that "war is not the answer." It may not be the *only* answer. But no valid alternate to war can be a mere ungrounded velleity, a frivolous hope that nothing bad will happen no matter what we do or do not do. Any presumed alternative to war, by other supposedly more effective methods, has to stop what war seeks to prevent by its own reasoned use of measured force. The general opinion of most sensible men in most of history is that war certainly is one answer, even a reasonable answer, in the light of actual alternatives and consequences that would likely ensue without it. Not a few unfought wars have made things considerably worse. Not a few fought wars have made things better. The honor classically associated with war heroes is explained by the following proclamations: "Our cause is just." "Give me liberty or give me death." "Eternal vigilance is the price of liberty." "Walk softly, but carry a big stick."

We often, and rightly, ponder the horrors of war. It is a growth industry, particularly for those who do not choose to fight in wars. Soldiers usually know more about the horrors of wars than journalists. They also know more about what it is like to live under a tyrannical system. The gulags and concentration camps ought also to cause us to reflect deeply on what happens when unjust regimes acquire and remain in power. September 11th could have been prevented with but a small use of force had we known that we had an enemy who could utterly surprise us by using passenger planes as weapons of war.

A Nietzsche, since he thought Platonism and Christianity had failed because both lauded weakness, will see, as a replacement, a certain nobility to wars and power for their own dramatic sakes. Nietzsche, like many moderns, did not think there is any order in the universe except that imposed by his own will. Most sensible people, however, can see that the major way to prevent any form of unlimited power coming to pass, or to remove it once established, is the legitimate use of adequate force against it. Often we do this reflection about war's atrocities in isolation from real situations and without balance. Peace is not simply the absence of war. "No war" can, and not infrequently does, mean the victory of tyranny and the subsequent disarming of any opposition to itself. "No moral use of war" can, by the same logic, result in no freedom, no dignity.

We need more serious reflection on what happens, both to ourselves and to others who rely upon us, when we lose wars or fail to act so that, as a result, something worse happens. Those who cry "peace, peace," often have unacknowledged blood on their hands because they failed to use adequate force when needed. "To the victors go the spoils" is an ancient principle of fact, not rightness. Cowardice has never been considered a virtue. Nor has "turning the other cheek" served as an excuse for allowing some evil to continue or conquer, one that we could prevent except that our theories or fears prevented us from trying. Not a few worthy things have been eradicated forever because a war was lost. Eternal vigilance remains the price of liberty and of much else that is worthy.

In reading ancient history, as we should and for this very reason, we can still meditate with profit on the enormous cultural consequences of the final success of Xerxes in Greece, had Sparta and Athens not successfully defended themselves. Nonetheless, good causes do not always win wars; neither, to say the same thing, do bad causes always lose them. The "God of Battles" is often ironic. Fortune is difficult to conquer. Nor do its consequences guarantee justice. St. Paul, as Dawson reminds us, even suggests that wars and the sword punish our wrongdoings. John Paul II observed that we live in a world in which we want to deny that we commit any wrongs or sins, and hence we lack any reason for correcting them within ourselves. Sins have dire consequences even if we call them virtues, as we often do.

Still, we are not free not to think about this consequence that failure to act can make things worse. Nor can we deny that there is a comparative difference between "bad" things and "terrible" things. We can be as immoral and as inhuman by not acting as by acting. The history of lost wars is as important as the history of victorious ones, perhaps more so. And the idea of an absolutely warless world, a world "already made safe for democracy," is more likely, in practice, to be either a sign of utopia or a madhouse. A world in which war is "outlawed" is more likely to mean either that we are no longer in the real world or that the devils and the tyrants have finally won. They allow us only to agree with them and do as they say. We are naive if we think that formal democratic procedures, lacking any reference to the content of laws, cannot have deleterious effects. A democratic tyranny is quite conceivable, many think likely, and on a global scale. Globalization is not neutral. Not a few of the worst tyrants of history have been very popular and have died peacefully in bed in their old age, midst family and friends.

III.

More than anything else, the frontiers of most states of the world are where they are because of war, won or lost. This factor is true even of, say, the relatively peaceful Canadian-American border, whose drawing, even whose existence, is related to the American Revolution, to the War of 1812, and to "54.40 or Fight!" The northern Mexican border does not include California, Texas, Arizona, or New Mexico, as it once did, because a war was lost. I have seen Mexican maps that still include these states within Mexican frontiers. This means that many Mexicans think present borders are unjust; thus we are not wholly at peace. Lord Acton thought that had the South won the American Civil War, it probably would have taken over Mexico.

The "evil empire" covered a quarter or more of the globe because of war and revolution. Ironically, it got its start when Lenin precipitously pulled out of bloody World War I to eradicate his domestic enemies on the right and the enemies of his Bolshevism on the left. The demise of the Soviet Union surprised all the social scientists in that it was not destroyed by war or by any force found in their analytic methods. However, as we were reminded by the Reagan funeral, a major cause of the demise of communism, besides the spiritual one for which the Polish pope stood, was the massive American preparations for war, including nuclear war. They were sufficient to convince the Soviets finally to recognize communism's own internal bankruptcy. Many, at the time, thought this buildup was itself "immoral." Had it not occurred, the Soviet Union might well still be in existence, and its demise might not have been so peaceful, if indeed it was not victorious.

In the case of World War II, we can surely "thank" the lack of early French and English preparedness for and initial unwillingness to engage in war to be a major cause of the more lethal war that, by almost any standard, had to be fought and fortunately won, but only with the aid of others. "Peace in our time," the slogan of the British prime minister, led to World War II. "War was not an answer?" What is the "answer" to terrorism if not war at some level? Terrorists, as they often testify, think that terrorism is a legitimate, even God-commanded duty. Is capitulation the answer? Roman history, in fact, is filled with such wars and capitulations.

In the abstract, the view that noncombatant alternatives to war are always available may well be true. But there are things worse than war. Not to know what they are is tantamount to losing any real contact with or understanding of human experience or history. The "history of war" was not studied by Machiavelli for nothing. Many "peaceful" alternatives to war are not always happy ones. One of them consists in being conquered by a hostile power, another in the complete destruction of civilization. We read of Muslim and Mongolian armies before whose swords we would not like to fall, knowing that if we did, our culture, religion, and way of life, not to mention many of our lives, would disappear. No one in the decade before the sudden appearance of Mohammedan armies in the seventh century could have imagined the configuration of the world map today, a configuration in many areas due precisely to the permanent conquests of these earlier and later armies. The modern integrity of Europe is unimaginable without two victories over Muslim forces, one at Tours in France, one at Vienna.

IV.

In these reflections, however, I do not propose to bring up again or define further the now rather exhausted discussion of the conditions of just war in the modern age of mass weapons. The most "lethal" weapons are today turning out to be car bombs and ordinary passenger planes. But the problem with nuclear weapons was never really the weapons themselves but the will and purpose for which they might or might not be used. Reading the American bishops' documents on nuclear war in the retrospective light of the bombing of the World Trade Centers makes them seem almost irrelevant. The fact is, deterrence did work, however reluctant we are, usually for ideological reasons, to admit it. Such earlier considerations of "absolute weapons" also seem wholly out of touch with what has become the problem of the defense in the twenty-first century.

We do have a concern that "terrorists," as we are wont to call them in lieu of calling them what they call themselves, will gain possession of nuclear weapons. We could reasonably suppose that communists did not want to be destroyed. We are not so sure about Muslim war planners. The "suicide bomber" may prove to be more lethal, and more intellectually perplexing, than any nuclear weapon ever was.

Nuclear and conventional weapons, in fact, have become so accurate, so downsized, so controlled that all the elements of the just war theory devised by the most scrupulous moralist are in place and in operation. One might even argue that current American weaponry is constructed the way it is precisely because it is living up to just war concerns. Again, the problem is never the weapons themselves, but who uses them. The knowledge of how to make such weapons simply exists, along with the technology to make them. We cannot think these plans out of existence without thinking much of modern science out of existence. And we have no reason to think that present day terrorists, who have a different religious philosophy, will not use nuclear weapons if they can, even if they destroy themselves in the process.

What is not in place today is how to deal with or even understand the "suicide bomber." Just war theory is relatively useless in this area. As I read somewhere, what, after all, does a fully armed G.I. do in confrontation with a pregnant Muslim woman who has bombs strapped inside her dress and intends to blow him, herself, her baby, and dozens of other up? All the literature and normal understanding about "innocent women and children" have become, if not irrelevant, at least maddeningly difficult to apply in such increasingly common cases. And the reason for this problem is not, I think, military, but ideological or theological.

The answer to the question of why a Muslim man or woman will blow him or herself up is not simply political or military. Aristotle had said that if someone is willing to die in the process, no one can really prevent him from trying to kill us. Augustine had a similar problem with the Donatists. A Muslim blowing himself up along with fifteen others, can pretty much rest assured that this same utterly irresponsible type of weapon will not be used against his own people. This is a civilizational divide, not just a matter of taste, or even of the end justifying the means. It is the consequences of a faulty theology that has to be addressed at that level.

The real issue is Dawson's question from the 1930s, namely, is this current situation a new war of civilization? Much vested interest is devoted to the proposition that it is not. This insistence that it is not is itself an ideological question. Our leaders, both civil and religious, have been loathe to designate it as a civilizational war. Islam is a religion of peace. To suspect that it is a threat on a much broader scale is one of those things that must be classified as "secret writing." It goes against the dominant religious mood, namely, ecumenism, and against the liberal mode, namely, tolerance, according to which all issues can be resolved without war. But neither of these viewpoints is proper to certain Muslim ways of looking at the world which, in their missionary view, ought to be Muslim, even if by war, even by suicide bombings. War can be precisely "holy." Until we can understand that, we simply will not be able to grasp the essence of the problem.

There is considerable talk both in the West and in certain sections of the Muslim world that Islam can be made over into politically acceptable forms without its having to change any of what are considered its basic beliefs. This radical reconstruction of Islam is said to be the main "neoconservative" project. This rewriting or refounding of Islam is certainly the import of identifying the current military attacks as coming from a minority "terrorist" movement and not from Islam in any genuine form.

One can, I think, defend this program on prudential grounds. No one, including the churches, is willing to examine in a serious way the truth claims of Islam, not only its own understanding of Allah and its understanding of Judaism and Christianity, but also its practiced way of life and its direct relation of its religion and its politics. Until this latter effort is undertaken in a much more serious way, the prudential approach can be justified as a holding operation. But even in the effort to provide models and forms of "democratic" and "free" political systems, what is ultimately behind this thinking is the effort to undermine those teachings and customs of Islam that cause the problem. The first of these issues is the claim of the truth of Islamic revelation and its understanding of the absolute will of God as arbitrary. In this sense, MacArthur was right. Political problems often have theological import at their basis.

The Italian paper *Il Giornale* recently published an interview with Caesare Mazzolari, Bishop of Rumbek in the Sudan, a place in which Christian-Muslim relations are those of war, war against the Christians. His remarks perhaps serve to contextualize this issue, particularly in the light of the Dawson thesis:

Q. "Is there a clash of civilizations?"
A. "The Church has defeated communism but is just starting to understand its next challenge—Islamism, which is much worse. The Holy Father has not been able to take up this challenge due to his old age. But the next pope will find himself having to face it."
Q. "Some bishops in Italy have allowed chapels to be used a mosques."
A. "It will be the Muslims who convert us, not the other way around. Wherever they settle down, sooner or later they end up becoming a leading political force."
Q. "Does it make sense to export our democracy to agricultural and sheepherding societies that make no distinction between religion and politics?"

A. "No. This is idiotic. Islamic people base their decisions only and exclusively on the *umma*. They don't even know what individual rights are."[2]

This is, no doubt, a blunt analysis from someone located in a country where over two million people have been killed in Muslim attacks on Christians and their own dissidents. Whether we look on such events as the wave of the future or an exceptional, isolated case will pretty much decide the kind of attitude we have to war and the necessity of the retention and use of military power.

V.

My topic here, however, is not Islam but war. Essential to this discussion, of course, is the current understanding of what Islam is and intends, of how we know. Islam is not the only civilizational problem, of course, and it is not necessarily unified with itself. Western secularist ideology is as absolutist in its own way as Islam. The thesis that the "terrorists" are merely a sideshow, a tiny minority, which will naturally pass away, is an easy way out of considering the more basic problem of Islam's religio-political movement and what to do about it. This consideration is written against the background that Islam is a confident movement that is suddenly aware of a possibility that, in the judgment of many of its radical leaders, it can continue its historic mission of spreading the religion by force or other means throughout the world.

The question of how to "disarm" or to "dissuade" this expansion, which now has a demographic component through immigration into Western nations of low birth rates, is bound up with the question of a continued capacity and willingness of a nation to defend itself. It is still necessary actually to disarm or destroy those who hold these violent positions as a question of legitimate political aggression through means of "terrorism," no matter how small or large we think their forces might be. We are in what is to us the paradoxical situation of realizing that "peaceful" means of dissuasion will not in fact always or automatically work to protect innocent people from the mission of these "terrorists," as we insist on calling them.

Dealings with terrorists remind us also of Augustine's further dealing with the Donatists in which, after exhausting all possible peaceful and accommodating means to deter them, he had to conclude that they must

2. Interview of Stefano Lorenzetto with Msgr. Caesare Mazzolari, May 26, 2004, http:// chiesa.espresso.repubblica.it/articolo/7044?&eng=y.

change their minds even with the use of force at least to pacify them. Augustine has taken much heat for this conclusion. But even assuming that it does work, which is dubious, it is clear that those with whom we deal today are never "converted." They look upon suicide bombing in their cause as a martyrdom and an entrance to heaven. The fact that this position seems preposterous to many of us is one of the main reasons we cannot well deal with it.

A common, oft-heard theory about war today is that we have "grown" or progressed out of it. The claim that war may still be needed is looked upon as "anti-progressive," a sin against "history." No "reasonable" person can hold such a view that war may be necessary. This "we-have-outgrown-war" position, with its Hegelian overtones, is an aspect of an evolutionary hypothesis that, generally speaking, holds that the world is getting morally better. Whether it is or not, however, is another question, by no means obvious to an honest observer. Still, it is said, certain things like war are not now "necessary." We have learned how to "overcome" them with dialogue or discussion or psychological counseling. The older realist hypothesis, by contrast, more attuned to the Fall and the natural difficulties of the practice of virtue, maintained that as the world improved in technological or political means, its potential for greater evil also increased. We would thus never be in a situation where some use of force or power would not be needed for the achievement of what limited good we could and should attain.

The hypothesis is that war is no longer necessary and has little justification. Behind this view, we find operative an ancient controversy about the logic of the world state as the primary inner-worldly purpose of mankind. Indeed, on denying some transcendent purpose, it becomes the only purpose of mankind. The framework of "world" or "global" government is now said to be already in place. Though the United Nations was not legally erected to be a "world government" or "world state," no political controversy involving war, it is now claimed erroneously, can be "unilaterally," and hence morally, decided outside of its jurisdiction. This view is designed to take away any consideration of national self-interest or independently coming to the aid of those evidently under attack. This newly found veto on war evidently comes from custom, not law, though even there it is difficult to know how such a momentous structural change could be legitimated in this unarticulated way.

This assumption of a benign United Nations already legally established depends on a one-sided view of the United Nations and the ideological currents within it. Many positions on life and economic questions within the United Nations are extremely troubling. There are "missionary" efforts to impose these ideas on the world. This position also implies that neither truth nor good will ever have to be protected *against* the United Nations, which logically should and indeed would like to absorb all the world's military capacity within itself. United Nations citizenship and courts should replace national citizenship and courts. The ultimate appeal, in this view, ought not to be to national courts but to international courts, which would become the ultimate arbiters of law within the world and within each lesser jurisdiction. International criminal and civil courts would be the primary arbitrators who decide justice within the nations. International courts would claim immediate jurisdiction over all rights cases wherever they occur. Any appeal to national "self-interest" against their decisions would be looked upon as a crime against humanity.

In his discussion of "restitution," the primary act of justice in all its forms, Josef Pieper made the following observation:

The dynamic character of man's communal life finds its image within the very structure of every act of justice. If the basic act of commutative justice is called "re-stitution," the very word implies that it is never possible for men to realize an ideal and definitive condition. What it means is, rather, that the fundamental condition of man and his world is provisory, temporary, non-definitive, tentative, as is proved by the patchwork character of all historical activity, and that, consequently, any claim to erect a definitive and unalterable order in this world must of necessity lead to something inhuman.[3]

This "something inhuman" is what we are concerned about when we address the question of whether war is obsolete. The grounds of this latter assumption are that we actually do have in place the means to prevent war. The historic realism that argued that war would always be with us is now said to be effectively bypassed.

In this regard, let me further cite the following summation of Herbert Deane about Augustine's view of war. "Wars are inevitable as long as men and their societies are moved by avarice, greed, and lust for power, the permanent drives of sinful men. It is, therefore, self-delusion and folly to expect that a time will ever come in this world when wars will cease and 'men will beat their swords into ploughshares.'"[4] In this light, we are asked to maintain that the institutions designed to replace the national state will

---

3. *Josef Pieper: An Anthology*, 63.

4. Herbert Deane, *Political and Social Ideas of St. Augustine* (New York: Columbia University Press, 1956), 155.

not themselves be threats against freedom and justice. The question becomes whether the world and, indeed, ourselves are better off with national states that can maintain their own judgments and forces. Thus, it would be my position that whatever the logic of the international state, its practice is too dangerous both on the large scale and on the small scale ever to trust it with anything more than minimal powers, and these most advisory. For the most part, when it comes to modern tyrannies, international organizations have not been successful, as they are often part of the problem.

Jean Elsthain has written, "I would argue that true international justice is defined as the equal claim of all persons, whatever their political location or condition, to having coercive force deployed in their behalf if they are victims of one or the many horrors attendant upon radical political instability."[5] What Elsthain implies is that there is and must be room for the existence and use of force that understands and works for right order. I would maintain, therefore, that much of the thinking about how war is obsolete is itself a major contributor to war, particularly to the new kinds of war that we see in the twenty-first century. Such a view prevents quick and effective action. Without denying that this alternative can also be abused, we can never arrive at a clear concept of what the problem is because the mechanisms designed to address this problem include the problem.

VI.

In conclusion, where does this leave this discussion? We are left with the need to see force and power as actual servants of justice. C. S. Lewis wrote in his essay, "Why I Am Not a Pacifist":

It is arguable that a criminal can always be satisfactorily dealt with without the death penalty. It is certain that a whole nation cannot be prevented from taking what it wants except by war. It is almost equally certain that the absorption of certain societies by certain other societies is a great evil. The doctrine that war is always a greater evil seems to imply a materialist ethic, a belief that death and pain are the greatest evils. But I do not think they are. I think the suppression of a higher religion by a lower, of even a higher secular culture by a lower, a much greater evil. . . . The question is whether war is the greatest evil in the world, so that any state of affairs, which might result from submission, is certainly preferable. And I do not see any really cogent argument for this view.[6]

5. Jean Bethke Elshtain, *Just War against Terror* (New York: Basic Books, 2003), 168.
6. C. S. Lewis, "Why I Am Not a Pacifist," in *Weight of Glory and Other Addresses* (New York: Macmillan, 1965), 43.

Lewis, as usual, on the grounds of principle, had it about right. War is not the greatest evil, but at times the only means to prevent it. This is true on both a large and small scale. What we are left with is that the effective use of force is still best and most properly left in the national state. This is not the war of all against all, but the war of those who can limit terrorism and tyranny when and where it occurs. The worst modern tyranny in the twenty-first century will not come from armies but from their lack or, better, from the lack of capacity and courage to use them wherever needed to protect justice, freedom, and truth.

PART VII

WHERE DOES IT LEAD?

20   ON CHOOSING NOT TO SEE

Purely intellectual activity cannot occur without some action by our sensitive powers, but the content of our conceptual thought is not affected by it. We can think conceptually of that which is not sensible at all, and not imaginable.

—Mortimer Adler, "Sense," *Philosophical Dictionary*

I.

One of the most instructive passages I have ever read is that found in C. S. Lewis's *The Abolition of Man* about the textbook writers and the waterfall. The story goes that the English poet Coleridge records the reaction of two ordinary tourists on first seeing a particularly lovely waterfall. One of these tourists called it "pretty," while the other called it "sublime." Coleridge, of course, thought the tourist calling it "sublime" was correct, while the one calling it merely "pretty" was lacking in some perception or appreciation of the reality before him. There was a note of "culpability" in Coleridge's reaction, as if the said tourist ought to know that something more than "pretty" was before him.[1]

Words mean things, just as paintings or drawings in a different way refer to things that words given to the same things indicate. However, we can have paintings of waterfalls that are themselves as artifacts "pretty" or "sublime." In this latter case of the paintings or drawings, they have their own existence, outside the mind and independent of that which they depict. I suppose it is possible to have merely a "pretty" painting of what is in fact a "sublime" waterfall or a "sublime" painting of a pretty waterfall. But in either case, of the waterfall itself or of the painting, what merits the word used is the objective reality of a thing in nature or in art.

The first thing to notice about this passage in Lewis, however, is the

This essay was originally published online in *New Pantagruel* 2, no. 3 (Summer 2005), www.newpantagruel.com/issues/2.3/on_choosing_not_to_see.php. The essay was republished in *Telos* 136 (Fall 2006): 167–72.

1. C. S. Lewis, *The Abolition of Man* (New York: Macmillan, 1962), 13–35.

possibility that a real waterfall standing before us may be in fact only "pret-ty," as opposed to other waterfalls that are "sublime." It is a question of fact. "Pretty" waterfalls are both possible and do exist. I have seen them myself. Evidently, these tourists of whom Coleridge spoke were, in his es-timate at least, overlooking not just an ordinary falls but a grand one in the order of Niagara, Victoria, or Yosemite. The proper human response to what was before them thus required some description more than merely "pretty," itself a perfectly good word that can be used to describe many ex-isting things from ladies to flowers to music.

The contradictory of "pretty" is not "sublime" but simply "not-pretty." "Sublime" does not deny prettiness in things but grasps the degrees of glo-ry within things themselves. We seek to distinguish properly and name accurately what we observe, *what things are*. This is the reason, or one of them, why we are given minds and, indeed, why we enjoy using them. It makes a difference how we say what we see or hear. We know that the same reality can use different words in different languages or even within the same language. Still, the words we use have a firmness of meaning about them such that "pretty" does not mean the same thing as "sublime," both good words, but different.

To make the same point in another way, in a 1954 *Peanuts*, Lucy has just discovered the funny curly marks on her fingertips. Charlie Brown tells her that they are "fingerprints." As she continues to look at them in some fas-cination, Charlie observes, "Still studying your fingerprints, Lucy?" She replies, "Uh huh. Let's see yours, Charlie Brown." She carefully examines Charlie's fingertips. Finally, she concludes triumphantly to a dazed Charlie, "Mine are prettier!" (September 4, 1954). We are amused here not because we should have used "sublime" but because the word "pretty" or "sublime" is not used to describe things like fingerprints. Again, words have meanings that are designed to get at what is there in the waterfalls or fingerprints.

But the problem that Lewis originally presented was of another order than that of the proper use of words. Rather, he presented the problem of whether we can ever get outside of ourselves in our knowing processes. If we cannot, when we spell out its implications, it is a rather frightening prospect. It seems that the writers of English textbooks for schoolchildren explained this passage from Coleridge in quite an odd fashion. For them, the problem was not whether the waterfall, in its own objective grandeur, was "pretty" or "sublime." Neither of these two words, in these authors' view, referred to the waterfall at all. They referred to the thoughts or emo-tions of the tourists about the said falls. These thoughts were, evidently, themselves either "pretty" or "sublime" according to the inner "feelings" the observers imposed on them.

In other words, in shades of epistemological theory, the tourists were not seeing the waterfall at all but only their thoughts about the waterfall. Whether they knew the actual waterfall at all was not the problem of the textbook writers, however much it is the problem of epistemology itself. As Lewis quipped, in effect, if someone says that "you are ugly," it does not refer to you at all. Rather it refers to the observer's thoughts about you. It means "my thoughts about you are ugly," whatever in fact you might look like, even "pretty" or "sublime." Such a theory is delightfully absurd.

But such theory is not harmless. Its real effect is to deprive us of the world itself, including the waterfall, sublime, pretty, prettier, or even ugly. We thus walk about in a world in which nothing, as it is in its objective being, can affect us. Things are not *what they are* but what we think they are. And if we think that a waterfall is "pretty," who can disagree with us, since there is no objective order available to us, as there evidently was to Coleridge, by which we can inquire whether our ideas correspond to reality. We cannot be moved by *what is*, because reality does not get through to us. We are not concerned about what our thoughts refer to. We are concerned with the thoughts themselves and try to describe them, not what they are said to know.

We are, so it is said, "free" of reality. We are liberated from things. They do not impinge on us for their truth, but we make them what they are. In looking at our thoughts about waterfalls, then, we are only looking at our own feelings as if they mattered, not the waterfalls. Just how we know these "feelings" are even about waterfalls themselves is not clear. The content of our feelings is said to be imposed by us on ourselves, not by the waterfalls. If we cannot distinguish between "sublime" and "pretty," why can we distinguish between a waterfall and, say, a tree or a goat? What is there to respond to besides ourselves and our feelings?

II.

Aristotle thought that our "feelings" or "passions" are indeed an elemental part of our being, of *what it is to be man*. But these passions in turn are not ordered simply to themselves. They are ordered to whatever is out there. We are primarily concerned about the things that are there. Reality, *what is*, thus, included not merely the world of things, but a being within it who had powers to know and react to these things as they are. Through knowledge man could "become" the thing without changing it. Some fundamental relation between word and thing seemed to exist in the structure of things. But simply because the world existed and we had power to know it, it does not follow that we always used our minds or explained our passions about reality adequately or accurately. Hence, like Coleridge, we could talk, in the area of senses, of an education in "taste," because it was not right to use words inaccurately.

This position is not to deny the principle, *de gustibus non est disputandum* (about taste there is no disputing). If someone insists on disliking lovely ripe tomatoes in the summer or in liking garlic ice cream, we cannot simply call him mad. But we are probably not wrong in suspecting that something is wrong with his evaluation of these things, which, in our evaluation of them, will always have something objectively to like or dislike about them. The accurate naming of things what they are is a work given to man even from Genesis in Adam's naming the animals. We cannot act unless we know what things are and are able to speak what they are to those who understand us.

On the other hand, we are to like what is to be liked. We are to enjoy what is to be enjoyed. A proper response to things is something we must cultivate, if we do not have it spontaneously. If our teeth are crooked, we straighten them out. If our taste is skewered, we, analogously, do the same thing, always granting the possibility of a better objective appreciation of things. We may have to learn to appreciate a fine French wine or the gait of a thoroughbred horse or the music of Mahler. Few of us lack the experience of gradually coming to appreciate what we once thought distasteful. The opposite is probably also true; we learn to dislike what we once thought quite good. Both movements imply that there are standards or criteria by which we can judge whether our response to things is adequate or fine, yes, "pretty" or "sublime." We exist that the highest things be appreciated highly. But we also exist that ordinary things can be appreciated ordinarily. Pretty things ought, in fact, to be called precisely "pretty." And indeed, some pretty things are prettier than others.

III.

But I am not so much concerned here with an epistemological theory that would, when spelled out, cause us so to doubt our senses that we can really say nothing of anything outside of ourselves, even whether there be things outside of ourselves. Rather I am concerned with something that I found in Aristotle, among other places. It is not directly a problem of epistemology or even of metaphysics, but rather of morals, of choice. Indeed, I often think that, for most people, thinkers included, the epistemological and metaphysical theory comes from the morals, not vice versa. I think that most of such intellectual aberrations are consequences of an effort to defend what one does or chooses to do. They are not derived directly from perplexity about objectively understanding *what is.*

Why, we might inquire, if there is one world, one human nature in which we all participate, are there so many convoluted and contradictory theories about how to live the one life we are given in the one world we all inhabit? Modern "tolerance" theory wants us not to "judge" other views in terms of good or bad, truth or falsity, but only in terms of "different" and "very different." Still, we cannot help notice that one claim always serves, within this world of universal tolerance, to cause bitter antagonism. That is the notion that there is a right way to live. There is a right and wrong that is objective and grounded in *what is.* This "right" way, moreover, is not merely another human concoction or confabulation. And if there is a right way, there must be likewise a wrong way to live. This view, which has ancient roots, as do the modern theories that oppose it, is more and more looked upon as the principle that undermines modern culture. Insofar as modern culture is based on simple, naive relativism, this is true.

Normally, if someone is not living as he should, as some objective criterion would seem to suggest that he live, we should think that that person would be glad to have his erroneous ways pointed out to him so that he could correct himself. He would, in other words, want to call "sublime" things precisely "sublime," true things true. We soon discover, however, that most people do not like to be confronted with the notion that their way of living is not the best, and even may be quite wrong. If we know of the meaning of "original sin," we should not be at all surprised at this situation. Charges of arrogance and hypocrisy go back and forth. It all seems like a futile effort. What are we to make of it?

In the *Idler* for Saturday, October 21, 1758, Samuel Johnson made the following very Socratic observation: "It has been the endeavour of all those whom the world has reverenced for superior wisdom, to persuade man to be acquainted with himself, to learn his own powers and his own weakness, to observe by what evils he is most dangerously beset, and by what temptations most easily overcome."[2] Behind this "know thyself" ob-

---

2. Samuel Johnson, *Selected Essays,* edited by David Womersley (Harmondsworth, England: Penguin, 2003), 425.

servation is the frank realization that, on self-reflection, we realize that we not only do things that are wrong or evil, but that we are tempted to do so even if we do not do them. We must then take steps both to understand the dimensions of the evil to which we are tempted and how to deal with them.

Very few of us, Johnson tells us, can "search deep into their own minds without meeting what they wish to hide from themselves." So what do we do? We devise theories that apparently explain that what we actually do, whatever it is, is quite fine. Many simply try to avoid the issue of conscience or guilt. We can put pressing things aside. Others will be struck by examples of goodness and their own actions in relationship to them. "These are forced to pacify the mutiny of reason with fair promises, and quiet their thoughts with designs of calling all their actions to review, and planning a new scheme for the time to come. There is nothing we estimate so fallaciously as the force of our own resolutions, nor any fallacy which we so unwillingly and tardily detect." In other words, the bitterness we find in reactions to any claims of truth has its roots here in our defensive intellectual reaction whereby we construct an alternate truth to the truth of *what is.*

Johnson put the main blame for our refusal to recognize what is right and change our ways to the very Aristotelian difficulty of changing any habit once we are set in it. We think it is an easy thing to reform, but for most people, it is not. Yet, beyond this difficulty, there are those who actively seek to defend, at all costs, their option for a freedom that supplies the content of their actions. They do not discover this content but define it. They are autonomous. This counter formulation is no easy task, to be sure. "Those who are in the power of evil habits, must conquer them as they can, and conquered they must be, or neither wisdom or happiness can be attained."[3]

What interests me about that passage, in conclusion, is the relation that Johnson draws between the possibility of "wisdom or happiness" and our failure to conquer our own evil habits. He leaves those of us in evil habits no alternative: either we conquer them or they stimulate us to establish theories counter to the truth of what happiness and wisdom are. We then proceed to live according to our own theories, themselves concocted precisely to justify what we do. They are formulated against what is classically defined as good or true.

3. Ibid., 427.

In the beginning, I cited Mortimer Adler, who told us that "we can think conceptually of what is not sensible." In context, this observation was merely a summary of the relation of our senses to our intellect. But in view of what I have been saying, there is perhaps a more sinister implication. We can think conceptually of a world we create for ourselves that is not itself connected with the world, "pretty" or "sublime," that is revealed to us by our senses. In this conceptual world, we define what is good and what is evil by denying that such realities are discoverable as not ours to formulate.

Deep in our minds, as Johnson told us, we seek to "hide things from ourselves." This is what happens when we choose "not to see." We have the uncanny power, because of our evil habits, according to which we seek not only to live but to justify the world we construct in order that we may live this way. We establish our own content of what is called "wisdom" or "happiness." It is this power that, more than anything else, rules the modern world. The only proper anecdote is our ability to "know ourselves," to be able properly to distinguish between what is "pretty" and what is "sublime," what is true and what is false, not of our own making.

21 "THE ULTIMATE MEANING
OF EXISTENCE"

It might well be that at the end of history the only people who will examine and ponder the root of all things and the ultimate meaning of existence—i.e., the specific object of philosophical speculation—will be those who see with the eyes of faith.

—Josef Pieper, "The Possible Future of Philosophy"

The world hates Christians.

—St. Cyprian, Bishop (d. 258 AD), "Sermon on Man's Mortality"

We who are Christians never knew the great philosophic common sense which inheres in that mystery until the anti-Christian writers pointed it out to us. The great march of mental destruction goes on. Everything will be denied.... We shall be left defending, not only the incredible virtues and sanities of human life, but something more incredible still, this huge impossible universe which stares us in the face. We shall fight for visible prodigies as if they were invisible. We shall look on the impossible grass and the skies with a strange courage. We shall be of those who have seen and yet have believed.

—G. K. Chesterton, *Heretics*

I.

The most penetrating question that a man can inquire of himself about himself is the obvious and simple inquiry, "Why do I exist?" Or to state it another way, "Why am I rather than am not?" No subsequent question is asked that does not anticipate and expect a prior answer to the existence question. I am quite well aware that I do not cause my own existence. I am likewise aware that "existence" is a special kind of word that refers to an "aspect" of our being unlike anything else about us. My existence belongs to me, no one else.

Even if it is phrased as a general noun, "existence" is really a verb that

This essay was originally published in the *Fellowship of Catholic Scholars Quarterly* 29 (Spring 2006): 29–34.

we have abstracted from its reality and universalized. "To exist" means to stand outside of nothingness. It is an act. It is the most vivid and radical of the predicates we can apply to ourselves, the affirmation that "I am." This predicate is different from all the other possible predicates, the one without which nothing else much matters, at least to us. Without it, we are not. We realize, likewise, that it is possible for us not to be. We are somehow fragile, contingent beings. Not only is it true that we are, but *what we are* also stands outside of our own powers to accomplish or formulate. We can only recognize it. We do not make either what it is to be a man or that even as a man, "I am" at all. Yet, we are both one and the other. We are what we are and we exist.

"Why am I, rather than am not?" Of course, if I were not, the question of existence, mine or anyone else's, would hardly have arisen. "Not-being" does not blithely ask questions about its own "nonbeingness." Only existing beings that also have within them a rational power can ask about *what is* and *what is not*. Even to arrive at the notion of "nonbeing," we have to begin with something *that is* that we already know. We then proceed mentally to deny of it existence, while recognizing that this denial does not happen in reality, only in our minds. No nonexisting or nonrational being can ask questions of any sort. Those beings that can and do ask such questions seem to have a special place in existence, in the levels of being. These are the beings that add something to mere existence, namely, its articulated relation to mind and will. Limited existence by itself implies a relation existence that is not limited.

Many things exist. Things come to exist and cease to exist. Not many of these things have the powers to ask, "Why do I exist?" And, of course, if I can ask, "Why do I exist?" I have to wonder "Why do you, someone not me, exist?" Failure of attentive inquiry about our "to exist" implies, I suspect, a fear to know the answer to this question in case such knowledge of existence would put certain untoward demands on us. It might make us, in some fundamental sense, responsible for what becomes of us, not just immediately but ultimately. We can theoretically protect ourselves from the implications of these questions only by embracing philosophical positions that systematically deny any order or meaning to existence and hence to existence questions.

The easiest and most common way to accomplish this avoidance is to embrace a theoretic relativism or determinism that concludes that no particular reason can be found either for "why *what I am* could not be otherwise" or for "why I, as a unique being, exist at all." But if either of these latter propositions is true, that what I am is not an order, that I exist only by chance, it makes no sense to ask questions or to anticipate answers to them. Philosophy of this persuasion is an illusion, especially if its purpose or "reasoned" conclusion is to inform us that there is no reason in things. It has the dubious audacity to give us a "reason" why there is no reason.

II.

Josef Pieper remarks that, in the end of history, the only people who really will philosophize by taking reality as their starting point are likely to be those who also believe, who believe that there is a purpose to existence, particularly our own existence. They are not afraid of genuinely philosophical questions because such questions are also demanded by the faith itself to be confronted philosophically. We do not know whether there are answers given to philosophic questions given by revelation until we first know the adequacy of the answers philosophy gives to its own inquiries.

Chesterton puts it even more graphically. In the end, it will take faith not only to philosophize, but yea, even to affirm that the grass is green and the skies are blue. If we do not want to know why we are, we must, to be safe, systematically doubt even our own powers to know, beginning with the capacity of our senses to manifest to us what is seen or heard, touched or smelled or tasted. If we cannot pass from our mind to things in such a way that things first indicate to our minds *what is,* then we are left with the apparently exhilarating conclusion that we can create our own world. If we do not actually know *what is,* nothing can contest the world we make for ourselves. We are free from any fear that our lives should be ordered on principles that we did not give ourselves, which might happen if the world really existed and we could know it.

St. Cyprian, the Bishop of Carthage, early on, said, almost as if it were an abiding truism that was obvious to anyone, that the world "hates" Christians. We find such statements blunt and upsetting. It goes against our democratic instincts. We like to think that if we are good, we will automatically be loved. Indeed, we like to think we are loved no matter what we do or hold. But it is not so. Good people can be and in fact often are hated precisely because they are good. The good can be hated insofar as it is opposed to my good as I define it.

Christ, in the Gospel of John, said pretty much the same thing: "If the world hates you, know that it hated me before it hated you" (15:18). Such frank affirmations go against the grain of modern multicultural tolerance and ecumenical theory wherein we are supposed to be abidingly nice to each other. All things can be resolved by "dialogue." How seriously, then, are we to take these warnings about the hatred of the world? Even after we distinguish the several usages of the word *world*—what is created, the totality of existing things, what is not the Church—we are today little prepared, in spite of much evidence to the contrary, to accept the truth of Cyprian's rather laconic observation that "the world hates Christians."

Yet, I suspect that some subtle relation exists between the epistemological problems of modern philosophy by which we defend ourselves against the truth of things by doubting that we can know things—"all is relative"—and what Pieper and Chesterton predicted, that finally only believers would also philosophize. They held that it is largely believers today who can be or are in fact the metaphysicians, the only ones still capable intellectually, on the basis of reason, of affirming of *what is* that it is. The fear of knowing why we exist leads to a denial of any ordered existence but what we ourselves project into reality. This projection provides the theoretical background that allows us to do whatever we wish, no matter how contrary to any objective order in things. It leads to the claim that whatever we do is a "right," and, as a consequence, leads to and grounds the establishment of "democracy" on its basis. In this sense, democracy is designed precisely to prevent any serious existence question from being asked. Its purpose is to protect "rights," whatever they are.

We live in a liberal and ecumenical age, at least if we are in North America or Europe. The Chinese, Indian, and Islamic worlds, strikingly larger than our own, are not nearly so open to these "democratic" values and rights that have no content but what is willed to be there. Or perhaps better, they have their own versions of these said "rights," ones equally as arbitrary. We believe in a multiculturalism and diversity that presuppose no standards or measures even more than we believe in God, the Father Almighty, maker of Heaven and Earth. Indeed, we believe in the former, in "rights" and "values," so that we do not have to admit the truth of the latter as a source of order.

Yet, more than one author have pointed out that Christians, insofar as they hold and practice what is laid down in their books (not all do), are in fact hated and, yes, feared. To the Muslim, they are the hated Crusaders. To the liberal, they are the one legitimate object of bigotry and intolerance precisely because they stand for something definite as true. Ultimately, the Christians are the ones who have, as Nietzsche suspected, inherited the Socratic principle: "It is never right to do wrong." This principle is the

one that multiculturalism and diversity theories hold to be most dangerous and the main source of "fanaticism."

When Nietzsche told the Europeans, in words that remind us of nothing so much as their recent debates over the constitution of the European
Union, that "God is dead," he did not address this proclamation to God or
metaphysics. He addressed it to those who did not live and act as if God
existed even when they still claimed to believe in Him. This lack of authen-
ticity was what scandalized Nietzsche about Christians. The limits of tolerance are quickly found when we affirm that something is indeed true, true
not just for us, but true for any mind, for any culture, for any public order.
This claim was at the heart of natural law theory. Its denial results in the establishment of cultures and nations whose diversity is at bottom radical,
based on the impossibility of moral absolutes, and hence the impossibility
of criticizing or judging any culture. It also excludes any rational discourse
other than that of interest or power as a means to resolve controversy and
disagreement. For with no common ground, there is nothing on which to
agree.

III.

In the New Testament we read that the children of light are less enterprising than the children of darkness. We wonder about this resourceful-
ness of what are called "the children of darkness," even if it seems observa-
tionally true that such energy against what is good exists. A friend of mine
remarked:

Here is the mystery: why does wrong have more energy than the right side? Or
so it seems to me. The standard situation is that those most committed to disorder, such as the homosexual agenda, heresy, Islam, eliminating the name of Christ
from all Christmas displays, spend or have more energy than "we" do to combat
their efforts, we, who are hopefully on the right side of the issues. Why is this?

One only need to think of the abortion, euthanasia, and human experi-
mentation movements to affirm the truth of this penetrating observation,
already touched on in the New Testament itself.

Such wonderments are, as I said, modern formulations of an ancient
problem. We have been curious from the beginning, for instance, about
why the fallen angels not only had great power but great energy and zeal
to achieve their will. They were pictured as not content with their expulsion from their Paradise. They went about seeking to poison the Paradises

and Edens of other races, particularly our own. In the Epistle of Jude we read, "Sodom, Gomorrah, and the town thereabout indulged in lust, just as those angels did; they practiced unnatural vice. They are set before us to dissuade us, as they undergo a punishment of eternal fire."

In more and more political jurisdictions today, such a passage, and those similar to it in Scripture, cannot be read in public discourse or perhaps even in the Church. The Bible, it is said, has to be "amended" according to a higher political doctrine, generally that of the notion of "rights." Many rights are defined by the individual and protected by the state from any criticism even of public opinion. Churches increasingly censor themselves so that what Scripture contains is either not published or not commented on. The new culture defines what elements in the old religion can be retained.

The question at hand is not an issue of what is right and what is wrong. Rather it concerns the energy shown by those whose views, by explicit teachings of revelation or the normal conclusions of reason, are erroneous. Burke is famous for stating that evil will prosper when those good men who oppose it do little or nothing to combat it. The energy that goes into efforts to insist that homosexuality is perfectly "normal" or that Christmas should be removed from public expression is not just that effort devoted to a normal political or economic cause. We do not need to seek too far in the proponents of these movements to find a hatred for Christians for being so rash as to uphold what they are understood to stand for. Christians who compromise on these issues are fine. Again, why this lethargy on the part of believers to acknowledge that they are under attack, that they are indeed hated? Why this energy that insists that Christian principles be politically forbidden?

In the case of Islam, if we read its history, the lesson that clearly comes across is that it is very dangerous, personally dangerous, to oppose it, particularly when it has gained political power. There is remarkably little organized attention from Christian sources over the persecution and civic disabilities of fellow Christians in Islamic states over recent decades. And when there is, it is often the result of prodding by Jewish sources. Islam generally speaking makes no bones in affirming that the world should be Muslim. Its history of holy war had no other object than to carry out this belief. It is still very much a goal of many Muslim movements.

In the West the sort of "death" that arises from opposing an evil is more in the nature of an attack on one's reputation or style, of not being with the cultured or the powerful. It is very unpopular to oppose abortion either in the clinics where it is regularly performed or in courts and leg-islatures where it is proposed as a good, as a "right." Leading proponents of abortion in the public order are often those who claim religious belief, not a few Catholics among them. Needless to say, it is also very difficult to oppose intrinsic corruption in civil bureaucracies. For many states in the world, crime and corruption are the major issues, particularly when the control of dope and other large-scale vices are at stake. The ability of police and army to stay ahead of organized crime is often limited. And be-hind this corruption lies the demand within a citizenry for those things that usually make crime possible by financing it—drugs, prostitution, theft, or pornography.

The question of good government thus unavoidably brings up the more fundamental concern about "what is good?" Already in Plato and Aristo-tle, we are aware that government can be in the service of almost any end, whether it be decent or corrupt. We will never have a world in which these tendencies to promote what is evil do not exist. No doubt, this fact is not a formula for doing nothing. But it does remind us of the meaning of Paul's remark that our warfare is not against flesh and blood but against princi-palities and powers. Paul seems to be aware that evil is not an abstraction but somehow an option, a choice that evidently wants to justify itself, that makes a case for itself as something good. Somewhere, I think, C. S. Lew-is said that the greatest evil would be the effort to define what is evil to be good and what is good to be evil. Perhaps we should say that those who do define what is evil to be good are endowed with a surprising energy and zeal, almost as if to say that error has no alternative but to justify and pro-tect itself both with philosophical arguments and with political power.

We hear much about the fact that "terrorists," as they are quaintly called, seem to epitomize what is evil in a world in which the content of evil is not discussed or defined. That the "terrorists" themselves do not think they are terrorists seems remarkable. In their own terms, they are pursuing a good cause by necessary means. They reject the standards by which we define them as terrorists. If they succeed, however, the world will be at "peace," and there will be no more violence. Violence is caused by those who oppose this effort to subject the world to Allah, not by the terrorists.

Moreover, since, presumably, there is no universal culture, no natural law, what principles are defined as "rights" in any given culture are as good as those in any other culture. To pursue a cultural good by means accept-ed and fostered by the culture is itself a good that cannot be opposed on the basis of some other view that has as much or as little status as the cause embraced by "terrorists."

Josef Pieper also wrote, "Non-violent totalitarianism is the most inhuman form of totalitarianism—among other reasons because it can always cite what appear to be valid arguments to prove that it is not what in fact it is."[1] We often hear that war is the greatest evil. But it is suggested here that it is precisely when war is no longer possible that the worst evils will come about. If we mean by "peace" no fighting, and no possibility of fighting, we are already in an absolutist state. Peace never meant "no fighting." Rather, it meant no unjustified fighting.

IV.

At the end of his essay explaining the basic outlines of his work, Hans Urs von Balthasar wrote:

All true solutions offered by the Christian Faith hold, therefore, to these two mysteries (Trinity and Incarnation), categorically refused by a human reason which makes itself absolute. It is because of this that the true battle between religions begins only after the coming of Christ. Humanity will prefer to renounce all philosophical questions—Marxism, or positivism of all stripes, rather than accept a philosophy which finds its final response only in the revelation of Christ. Foreseeing that, Christ sent his believers into the whole world as sheep among wolves. Before making a pact with the world it is necessary to meditate on that comparison.[2]

Here, St. Cyprian's "the world hates Christians" links up with von Balthasar's warning about making a pact with the world. We also see in this passage just why it is that a realist philosophy must be rejected at an early stage lest it is forced to see the relation between, what John Paul II called in his famous encyclical, *Fides et Ratio,* faith and reason.

What is also significant about von Balthasar's remark is the implication that a failure of philosophers to defend reality with their minds would in fact justify Christ's remark about sending us as sheep among wolves. Christians think that they are hated because of some defect or sin that they have committed. The lesson of Christ was rather the opposite, namely that a believer would be persecuted and ostracized precisely because of what

---

1. *Josef Pieper: An Anthology,* 228.

2. Hans Urs von Balthasar, "A Résumé of My Thought," translated by Kelly Hamilton, www.ignatiusinsight.com/features2005/hub_resumethought_mar05.asp. The essay originally appeared in *Communio* 15 (Winter 1988).

was good. The fact that someone is good does not guarantee that he will not be persecuted on the grounds that he is evil.

"We shall be of those who have seen and yet have believed." It will take courage to say of *what is* that it is. The reason for this intellectual courage is precisely because the human mind anticipates where it does not want to go, even if reason points in that direction. What modern philosophy and ideology primarily are, I think, is an effort to provide an alternate world to the one *that is,* in order to be exempt from any relationship to or obligation to an order to which man is related. It must aggressively formulate and impose its philosophy. Otherwise, the mind, reflecting on *what is,* does point thought in the direction of what is found in revelation.

Von Balthasar's very sober reminder of what it actually says in Scripture makes solemn reading. Both in Plato and in the New Testament, we have incidents—the one of Alcibiades at the Symposium, the other at the stoning of Stephen—in which men closed their ears so that they would not hear the truth. Instead of doing anything quite as dramatic as putting our hands over our ears so that we would not hear, we accomplish fundamentally the same thing by formulating a philosophical position that does not have to confront the implications of revelation to reason.

So, in conclusion, what is the source of the energy that is displayed by the children of darkness, an energy that we see displayed with growing force in our world? Basically, it is the conflict between creating a world of our own and acknowledging a world of gift that is already presented to us as something better than anything we could concoct for ourselves. The hatred of Christianity is the necessary product, I think, of a bad conscience that suspects that these man-chosen worlds do not compare to the one that is revealed to us. The philosophy that must be true if Christian revelation is true is a philosophy of realism nowhere better outlined than in Aristotle. If we suspect this relationship between realism and revelation, in order to protect from admitting the implications of the relationship, philosophy itself must be rejected. This conclusion leaves us with the suspicion that the only people still defending philosophy, as such, are the believers. They defend it both on philosophical and theological grounds.

Let me again refer to the growing opposition to any public expression of Christmas, the loveliest of feasts and the most basic of the truths that indirectly ground philosophical realism. Chesterton remarked that on Christmas Eve, we should close our doors and spend the time with those we love. But it is the truth of the Nativity, of "a Son is born to us," that makes this feast so joyous. Those who do not believe in Christmas, in its truth and therefore in its reason for celebration, insist on taking all of what makes Christmas out of the public order. So we have "winter holidays," not Christmas. We have Christmas songs and symbols without Christ. Even those signs that could be seen as symbols are stripped of their significance. The real reason of the opposition of Christmas as a celebration is that those who reject its truth cannot stand its celebration, cannot understand the joy that comes with this feast.

"At the end of history the only people who will ponder *the ultimate meaning of existence* will be those who see with the eyes of faith." Whether it is the "end of history," I shall not claim knowledge. But whether philosophy is now more and more related to the stand we take on revelation's basic truths, I have no doubt. The world "hates" Christians because they affirm its own proper and philosophic meaning in the light of their revelation. At bottom, however, the invention of alternate philosophies is a deliberate construct made necessary by the fact that the philosophy that revelation points to is a realism of *what is*. If we suspect that there is an order in things that makes demands on us for our own good and salvation, we must reject philosophy first if we realize that it does lead to truths that are presented to us as gifts. We are sent as sheep among wolves because the world cannot bear the fact that ultimately it chooses not to accept what it is. This profound unsettlement is, I suspect, the real cause of the strange energy of the children of darkness.

22 "THE BEGINNING OF THE REAL STORY"

And for us, this is the end of all the stories, and we can most truly say that they all lived happily ever after. But for them, it was only the beginning of the real story. All their life in this world and all their adventures in Narnia had only been the cover and the title page.

—C. S. Lewis, *The Last Battle*

The ungentle laws and customs touched upon in this tale are historical, and the episodes which are used to illustrate them are also historical. It is not pretended that these laws and customs existed in England in the sixth century, no, it is only pretended that inasmuch as they existed in the English and other civilizations in far later times, it is safe to consider that it is no libel upon the sixth century to suppose them to have been in practice in that day also. One is quite justified in inferring that whatever one of these laws or customs was lacking in that remote time, its place was competently filled by a worse one.

—Mark Twain, preface to *A Connecticut Yankee in King Arthur's Court*

I.

Narnia, too, like our own fallen world from which it differs in many ways, was not intended to last forever. This truth does not mean that there is no everlastingness, only that it is not ultimately found in Narnia or in this world. Yet, intimations of forever are found both in Narnia and in this world in which our own dramas are played out. Our own existence, as Chesterton put it in "The Ethics of Elfland," reveals "a hairbreadth escape: everything has been saved from a wreck. Every man has had one horrible adventure: as a hidden, untimely birth he had not been, as infants that had never seen the light."[1] The fairy tale makes us aware that we need not be; the "might-not-have-beens" include our own "hidden, untimely births."

This essay, "The Beginning of the Real Story," was originally published in Shanna Caughey, ed., *Revisiting Narnia: Fantasy, Myth and Religion in C. S. Lewis' Chronicles* (Dallas: Benbella Books, 2005), 147–58.

1. Chesterton, *Orthodoxy*.

Our, to us, unexpected existences teach us both a gratefulness that we are at all and a deep awareness of the risks of our being what we are, of our freedom. "Living happily ever after" is not a sure thing because, as all good fairy tales teach us, it depends on how we ourselves choose to live.

Mark Twain was aware of what we do with our freedom, of the abiding disorders of our world, present, past, and, no doubt, future, a world full, as it is, of "ungentle laws and customs." Indeed, Mark Twain suspected, like Augustine, that, as this world grows older, it will manifest, in human terms, mostly things that are worse than the world our ancestors knew. Not a few ancient tales pictured the world as a continual declination from an aboriginal good. Later thinkers of liberal or Marxist persuasions maintained, on the contrary and in spite of considerable evidence, that history is a progress to an inner-worldly good not yet achieved, one achieved solely by our own efforts. The Garden of Eden and what happened there, however, was a "beginning," that did not cause itself. We all still have, as Chesterton said, some sense of a primordial "wreck" in which we participate.

Yet, the story of our achievements and joys, of our sins and disorders, is a "real story" into which we are caught up by the very fact that we are born into this world as human, rational beings, not something else. How do we live with these signs of disorder found everywhere around us? Can we escape them? On what terms? In *The Last Battle*, the last of the Narnian tales, C. S. Lewis suggested that the story that we are living out in our lives is not the one we would describe ourselves to be experiencing. We omit so much from our autobiographies, most often the part that urgently needs repentance. We find it odd that the first thing that the Gospels tell us to do is precisely to "repent." Still, we long to see and know this "real story," *our own story*. We wonder, in the light of this dire record, why we have this unsettling idea of happiness in the first place. And why do we think that somehow this record of how, in practice, we define our happiness by our choices relates to our personal destiny? Still we wonder whether the picture that we make for ourselves is the one that is really best for us, the one that is seen by what sees the order of things.

Readers of the *Republic* of Plato are aware of the "shadows" on the wall of the Cave, shadows that imply that the ordinary opinions and lives of normal citizens in any real city, however vivid, obscure something more fundamental about their lives. Knowing our Plato and the *Republic*, the most fundamental book of our philosophic tradition, we again read (I presume everyone has read it before), in the last book of the *Chronicles of Narnia*: "'There *was* a real railway accident,' said Aslan softly. 'Your father and mother and all of you are—as you used to call it in the Shadow-Lands— dead. The term is over: the holidays have begun. The dream is ended: this is the morning.'"[2] Here are Plato's "shadows" again. Here is again the same image of light that the philosopher who turned around in the Cave beheld in the Sun, the Good.

This tradition of intense searching through the shadows, through the "Shadow-Lands," goes on, looking for the reality that such shadows seem to obscure, yet imply. However, in Narnia, this desire for clarity and sight, the end of the Shadow-Lands, is presented not so much as light but as sacrifice. "The light came into the world, and the world comprehended it not." The heart of the first book of the *Chronicles of Narnia*, with its incident that runs through all the other six tales, shows the evil White Witch killing Aslan on the Stone Table. Did she succeed? Is evil stronger than good? Aslan dies, but He really cannot be permanently killed by creatures.

On initially discovering the truth and reality of Aslan, Susan wants to know what it means. Aslan replies:

It means that though the Witch knew the Deep Magic, there is a magic deeper still which she did not know. Her knowledge goes back only to the dawn of Time. But if she could have looked a little further back, into the stillness and the darkness before Time dawned, she would have read there a different incantation. She would have known that when a willing victim who had committed no treachery was killed in a traitor's stead, the Table would crack and Death itself would start working backward.[3]

Here, we are already beyond philosophy without leaving it unnoticed. Socrates, in the *Apology*, did not fear death because he did not know if it was evil or not. All he knew was that to do evil was wrong, even more wrong than death, a death he, as the philosopher, suffered rather than do evil. Philosophy takes us this far.

Without philosophy, without discovering things it cannot answer, moreover, we do not know that it (philosophy) does not itself answer all the questions. Attempted answers, though not always true, are preparatory for true answers. They reveal our puzzlement. Sophocles had said that "man learns by suffering," perhaps only by suffering. Thought alone, as Aristotle said, moves nothing. The Innocent Victim is connected with what is before Time and likewise with the beginning of the elimination of death, through death. The Innocent Victim is betrayed and put to death, not un-

2. Lewis, *Last Battle*, 183.
3. C. S. Lewis, *The Lion, the Witch and the Wardrobe* (New York: Collins, 1950), 159–60.

like what Glaucon, in book 2 of the *Republic,* intimated to be the fate of any just man appearing in any actual city. The Innocent Victim is "willing," obedient. What is the command He follows? We know it leads to death. Yet, as Dylan Thomas said, following St. Paul, "Death has no dominion." After the killing of Aslan at the Stone Table, "death itself would start working backward." What is "backward" from death must be life, must be the "title page," a new adventure just begun.

II.

We are used to fairy stories. We are fortunate if someone reads them to us in our youth, even more so if we read them, reread them ourselves as adults. "You have not read a great book at all if you have only read it once," Lewis himself once said. Fairy tales—themselves often truly great books—take place in "never-never land," however it be called, even in Narnia, even on Earth. We are startled when, on reading such far-fetched, presumably "childish" narratives, they tell us more about ourselves and our world than do our latest conversations in the city in which we live, or in the universities in which we study, or in the media that we watch. This *reality-in-fairy-tales* seems peculiar to us, unsettling even. The world of fantasy is a world full of truth, often of truth that we are not aware of, or even allowed to speak of in existing cities.[4] It is also full of truths that we often choose not to know if we do not want to learn our real stories.

"People who have not been to Narnia sometimes think that a thing cannot be good and terrible at the same time."[5] We read these words in the first of the Narnia Chronicles. The good can be terrible both because it can freely be rejected and because we did not ourselves constitute its validity. When we reject it, we must defend ourselves and make as if what we rejected was not good, even if it is. In the fairy tales themselves, the rejection of the good is never so easily resolved. Free decisions have consequences both for good and for ill, both to ourselves and to others, consequences that the tales trace out for us. Good deeds, paradoxically, can cause hatred; evil ones can incite remorse. We somehow suspect that this inevitable result of free decisions is also true in our own personal world, though we are

---

4. James V. Schall, "On the Reality of Fantasy," in *Tolkien: A Celebration,* edited by Joseph Pearce (London: Fount/HarperCollins, 1999), 67–72. See also Schall, *Unseriousness of Human Affairs.*

5. Lewis, *Lion, the Witch, and the Wardrobe,* 123.

not often told this. Indeed, every effort is made to obscure this realization from our active attention. Choices have consequences. We are loathe to be held responsible. Yet without responsibility for our deeds, we cannot be what we are.

In tales, we notice, things always work their way to a happy or tragic ending, even worse than "tragic" for those who willfully oppose what is good. The evil figures in fairy tales, who are often directly involved in the cause of the ongoing plot, the White Witch in Narnia, for instance, are not, in the end, "saved." And we are not somehow disappointed that they are not. Though there are happy endings, not everyone ends happily. Fairy tales do not pretend that no one is lost, though they do intimate that no one is lost except through his own volition, a truth seen in the lives of the rulers of Mordor in the *Lord of the Rings*. Or as it is said in the *Lion, the Witch and the Wardrobe,* in the land of the White Witch, "it is always winter and never Christmas."[6]

The order of the universe includes places where there is no Christmas, not because Christmas was not offered, but because it was rejected by at least some of our kind and not a few those of other free species beyond our limited powers. Plato said the same thing at the end of the *Republic.* The world would not be complete if what was not just was not exactly identified and punished, if what was good was not specifically rewarded.

This overall sense of what is "just" is often why those who want to prevent children from reading, say, Grimm's fairy tales, with their many frightening figures, on the ground that they are too scary, really work to prevent children from understanding what the world is really like. Chesterton put the theoretical consideration behind such objections well. The first time children realize the disorder in the world is not from tales they read.

Fairy tales, then, are not responsible for producing in children fear, or any of the shapes of fear; fairy tales do not give the child the idea of the evil or the ugly; that is in the child already, because it is in the world already. Fairy tales do not give a child his first idea of bogey. What fairy tales give is the first clear idea of the possible defeat of bogey. The baby has known the dragon intimately ever since he had an imagination. What the fairy tale provides for him is a St. George to kill the dragon.[7]

---

6. Ibid., 56.
7. G. K. Chesterton, "The Red Angel," in *Tremendous Trifles* (New York: Dodd, Mead, 1910), 129–30.

A human being cannot avoid knowing that something is wrong with himself and his world, even if he knows that both himself and the world are created to be good. What any person needs to wonder about is whether this is all there is. This wondering is where fairy tales provide us with a suspicion that, even if we cannot save ourselves, it does not follow that there is nothing that will save us. Both the dragon and St. George exist.

III.

In *Prince Caspian*, Lucy wants Aslan to perform deeds he had previously done. She also wants to know how things might have turned out all right. "'To know what *would* have happened, child?' said Aslan. 'No, Nobody is ever told that.'"[8] In the order in which they are made, our choices are always final, irreversible. As the logic textbooks say, "Once Socrates has sat down, it is eternally true that he sat down, even though he need not have sat down when he did." The world now includes made choices. This does not mean that what could have been otherwise was not a real possibility. It was, for good or ill. We are judged on what we do, including our not doing what we ought to do. We are not judged on what we might have done. Yet, what might have been is part of our choices, though we are, no doubt, mercifully at times, spared from knowing what might have been. We cannot forget that the Angel of Light, perhaps the brightest of the angels, need not have chosen as he did. The mystery of evil is directly related to the mystery of free choice, to the mystery of why there is something rather than nothing. The drama of Aslan at the Stone Table is a consequence of what need not have been, but was.

Narnian Chronicles are a fairy story within the story of young English students in a common English town. The Chronicles constantly suggest that the disorder in the actual English school world of the young heroes, and *a fortiori* of England itself, is more of a problem than the Narnia that confronts the heroes and heroines of the adventure. The great fairy tale question is asked: "How did the adventure begin?"[9] It began like all stories, even like all knowledge, with curiosity and wonder, with what is behind a door. But before the children discovered the door, there was their school.

At the beginning of the *Silver Chair*, Jill Pole is crying behind the gym.

8. C. S. Lewis, *Prince Caspian* (New York: Collier, 1951), 137.
9. Lewis, *Lion, the Witch, and the Wardrobe*, 4.

Why? Other students have been "bullying her." We are merely told that we shall "say as little as possible about Jill's school."[10] What kind of a school was it?

It was "Co-educational," a school for both boys and girls, what used to be called a "mixed" school. Some said it is not nearly so mixed as the minds of the people who ran it. These people had the idea that boys and girls should be allowed to do what they liked. And unfortunately what ten or fifteen of the biggest boys and girls liked best was bullying the others. All sorts of things, horrid things, went on which at an ordinary school would have been found out and stopped in half a term, but at this school they weren't. Or even if they were, the people who did them were not expelled or punished. The Head said they were interesting psychological cases and sent for them and talked to them for hours. And if you knew the right sort of things to say to the Head, the main result was that you became rather a favourite than otherwise.[11]

Condensed in this brief description is already found a blunt critique of the modern world and its principles and language—the notion of Rousseau that we should let the young do what they want, the substitution of psychology for common sense, the belief that punishment has no purpose.

Narnia exists, as it were, over and against a world that is unable to see its own disorders. *The Silver Chair* has to do with the reeducation of Eustace, a cousin who typifies the student who at first believes in the education given at Experiment House. In the end, Prince Caspian, who has died, still wants to see something of the world in which Jill and Eustace came from, "if that would not be wrong." Aslan tells him, "You cannot want wrong things any more, now that you have died, my son."[12] So Aslan explains about the school, Experiment House, to Caspian. But Aslan sends Caspian, Jill, and Eustace back to it, where they immediately get rid of the bullies.

And what happens to the Head? Eventually, after Caspian goes back to his land and Aslan repairs the damage, the Head is fired but her friends make her the Education Inspector, a kick upstairs. "And when they found she wasn't much good even at that, they got her into Parliament where she lived happily ever after."[13] With this amusing comment, we see that Lewis hints that the disorder of our world reaches its very topmost ranks and constantly recurs.

10. C. S. Lewis, *The Silver Chair* (New York: Collier, 1953), 1.
11. Ibid., 1–2.   12. Ibid., 214.
13. Ibid., 216.

IV.

All of the central real-world figures in the Narnian tales have about them a sense of longing. They are aware that something is not right or complete with what they know. This feeling is true of Shasta in *The Horse and His Boy:* "But he was very interested in everything that lay to the north because no-one ever went that way and he was never allowed to go there himself. When he was sitting out of doors mending the nets, and all alone, he would often look eagerly to the north."[14] Again we have a sense of adventure, of concern why something is forbidden to us, of a sense that something lies beyond our ken, something that concerns us.

In fairy tales there is found this sense of an adventure not yet begun. We find also a need to retell, appreciate what was once done. We need to retell and relive a tale that is now completed, as if we need to comprehend again and again what has happened to us. We love to know our part of the adventure in which all men are engaged. We know that our part was real and yet only a part.

And the wine flowed and tales were told and jokes were cracked, and then silence was made and the King's poet with two fiddles stepped out into the middle of the circle. Aravis and Cor prepared themselves to be bored, for the only poetry they knew was the Calormene kind, and you know not what that was like. But at the very first scrape of the fiddles a rocket seemed to go up inside their heads, and the poet sang the great old lay of Fair Olvin and how he fought the Giant Pire . . . and won the Lady Liln for his bride; and when it was over they wished it was going to begin again. . . . And Lucy told again . . . the tale of the Wardrobe and how she and King Edmund and Queen Susan and Peter the High King had first come into Narnia.[15]

The retelling of the beginning is necessary to retell the end of the adventure. But all retelling of the past is in the present as if to say, as fairy tales do say, that it is the ending that counts.

We likewise find a great sense of longing in Reepicheep, the gallant mouse in the *Voyage of the Dawn Traeder.* "I will gladly tell you that, my son," said the Old Man. "To break this enchantment you must sail to the World's End, or as near as you can come to it, and you must come back having left at least one of your companions behind." "And what is to hap-

---

14. C. S. Lewis, *The Horse and His Boy* (New York: Collier, 1954), 2.
15. Ibid., 214–15.

pen to that one?" asked Reepicheep. "He must go on into the utter east and never return into the world."[16] This "going on" is precisely what Reepicheep does. He is the one who is left behind. He is the one who has the courage and the faith to go on eastward to "never return into the world." But this "never returning," we are aware, would not be possible if the voyage of Reepicheep was not to a better world, to the "world's end."

The reading of fairy tales, the reading and rereading of Narnia, as I have suggested, reveals to us truths that we do not otherwise see in our daily living. Why is this? We read in *The Magician's Nephew:* "For what you see and hear depends a good deal on where you are standing: it also depends on what sort of person you are."[17] It depends on where we are standing, but also on "what sort of person" we are. That we are human persons is not under our control. That is what is given to us by our birth. We do not make ourselves to be what we are. But what we do with what we are is indeed ours to fashion. We can not see the light because of where we are standing. But we can also reject it because we do not want to see by it. Fairy tales are full of blind characters who will not see what is there to be seen. "'You see,'" said Aslan in the *Last Battle,* "'they will not let us help them. They have chosen cunning instead of belief. Their prison is only in their own minds, yet they are in that prison; and so afraid of being taken in that they cannot be taken out.'"[18] In fairy tales, the ultimate prison is self-made.

Time ends. Indeed, Father Time does wake up "on the day the world ended."[19] One would expect the opposite expression, namely, that time would end when the world ended. Instead, that is only when time wakes up. Yet, as I recalled in the beginning of this chapter, Narnia itself ends.

"So," said Peter, "Night falls on Narnia! You're not *crying?* With Aslan ahead, and all of us here?"

"Don't try to stop me, Peter," said Lucy, "I am sure Aslan would not. I am sure it is not wrong to mourn for Narnia. Think of all that lies dead and frozen behind that door."

"Yes and I *did* hope," said Jill, "that it might go on forever. I knew *our* world couldn't. I did think Narnia might."

"I saw it begin," said the Lord Digory. "I did not think I would live to see it die."

16. C. S. Lewis, *The Voyage of the "Dawn Traeder"* (New York: Collier, 1952), 179.
17. Lewis, *Magician's Nephew,* 125.
18. Lewis, *Last Battle,* 148.
19. Ibid., 150.

"Sirs," said Tirian. "The ladies do well to weep. What world but Narnia have I ever known? It were no virtue, but great discourtesy, if we did not mourn."[20]

Shadow-lands—how are these things to be explained? In their trying to figure out the reality of the Narnia, they knew, the Unicorn remarks, "'the reason why we loved the old Narnia is that it sometimes looked a little like this,'" that is, our "real country."[21] Lord Digory had just said to Peter, "'Listen, Peter. When Aslan said you could never go back to Narnia, he meant the Narnia you were thinking of. But that was not the real Narnia. That had a beginning and an end. It was only a shadow or a copy of the real Narnia, which has always been here and always will be here, just as our own world, England and all, is only a shadow or copy of something in Aslan's real world.'"[22] So there is the imaginary Narnia, the real Narnia that ended, and another more "real" Narnia that all the others imitated.

This is all familiar, or should be. But Digory, who has a reputation of being a bit pedantic, added, "under his breath," still loud enough for the others to hear, "'It's all in Plato, all in Plato: bless me, what *do* they teach them at these schools!'"[23] Everyone about him laughs at Digory's classical reference. He laughs himself. But he becomes "grave again." He recalls that "'there is a kind of happiness and wonder that makes you serious.'" It is not merely a "joke." In the *Republic* of Plato we are told that our human affairs are not "serious." And in the *Laws*, we are told that only one thing is "serious," against which all things will seem insignificant, and that is God. This is what Aslan is all about.

We are to love those things we know, and mourn for them when they cease, because they are loveable in their own order. But the reading of the tales of Narnia brings us to the "beginning of the real story," to the living happily ever after. Perhaps it is in fairy tales, which he himself so severely criticized, that we first encounter what Plato was talking about. But the Stone Table we do not find in Plato, though there are intimations of it. We do find it in Narnia, and indeed in our own world, if we, with grace, but will to see it.

Such are the themes and warnings and sights and songs that we are left with on our passage through Narnia:

"One is quite justified in inferring that whatever one of these laws or

20. Ibid., 158.
21. Ibid., 171.
22. Ibid., 169.
23. Ibid., 170.

customs was lacking in that remote time, its place was competently filled by a worse one" (Mark Twain).

"The baby has known the dragon intimately ever since he had an imagination. What the fairy tale provides for him is a St. George to kill the dragon" (G. K. Chesterton).

"But for them, it was only *the beginning of the real story*. All their life in this world and all their adventures in Narnia had only been the cover and the title page" (C. S. Lewis).

CONCLUSION
ON BEING ALLOWED TO READ
MONTE CRISTO

A boy can spend hours in the school library reading Monte Cristo if he wants to. Nobody cares. But supposing everyone cared and thought it a disgrace not to like Pindar, nobody would be allowed to read Monte Cristo or Sherlock Holmes. The tyranny of the intellect is the worst of all.

—Maurice Baring, "Eton"

The introduction of this book began, from Samuel Johnson, with the amusing and paradoxical consideration of madness and enthusiasm, of "praying always" and "not praying at all," of how what is sane can seem to be insane and of how what is maniacal is seen by many to be sensible. This same point is made again in considering Chesterton as the "real heretic," the man whose views were considered most outlandish precisely because they were really the ones closest to the truth. Chesterton had learned this paradox, to use his word, not from reading Scripture or apologetics but from reading the "heretics" themselves, as he called them, only to be puzzled by their inconsistencies.

In his great book, *Enthusiasm,* another book not to be missed, Ronald Knox wrote that "more generally characteristic of ultrasupernaturalism [great word!] is a distrust of our human thought-processes. In matters of abstract theology, the discipline of intellect is replaced by a blind act of faith."[1] What these varied reflections have intended to suggest is that

---

1. Ronald Knox, *Enthusiasm* (1950; Westminster, Md.: Christian Classics, 1983), 585. Benedict XVI made a similar point: "With the advent of Illuminism (the Enlightenment), Western culture began to drift more and more swiftly away from its Christian foundations. Especially in the most recent period, the break-up of the family and of marriage, attacks on human life and its dignity, the reduction of faith to a subjective experience and the consequent secularization of public awareness are seen as the stark and dramatic consequences of this distancing." Benedict XVI, "To the

for the "mind that is Catholic," what is expected is both a trust in "human thought-processes" and a trust that faith is itself addressed to these processes for their own perfection. We do not begin by doubting that anything can be known or whether we have powers to know. We begin in the confidence that things exist and we know them. Faith is by no means "blind" in that to which it leads, even though we make no claims that our own human intellects are the highest intellects in the universe. We merely claim that they are intellects and that we are free to use them.

At the conclusion of this book, I have cited a passage from the great English diplomat and writer, Maurice Baring, a man who was a friend of Belloc and Chesterton. I had once read Baring's delightful *Lost Lectures* but had not seen the book in years. A friend of mine was visiting London and, remembering that I had mentioned the Baring book, found it in a used book shop, an inestimable gift. On rereading it, the book's charm is everything that I remember about it.

Baring's recollections of his school days in Eton could hardly be more amusing. Here he talks about the relation of sports and study, something we have touched on in these pages. He is delighted that sports took his companions' attention so that he was left free to read what he wanted in the school library. His soul was not limited to what he "had" to read. He thinks, as did Samuel Johnson, that a boy must not be overly regimented in his learning. Baring says, wisely, that if the boy wants to read *The Count of Monte Cristo* or Sherlock Holmes, "Well let him read them!" Baring feared what he called "the tyranny of the intellect." He doubted that we will really learn much if we do not first delight in learning and in truth.[2] This point was actually made both by Plato and Aristotle. Hopefully, these considerations about "the mind that is Catholic" are seen by any reader in this same spirit. We are concerned with the delight of truth, the truth of things, nothing more, but nothing less.

At the very beginning of this book, six citations were listed, favorites of mine. One was from Plato, one from Augustine, one from Joseph Ratzinger, one from Chesterton, one, left in French, from Jean Daniélou, and one from Aristotle. I would hope that the reader sees in these pages devoted to thinking, to Plato, to friendship, the Trinity, political philosophy, intellec-

Media of the Italian Bishops' Conference" (lecture, June 2, 2006), *L'Osservatore Romano*, English ed., June 14, 2006, 5.

2. I have said something along these same lines in "Seneca on Personal Libraries: Some Thoughts on Reading Widely and Reading Well," *Vital Speeches* 72 (February 1, 2006): 248–53.

tual vocation, revelation, even to war and Narnia, the spirit found in these often famous beginning passages.

The citation from Daniélou tells us not to make politics absolute, a major concern of this book.[3] We are not to be forbidden from seeing something transcendent to politics. Yet, Plato rightly says, in the famous prayer, that we too seek to be beautiful inside. We hope our external possessions are in "friendly harmony" with our inner life. Revelation itself takes up the theme that what goes on inside of us is that from which our outside contact flows. No reform of politics will work that does not understand the soul of free men and its inner beauty, its inherent orientation also to what is beyond politics.

Augustine, following Plato and scripture, is always best at reminding us of the "longing" that abides in all of our lives, something found in all men and in all ages. But "longing" is not just "longing" for its own sake. That too would be deadly, a kind of insanity. We are realists especially in our longing. Our questions about *what is* seek not merely "answers" but the reality itself that *is* the answer, particularly the reality of others in friendship. The point of transcendence is not primarily to tell us we have here no lasting city, something that really seems obvious, but to tell us finally that we do have a City of God, an eternal life.

Joseph Ratzinger (Benedict XVI) is blunt with us. We do not ourselves "concoct" what we are told in revelation. We do not make up what we believe. Faith is objective. What we are told is given us to guide us in explaining *what is*. Revelation is a freedom to begin and to continue to think, not to stop thinking. Revelation is not opposed to thinking and to thinking well. Rather, it incites us to understand what is given, what is explained by ultimate things in revelation. In sorting it out, we learn to think more fully, more incisively.

Chesterton, like Baring, looked at the playing fields of the English schools. It is the great teaching, best seen perhaps in Josef Pieper, but also in the heart of our theology, that our existence, our very cosmos, need not be.[4] "The real end and final holiday of human souls" is seen more clearly in

---

3. "In other words, the problem is to know whether the final reference [of reality] is political or if there are ultimate references by which politics itself is judged. This problem is perhaps the essential problem of today. But if we hold that this reference is to God, there is a cause for it. It because we think that a world in which the political reference would be the final reference would be a world where liberties would no longer be possible" (author's translation of epigraph from Jean Daniélou). Benedict XVI makes much the same point in *Jesus of Nazareth*, 46–56.

4. Pieper, *In Tune with the World*. See also Rahner, *Men at Play*.

play than perhaps any other way. Again we learn, with Aristotle, that delight is given to us. Things like games, like ourselves, exist for their own sakes. As Chesterton said in *Dickens,* as we have often seen, the road leads to the inn, not the inn to the road. We do hope to drink again from those great flagons at the inn at the end of the world. As it says in *Narnia,* we are in truth only at the "beginning of the real story."

Finally, the great Aristotle teaches us so much about what friendship is. This teaching is what, as Aquinas also saw, brings us most directly to the heart of revelation itself. Aristotle, to be sure, did not know such a connection, that we would also be called God's "friends." Yet, what revelation tells us about friendship follows, in its own way, from what Aristotle wrote. Moreover, as he knew, our minds are open to the cosmos. Even the ugliest and seemingly most senseless of things cause us to think, to see "links of causation," to "incline" ourselves to philosophy so that we might wonder about the whole, about *what is.*

The "mind that is Catholic," in conclusion, is a mind that is open to *all that is,* as Aquinas told us. We should not let the "tyranny of the intellect," an intellect closed on itself, prevent us from opening our minds to what we discover and cannot explain wholly by ourselves. The doctrine of grace is itself dedicated to the Platonic prayer that we may also be "beautiful inside." This inner beauty, which we must also choose, seems to be the reason we are created, in order, as Plato also said, that in knowing itself, the mind may, in that very act, praise the *what is* of its own personal being that it did not itself create.

The sober Aristotle told us, when talking about riches, that most of us would need some riches if we were to practice virtue. The things of this world are worthy. Politics is the "highest of the practical sciences." But it is in pursuing justice and friendship that we unexpectedly experience a "longing" in the very highest things we confront. We begin to realize that we do not find final satisfaction in this world in any of the alternatives proposed to us by the philosophers or the politicians. We can only receive it, not make it. Revelation tells us the same thing. This is why we begin to pay attention to it.

As Daniélou remarked, the "ultimate references" are not political. A world in which "politics is the ultimate reference is a world in which liberty is no longer possible." Yet, we are asked to think accurately about political things precisely because we find, in our lives, a liberty, a longing for things that political life, by being what it is, only points to. It all becomes clearer when we know that God is Trinity, that the world is not "necessary." God does not need the world to overcome any inner loneliness of His own.

The *mind that is Catholic* knows that it is a mind that also need not exist, but it does exist. It finds its ground in a delight that it is given the power to know and in the fact that it does know. The best way to avoid both the tyranny of politicians and the tyranny of intellect closed on itself is to have a mind open both to *what is* and to what is revealed to us about *what is*.

APPENDIX
POLITICAL PHILOSOPHY'S
"HINT OF GLORY"

INTERVIEW OF JAMES V. SCHALL BY KENNETH MASUGI:

KM: You are still teaching at an advanced age while in most other countries, even in Roman Church institutions, one is required to retire at your age. Why are you still teaching when you should be enjoying retirement or otherwise turned out to pasture?

JVS: But I still enjoy teaching. There is something to be said for enjoying what is to be enjoyed, as Aristotle said. And there is also something to be said for dying with your boots on. Besides, we live in almost the only country in the world in which the elderly are not discriminated against. They are allowed to do what they can, even legally.

I have all my students read Cicero's wonderful, politically wise essay "On Old Age." I tell them to read it to their grandfathers when they finish. Likewise, my students are familiar with the elderly Cephalus in the beginning of the *Republic*. Socrates wanted to talk to him because he, as an old man, has been down a path we will all have to follow. So it is good to know what it is like along this path. Too, we are aware, as Scripture often tells us, that some correlation exists between increasing age and a certain amount of wisdom. But everyone needs to read this implied praise of old age carefully. He does well to keep in mind, as not totally impossible for himself, the famous adage: "There is no fool like an old fool."

Samuel Johnson said somewhere that, as we become older, many of our friends die, so that we should be constantly making new friends. Cicero said

This interview of me by Kenneth Masugi, December 2003, is reprinted by permission of the Claremont Institute, Claremont, Calif . Under the title, "Political Philosophy's 'Hint of Glory': Love of God as the Completion of the Love of Wisdom," a shorter version of the Interview appeared in *Perspectives on Political Science* 33 (Summer 2004): 164–68. Other Interviews with Kenneth Masugi and myself on natural law, faith and reason, and the Regensburg Lecture, can be found at www.claremont.org. I include this interview here as an appendix at the suggestion of Professor Bradley Lewis at the Catholic University of America, as a more relaxed instance of doing philosophical and political things.

that we are fortunate if we can surround ourselves with the young. They give us an opportunity to speak what we know, listen to what they know. Of all places in the world, a university is often most congenial to the normal occurrence of this relationship of old and young.

Ralph McInerny at Notre Dame had a wonderful column on this topic of academic retirement in the December (2003) *Crisis Magazine*. "Plato said that philosophizing was learning how to die. He did not say learning how to retire," McInerny quipped, rather profoundly, as is his wont. When and if McInerny retires, I figure that it will be a greater blow to Notre Dame's intellectual standing than the combined defeats of Faust, Davies, and Willingham on its football standing.

In this matter, I am, in fact, rather partial to the view of Coach Joe Gagliardi, the most winning football coach in college history (414). After his team at St. John's University in Minnesota won the Division III national championship over a heavily favored, and rarely defeated, Mount Union College, Gagliardi, 77, four years younger than Plato when he died, was asked about retiring. "I'm not going into the sunset," Gagliardi affirmed, "because I'd miss all these guys (players). What? Go on a park bench and play checkers with some guy that can't hear me?" (*Washington Post,* Dec. 21, 2003). Cicero, less colorfully, said the same thing. Athens killed Socrates rather than letting him go on further into old age. And Christ was executed as a young man.

KM: Do I understand that you taught a course in Plato last semester?

JVS: There is simply nothing like Plato. There is no such thing as a university in which Plato is not constantly being read by both professors and students, and not just in the philosophy department, especially not in the philosophy department. This emphasis is not in any way to downplay Aristotle, Cicero, Augustine, or Aquinas, each of whom I love dearly, but none of them would be what he is without Plato.

Plato still turns us around, makes us examine our souls; he even tells us that we have souls when no one else, even psychology departments, will mention the topic. No other philosopher comes near to him in this dramatic capacity of turning us around, except perhaps Augustine, and that for the same reason. The two young potential philosophers in the *Republic,* Plato's brothers, Adeimantus and Glaucon, with their friends had it about right. They could figure out what was wrong by themselves, but knew not how to get the whole picture right. For this latter, they needed to talk with Socrates. We still need him. I think now that anyone who graduates from college or graduate school without a serious, sympathetic, and genuine reading of Plato has pretty much wasted his time. He deserves a refund.

KM: Tell us about your new book.

JVS: Well, to tell you about a new one probably entails telling you about the old ones. But I will spare you Schall's version of Schall. You couldn't bear it. Actually, I have several projects in mind. One is called *The Life of the Mind*, the second *The Sum Total of Human Happiness*, the third a collection of essays called *That All Tales May Come True*, and finally something I want to call *The Order of Things*, which I hope to get to next year, if I can put order in my own days. [See bibliography for these projects.]

However, the present book has a succinct, terse, even provocative title. I call it *Roman Catholic Political Philosophy* (Lanham, Md.: Lexington Books, 2004). It won't make the Style section, let alone the Book Review section, too dicey. That Roman Catholicism is also a revelation of intelligence to intelligence shocks many. But that communication of mind to mind, of course, is what it also is, among other things. At first sight, the topic will seem like mixing apples and oranges. But there is a point to it. At some level, these peculiar apples and oranges do belong together.

The thesis is straightforward. It is not intended to scandalize, at least not too much, either the pagans, the pious, or the tepid, let alone the Muslims, the Baptists, the Buddhists, the Jews, the Mormons, the Unitarians, the Confucianists, the Latitudinarians, the politicians, the hierarchy, the "think-tankites," or, only a little, the college professors. The book does not intend to invent a new brand of political philosophy, even less does it intend a radically divergent version of Roman Catholicism, which already has enough of these divergences lying around. I find both Roman Catholicism and political philosophy in their classic statements about themselves and their intellectual dimensions to be rather persuasive, indeed exciting. I, for one, would like to keep them both. I think the "keeping" of them has something to do with seeing them together.

KM: What do you mean, "seeing them together"?

JVS: First, I conceive this book to be a book in political philosophy. My concern is what the mind knows. Political philosophy has a certain breath that allows, indeed requires, it to know more than itself to be itself. To understand this "discipline," if I might call it that, one not only needs to know the "brilliant errors" from the history of political thought, about which Strauss spoke, but also theology, philosophy itself, practical and theoretical, history, literature ("the ancient struggle between poetry and philosophy," of which Plato spoke in book 10 of the *Republic*), science, and just about anything else.

Of course, one needs to be something more than a genius to know such things well. It would be rash to suspect that one knows them all. But still, philosophy is a knowledge of the whole, and political philosophy ends up, at its highest level, with the question of the activities of leisure that are allowed freely to happen in certain existing regimes. I think that Dostoyevsky, Solzhenitsyn, David Walsh, and others have also shown that sometimes we can only see, are only willing to see, the highest things after suffering in the worst regimes or better because of them. Plato taught that same lesson too in his own way when he finally concluded that the tyrant could not really be happy, and Glaucon agreed with him.

In any case, by "seeing them together," I mean that there are two bodies of explication about reality, one whose source is in reason, best exemplified, I think, by Aristotle, and one in revelation, best exemplified, in summary from Scripture, by the Nicene Creed. The truth of one is not necessarily in contradiction to the truth of the other. What I argue is that political philosophy and philosophy are human spiritual activities that seek to know the truth of things. In order to find out this truth, they systematically and intuitively pose questions to themselves and seek to discover coherent answers to them.

In this sense, I argue that we will not know, intellectually, if revelation has happened, unless we have first taken the trouble to examine the questions that arise in the experience of political and human things together with the varieties of answers that have been given to these questions by the philosophers. This effort recalls what Aristotle did in book 2 of his *Politics*. What I conclude is that a number of central questions that do arise in the classical political philosophy books have answers to them. But the answers, on reflection, are either inadequate or implausible. I like to say that the study of political philosophy ought to bring such questions forward in our souls so that there is a kind of longing or searching that arises from the suspicion that none of the answers so given have been complete or adequate.

In the case of Plato, I generally argue that even when Plato was wrong in his answers, he was always disturbingly close to the truth, so much so that I am in much sympathy with those ancients or moderns who wonder if Plato himself did not receive some kind of revelation. Indeed, it is revelation that generally makes us see how very close to the truth Plato actually was. I have argued an aspect of this point many long years ago in *Human Dignity and Human Numbers* and more particularly in an essay in the *Downside Review* entitled "The Christian Guardians." (This essay is found in my *Politics of Heaven and Hell*.) The essay deals with the prophetic book 5 of the *Republic*. That book, when taken literally, and, I think, erroneously so taken, makes Plato almost the cause or inspiration for what is happening to family and moral life in contemporary society from genetic engineering to women soldiers and state-controlled day-care centers. I do not think Plato to be the origin of "fascism" or other ills, but, as I said in my essay "On Teaching the Political Thought of Plato," in *Another Sort of Learning*, "one cannot refute Plato without Plato." He has uncannily already anticipated all the alternatives. Reading Machiavelli is *déjà vu* if we have read the *Apology*, the *Gorgias* or books 1, 8, and 9 of the *Republic*." (See above, chapter 14.)

KM: Isn't philosophy "autonomous"? So what is this odd business of seeing philosophy and revelation together?

JVS: John Paul II, in *Fides et Ratio,* a discussion of which encyclical is the final chapter of *Roman Catholic Political Philosophy,* dealt quite well with this question of the relative autonomy of philosophy. If philosophy is not what it is, that is, a statement or illumination of what the mind can know "by itself," it is of absolutely no use to revelation, or anything else, for that matter. Plato and Aristotle still occupy a unique place in philosophy for having thought about *what is* before revelation, as we normally conceive of it, was a major factor. This very fact makes some of us, at least, wonder about the timing of revelation itself, the problem of the philosophy or theology of history. We wonder, that is, if it was "timed"—"And it came to pass in those days, that there went out a decree from Caesar Augustus, that all the world should be taxed," as we read in the King James version of Luke (2:1) about the world's most peculiar use of the taxing powers of the state.

One still must be careful not to be a Pelagian or a fideist in these matters. There are rather more of both of these about than either of the peculiar names we give such ideas would indicate. That is, the theoretical openness and empirical incompleteness of philosophy ought to make us suspicious of any closed philosophical system that claims the absolute human autonomy to decide everything, including being itself, and particularly human *being* and that to which it is open. The openness of philosophy to any truth, no matter what its source, is not compatible with a system that, on narrow rationalist grounds, refuses to consider something, however implausible, proposed as true from whatever source, a point Josef Pieper tellingly made in his brilliant book, *In Defense of Philosophy.*

At the same time, however insightful and even authoritative revelation might be in itself, however much it is also addressed to the nonphilosopher as itself a separate philosophic problem, the meaning of the destiny of every human person, not just the philosopher, still needs some basic philosophical grounding. This basis would allow us to grant, not just its theoretic coherence within itself, but also its relation to what we do know of reality. One of the basic positions that revelation must hold, if it is to have any claim on our minds at all, is the principle of contradiction that flows into Aquinas's famous dictum that faith does not contradict reason but, as he implies, causes it to flourish, perfects it.

Moreover, if our personal philosophy makes us doubt the existence or intelligibility of a real world, the general dimensions of which we can know by our own powers of sensation and intelligence, we have no business wondering whether the Son of God was born into such a world. Our prior philosophy, in this case, makes it impossible for us really to understand what is at issue in the reason and revelation relationship. One even suspects that, at times, such antirealist philosophies are invented or held precisely so that those who hold them would not have to take seriously the claims of revelation on reason.

KM: You've written extensively on these themes before. What did you teach yourself in writing this book (that is, *Roman Catholic Political Philosophy*)?

JVS: That is an interesting expression: "What did Schall teach Schall in writing this book?" The skeptics will recall the famous philosophic phrase, *Nemo dat quod non habet!* But this question reminds me of the observation that Rebecca West once made when she was asked about how long it took to write a book. She replied, "a couple of years and all of my life." In some sense, this present book goes back to the old-age question of whether a basic thing that we thought was true when we were twenty is still true when we are past the age of Socrates at his trial.

The very first serious academic essay that I ever wrote, itself part of an M.A. thesis under the late Clifford Kossel, S.J., one of the most intelligent men I ever met, was published in 1957, in *The Thomist*, entitled "The Totality of Society: From Justice to Friendship." (See above, chapter 9.) That maddening, unsettling, glorious theme of justice and friendship appeared again in my first book, *Redeeming the Time*. And it is, in fact, what is behind the thesis of the present book. So perhaps I may not have changed very much. Schall may not have evolved into Schall at all. The relation of justice to friendship is at the heart of Aristotle's *Ethics*, not to mention the heart of Plato, though I did not know Plato that well at the time. I have returned to this theme often as it is one of the most fertile and fascinating of all human and divine topics. There is a chapter on friendship in my *What Is God Like?*, another in *At the Limits of Political Philosophy*, and also an essay, "Aristotle on Friendship." (See above, chapter 8.)

In the *Ethics*, there are two questions asked by the man whom Aquinas called simply "the Philosopher," questions that must be asked again and again by anyone who even begins to examine himself—"the unexamined life is not worth living," to recall a famous passage in Plato—about *what is*, the great metaphysical question. One question is whether we would want our friend to become someone else, a god or a king, perhaps? The other is Aristotle's wonder about whether God is lonely, and therefore whether He lacks some perfection that human beings seem to possess. The thesis of *Roman Catholic Political Philosophy* is essentially that no human mind can fail to ponder these questions and still be loyal to itself, to philosophy.

"What I suggest is that, without implying in any manner that we can conclude from philosophy to revelation, these two questions, arising in philosophy, do have plausible answers in revelation. Then, going back to the subtitle of my book *At the Limits of Political Philosophy*, namely, *From "Brilliant Errors"* (Strauss) *to the Things of Uncommon Importance*, I suggest that the history of philosophy and indeed of religion, subsequent to rejecting the Christian answers at any level of encounter, results in a record of sometimes interesting, often silly, rarely satisfying, answers to the questions as posed. Such tentative answers explain or try to make us accept an answer to these questions that arise in political philosophy but are not adequately answered there.

Aristotle himself, to his credit, as Aquinas saw, both asked the proper questions and suggested tentative, sensible answers. Aquinas's view was that such Aristotelian answers were about the best that the human mind, by itself, could come up with. In that regard, Aquinas was most respectful of Aristotle. He did him the honor of taking his views seriously, an honor that entailed disagreeing with Aristotle on certain points when reasonable. Indeed, the proper relation of Aquinas to Aristotle is not that Aquinas is great because he kept Aristotle "alive" for subsequent philosophical consideration, though he did that.

Rather it is that Aquinas carefully corrected Aristotle's few philosophic errors not in the order of theology, but in the order of philosophy itself. There are some who think that Aristotle would have been annoyed by Aquinas's corrections. I suspect that he would have been delighted, as he would have been on learning that Aquinas agreed with him on the question of the theoretic possibility of the eternal existence of the finite world, even if in fact the world was creates *ex nihilo*.

The point I make in the present book, as I have touched on also in *Reason, Revelation, and the Foundations of Political Philosophy*, is that the doctrine of the Trinity is the only real response, qua response, even though it comes from revelation, to Aristotle's question about the loneliness of God. As I tried to show in *Redeeming the Time*, "God is not alone." (See above, chapter 10.) Therefore, what is not God does not exist because of any lack in God. This is what the Trinity means.

Likewise, a central teaching of the Last Supper was that "I no longer call you servants but friends." Thus, the question of our not being able to be friends with God was answered not on the philosophic side but on the side of revelation with the reality and doctrine of the Incarnation, the man-God. This latter doctrine is also the only possible satisfying response to Aristotle's suggestion that we want our friends to remain what they are, not just souls, but complete persons. The fact that Aristotle's First Mover could move by "knowledge and desire" is something that both Aquinas and Augustine could deal with. Plato's discussion of *Eros*, moreover, seems fully intelligible only in terms of the dimensions of revelation. I do not argue from the fact that a thing "might" seem fitting to its being therefore true, a version of the ontological argument. There always must be grounds for accepting the truth suggested by fittingness.

KM: You don't think anyone besides you believes this stuff, do you?

JVS: That is rather a different question, of course. I suppose that I could say that if my argument is anywhere close to the truth, I don't particularly care. I do think that you will spend a rather lonely life in modern academia if you do think there is something to these views, but that is not any really any reason not to hold them. In fact, it may be an argument in its favor. *Amicus Plato, Amicus Aristoteles, Magis Amicus Veritas.* But the spirit of *Roman Catholic Political Philosophy* (as of its predecessors, *At the Limits of Political Philosophy; Reason, Revelation, and the Foundations of Political Philosophy;* and the *Politics of Heaven and Hell*), is not polemic. I wanted to spell out what I thought of this topic.

Indeed, after I had finished this manuscript, I taught a course with the same title, something I had never done before. It dealt with a good number of books or authors that were more or less in the same general area, ones that do not directly enter *Roman Catholic Political Philosophy.* Without being exhaustive, they were the Hittingers, Kraynak, Walsh, Schindler, Lawler, Sokolowski, Rowland, Slade, Nicgorski, Novak, Royal, Haggerty, the O'Donovans, Fortin, Manent, Goerner, Canavan, Pickstock, Budiziszewski, Mahoney, Tom Smith, Nichols, Redpath, Schrems, Hanus, Orr, Rhodes, McInerny, and Neuhaus, not to mention the older generation of Maritain, Simon, Gurian, Percy, O'Connor, Rommen, Molnar, Wilhelmsen, Dawson, Murray, Briefs, Hallowell, Gilson, de Koninck, and, of course, my favorites, Lewis and Tolkien, Chesterton and Belloc.

To me, the two most important thinkers on specifically political philosophy have been Kossel, whose studies on the metaphysical category of relations are so important for understanding the being of society and the life of the Trinity, and Charles N. R. McCoy, whose *Structure of Political Theory* remains fundamental. I have to put in a special word of admiration both for the late Ernest Fortin and for Josef Pieper, whose book *On Love* is unsurpassed on that noble topic. Nor here, though it is not my purpose to examine their views, do I intend to overlook my debt to Voegelin and Strauss, and their schools, who have largely made consideration of reason and revelation, not to mention political philosophy itself, at least a feasible, and certainly lively, topic in academia, or sometimes, in spite of it.

And I must confess a covert attraction to Nietzsche, who seems to have pointed out better than anyone else that in modern philosophy, what could go wrong, did go wrong. Nietzsche, as I see it, did not really reject Plato or Christianity. He was more a disappointed lover because no one seemed to be willing to follow Christ or Plato. He thought Christ came to make us sinless, not to redeem us from our sins, which upsettingly go on in every age, obviously in our own. "The last Christian died on the cross" seems a rather appropriate witticism for an age seemingly upset by a movie on the "Passion" [*The Passion of the Christ*] of which, as Peggy Noonan reported, the pope (John Paul II), when he saw it, simply said, "It is as it was."

In one sense, *Roman Catholic Political Philosophy* is what the world looks like if this is true, "if it is as it was," if the Incarnation and Redemption on the cross happened to a man who was indeed the Son of God, if the inner life of the Godhead is Trinitarian, not monolithic as our Muslim friends keep insisting with rather too much force to make their alternative seem feasible. When we hold that the account of revelation is not true, for whatever reason, and there are millions of them that we can conceive if we choose, we fill the world with myriads of theories, movements, polities, and lifestyles, with "brilliant errors," all of which are worthy of examination, but none of which really answers the real questions posed by political philosophy to philosophy and to the sources of truth that may be addressing us, even our minds.

By this argument, I am not particularly trying to "convince" anyone of anything in any pejorative sense of that word. It is not a polemic with, say, Islam or Buddhism, or Judaism, or whatever, even though we need someplace where such differences can be confronted and met, something John Paul II sought to do in various ways by his consultations with anyone who would peacefully consult with him. It is interesting that it is a pope, not academics, who is encouraging this mutual exchange of ideas. (The thought of Benedict XVI is also grounded in these issues.)

Intellectual freedom, in the end, means that we are at liberty to make an argument in our own terms and seek to make it plausible and intelligible to others, because it is plausible and intelligible to us. We need not claim that we make no errors of fact or logic, only that we will correct them if they are pointed out and are valid. At the level I am dealing with here, I think political philosophy and its dimensions and relation to philosophy is pretty much unknown among the theologians. The whole, even ongoing, saga of theologians and liberation theology even makes one want to weep in this regard they were so naive about what stood behind Marxism. (See my book *Liberation Theology*.) The current enthusiasms for "justice" and "rights" are almost as bad if not worse to the degree that modern concepts of these terms, thanks largely to Hobbes, can undermine any possibility of either dignity or transcendence.

Father Ernest Fortin was particularly good the dangers of both of these issues. This lack of a dimension in political philosophy is why, I suspect, we find cardinals, even, making so many outlandish mistakes and errors of judgment about everything from war to development to family to scandal. Academic life is pretty generally known for being a rather closed shop, in any case, in spite of its protestations to the contrary. But the ignorance of theology in academia is, likewise, legendary and mostly chosen. One should thus be content here with this minority report about what seems to be the real relation of revelation and philosophy—"notes from the underground" would be too pretentious a name for it.

KM: Is this a correct summary of your point: that one can know the natural only when one accepts the supernatural—that is, revelation in a sense precedes reason?

JVS: Not quite. There are two famous and classical sentences that are pertinent here: The first is, *Homo non proprie humanus sed superhumanus est.* The second is, *Nulla est homini causa philosophandi nisi ut beatus sit.* I found both of these statements, in Latin yet, in E. F. Schumacher's very useful book, *A Guide for the Perplexed.* The first is, I believe, from St. Thomas and the second from the nineteenth book of Augustine's *City of God.* Man, as we know him (including ourselves), was never in fact in any purely "natural" state, with a purely natural destiny. His end was always directed to something higher than his own natural powers could in fact have ordered him. This situation implies that any truth that he acquires by the use of his reason, and this is not a little, always points to something more, something further. It is Augustine's "restless heart," and Chesterton's "homesickness at home." Why do we go about pondering over all these questions anyhow? We do, I think, because we want to know the truth, to be happy. Chesterton remarks somewhere that whenever man starts out to be purely natural, he ends up being somehow precisely "unnatural," but he insists on calling it normal. This is, I suspect, the explanation of our time.

I would not say that "revelation precedes" reason. They both have the same source. I am comfortable with the idea that in the dispensation we have, as far as we are concerned, reason came first, hence Plato and Aristotle. But this is a reason related to what is known as the Fall, the account of Genesis remains amazingly insightful when it comes to the question of what man is doing when he chooses himself, chooses to make himself the cause of the distinction between "good and evil." He is never, contrary to Nietzsche, "beyond" good and evil, but, like Nietzsche and Machiavelli, someone who claims that it is his duty to establish an alternate view, alternate to the one found in his being—Socrates' "it is never right to do wrong." This alternative, repeated again and again, in personal and corporate existence, allows autonomous will to establish the distinction between good and evil on whatever basis it chooses.

Revelation, in fact, is addressed to reason, but to a reason with its own questions, hence philosophy and political philosophy. Philosophy, and this is the thesis of the book, cannot deny its own unanswered questions. Nor can it, *a priori*, exclude any answers proposed to it simply on the grounds that they are proposed by what is called revelation. This conclusion on strictly philosophical terms only necessarily concludes to the fact that here is a "feasible" or "interesting" alternative, not to a necessary conclusion as to its truth, which, even in theological terms, requires faith, itself containing its own criteria of credibility.

Thus, what one "knows" when one accepts the supernatural, to use your terms, is how the whole fits together, at least in its general outlines. So when I speak of a "Roman Catholic political philosophy," I do not imply that Roman Catholics are sinless—God save us! I do imply that, crucial to their own concept of revelation, one of its purposes was the forgiveness, not the elimination, of our sins. When Chesterton, a man who seems particularly good and even sinless by most of our standards, became a Catholic, he was asked why he did so. His answer was simply, "I wanted to get rid of my sins." So the notion that we can reject revelation because of the splendidly bad example of particular Catholics, whether clerical or lay, is simply a failure to understand what, in fact, revelation is about on this score. We have here no lasting or sinless city, but that does not necessarily mean, as Augustine taught us, that there is no such city.

A "Roman Catholic political philosophy" is the mildest effort to suggest that certain fundamental coherences do exist if we are willing to look at them. Revelation does "precede" reason merely in the sense that it includes within itself the order of all things, all things being originally intended for an end higher than we might expect. These ends in fact have to do with the curious questions or observations that Aristotle, among others, posed about whether God is lonely or whether we want our friends to become gods, or whether our loves, as Plato intimated, have a touch of immortality about them.

But this "touch," as it were, since the Incarnation includes not just the immortality of the soul, but the Resurrection of the body, a doctrine that St. Paul, no mean philosopher in his own right, implied was indeed foolish to the philosophers even though it made perfectly good sense to want it if we could have it. From my point of view, after watching frantic clone research or the recent controversy over the baseball star Ted Williams being frozen in Phoenix in the hope that science will someday find a formula to bring him back, still swatting the ball, the orthodox view is no more silly than what else is going on about us. After taking a look at the alternatives, in fact, the orthodox view looks better and better, whatever else one might think of it.

What about the question that you cannot expect a philosopher or believer in another faith to know or even be concerned about the incredible intricacies of Catholic positions? Briefly, if I, as a Catholic, talk about a Hindu position, or a Hegelian one, I can be expected to have the basics of the position down fairly accurately. All I ask here for the purposes of this book is that, when agreeing or disagreeing with a typically Catholic position, what that position is be stated carefully and accurately.

Thus, one might say, for instance, that "all those stories about miracles in the New Testament must be silly because no mere man could perform them." No Catholic would have the slightest problem in agreeing with such a statement as a principle. The only problem with it is if that is the reason one does not agree with a Catholic position, then he must realize that Catholics also agree in rejecting such a view. The problem is not whether a man could do it, but rather "Who was this Man?" One need not be a Catholic (or Marxist) to state accurately what it holds, even if one does not "agree" with it. It may be quite unlikely that there are "persons" in the Godhead, in the inner life of God. But, in the logic of things, both historically and philosophically, if there are no persons in the Godhead, it is highly unlikely there is any anywhere else, for our origin of what it is to be a person has such theological roots in the explication of the inner life of the Trinity.

And we may reject all this silliness about a hell, even if Plato talked about it. But when we do reject it, we have to suffer the intellectual consequences of undermining any ultimate meaningfulness to our individual actions. When Plato dealt with this topic, and revelation merely repeated its essentials, it was to confront what is essentially a problem in political philosophy. This dilemma is stated as follows: either, without a doctrine of hell, many unjust actions ultimately go unpunished, as they are not punished in this life, and therefore the world is created in injustice, or that we license the state take it on itself, like the recent Belgian courts, to punish all crimes in this world. Hence, in this latter case, we create an incipient tyranny because we cannot acquire that sort of knowledge sufficient to carry out the task of knowing and punishing all crimes. Aquinas was much wiser. The state, he thought, can only deal with certain obviously dangerous external crimes that would undermine the possibility of civil living, those that the generality of men can observe. The rest we should leave to freedom and virtue and the practical and fallible prudence of existing states, a prudence not all have, to be sure. Ultimate justice is found only in the transcendent order.

KM: What is the most revealing comment you've ever heard a student make?

JVS: It is, after having dutifully passed out, on the first day of class, a syllabus with all the pertinent information on this very subject, to get, during the last week of class, an e-mail from a student wanting to know "whether there would be a final and when it would be held?" From this brief exchange, one concludes either a) the student cannot read, or b) that he chooses not to read.

KM: What is the most interesting comment you've ever heard a student make?

JVS: When I taught in Rome, during the Communist era, I was teaching a class in which Plato came up. There was a Hungarian cleric in the class along with several would-be liberation theologians, then a current fad. After the class, the Hungarian student calmly told me that "in my country, they would never allow you to teach that class." "Why?" I asked. "Because you cannot ask about the best regime in an already perfect state," he replied. No observation reveals more of what political philosophy is about than this one.

KM: What is the most profound remark you've ever heard a student make?

JVS: A student from a very good and happy family returned home for school vacation. It seems that, while she was away at college, her old room, remembered from childhood, was taken over by her younger sister. Even though she had a place to stay in her own home, she suddenly realized that "this is no longer my room, my home. I no longer really live here." Then she added, "I also know that the college is not my home even though I live there for a while." This experience is all in Aristotle, of course, and repeated in Jennifer Roback Morse's insightful book, *Love and Economics*. It is about seeking a friend for life with whom to live, about the purpose of parental authority finally to disappear, about founding new homes, about growing up, becoming a citizen, leaving home, finding a worldly task, wondering about the ultimate things, making decisions, knowing that we too will, soon enough, have to travel down that path about which Socrates spoke to Cephalus in book 1 of the *Republic*, about the mystery of Chesterton's "homesickness at home," and Augustine's "restless heart."

BIBLIOGRAPHY

This bibliography includes three sections: (1) the author's previously published books that also contain or develop many of the principal themes of this present book. (2) A selection of the author's essays and chapters of books not included in this book. These essays deal in one way or another with academic intellectual issues. For a complete listing of essays, chapters in books, columns, and other written materials, see the web site: www.moreC.com/schall. The Schall Special Collection at the Lauinger Library at Georgetown University has copies of all the published material. (3) A short list of books that, in their own independent ways, serve to bring out the broader point of my own book. (I included such lists in my previous books *Another Sort of Learning; On the Unseriousness of Human Affairs; A Student's Guide to Liberal Learning;* and *The Life of the Mind.)* These books, as well as many of those cited in the text, help illuminate the argument I am trying to make about the openness to a quest for knowledge of the whole, its limits and its delight.

Other Books by the Author

Redeeming the Time. New York: Sheed & Ward, 1968.

Human Dignity and Human Numbers. Staten Island, N.Y.: Alba House, 1971.

Play On: From Games to Celebrations. Philadelphia: Fortress Press, 1971.

Far Too Easily Pleased: A Theology of Play, Contemplation, and Festivity. Los Angeles: Benziger/Macmillan, 1976.

The Praise of "Sons of Bitches": On the Worship of God by Fallen Men. Slough, England: St. Paul Publications, 1978.

The Sixth Paul. Canfield, Ohio: Alba Books, 1977.

Welcome Number 4,000.000,000. Canfield, Ohio: Alba Books, 1977.

Christianity and Life. San Francisco: Ignatius Press, 1981.

Christianity and Politics. Boston: St. Paul Editions, 1981.

Church, State, and Society in the Thought of John Paul II. Chicago: Franciscan Herald Press, 1982.

Liberation Theology. San Francisco: Ignatius Press, 1982.

The Distinctiveness of Christianity. San Francisco: Ignatius Press, 1983.

The Politics of Heaven and Hell: Christian Themes from Classical, Medieval, and Modern Political Philosophy. Lanham, Md.: University Press of America, 1984.

Unexpected Meditations Late in the Twentieth Century. Chicago: Franciscan Herald Press, 1985.

Reason, Revelation, and the Foundations of Political Philosophy. Baton Rouge: Louisiana State University Press, 1987.

Another Sort of Learning. San Francisco: Ignatius Press, 1988.
Religion, Wealth, and Poverty. Vancouver, B.C.: Fraser Institute, 1990.
What Is God Like? Collegeville, Minn.: Michael Glazer / Liturgical Press, 1992.
Does Catholicism Still Exist? Staten Island, N.Y.: Alba House, 1994.
Idylls and Rambles: Lighter Christian Essays. San Francisco: Ignatius Press, 1994.
At the Limits of Political Philosophy: From "Brilliant Errors" to Things of Uncommon Importance. Washington, D.C.: The Catholic University of America Press, 1996.
Jacques Maritain: The Philosopher in Society. Lanham, Md.: Rowman & Littlefield, 1998.
Schall on Chesterton: Timely Essays on Timeless Paradoxes. Washington, D.C.: The Catholic University of America Press, 2000.
Students' Guide to Liberal Learning. Wilmington, Del.: ISI Books, 2000.
Reason, Revelation, and Human Affairs: Selected Writings of James V. Schall. Edited and with an introduction by Marc Guerra. Lanham, Md.: Lexington Books, 2001.
The Unseriousness of Human Affairs: Teaching, Writing, Playing, Believing, Lecturing, Philosophizing, Singing, Dancing. Wilmington, Del.: ISI Books, 2002.
Roman Catholic Political Philosophy. Lanham, Md.: Lexington Books, 2004.
The Life of the Mind: The Joys and Travails of Thinking. Wilmington, Del.: ISI Books, 2006.
The Sum Total of Human Happiness. South Bend, Ind.: St. Augustine's Press, 2006.
The Regensburg Lecture. South Bend, Ind.: St. Augustine's Press, 2007.
The Order of Things. San Francisco: Ignatius Press, 2008.

Academic Essays Not Previously Included in This or Other of the Author's Books

Journal Articles
"The Political Philosophy of Reinhold Niebuhr." *Thought* 33 (Spring 1958): 62–80.
"Generalization and Concrete Activity in Natural Law Theory." *Archiv für Rechts- und Sozialphilosophie* 45 (Mai 1959): 161–92.
"Cartesianism and Political Theory." *Review of Politics* 24 (April 1962): 260–82.
"The Abiding Significance of Gnosticism." *American Ecclesiastical Review* 147 (September 1962): 164–73.
"The Significance of Post-Aristotelian Thought in Political Theory." *Cithara* 3 (November 1963): 56–79.
"Christian Political Approaches to Population Problems." *World Justice* 7, no. 3 (1966–67): 301–23.
"The Modern Church and the Totalitarian State." *Studies* (Dublin) 57 (Summer 1968): 113–27.
"Ecology: An American Heresy?" *America* 124 (March 27, 1971): 308–11.
"Second Thoughts on Natural Rights." *Faith & Reason* 1 (Winter 1975–76): 44–59.
"Possibilities and Madness: A Note on the Scope of Political Theory." *Review of Politics* 37 (April 1975): 161–74.
"Apocalypse as a Secular Enterprise." *Scottish Journal of Theology* 29, no. 4 (1976): 357–73.
"The Non-existence of Christian Political Philosophy." *Worldview* 11 (April 1976): 26–30.
"The Best Form of Government." *Review of Politics* 40 (January 1978): 97–123.

"The Recovery of Metaphysics." *Divinitas* 23, no. 2 (1979): 200–19.
"Political Theory: The Place of Christianity." *Modern Age* 25 (Winter 1981): 25–33.
"Human Rights: The 'So-Called' Judaeo-Christian Tradition." *Communio* 8 (Spring 1981): 51–61.
"Central America and Politicized Religion." *World Affairs* 144 (Fall 1981): 125–49.
"Metaphysics, Theology, and Political Theory." *Political Science Reviewer* 11 (Fall 1981): 2–25.
"Revelation, Reason, and Politics: Catholic Reflections on Strauss." *Gregorianum* 62 (part I, no. 2, 1981): 348–66; (part II, no. 3, 1981): 469–97.
"Luther and Political Philosophy." *Faith & Reason* 8 (Summer 1982): 7–31.
"Natural Law in the Medieval Intellectual Context." *Modern Age* 28 (Spring/Summer 1984): 228–36.
"Immortality and the Political Life of Man in Albertus Magnus." *The Thomist* 48 (October 1984): 535–68.
"Political Philosophy and Catholicism." *Divus Thomas* 87, no. 3 (1984): 153–64.
"'Man for Himself': On the Ironic Unities of Political Philosophy." *Political Science Reviewer* 15 (Fall 1985): 67–108.
"Plotinus and Political Philosophy." *Gregorianum* 66, no. 4 (1985): 687–707.
"Human Rights as an Ideological Project." *American Journal of Jurisprudence* 32 (1987): 47–62.
"Last Medieval Monarchy: Chesterton and Belloc on the Philosophic Import of the American Experience." *Faith and Reason* 15 (Summer 1988): 167–86.
"Born to Die: The Alternative to Ideology." Catholic Commission on Intellectual and Cultural Affairs, *Annual* (1988), 40–50.
"Intelligence and Academia." *International Journal of Social Economics* 15, no. 10 (1988): 63–71.
"Nature and Finality in Aristotle." *Laval Théologique et Philosophique* 45 (Février 1989): 73–85.
"Albert Camus: Deprived of Grace." *World and I* 4 (June 1989): 543–63.
"On the Teaching of Political Philosophy." *Perspectives on Political Science* 20 (Winter 1991): 5–10.
"The Law of Superabundance" (on Maritain). *Gregorianum* 72, no. 3 (1991): 515–42.
"Natural Law and the Law of Nations: Some Theoretical Considerations." *Fordham International Law Journal* 15, no. 4 (1991–92): 997–1030.
"'On Being Dissatisfied with Compromises': Natural Law and Human Rights." *Loyola Law Review* 38 (Summer 1992): 289–309.
"The Importance of Political Philosophy to Catholicism." *Louvain Studies* 18 (1993): 56–71.
"The Intellectual Context of Natural Law." *American Journal of Jurisprudence* 38 (1993): 85–108.
"The Teaching of *Centesimus Annus*." (John Paul II) *Gregorianum* 74, no. 1 (1993): 17–43.
"Culture, Multi-Culturalism, Culture Wars, and the Universal Culture." *Journal of Texas Catholic History and Culture* 5 (1994): 11–24.
"The Secular Meaning of *Veritatis Splendor*." (John Paul II), *Seminarium* 34, no. 1 (1994): 151–62.
"The Natural Law Bibliography." *American Journal of Jurisprudence* 40 (1995): 157–98.

"The Right Order of Polity and Economy: Reflections on St. Thomas and the 'Old Law.'" *Cultural Dynamics* 7 (November 1995): 427–40.

"Ratzinger on the Modern Mind." *Homiletic and Pastoral Review* 9 (October 1997): 6–14.

"On the Will to Know the Truth: Newman on Why Men of Letters Do Not Believe." *Dossier* 4 (January/February 1998): 30–35.

"Aristotle: Religion, Philosophy, and Politics." *Perspectives on Political Science* 27 (Winter 1998): 5–12.

"On the Most Mysterious of the Virtues: The Political and Philosophical Meaning of Obedience in St. Thomas, Rousseau, and Yves Simon." *Gregorianum* 79, no. 4 (1998): 743–58.

"Structures of Evil—Structures of Good: On the Centrality of Personal Sin." *Fellowship of Catholic Scholars Quarterly* 23 (Winter 2000): 7–14.

"On the Meaning and Conservation of Human Things." *Modern Age* 43 (Winter 2001): 71–78.

"On the Academic Discipline of Political Science." *Perspectives on Political Science* 30 (Spring 2001): 69–72.

"'Islam Will Not Be the Loser.'" *Dossier* 8 (January/February 2002): 8–14.

"Newness of the *New Jerusalem*." *Chesterton Review* 28 (Winter 2002): 503–19.

"Plato's Charm: On the Audience for Political Philosophy." *Fides Quaerens Intellectum* 2 (Spring 2003): 269–304.

"Justice: The Most Terrible Virtue." *Markets and Morals* 7 (Fall 2004): 409–21.

"On Testing the Test: On the Kind of 'Work' Metaphysicians and Doctors of the Church Do." *Fellowship of Catholic Scholars Quarterly* 28 (Spring 2005): 16–20.

"(The) Corporation: What Is It?" *Ave Maria Law Review* 4 (Winter 2006): 105–22.

"Aquinas and the Life of the Mind." *New Blackfriars* 87, no. 1010 (July 2006): 406–17.

"Is Christianity a Comfortable Religion?" *Homiletic and Pastoral Review* 106 (August/September 2006): 8–14.

"Liberal Education and 'Social Justice.'" *Liberal Education* 92 (Fall 2006): 44–47.

"Politics and *Eros*: Beyond Justice." *Telos* 138 (Summer 2007): 8–42.

Chapters in Books

"Truth and the Open Society." In *Order, Freedom, and the Polity: Critical Essays on the Open Society,* edited by George W. Carey, 71–90. Lanham, Md.: University Press of America, 1985.

"Catholicism and the American Experience." In *Best of This World,* edited by Michael Scully, 1–13. Lanham, Md.: University Press of America, 1986.

"From Catholic 'Social Doctrine' to the 'Kingdom of God on Earth.'" In *Readings in Moral Theology,* 5. Official Catholic Social Teaching, edited by Charles E. Curran and Richard A. McCormick, 313–30. New York: Paulist Press, 1986.

"On Things Worth Doing Badly." Introduction to *What's Wrong with the World.* Vol. 4 of *The Collected Works of G. K. Chesterton,* 11–29. San Francisco: Ignatius Press, 1987.

"Mystery of the 'Mystery of Israel.'" In *Jacques Maritain and the Jews,* edited by Robert Royal, 51–71. Notre Dame, Ind.: University of Notre Dame Press, 1994.

"Post-Aristotelian Political Philosophy and Modernity." In *Aufstieg und Niedergang der Römischen Welt,* Teil II: Principat, Band 36.7, 4902–36. Berlin: Walter de Gruyter, 1994.

"On Post-Modernism and the 'Silence of St. Thomas.'" In *Post-Modernism and Christian Philosophy,* edited by Roman Ciapolo, 218–29. Washington, D.C.: American Maritain Association / The Catholic University of America Press, 1997.

"Immanent in the Souls of Men." Introduction to *Acquaintance with the Absolute: Philosophy of Yves Simon,* edited by Anthony Simon, 1–16. New York: Fordham University Press, 1998.

"The Person and Society: John Paul II on Substance and Relation." In *Prophecy and Diplomacy: The Moral Doctrine of John Paul II: Jesuit Symposium,* edited by John Conley and Joseph Koterski, 2–20. New York: Fordham University Press, 1999.

"On the Reality of Fantasy." In *Tolkien: A Celebration,* edited by Joseph Pearce, 67–72. London: Fount/HarperCollins, 1999.

"Was Maritain a Crypto-Machiavellian?" In *The Failure of Modernism: The Cartesian Legacy and Contemporary Pluralism,* edited by Brendan Sweetman, 87–100. Washington, D.C.: American Maritain Association/The Catholic University of America Press, 1999.

"On Merely Being Intelligent: Canavan's Views and Reviews." In *A Moral Enterprise: Politics, Reason, and the Human Good: Essays in Honor of Francis Canavan,* edited by Kenneth L. Grasso and Robert P. Hunt, 321–32. Wilmington, Del.: ISI Books, 2002.

"The Natural Restoration of the Angels in the Depths of Evil: Concerning the Obscure Origins of Absolute Human Autonomy in Political Philosophy." In *Faith, Scholarship, and Culture in the Twenty-first Century,* edited by Alice Ramos and Marie George, 251–68. Washington, D.C.: American Maritain Association / The Catholic University of America Press, 2002.

"From Curiosity to Pride: On the Experience of Our Own Existence." In *Faith and the Life of the Intellect,* edited by Curtis L. Hancock and Brendan Sweetman, 187–209. Washington, D.C.: The Catholic University of America Press, 2003.

"What Are the Liberal Arts?" In *A Student's Guide to the Liberal Arts,* edited by Wilburn T. Stancil, 1–19. Kansas City, Mo.: Rockhurst University Press, 2003.

"On the Prospect of Peace on Earth: Maritain on Action and Contemplation." In *Truth Matters: Essays in Honor of Jacques Maritain,* edited by John Trapani, 12–25. Washington, D.C.: American Maritain Association/The Catholic University of America Press, 2004.

Books by Others

Thirty-two books, plus one essay, that reflect the "mind" of a Catholic in the broad spirit of the approach in this book. (Classical authors such as Augustine, Aquinas, the Church Fathers, and Newman are taken for granted and not included here.)

Belloc, Hilaire. *Path to Rome.* 1929. Garden City, N.Y.: Doubleday Image, 1956.

Chesterton, G. K. *Orthodoxy.* 1908. Garden City, N.Y.: Doubleday Image, 1956.

De Lubac, Henri. *Catholicism: Christ and the Common Destiny of Man.* 1947. San Francisco: Ignatius Press, 1988.

Gilson, Étienne. *God and Philosophy.* New Haven, Conn.: Yale University Press, 1941.

———. *The Unity of Philosophical Experience.* 1937. San Francisco: Ignatius Press, 1999.

Guardini, Romano. *The Humanity of Christ.* New York: Pantheon, 1964.

Hittinger, Russell. *First Grace: Rediscovering the Natural Law in a Post-Christian World.* Wilmington, Del.: ISI Books, 2003.

Jaki, Stanley. *The Road of Science and the Ways to God.* Chicago: University of Chicago Press, 1978.

John Paul II. *Crossing the Threshold of Hope.* New York: Knopf, 1994.

Kraynak, Robert. *Christian Faith and Modern Democracy.* Notre Dame, Ind.: University of Notre Dame Press, 2001.

Kreeft, Peter. *The Philosophy of Tolkien.* San Francisco: Ignatius Press, 2005.

Langan, Thomas. *Catholic Tradition.* Columbia: University of Missouri Press, 1998.

MacIntyre. *After Virtue.* Notre Dame, Ind.: University of Notre Dame Press, 1981.

Manent, Pierre. *The City of Man.* Princeton, N.J.: Princeton University Press, 1998.

Maritain, Jacques. *Approaches to God.* London: Collier, 1962.

McInerny, Ralph. *The Very Rich Hours of Jacques Maritain: A Spiritual Life.* Notre Dame, Ind.: University of Notre Dame Press, 2003.

Morse, Jennifer Roback. *Love and Economics.* Dallas: Spence, 2001.

O'Connor, Flannery. *The Letters of Flannery O'Connor: The Habit of Being.* New York: Vintage, 1979.

Percy, Walker. *Conversations with Walker Percy.* Jackson: University Press of Mississippi, 1998.

Pieper, Josef. *In Defense of Philosophy.* San Francisco: Ignatius Press, 1992.

——— . *Faith, Hope, Love.* San Francisco: Ignatius Press, 1997.

——— . *Josef Pieper: An Anthology.* San Francisco: Ignatius Press, 1989.

Quinn, Dennis. *Iris Exiled: A Synoptic History of Wonder.* Lanham, Md.: University Press of America, 2002.

Ratzinger, Joseph. *Introduction to Christianity.* New York: Herder and Herder, 1969.

——— . *Jesus of Nazareth.* New York: Doubleday, 2007.

——— . *Salt of the Earth: Christianity and the Catholic Church at the End of the Millennium.* San Francisco: Ignatius Press, 1996.

Reilly, Robert. *Surprised by Beauty: A Listener's Guide to the Recovery of Modern Music.* Washington, D.C.: Morley Books, 2002.

Sokolowski, Robert. *Christian Faith and Human Understanding.* Washington, D.C.: The Catholic University of America Press, 2005.

——— . *God of Faith and Reason.* Washington, D.C.: The Catholic University of America Press, 1996.

Wallace, William. *Modeling of Nature: Philosophy of Science and Philosophy of Nature in Synthesis.* Washington, D.C.: The Catholic University of America Press, 1996.

Walsh, David. *The Third Millennium: Reflections on Faith and Reason.* Washington, D.C.: Georgetown University Press, 1999.

Wilhelmsen, Frederick D. *Paradoxical Structure of Existence.* Albany, N.Y.: Preserving Christian Publications, 1995.

One final essay is added to this list: von Balthasar, Hans Urs, "A Résumé of My Thought." *Communio* 15 (Winter 1988), also found at www.ignatiusinsight.com/features2005/hub_resumethought_mar05.asp.

INDEX

➤⬿

The Mind That Is Catholic: Philosophical & Political Essays
was designed and typeset in Arno by Kachergis Book Design of Pittsboro,
North Carolina. It was printed on 60-pound Natures Book Natural and
bound by Thomson-Shore of Dexter, Michigan.